FORTRAN 90
AND ENGINEERING
COMPUTATION

FORTRAN 90
AND ENGINEERING
COMPUTATION

William Schick
Fairleigh Dickinson University, Professor Emeritus

Gordon Silverman
Manhattan College

JOHN WILEY & SONS, INC.
New York   Chichester   Brisbane   Toronto   Singapore

Cover Art by John Jinks

Acquisitions Editor	Charity Robey
Marketing Manager	Susan Elbe
Senior Production Editor	Savoula Amanatidis
Design Coordinator	Laura Nicholls
Text Design	Lynn Rogan
Cover Design	Meryl Levavi/Levavi & Levavi
Manufacturing Manager	Susan Stetzer
Illustration Coordinator	Jaime Perea

This book was typeset in Times Roman by General Graphic Services, and printed and bound by R.R. Donnelley in Willard, Ohio. The cover was printed by Lehigh Press, Inc.

Recognizing the importance of preserving what has been written, it is a policy of John Wiley & Sons, Inc. to have books of enduring value published in the United States printed on acid-free paper, and we exert our best efforts to that end.

Library of Congress Cataloging in Publication Data
Schick, William.
    Fortran 90 and engineering computation / William Schick, Gordon Silverman.

      p. cm.
    Includes index.
    ISBN 0-471-58512-2 (paper)
     1. FORTRAN 90 (Computer program language)   I. Silverman, Gordon.
  II. Title.

QA76.73.F25S333   1994
005.13´3—dc20   94-30554
                                                 CIP

Printed in the United States of America.

10 9 8 7 6 5 4 3 2 1

To our wives, Jessica and Roslyn

Preface

A key objective of this text is to prepare engineers and scientists to function in the highly computerized industrial and scientific environment of the modern world. Problem solving using the digital computer is one of the important skills that students should acquire to attain this objective.

FORTRAN is currently the most widely used high-level programming language taught in technical educational institutions, and it is likely to hold this position for some time. It leads the most frequently taught high-level languages by more than two to one. It is well suited for teaching problem solving. The continued development of new versions of FORTRAN, most recently FORTRAN 90, attests to the recognition of its continuing value in industry. This text is organized around the use of a digital computer for solving engineering problems.

For about two decades, students entering the engineering programs at the university at which the authors were affiliated were introduced to the solving of engineering problems using the FORTRAN language early in their education, usually in the freshman year. For quite a long period, this program of instruction was supported by the text *Fortran for Engineering* by Schick and Merz. Although the present text is a sequel to that successful book, it differs from it not only because FORTRAN 90 is used in this text, but also because of new educational criteria set by the engineering accrediting agency (Accreditation Board for Engineering and Technology, ABET) and changing educational goals of institutions. Although problem solving continues to be important, there now is increased emphasis on engineering design. A relatively early start on teaching engineering design is encouraged. Thus, many of the examples in this book concern topics that are related, directly or indirectly, to the tools of engineering design.

- The authors are aware that the majority of users of this text will be freshmen or sophomores. Therefore, examples that contain design-related or somewhat advanced mathematical topics are preceded, where feasible, by explanatory discussion. For example:

In Chapter 6, a discussion of electric filter design begins with an explanation of the meaning of the terms *filter, signal, attenuation,* and *analog*.

In Chapter 7, a program that calculates permutations and combinations is preceded by definitions of these terms and examples of calculation of combinations and of permutations.

In Chapter 9, prior to a program involving diffusion, the terms *independence* and *mutually exclusive* which are used in probability theory are discussed, and examples of their use are given.

- The abundance and variety of example programs are sufficient to permit instructors to choose those best suited for their course. Also, they are of varying difficulty. Thus, the book should be accessible to students with a broad range of mathematical preparation.

Because the users of this text are likely to represent many disciplines, problems have been chosen from several subject areas to facilitate the instructor's ability to select appropriate examples:

- Chemical engineering
- Chemistry
- Civil engineering
- Computer science
- Electrical engineering
- Environmental science
- Industrial engineering
- Mathematics
- Mechanical engineering
- Physics

Some of the examples involve topics *that are applicable to several disciplines*. One such topic is reliability engineering. Another topic is simulation.

- In Chapter 6 reliability engineering is defined and exemplified by a program.
- Simulation, in the context of product testing and model testing, is discussed in Chapter 9. Several examples are given.
- Another topic that applies to several disciplines is signal analysis. This topic is discussed in Chapter 9, and a sufficient number of examples are given to make the topic understandable to beginners.

The programs in this book are written in FORTRAN 90, and its predecessor, FORTRAN 77, is mentioned in only a few instances. The committee that wrote the FORTRAN 90 standard, aware that a very large number of programs had been written in FORTRAN 77, made provision for the fact that in some instances it was not feasible to scrap these programs. Accordingly, the FORTRAN 90 compiler used by the authors is in accordance with the International Standards Organization (ISO) standard, which is tolerant to the use of FORTRAN 77 constructs. This practice will likely continue, at least for a few years.

Although a number of excellent texts use the FORTRAN language, they are not solely concerned with FORTRAN 90. At this writing, this text is the first devoted to engineering computation and design which is exclusively written using FORTRAN 90. All the programs have been tested according to the FORTRAN 90 standard and were compiled using the Numerical Algorithms Group (Nag) compiler (version 1.21).

The organization of the book is as follows:

- Chapters 1 and 2 provide the user with an introduction to organizing problems for computer solution and guide the reader through step-by-step compilation of a simple FORTRAN 90 program.
- Chapters 3 through 7 discuss the principles of FORTRAN 90. After principles are stated and explained, generally two or more programs are given using these principles.
- Chapter 8 discusses and illustrates program testing and debugging. A comprehensive discussion of such topics is rarely given in texts of this type.

After discussing the principles of FORTRAN 90, Chapters 9 and 10 present engineering applications of FORTRAN 90 programming. This material gives the text a reference quality; it shows the students additional use of FORTRAN 90, and it provides an opportunity for the instructor to present challenges to superior students. The applications reflect significant topics that an engineer or a scientist is likely to encounter during his or her professional activities. They are, however, presented at a level suited for undergraduate study. Chapters 9 and 10 deal with:

- Simulation and Monte Carlo methods
- Estimation exemplified by least squares fit to data
- Interpolation and estimation (Lagrange and Taylor)
- Integration and double integration by Simpson's rule
- Introduction to the discrete Fourier transform
- Introduction to computer graphics
- Introduction to queuing
- Introduction to databases
- Introduction to expert systems
- Introduction to solution of differential equations

To the Instructor:

This text may be used to support a one-semester course in engineering computation using FORTRAN 90. To that end, Chapters 1 through 8 would provide the basis for a one-semester course. If appropriate, material can be selected from Chapters 9 and 10.

Alternatively, Chapters 9 and 10 can be used as the nucleus of a second course introducing engineering design in a variety of disciplines.

A solutions manual will be provided for instructors who adopt the text.

The authors are grateful to a number of individuals: Dr. Howard Silver, professor and chair of electrical engineering at Fairleigh Dickinson University, provided invaluable suggestions. Dr. Terrence Akai, assistant dean for computing at the University of Notre Dame, Jerry R. Bayless, associate dean of engineering at the University of Missouri-Rolla, Dr. Joseph Saliba, of the University of Dayton, and Dr. David Edelson of Florida State University all contributed important comments.

Contents

9   NUMERICAL APPLICATIONS   289

Part I: Simulation

Part II: Some Tools for Estimation

Part III: Tools for Interpolation and Estimation

Part IV: Integration

Part V: Introduction to the Discrete Fourier Transform (*Civil, Electrical, and Mechanical Engineering*)

1

Computer and Programming Fundamentals

The importance of the digital computer in our daily lives makes it one of the significant developments in the history of humankind. Increasingly, it has become a visible tool in science, engineering design and manufacturing, business, and leisure activities. One of its key attributes is its ability to repeatedly carry out tedious tasks rapidly and without error. Examples of such chores include mathematical calculations, control of other machines, and the management of large quantities of information. In short, it has the potential to improve the quality of our lives, relieve us of tiresome responsibilities, and expand our creative capacity. As with any tool, the user must learn how to employ it properly and explore some of its many applications, both of which are the aims of this text. *This introductory chapter will touch on the computer's history, describe how the machine works, and discuss how to go about organizing a problem for computer solution, including the introduction of the concept of a program.*

1.1 HISTORY

Two aspects of human behavior, commerce and war, have been important factors in the development of the computer. Although events that contributed to its evolution can be traced to ancient times, one of the first clear examples of a machine that resembles the modern computer may be found in the middle of the nineteenth century. Charles Babbage (1792–1871), with the help of Ada, the countess of Lovelace, produced the Difference Engine as well as the design for the Analytic Engine. Although the analytic Engine was never built, its design presaged the modern form of the computer. The Difference Engine, which was commissioned by the British government, was intended to compute (lunar) navigation tables automatically. In those days, ships were navigated by the position of the moon, which was presented in the form of tables; the British government needed to ship goods over long distances, and it was important that these goods arrive at the correct destination. The Difference Engine could carry out some of the calculations normally found in the arithmetic sections of its modern descendants.

The design for the Analytic Engine incorporated an ingenious invention made by Joseph Jacquard, namely, the automatic loom. By employing a series of "punched cards," Jacquard's device could program or direct the automatic manufacture of woven cloth; its political consequences were widespread, for it threatened the jobs of many people, an effect that has to be considered for the modern computer as well. A combination of the punched cards envisioned by Jacquard and the Difference Engine, with its mechanical calculator, can be regarded as the world's first primitive computing machine.

The next significant milestone in the history of the computer can be traced to the early 1940s and World War II. During this period, a fully electronic machine was developed that could rapidly calculate the angle at which to fire an artillery shell; to accurately aim the weapon required solution of a complex equation incorporating such factors as the type of propellant used, the temperature and density of the air, and the aerodynamic properties of the projectile.

As new technologies have emerged, the organization or *architecture* of the computer has continued to be refined; recent developments include the optical computer, very large-scale integrated circuits (VLSI) architecture, multiprogrammed and multiprocessor systems, structured languages, computer networks, and artificial intelligence systems—automata that make decisions in a way that seeks to imitate human thought processes.

The developers of computers were faced with problems related to the hardware of the machine. Early versions required a system of wires to direct the sequence of operations; the wires had to be changed for each new application, and this required considerable time as well as personnel. Thus, a parallel development in the history of the computer was devoted to ways of simplifying and speeding up this part of the computing operation. Gradually, *stored programs,* rather than wired or switching methods, were developed. Numbers stored within the memory controlled the sequence of operations carried out by the computer. Subsequent developments permitted the programmer to use symbols in place of the numbers. For example, the word (mnemonic) ADD could be used in place of the binary equivalent for the ADD operation (e.g., 010). The resultant sequence of instructions—the program—was translated into the numbers that were then stored within the memory. (The translation program is known as an *assembler*.) Ultimately, statements with characteristics much like those found in English ("English-like") for each operation or command were used. These also required a translation program to convert such *high-level language* (HLL) statements into computer readable form. (The conversion programs are known as *compilers* or *interpreters,* depending on the translation method.)

One of the earliest programming languages of this type is FORTRAN whose name is a contraction of the words *for*mula *tran*slation. In the near future we will celebrate the fiftieth anniversary of its origin. Its first formal appearance occurred in 1957, although it was under development by John Backus before that. Despite the development of numerous HLLs, FORTRAN retains viability and can be found in countless applications. Consider, for example, that its formal specification has undergone several revisions; this text will employ its most recent formulation, *FORTRAN 90,* as the vehicle for explaining how scientists and engineers use the computer as a powerful tool in their work.

1.2 EXAMPLES OF COMPUTER USAGE

In this section we present several examples that demonstrate how the computer can be a powerful tool for solving scientific and engineering problems.

EXAMPLE 1.1 Automated Analysis of Chemical Substances

 A robotic arm, coupled to a computer that controls its actions, can be used to completely automate the analysis of chemical substances. (This idea can be extended to examples such as process control or manufacturing environments that may be hazardous to human health.) A sketch of the complete system is shown in Fig. 1.1. A key element of the design is a robotic, articulated arm.

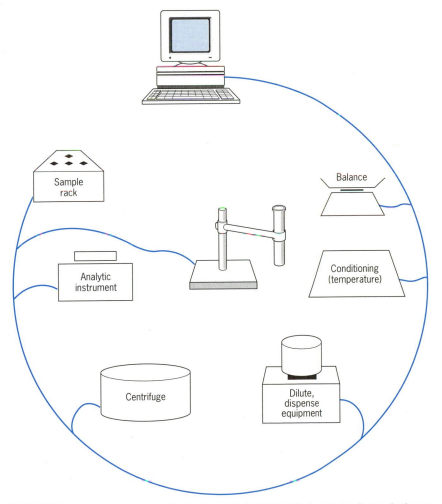

FIGURE 1.1   A computer-controlled automated substance analysis system using a robotic arm.

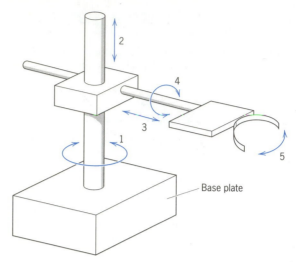

FIGURE 1.2   Representative articulated arm with five independent motions.

Articulated arms are meant to emulate the motions of a human hand/arm combination. A variety of arrangements for accomplishing this representative arm are possible, and Fig. 1.2 depicts one simple example. The five independent arm motions are as follows:

The entire arm can rotate on the base plate.

The arm can be raised or lowered.

The hand (grippers) can be extended or withdrawn.

The hand can pronate (or rotate the "wrist").

The fingers of the hand can open and close ("yaw").

Consider this robotic arm working within the system shown in Fig. 1.1. All instrumentation necessary for automated analysis is located within a radius that is included in the range of motion of the robotic arm. The instruments as well as the robotic arm are under direct control of the computer. The instruments whose combined functions support automated analysis of chemical substances include a centrifuge (which can be used for such purposes as blood analysis); an analytic instrument such as a spectrophotometer or chromatograph; a rack to hold the chemical samples; a balance; a conditioning unit, quite possibly a stirrer or temperature oven; and an instrument for dispensing, extracting, or diluting chemicals.

Commands, in the form of electrical signals, can be sent to the robotic arm. These signals represent precise actions or steps that the arm follows. The overall result is an automated analysis of a chemical substance. For example, the following sequence of operations describes automated analysis of blood serum.

• Specimen is placed in sample rack (by human operator).

• Reagents for desired tests are also placed in sample rack.

• Robot arm moves specimen to dispensing equipment where the following operations are completed: serum is aspirated and combined with reagent; diluent is added.

• Robotic arm moves prepared sample to conditioning instrument (heater).

- After appropriate delay, sample is moved to analytic instrument, which in this case is a photometer.
- Photometer reading is transmitted to computer where result is registered.
- Sample is removed from photometer by robotic arm and moved to disposal unit, which is not shown in the figure.

This simplified program of steps is carried out under the control of the computer. Though not explicitly cited, the program must take into consideration the tasks to be carried out by each instrument and include time delays where appropriate. (When the computer does not obtain ongoing status information from an instrument, the resultant arrangement is referred to as "open loop" control. The computer may also receive signals from the various statements that advise the program of their status; this is referred to as "closed loop" control, which is generally more desirable than the open loop operation.)

A complete description of the motion of the robotic arm requires many detailed steps for even relatively simple tasks. This description can include literally thousands of operations or instructions (e.g, pronate the hand 10 degrees, followed by closing the fingers 30 degrees, etc.) To complete such a description prior to successful operation of the system would take the user a prohibitively long time, for it would require the user to accurately predict the precise coordinates of all axes of motion for each desired position. Instead, robotic arms usually come with computer-based aids that greatly simplify the task; such aids are referred to as training programs. The computer can be used to track the position of each member of the robotic arm. The user positions the arm and its members manually, using a mechanical "pointing" device or reserved keys in combination with numerical information. When the user is satisfied with the successive motion that the robotic arm is to make, the data—as tracked by the computer—are stored in the computer's memory section. In this way a complex sequence of motions can be readily generated. Such motions, coupled with commands to individual instruments, support automated procedures for chemical analysis or processing.

EXAMPLE 1.2 Simulating an Oil Transportation Facility

The computer can be a powerful aid when planning large engineering projects. It permits the designers to answer a variety of questions pertaining to the strategies to be employed in the development. Normally, the facts and circumstances of the enterprise are provided to the computer in the form of a number of relationships between various parts of the project. The computer can assess the consequences of these relationships, and this approach is referred to as a *simulation*. A variety of constraints and parameters may be varied, and the results used to modify construction. (Such questions are referred to as "what-if" queries.) Using a computer in this way provides a less expensive alternative to actually building the facility only to discover that it is inadequate. Consider the design of an oil transportation facility that is to be simulated on the computer.

A petroleum transportation company is considering bidding on an oil shipping contract. What follows is a simplified list of factors and constraints that must be taken into consideration when planning for the project.

- There are three loading berths available which can service any size tanker.
- Three types of tankers can be used: small, medium, and large. They have the following characteristics:

Type of Tanker	No. Owned	Time Required to Fill (hours)	Total Travel Time (hours)	Relative Profit per Trip
Small	7	18 ± 2	240 ± 24	1
Medium	5	24 ± 4	360 ± 28	1.3
Large	3	36 ± 6	420 ± 30	1.4

- There is only one tugboat at the loading dock; it must move tankers from the harbor to the berths and back again once they are loaded. It takes one hour to move a tanker, but the tug only takes a quarter of an hour to move between harbor and berth when not escorting a tanker. (The tub may have just moved a tanker to the harbor, and another is just finished loading; the tug requires an addition quarter hour to return to the berthing area.)

- Unfortunately, the loading area is subject to frequent storms. They last from two to six hours once they arrive, and they arrive at random intervals, at an average interval of 48 hours. (The distribution of arrival times is assumed to be known.) Loading continues during storms, but the tug cannot move ships. (If a storm occurs while the tug is moving a tanker, the operation is completed before service terminates.)

Among the questions that the company wishes to answer before bidding on the contract are

- How many tankers should be used as well as the mixture (small, medium, large)?
- Can the efficiency of the operation be improved, such as adding a communication system to the tug which might reduce its service intervals?

The computer can help management to make decisions by simulating what might happen over the course of a year's operations for a varying number of tankers. It does so by generating a series of random numbers to represent events such as a tanker's arrival at the loading facility; a tanker's completion of loading; the tug's movement of the tanker in or out of the facility; a storm. These events are retained on lists of events that are normally referred to as *queues,* which grow or empty according to the events that occur. The results can then be used to help management make reasoned choices.

Other examples where computer simulations (Fig. 1.3) are important include the following.

- **Inventory policies** for retaining parts in a manufacturing facility. When and how often are orders to be placed?
- **Communication systems**   The telephone company needs to know how many trunk lines to install and maintain in order to assure subscribers that their call will get through 98 percent of the time without experiencing extensive delays. Does a computer network have sufficient capacity to support the number of nodes in the system?
- **Building design**   How many elevators are needed to service a given building design? Where does one locate ("park") the elevators when they are not needed? How does one schedule responses to passenger service calls?
- **Laboratory testing facilities**   Samples arrive at different times from subscribers with varying numbers and types of tests to be performed; how should these be scheduled, and how much test equipment should be acquired?
- **Weather forecasting**   Given such factors as wind direction, humidity, tempera-

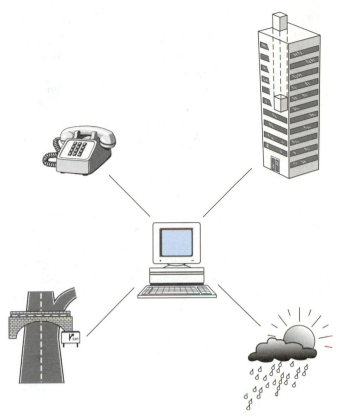

FIGURE 1.3   Computer simulations are important for improving the quality of our daily activities.

ture, cloud cover, and pressure, have the computer determine whether severe weather will develop. Where are such storms likely to occur?

- **Architecture**   How well will a given design for a building frame be able to withstand vibration either from traffic or, more importantly, from wind or earthquakes?
- **Civil projects**   What highway entrance ramp design will best provide for smooth access and transition into the traffic stream?

This represents a very modest sample of occasions in which computer simulation can be helpful. A great many additional examples can be found in the technical literature. (A few examples are described in Chapter 10 of this text.)

EXAMPLE 1.3 A Computer Database

Retaining large amounts of information is another area where computers can be very useful. Structured data arrangements of considerable size are referred to as *databases*. Consider the needs of various users of an information base in a manufacturing plant:

- **Engineering**   need access to schematics, design drawings, parts lists, vendor information, design aids, quality control reports, repair reports, manufactured parts inventory.
- **Manufacturing**   design drawings, production drawings, parts inventory, tool inventory, engineering reports, materials inventory, manufactured parts inventory.

- **Management**   engineering reports, quality control reports, parts inventory, sales reports, accounting reports, customer lists, current price structure.
- **Sales**   manufactured parts inventory, design drawings, parts specifications, customer lists, current price structure.
- **Receptionist**   personnel directory, personnel schedule, appointment schedule, customer lists.
- **Personnel**   payroll information, employee records (health, benefits, vacation, personal information), employment needs (positions to be filled).
- **Accounting**   payroll records, billing, inventory, receivable accounts, disbursements, bank account information.

This abbreviated list shows a variety of data needs for an efficient manufacturing plant. Notice that there are both common and unique database needs among the various constituent groups. An efficient database would include all the necessary forms that could be called upon from the computer so that a user (with proper protection and accessibility) could review or create various reports. For example, an engineer might wish to review a Failure Report for one of the products manufactured at the facility. This report could be displayed at the engineer's terminal and is likely to include such information as the nature of the failure, failure diagnosis (cause), the repairs that were made, and the length of time the unit had been in service.

Data for such computer-based installations must be accessible using relatively friendly, English-like statements, or by viewing a list of parameters and selecting the items to be searched and the information to be printed where appropriate. Such database systems might be linked to other company facilities, in the headquarters location, for example.

The examples shown here have been chosen with care; each of them is highly dependent on specific functional elements of the computer as discussed below. A summary of such applications includes the following.

- **Numerically intensive computations**   simulation, statistical calculations, artificial intelligence.
- **Memory-intensive systems**   databases, transaction applications.
- **Input/Output (I/O) intensive applications**   real-time control of the environment, speech recognition, image processing, computer vision systems, communications.

1.3 COMPUTER FUNDAMENTALS

The computer can be described from a variety of viewpoints including the electronic components that make up the machine, the functions of its various parts, the ways in which to control operation of the elements and to interconnect the machine to other machines and devices, and the applications that lend themselves to computer usage. This text is intended primarily to instruct the reader in the ways of solving scientific and engineering problems using a digital computer. To this end, some functional and operational descriptions of the tool (computer) are necessary. In particular, three topics need to be addressed; the hardware organization (*architecture*) of a representative machine (including a functional description), control of the machine by means of appropriate commands (the *operating system*), and preparation of a problem for solution on the computer. These topics are also covered in Sec. 1.4.

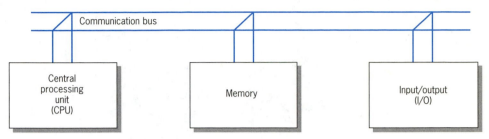

FIGURE 1.4   Functional organization of a computer.

1.3.1 Hardware

Hardware consists of the physical elements that direct the (electrical) energy associated with the processing of information. These elements may be grouped together according to the purposes they serve; one view of this organization is shown in Fig. 1.4. The four components included in the diagram are considered fundamental to all computers; in particular, they refer to a type of computer known as a *personal computer* or *PC*.

- **Central Processing Unit (CPU)**   The CPU is the logical heart of the PC, and its principal function is to control execution of the instructions in an orderly manner. To do so it must be able to complete a number of subordinate tasks: fetch instructions (from memory), decode (decipher) them, and execute them. In order to execute instructions, the CPU will issue commands to transfer data to and from memory or external components (*peripherals*), make logical decisions, compare logical entities, and perform simple arithmetic calculations. (A printer is one example of a peripheral device.) Although it is important to know what the PC does, users need only interact with the machine by means of simple English-like commands.

- **Memory**   Memory is a hardware element whereby information is stored and from which the same data may be retrieved. The data can represent three distinct entities: (program) instructions, partial (or intermediate) operational or computational results, and final results. Although only a single functional element is shown in Fig. 1.4, memory is further divided into two functional categories. Some information is needed at the same (or nearly same) rate as the CPU executes instructions, and it is considered to be *primary* storage, or, more commonly, *main memory*. This function is relatively expensive and normally holds only limited amounts of information. An important aspect of main memory is that all the data items can normally be accessed (stored or retrieved) in approximately the same amount of time; as a result, it is referred to as *random access memory* (*RAM*). Alternatively, the *secondary* storage (memory) holds large amounts of data, but access to such information is slow. The time required to store or retrieve data is proportional to the data's position, and such organization is considered to be *sequential*. Considering the amount of data secondary storage systems can retain, its cost (per data item) is considerably less than main memory.

- **Input/Output (I/O)**   If the computer is to be of real value, it must be able to accomplish communications; this is the function of *input/output* or *I/O*. Data that the PC moves or transfers to the external world include electrical information as well as some that is ultimately converted to human speech, or visual images. The translation between the information within the PC and its ultimate form or use re-

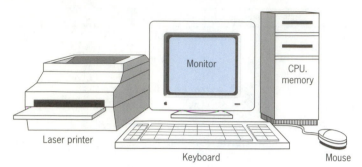

FIGURE 1.5   A typical computer station.

quires additional hardware and instructions (software), which is collectively called the *interface*. Two of the most important external components are the keyboard and monitor. The keyboard allows a user to enter alphanumeric (numbers and letters) data into the computer. The monitor, which looks like a television screen, allows the user to see the alphanumeric and graphical information that the computer generates. For historical reasons, the combination of keyboard and monitor may be referred to as the *terminal* device, even though they are separate elements from the computer's point of view.

• **System Bus**   The CPU, memory, and I/O have a common path by which they communicate with each other; this is the *system bus* (or simply, *bus*). For proper communication between the various functional elements of a PC, information on the bus should identify the source and/or destination of the information (*address*), the data to be moved, and finally a series of control signals normally referred to as *handshaking lines* for orderly transfer of the information. A sketch of a typical computer station is shown in Fig. 1.5.

1.3.2 Operating System Software

The computer hardware described above requires a series of electronic signals that are coded representations of numbers to complete any useful tasks. Without such information, the computer is virtually inoperative. A user cannot, for example, enter alphanumeric characters from the keyboard, or see text or graphic information on the monitor. When power is first applied to the computer, a series of commands are automatically loaded into memory to permit a user to control various hardware elements, including communication between keyboard and monitor, and management of the memory system (primary and secondary). These are two of the more important tasks performed by these instructions. Taken together, these instructions make up a series of software procedures that are referred to as the computer's *Operating System* (OS). A formal definition of the OS is: "A set of programs and routines which guides a computer in the performance of its tasks, assists the programs (and programmers) with certain supporting functions, and increases the usefulness of the computer's hardware."[1]

---

[1]McGraw-Hill *Dictionary of Scientific and Technical Terms* (Fourth Edition), Parker, S.P. (Ed.), 1989, McGraw-Hill Book Co., New York, NY.

We can think of the OS as a series of services that are available to a user and that fall into two categories:

- Operational control of the hardware.
- Supervision of the allocation of hardware (and software) facilities to user programs.

Of growing importance in OSs is the *Graphic User Interface* (GUI), which has supplanted the more traditional methods of entering commands via the keyboard with a combination of icons (graphical images). These icons move in correspondence with the movement of a "pointing" device (e.g., mouse, trackball, light pen), allowing the user to "point" at the desired task(s). These newer image-based OSs permit highly unsophisticated users to master the computer quickly. Examples of commercially available OSs include UNIX[2], MS-DOS, VM, VMS, Macintosh, and OS/2.

1.3.3 Files and File Systems

Many OS commands are concerned with user control of the secondary storage system. The secondary storage system—typically a hard disk—is divided into variable-sized logical groups called *files*, each consisting of *a collection of data with a common (logical) name*. The file management (software) resource may reference these files without regard to their size or physical location on the disk; such details are supervised by the OS, together with the disk hardware that controls the disk. A most important function of the OS allows users to *create, delete (erase), rename, copy, append*, or modify files and the data within. To manage this information, the OS maintains a *directory* of such files, which itself can be modified when necessary.

From the user's point of view, the file system and maintenance of his or her files is extremely important. As noted above, a file is considered to be a group of data (e.g., alphanumeric characters or binary coded numbers representing experimental results) that is assigned a single name—the *filename*. The syntax (format) of the file naming convention for one OS (MS-DOS)[3] is shown in Fig. 1.6.

File systems may be viewed in a way that is analogous to a document storage system with the following approximate relationships:

Conventional File System Entity	DOS "Equivalent"
File cabinet	Volume
File drawer	Directory
File folder	File

An important difference between a conventional document system and the OS file system (e.g., MS-DOS) follows from the possibility that a directory within MS-DOS may include (reference to) another directory that is subordinate to the first directory and is referred to as a *subdirectory*. A subdirectory is considered to be the *child* of the *parent* directory in which it is first referenced. This organization results in a *hierarchical* arrangement of files. A sample of such a system is shown in Fig. 1.7. Shown in the figure is the

---

[2]UNIX is a registered trademark of AT&T in the United States and other countries.

[3]A complete description of MS-DOS can be found in the *MS-DOS Encyclopedia*, edited by R. Duncan, (Microsoft Press, Redmond, WA, 1988). A summary of MS-DOS commands is included in Appendix A.

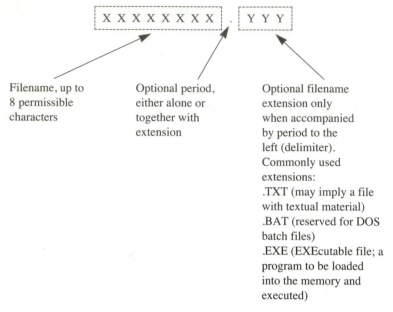

Filename, up to
8 permissible
characters

Optional period,
either alone or
together with
extension

Optional filename
extension only
when accompanied
by period to the
left (delimiter).
Commonly used
extensions:
.TXT (may imply a file
with textual material)
.BAT (reserved for DOS
batch files)
.EXE (EXEcutable file; a
program to be loaded
into the memory and
executed)

Filenames and extensions
include the following
permissible characters:

- Letters of the Alphabet
- Numbers 0 through 9
- Special characters
  $ # & @ ! % ( ) - { } ' _ ' ^ ~

Examples (must start with a letter)
experim.ent
day_1.dat
results.395

FIGURE 1.6 The file naming convention.

conceptual relationship of the directories, subdirectories, and files. The user can instruct the OS to display a listing of the files on the monitor (or direct it to print the list on a printer).

EXAMPLE 1.4 Obtaining an MS-DOS Listing of the Files in a Directory on the Monitor

When DOS is awaiting commands from the user, a prompt(ing) message is displayed on the monitor: the user response is shown in boldface, and is validated or completed by depressing the key marked variously Enter or ↵ on the keyboard.

```
C:\> dir
```

The prompt message indicates that DOS is addressing (accessing) the secondary storage system drive designed by "C:" and particularly its *base*, or *root directory* signified by "\". For the sample directory shown in Fig. 1.7, the computer will display the following on the monitor:

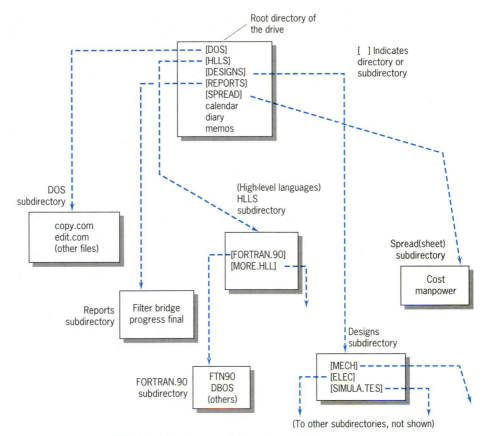

FIGURE 1.7   Conceptual view of a sample directory system.

```
DOS          <DIR>        04-23-93   4:25p
HLLS         <DIR>        03-04-94   9:15a
DESIGNS      <DIR>        02-28-95   10:21p
REPORTS      <DIR>        11-23-93   4:59p
SPREAD       <DIR>        02-12-94   8:25a
CALENDAR            250   06-22-95   12:01p
DIARY               512   10-19-94   3:00a
MEMOS              5225   05-10-95   8:25a
    8 file(s) 5987 bytes
                    85123072 bytes free
```

Included in the listing are the name of the file or directory, an extension if appropriate, the date as well as the time of the latest reference to the entity, and the size (specified by the number of bytes) of the files. (One example of a filename is filter.f90, where "filter" is the name of the file and "f90" is the extension.) A summary of the listing appears at the bottom and includes the number of items listed, the total number of bytes, and the space still available on the drive. (The term *byte* has various meanings; in this instance, it refers to the number of characters included in the file.) Other DOS directives for obtaining file/directory listings are possible:

dir c:\designs   Display the files in the subdirectory
                           "designs."

```
dir c:\reports > prn:    Have the file listing of the subdirectory
                             "reports" sent (printed) to the printing
                             device.
dir c:\calendar          Display a complete description of the file
                             named "calendar" (in the current
                             directory); this is one way to check for
                             the existence of a file.
dir c:*.exe              List the name of any file (indicated by the
                             asterisk (*)) whose extension is "exe."
                             This would produce a list of all
                             executable files.
```

In order to reference a particular file, its location (*path*) within the file system must be specified. The path may start with the particular secondary storage element on which to find the file—the drive indicated by a letter followed by a colon (:) (e.g., a:, b:, c:, d:, e:). Within Fig. 1.7, the path to the file named "filter" would be specified as

```
c:\reports\filter
```

assuming that it is located on drive C:. The symbol "\" is a reference to the *root* or starting point of the particular directory or subdirectory. Directories and subdirectories may be created or erased using DOS commands (or by pointing to appropriate symbols if using a *Graphic User Interface* (GUI) shell).

EXAMPLE 1.5 Creating a File (in MS-DOS)

There are a number of ways to create files within MS-DOS. For example, the DOS *copy* command may be used to create a file as follows:

```
c:\>  copy con: myfile
      This is an example for creating a DOS file.
      ^z
```

The *copy* command is shown as "copy"; the phrase "con:" advises DOS that the source of the data to be copied is the console device, namely, the combination of the keyboard and monitor. The data destination is specified by the next phrase—"myfile." This is the name of the file (in the directory c:\) that will be created if it does not already exist. If it does exist, it will be overwritten. (Each line in the example above must be followed by a carriage return.) All (alphanumeric) text following the command line ("This is . . . file.") will be stored in the file. The last line ("^z") is formed by depressing the keyboard key marked "Ctrl" and the key "z" at the same time; it is referred to by the name "control z." It is needed when using the copy command to signal the end of the file; it is the *end-of-file-mark*. It, too, must be terminated by a carriage return. The user should once again see the DOS prompt. This is not the preferred method for creating files. In the first place, the user cannot edit existing files in this way; they will be overwritten. A much better method makes use of a program (as distinct from the DOS "command") designed specifically for such purposes. A greater variety of such programs exist; they included *editor* programs of various descriptions as well as word processing packages. The editor program will be explored in more detail in Chapter 2 where it will be used to create a FORTRAN 90 program.

EXAMPLE 1.6 Some File or Directory Commands in Other OSs

The table shown below contains a brief listing of commands in some OSs.

Command	UNIX	MS-DOS	OS/2
Directory listing	ls	dir	dir
Copy a file	cp	copy	copy
Edit a file	ed	edit	edlin
	(text editor)		(line editor)
	vi		
	(screen-oriented		
	visual display		
	editor)		
Print a file	pr	copy filename prn:	type
		or	
		type filename	
Change the working directory	chdir	chdir	chdir

1.3.4 Some Limitations on Calculations

The computer will perform various numerical calculations in response to instructions included in a program (e.g., add two numbers). When solving a problem, the user must understand the limitations of such calculations. In particular, two concepts are relevant: *resolution* and *accuracy* of the information and the results.

The difference between the concepts of resolution and accuracy are depicted in Fig. 1.8. Number systems within the computer can be compared to an ordinary ruler, and numerical resolution describes the ability of the computing device to repeat a given result (Fig. 1.8a). The registration marks (e.g., measurement points on the ruler) are the numbers that the computer can reproduce. Suppose that the true answer to a problem is equivalent to the position represented by I_3. The computer has no number that is the equivalent of I_3; it must report either I_2 or I_1, depending on which is closer to the true answer. Resolution may be reported as the minimum change in numerical value. For example, if the smallest changes that can be reported correspond to 0.01, then the resolution is said to be "1 part in 100."

Alternatively, accuracy limitations come from errors that are introduced by the calculations (and/or measurement system); Fig. 1.8b shows the effect. If the computer were perfect, it would locate the registration marks at the position marked I_2. Because of accumulated errors within the computer, the registration mark for I_2 is reproduced as "I_2'," which is now "close" to the position of the true result. Had the computer not included errors, it would have reported I_1 as it should have, being naturally closer (by virtue of the resolution) to the true answer. I_2 is, of course, incorrect. Normally, computational errors are reported as a percentage of the range of possible answers. For example, if the numerical results can vary between 0.0 and 9.9, and limitations of accuracy make us unsure of the fractional portion of the answer, then we would specify the accuracy as 1 percent (or possibly 1 part in 100).

When processing data—restricted to decimal numbers for this discussion—the *significant digits* determine the accuracy. They are defined as follows.

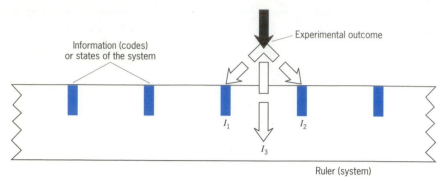

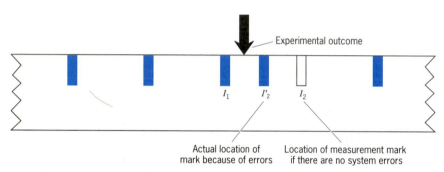

FIGURE 1.8 Resolution and accuracy in instrument systems. (a) Resolution concerns the ability of the system to repeat the required measurement. (b) Accuracy is a measure of the system's ability to repeat the correct measurement.

- All nonzero digits are counted as significant.
- Any zeros that are not used as placeholders for the decimal point are considered to be significant. For example, 0.213 has three significant digits because the leading 0 is a placeholder (by convention) and is therefore not significant. The number 0.05010 has four significant digits because the first two are merely placeholders, while the other zeros are not.

When carrying out arithmetic operations, the following rules should be observed.

1. When adding or subtracting, resolution is limited to the least precise number.
2. When multiplying or dividing, the result is only as accurate (number of significant figures) as the least accurate number.
3. The roots of a number are limited to the accuracy of the original number.
4. Exact numbers do not change the accuracy or precision of a calculation.

1.3.5 Number Systems Within the Computer

The decimal number system includes

- Ten distinct symbols, or digits: 0, 1, 2, 3, 4, 5, 6, 7, 8, and 9.
- A system of weights that is based on the position of the symbol within the number.

The standard format for a decimal number is

$$\cdots S_2(10^2) + S_1(10^1) + S_0(10^0) + S_{-1}(10^{-1}) + S_{-2}(10^{-2}) + \cdots$$

Normally, the powers of ten are omitted as well as the "+" signs, and a period (the *decimal point*) identifies the separation between positive and negative powers of ten. The number therefore appears as

$$- - -S_2S_1S_0 \cdot S_{-1}S_{-2}- - -$$

(e.g., 5725.62879). The *base* or *radix* of the number system is the weighting factor—10 in this case.

Although the decimal number system is convenient for users, computers require a numbering scheme that is limited to two symbols. The latter numbering scheme is implemented by the binary number system; it is called binary because it uses only two symbols, 0 and 1. The numbering scheme parallels the decimal system; it includes symbols and positional weighting. The standard format for the binary numbering system is

$$\cdots S_2(2^2) + S_1(2^1) + S_0(2^0) + S_{-1}(2^{-1}) + S_{-2}(2^{-2}) \cdots$$

with numbers represented in a way similar to the decimal number system (e.g., 1101.1010, with the period being referred to as the *binary point*). Each symbol used in the binary numbering system is referred to as a *bit,* which comes from *b*inary dig*it.* The least significant bit is the symbol at the right of the standard form, whereas the most significant bit is the symbol to the left.

EXAMPLE 1.7 Representing Negative Binary Numbers

Negative binary numbers are found by using the following steps.

1. Start with a given positive number.
2. Copy the least significant bit.
3. If the bit is 0, pass to the next most significant bit and repeat step 2; otherwise, copy the bit (which is a 1) and proceed to step 4.
4. Complement the remaining bits in the number. To complement a bit, change a 1 bit to a 0 and a 0 bit to a 1.

Carrying out this procedure for the binary number 01100—equivalent to the decimal number 12—will produce 10100. (An equivalent result may be obtained by complementing all bits in the number and adding 1 using the rules of binary addition.)

The binary numbers used in the computer are often unwieldly and difficult to interpret without effort. One compromise that has become widely accepted is to use the hexadecimal number system, particularly when some results are to be displayed to the user. (The octal number system is also used but will not be described; understanding octal numbers is readily inferred from the discussion of the hexadecimal system.)

As with all number systems, the hexadecimal system includes an appropriate number of symbols and weights. Hexadecimal numbers require 16 symbols, 0, 1, . . . , 9, A, B, C, D, E, and F. The standard format is

$$S_n(16^n) + S_{n-1}(16^{n-1}) + \cdots + S_0 + S_{-1}(16^{-1}) + \cdots$$

which is normally written

$$S_nS_{n-1} \cdots S_0.S_{-1} \cdots$$

The table below shows the 16 hexadecimal numbers and their equivalent binary and decimal representations.

Hexadecimal	Binary	Decimal
0	0000	0
1	0001	1
2	0010	2
3	0011	3
4	0100	4
5	0101	5
6	0110	6
7	0111	7
8	1000	8
9	1001	9
A	1010	10
B	1011	11
C	1100	12
D	1101	13
E	1110	14
F	1111	15

The hexadecimal equivalent of the decimal number 29 is 1D because the hexadecimal number is

$$1(16^1) + D(16^0) = 16 + D = 16 + 13 = 29$$

The last result follows from the fact that D is the hexadecimal equivalent of the decimal number 13.

EXAMPLE 1.8 Converting Whole Binary Numbers into Their Equivalent Hexadecimal Value

To perform conversion from binary to "hex," proceed as follows:

1. Starting with the least significant bit, arrange the binary number into groups of 4.
2. Replace each group with its corresponding hexadecimal number.

As an example, consider the following.

Binary number:	1101100101111011			
After step 1:	1101	1001	0111	1011
After step 2:	D	9	7	B

Conversely, if the original number was hex, replacing each (hex) digit with its binary equivalent would complete the conversion.

When converting decimal numbers to binary equivalents, it is sometimes easier first to convert the decimal number to its hex equivalent and subsequently from hex to binary.

This discussion of number systems is intended to provide some insights into the representation of information within the computer, as well as the conversions that are, at times, required of the user. Automatic calculators are available to perform these conversions automatically, but occasionally, "manual" conversions may be necessary.

EXAMPLE 1.9 Imperfect Conversions Within the Computer

Conversions of whole numbers from decimal to binary form is accomplished without error; this is not the case when converting fractional quantities. Fractional weighting in the decimal number system includes 10^{-1} or 1/10, 10^{-2} or 1/100, and so on. Fractional weighting in the binary number system includes 2^{-1} or 1/2, 2^{-2} or 1/4, and so on. The binary equivalent of the decimal fraction 0.5 is 0.1; in this case, the conversion is accurate. However, the decimal fraction 0.4 does not have an exact binary equivalent. The binary equivalent of 0.4 consists of the infinite sequence 0.0110 . . . 0110 . . . ; thus, it is not possible to express 0.4 exactly using a finite number of bits. For example, if the binary sequence is 0.011001, then the equivalent decimal number is 0.390625; the reader should confirm this. This results in an error of 2.34 percent. This conversion error leads to differences between expected computer calculations and observed results. Accuracy can be improved by adding more bits. If 11 bits are used to represent 0.4, the result is 0.01100110011 and the error is reduced to 0.0244 percent. (Note that an 11-bit binary number requires more storage than a 6-bit binary number.)

1.4 ORGANIZING A PROBLEM FOR COMPUTER SOLUTION

A *program* is considered to be a detailed, explicit set of directions for accomplishing some purpose, the set being expressed in a language suitable for input to the computer or as a set of (binary) numbers defined as *machine language*. A program must be able to serve two conceptually simple purposes:

- Specify what calculations and operations are to be performed (on the data).
- Specify the order or sequence in which calculations are to be performed.

(Although these are simple fundamentals that make programming "easy" on its face, programs can become exceedingly complicated as the number of operations—as measured by the number of lines of code—increases. It is not unusual for large programs to exceed 100,000 lines of code; in this text, we will only include programs of modest size while explaining relevant concepts.).

Operations that the computer can perform include data transfer or movement, arithmetic, and logical comparisons (e.g., determining whether two quantities are equal to each other). Unless otherwise instructed, the computer executes one instruction at a time in the order in which the instruction is encountered. The power of the computer comes from its ability to change this strict sequence. When developing a program, the user normally designs a logical solution to his or her problem—the *algorithm*. Language statements will support the underlying algorithm and, except in the most trivial examples, will include a number of *control structures* for altering the strict sequential order. There are six commonly recognized *primitive* control structures, and an interrelated sequence of these structures can be used to define the algorithm. (These primitive structures are themselves composed of several *basic* elements.)

Two methods have been used to implement algorithm designs; one is graphical and the second is linguistic. The graphic method for defining a program is embodied in a *flow*

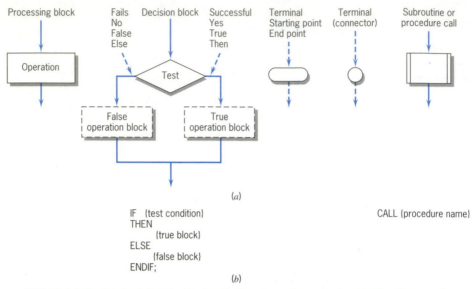

FIGURE 1.9   The basic building blocks of software control organization. (a) Flow Diagram. (b) Pseudocode equivalents where applicable.

diagram. The basic building blocks of Flow Diagrams are shown in Fig. 1.9*a* and include the following.

- **Processing block**   An operation to be performed is specified within the processing block.
- **Decision block**   A test, normally a comparison, is specified; if the test is passed, the program continues on the successful branch named, variously, *yes, true,* or *then;* if the test fails, program control is transferred to the (fails) branch named, variously, *no, false,* or *else.*
- **Procedure or subroutine**   A distinct body of code is specified within another flow diagram. Upon entry into such a block, control is transferred to the (program) name specified within the procedure block. Upon completion of the referenced code, the program continues on the branch leaving the procedure block.
- **Connector**   This specifies a program continuation and is especially useful for large flow diagrams that may be spread over several pages. Terminals with the same designator (e.g., "x") represent common continuation branches in a Flow Diagram.
- **Terminal**   This term specifies the start or end of a program and/or procedure.

(Some literature specifies additional symbols such as one for secondary storage operations; these are not particularly important for scientific or engineering problems, however, and the set described above is satisfactory for applications in this text.)

All languages include syntactical elements (statements) to support these blocks. Because the syntax varies from one language to another, many people use a generic form of these statements known as *pseudocode* in place of the flow diagram graphics. Algorithms are then described using this pseudocode rather than a flow diagram. The pseudocode equivalents of the flow diagram basic building blocks are shown in Fig. 1.9*b* and include

- The pseudocode for a decision block:

```
IF {condition}
      THEN
              {true block pseudocode statements}
      ELSE
              {false block pseudocode statements}
ENDIF;
```

The "{condition}" phrase will be replaced by the test to be made in any given application; {true block ... statements} and {false block ... statements} will also be replaced by appropriate actions, including the possibility for no action {absence of the THEN or ELSE branch) or another "enclosed" decision block (*nested* decision blocks).

- The pseudocode for a procedure block:

```
      CALL {procedure entity or name};
```

A specific object (name) will replace {procedure ... name} in a given application. The other basic building block flow diagram elements do not have pseudocode equivalents. However, the primitive control elements that are built from these basic elements do have pseudocode representation as described below.

The basic building blocks may be combined into a set of primitive structures as shown in Fig. 1.10a; also shown in the figure are the pseudocode equivalents (Fig. 1.10b). The simplest organization consists of *sequential* processing blocks; this is representative of the computer executing instructions one at a time, in the order in which they are encountered without deviation. The remaining primitives are all concerned with repetition in one form or another. There are three types of repetition:

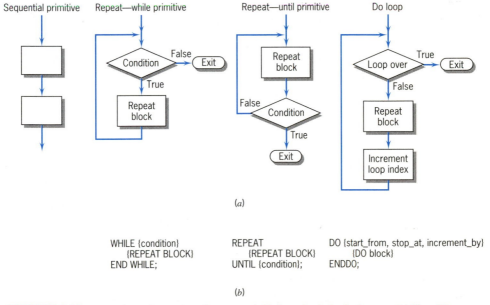

(a)

```
WHILE {condition}             REPEAT                    DO {start_from, stop_at, increment_by}
     {REPEAT BLOCK}               {REPEAT BLOCK}             {DO block}
END WHILE;                     UNTIL {condition};        ENDDO;
```

(b)

FIGURE 1.10   Primitive software control structures built from the the basic elements. (a) Flow Diagram. (b) Pseudocode equivalents where applicable.

- **DO LOOPs**   A DO LOOP may be employed when a group of instructions is to be repeated a fixed number of times. The loop is characterized by three parameters that determine the control of the *loop counter*: the {start} value is the initial setting of this counter; the {stop} value determines when the loop is terminated—the loop terminates when the number of repetitions *exceeds* the {stop} value; and for each repetition of the statements within the loop, the loop counter is incremented by an amount denoted by {increment}. The *loop block* includes the instructions to be completed; the block can consist of additional basic or primitive structures (e.g., another DO LOOP that results in a nested DO LOOP organization). Initially, control is transferred to the start of the loop; values for {start}, {stop}, and {increment} are determined by instructions prior to entry—this is *loop initialization*. On occasion, the initial value of {start} may exceed the value of {stop}; in such instances, the loop is not to be repeated at all. In most cases, the loop will be repeated one or more times. When it has been executed the requisite number of times, the loop is terminated—*exit*. (Within the loop block there may be additional programmatic tests that may result in an *abnormal* termination of the loop from some intermediate point in the block of code [program]. An example of such tests is checking for an error such as the presence of a negative result when none is expected.)

- **DO WHILE**   This is the first of two structures in which the number of repetitions of the *repeat block* may not be known in advance of its execution. For this architecture, a {condition} is tested at the beginning of the structure. If the condition is validated, ("true branch") control passes to the repeat block. This block contains other basic or primitive structures, one of which normally alters the test condition. (If it did not, the loop would never terminate.) The {condition} is tested again and if it fails, the loop is terminated.

- **DO UNTIL**   This is the second form of repetition where a modification within the loop determines whether the loop is to continue. It differs from the DO WHILE primitive in one important respect: the repeat block is executed *at least* once—{condition} is tested *after* processing of the repeat block. In other respects, it is similar to the DO WHILE primitive.

A given computer language may not include the entire repertoire of basic and primitive structures outlined above, but each includes the possibility of "emulating" the ones that it does not support directly.

There are two different "styles" of program development:

1. **Top-down**   Some users prefer to start from a "global" view of the problem solution and provide procedures to support the algorithm in increasing detail; each required process block is further decomposed into appropriate structures.

2. **Bottom-up**   Other users prefer to implement procedure details first and then combine these into a coherent program that supports the algorithm.

(Some programmers use a combination of top-down and bottom-up approaches, detailing code that supports more delicate aspects of the problem early in the development cycle in order to establish feasibility.) With the symbols and/or the pseudocode shown above, a user can readily specify the problem solution, as the following example demonstrates.

EXAMPLE 1.10 Designing a Computer Program to Study Animal Behavior

Various animal behaviors, including alcohol consumption, are to be studied, perhaps to gain insights into addictive behavior. (The pseudocode as well as the flow diagram to be described will support any number of animal studies—for example, obesity research.) Of interest are factors such as the amount of exercise (spontaneous locomotive behavior) these animals get; the nature of their caloric intake (e.g., calories from alcohol versus the quantity ingested from solid food); and the quantity of water ingested. The instrumentation setup is to include resources for a large population of animals (e.g., 128 stations). Each station includes a solid food feeder, several tubes filled with water and/or water–alcohol mixtures, and an exercise wheel that can be freely accessed by the animal. (For purposes of this discussion, mice are assumed to be the animals under investigation.) Each station is equipped with electromechanical devices that convert licking behavior into electrical information that can be detected by the computer. Experimental parameters include the following: the number of animals in the given experiment, how often each station is to be sampled, the starting time of the experiment, the stopping time of the experiment, and possibly some indication of experimental groups that represent alternatives (hypotheses) being studied (e.g., the susceptibility of a particular strain of animal to addiction).

The pseudocode is shown in Fig. 1.11. (All programming languages have some method for including comments within the code; in the case of pseudocode, any textual material preceded by an asterisk (*) will signal the start of a *comment*. The comment is considered to end at the next carriage return. The *end* statement is equivalent to the terminal element in a flow diagram.) The pseudocode is organized using the top-down programming style. The pseudocode is virtually self-documenting, but additional comments and explanations for each module may be helpful.

- **Main program**   The programming problem subsumes three procedures: the user must enter the parameters associated with the experiment (call to procedure parameter_input); continue collecting data from the stations during the experimental trial (call to procedure data_acquisition); and generate a printed tabulation ("hard copy") of the results (call to procedure report_generator).

- **Procedure parameter_input**   Logically, the module calls for the user to repeatedly enter the parameters of the experiment. (The pseudocode might even specify all the parameters to be entered, but such detail would overly complicate the example.) Entering parametric data requires the computer to prompt the user (e.g., "Please enter the number of stations"); the computer reads the value that is entered and checks the validity of the value. This last process block is included to make a point: a good program will often include checks on data that are entered from the keyboard. For example, suppose the particular data to be entered is a real number and the user enters alphanumeric data by mistake; the computer should recognize this error and prompt the user for an appropriate value.

- **Procedure data_acquisition**   The computer continues to collect data from all the stations—DO (station_1, last_station, increment_1)—from the start of the experiment until the end of experiment at times specified by time_to_sample. The symbols within the WHILE loop test condition (<> and >) stand for "not equal to" and "greater than," respectively. The procedure, "collect_counts," is included as a functional (logical) requirement, but corresponding code has been omitted for simplicity.

- **Procedure report_generator**   The final procedure supports the tabulation of results and provides a printed or hard copy of the data that have been collected. A heading is printed, summarizing general information (experimental name, date, parameter values, etc.). For each station the data that have been collected are first converted into appropriate units. (E.g., licks on the solid food dispenser are converted to calories, based on knowledge, of course, of the caloric properties of the

```
* Start of the main program
       CALL parameter_input;
       CALL data_acquisition;
       CALL report_generation;
END main;

* PROCEDURE parameter_input
       REPEAT
              prompt_user_for_parameter;
              read_value;
              check_for_errors; *wrong number
       UNTIL (all_parameters_read);

* PROCEDURE data_acquisition
       WHILE (current_time < > stop_time and current_time > start_time)
              IF (time_to_sample)
                     THEN
                            DO (station_1, last_station, increment_1)
                                   CALL collect_counts;
                            ENDO;
              ENDIF;
       END WHILE;
END data_acquisition;

*PROCEDURE report_generator
       print header; *experiment name, data, parameter values
       DO (station_1, last_station, increment_1)
              print station_number;
              print group_type;
              DO (start_time, stop_time, sample_time
                  compute calories_of_solid_food;
                  compute water_intake;
                  compute alcohol_intake;
                  compute exercise;
                  print calories_of_solid_food;
                  print water_intake;
                  print alcohol_intake;
                  print exercise;
              ENDDO;
       ENDDO;
END report_generator;

* Physical end;
```

FIGURE 1.11   Pseudocode for behavioral study.

food as well as the sample taken with each lick.) This is followed by a print statement for each of the collected variables.

Although programming details have been omitted, the pseudocode provides the programmer with a logical framework in which to specify syntactical statements within the programming language. It is an important aid for anyone who must understand the program details and who is asked to modify the program at a later date. The algorithm is depicted as a flow diagram in Fig. 1.12.

The CPU, memory, I/O, and system bus constitute the basic functional (hardware) components of the modern computer. The OS provides control of these elements. A primary function of the OS is management of the file system that is found in the secondary

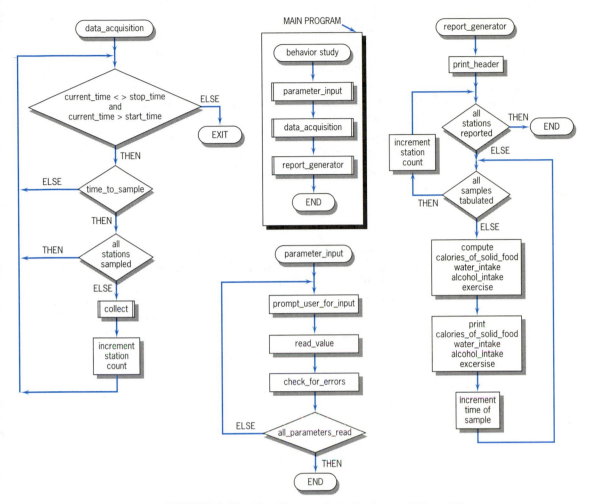

FIGURE 1.12   Flow Diagram solution for data acquisition problems.

storage facility of the computer system and that ultimately retains (soft) copies of a user's files. Files can include a program (in both executable form or in its original version), or a collection of data that are generated as a result of executing a program (e.g., the results of a FORTRAN 90 program or a report that is produced by a word processing program). A user must be able to judge the significance of a computer's output, particularly through an understanding of the resolution and/or accuracy of the numbers involved in the calculations. For a scientific or engineering problem, the algorithm may be specified using a series of generic symbols or phrases. When using symbols, the result is a flow diagram; when using English-like phrases, the outcome is called a pseudocode program.

PROBLEMS

1.1   Name at least five computer applications from distinct scientific or engineering disciplines. Be explicit and provide details to support your answer for using a computer program in each instance.

1.2 Design a file system that might be suitable for a manufacturing plant. In particular, organize the system as a logical series of directories and subdirectories in which to retain the organization files. Take into account the following.

- The system should be limited to the following technical departments: engineering, production, test, and field service.
- Within the engineering departments, provision should be made for both electrical and mechanical engineering.
- The engineering departments need files to be stored according to either specification, design, or documentation files.
- The field service department has to keep reports from different regions of the country.

1.3 **(a)** A file system has the following (partial) organization:

- The root directory includes a subdirectory named RADARS.
- Within the subdirectory named RADARS is a file called X_band.

What DOS command will cause the file X_band to be displayed on the computer's monitor? (Assume that the current directory is the root directory.)

(b) Indicate two distinct methods (DOS commands) that would reproduce the contents of the file X_band to be printed on a printer rather than being displayed on the monitor.

1.4 What DOS command will generate a "hard" or printed copy of the current directory?

1.5 What is a file?

1.6 **(a)** Write the DOS command that will create the (sub)directory named "simulate."

(b) Is there anything wrong with the subdirectory named "simulations"?

(c) Write the DOS command that will erase ("remove") the (sub)directory named "simulate." *N.B.*: You must erase or delete all files in a subdirectory before removing it.

(d) What DOS command will erase the file named "oldstuff"?

1.7 How many significant digits are contained in the following numbers?

2319

−89.9

13500

0.0674

0.001

25.010

1.8 Calculate each result and adjust the answer by applying the rules for significant digits:

(a) $3.15 + 2.061 + 3.2$

(b) $81.18 * 2.93 * 3.6$ (The asterisk "*" indicates a multiplication operation.)

(c) $8.731 - 2.14 + 0.22$

(d) $(6.3200)/(1.100 * 3.250)$

(e) $100.1 - 7.02 + 5.132 * 6.02$

1.9 Determine the resolution for each of the following numbers:

    (a) 0.080

    (b) $11.5 * 10^3$

1.10 Calculate the decimal equivalent of the following binary numbers.

    (a) 11011011

    (b) 10.11

1.11 Compute the negative of the binary number 01101101 and find its decimal equivalent.

1.12 Convert the binary number 10011001 to decimal by first converting it to hex and then from hex to decimal. Check your answer by direct conversion and from binary to decimal.

1.13 Convert the decimal number 213 to binary by first finding its hex equivalent and then converting the hex to binary.

1.14 A falling body normally encounters air resistance that causes the resultant velocity to differ from its value when falling in a vacuum. The following equation governs the velocity of a body falling through air:

$$m\frac{v_{n+1} - v_n}{h} = mg - mrv_n$$

In this equation,

    m is the mass of the falling body,

    v_n is the velocity of the falling body at time t_n,

    v_{n+1} is the velocity of the falling body at time t_{n+1},

    h is the small time interval ($t_n = nh$, $n = 0, 1, 2, 3, \ldots$),

    r is the constant that governs the air resistance, and

    g is the acceleration of the body due to gravitational forces ($g = 32.3$ ft/sec^2)

    (a) Draw a Flow Diagram that can be used as a basis for a computer program for solving this equation for the final, or terminal, velocity value. Assume that an initial velocity v_0 is given.

    (b) Write an equivalent pseudocode fragment.

1.15 A high-quality product is one that operates trouble-free for long periods of time in a variety of environments (e.g., in hot or cold temperatures, varying humidity, etc.). One measure of reliability is to estimate the Mean Time Between Failures (MTBF) of the product. The following procedure describes the computation:

    1. Obtain inputs (from the user) for

       • The number of components of each type in the circuit (n_i) where i is the type.

       • The mean (expected) failure rate for each type of component, f_i.

       • The environmental stress factor for each type of component, w_i.

       • The time over which the MTBF is to be calculated, t; this is the so-called mission time.

    2. Compute the component failure rates for each type of component, as follows:

$$n_i * f_i$$

3. Calculate the unadjusted total failure rate as

$$\sum_{i=1}^{n} n_i * f_i$$

4. Compute the adjusted total failure rate as

$$\text{Total failure rate} = \sum_{i=1}^{n} n_i * f_i * w_i$$

5. Calculate MTBF as

$$MTBF = \frac{10^6}{\text{results of step 4}}$$

Note: Most components should have failure rates that extend over millions of hours. Therefore, MTBF includes 10^6 in the numerator so that the result will have units of hours.

6. Print the MTBF and the product reliability which is given by

$$\text{Product reliability} = \epsilon^{-\frac{t}{MTBF}} * 100 \quad (\%)$$

where t is the mission time.

Write a pseudocode program that permits a user to calculate MTBF. Draw an equivalent flow diagram.

1.16 Engineers and scientists are often involved with the design and operation of various processing facilities that produce chemicals and materials (e.g., sulfuric acid,

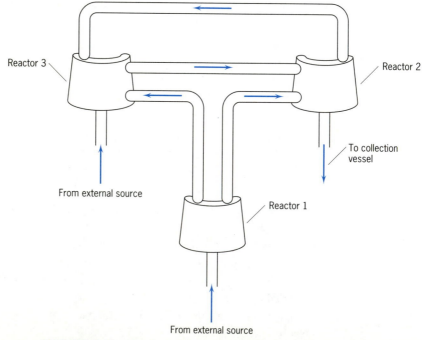

Reactor 3

Reactor 2

To collection vessel

From external source

Reactor 1

From external source

FIGURE 1.13   Sample chemical processing arrangement for Problem 1.16.

paper, polyester). To do so requires a series of steps in which ingredients flow into or out of a reaction vessel (or reactor). It is necessary to ensure that (in the "steady state") the mass inflow equals the mass outflow for each reactor. To confirm this, a number of linear and nonlinear algebraic equations must be solved; these are mass, material, and energy balance calculations. Reactors may be connected to each other in various ways (by pipes), and in the steady state mass balance and mass transfer into one reactor should equal transfer out of the reactor. The rate of transfer of chemicals through the pipes is given by the product of the flow rate and the concentration of the chemicals. (An example of such an arrangement is shown in the Fig. 1.13.) Write a program using pseudocode and draw the corresponding flow diagram that permits a user to compute the concentrations in each reactor. (Solve the problem in general and not just for the arrangement shown in the figure.) Take into account the following:

1. Input from the user:
   - Number of reactors and their interconnections.
   - Flow rate from external sources into each reactor.
2. Write a mass balance equation for each reactor:

$$\text{Mass in} = \text{Mass out}$$

   where masses are computed as flow rate * concentration.
3. Calculate concentrations for each reactor. (*Hint*: Because of feedback between reactors, several iterations may be needed. These should be outlined in your solution. For example, the concentration of reactor 1 may depend in part on the concentration in reactor 2, which itself may depend on the concentration in reactor 1.)
4. Print concentrations for all reactors.

1.17 One programming control structure that can be built up from the primitive architectures is the IF-ELSEIF statement. Its pseudocode is given by

```
IF {condition_1} THEN
        {condition_1 block}
ELSE IF {condition_2} THEN
        {condition_2 block}
ELSE IF
        ---
        ELSE {condition_n}
        {condition_n block}
END IF
```

It operates as follows:
   - Each condition is tested in the order in which it is encountered in the statement.
   - If the test passes, the corresponding {condition_i block} is executed; once completed, the algorithm proceeds to the process that follows the END IF code.
   - If the test fails, control passes to the next test condition.
   - The ELSE test (block) need not be present.

Draw a flow diagram for the IF-ELSE IF control structure.

2

FORTRAN 90
Programming
Procedure

A *program* consists of a detailed and explicit set of directions for completing some task. In the case of FORTRAN 90, these instructions are initially expressed using "English-like" expressions that, taken together, form the *source program* (or source code and informally referred to as "the source"). In order for the user's intentions to be successfully executed, the source program must first be entered into the computer's memory and subsequently translated by software into a form that the computer can ultimately execute. The translation program is called a *compiler*, and the code it produces is called *object code*. The object code goes through one additional processing step (*linking*) that readies the program for execution once it is loaded (from the secondary storage system) into the computer's main memory. If any errors are introduced at any time during these steps, they must be corrected; otherwise, the program will not execute successfully. It is important to test the resultant program; once this is completed to the user's satisfaction, the executable code is available to be used at will. *This chapter will provide an overview of the FORTRAN 90 program development cycle, including designing a simple program, creating the source code using an editor program, translating (compiling) of the source code, and executing or running the program.*

2.1 STEPS IN PROGRAM DEVELOPMENT

Figure 2.1 presents the steps that are needed to develop a FORTRAN 90 program successfully. The computer's secondary storage system contains all the programs that are required for translation and execution; these have (previously) been installed and include an editor, a compiler, and a linker/loader. We now discuss these terms.

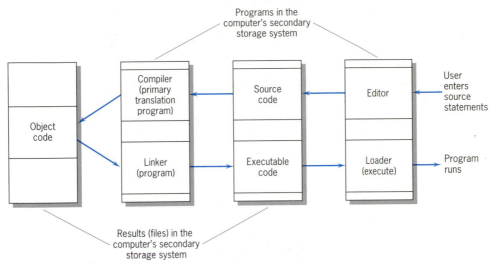

FIGURE 2.1 The steps, facilities used, and results generated in the course of the development of a FORTRAN 90 program.

- *Editor* **(program)** By means of this program, a user may enter and/or correct (insert or delete) the textual material that comprises a new or existing source program. The source program resides in a file to which the programmer assigns a name (e.g., CALC_AVG.F90).

- *Compiler* **(program)** A compiler accepts the source code (which has been produced by the editor) and produces another code that is the first step toward ultimately creating a machine language (executable) version. Initially, the compiler generates a form of machine code known as an *object program*. Instructions within the object program can refer to FORTRAN 90 programs that are located elsewhere in secondary storage—in particular to certain modules (called *procedures* or *routines*) that are contained in a *library* of such utilities. An example of such a module is the one that can calculate the square root of a number. A program is needed to perform this computation, and it is normally written by the manufacturer of the FORTRAN 90 compiler; it is subsequently stored in the library where it may be called into action by a user's program.

  The compiler accepts a source file and produces a second file that is (automatically) stored in the computer's secondary storage system. The name assigned to the object file is normally the same as the source file with a minor modification that identifies it as an object file. (For example, if CALC_AVG.F90 were the name of the source file, then CALC_AVG.OBJ would be the name of the object file. Notice that the software has changed "F90" to "OBJ.")

- *Loader* **(or linkage editor)** The second stage of the complete translation process is carried out by another program called a *linkage editor* (or more commonly known simply as a *linker*). This program acts to replace any unresolved references within the object file with the proper code from the library routines. A new file is then created and stored in the secondary memory. (Continuing with the example cited previously, the name of this new file will become CALC_AVG.EXE. The "EXE" designation identifies this file as one that can be stored (*loaded*) in the computer's main memory where it is conveniently *executed* or *run*.)

The physical steps that are required to develop a FORTRAN 90 program are summarized in Fig. 2.1. It is important to note that the figure does not include any of the conceptual thinking that is required prior to compilation. Nor does it include the thorough testing that is required to confirm the reliability and accuracy of the executable version.

Step 1   User invokes (runs) the editor, enters the source text, and stores the results in a file.

Step 2   A command to the computer's Operating System (OS) starts the compiler; part of the command includes the name of the source file. If there are no errors, an object file will be produced. If the compiler encounters violations of the FORTRAN 90 rules, a message will appear on the computer's monitor citing the difficulty. The user must go back to step 1 to rectify the problem.

Step 3   The loader is invoked with the name of the object file appended to the command. If no errors exist—such as a reference in the object code to a procedure that cannot be found in the secondary storage system—the computer will produce a file that can be executed.

Step 4   To execute the program, the user simply enters the name of the executable file.

2.2 CREATING THE SOURCE CODE

Editor programs that are compatible with an OS-DOS—in this case—range from some that have few commands to those that are powerful and relatively easy to use. (In fact, DOS itself can be used to create a source file using the *copy* command. This will not be described, however, because, among other deficits, it has very little provision for changing text.) Most modern versions of DOS include an editor program that is easy to use and is representative of many others.

2.2.1 A Sample Problem

The sample program described here will be used as the model for creating the source program, compiling it, and loading and executing the target program. This program is not designed in the most efficient way. It minimizes the number of different FORTRAN 90 statements that the reader must understand at this point. Instead, the emphasis will be on the steps previously described and summarized in Fig. 2.1. The FORTRAN 90 statements themselves will be explained with regard to their intent; formal presentation of the syntax (or rules of the language) are described in the chapters that follow. Because a FORTRAN 90 program includes many statements that resemble ordinary English, reading and following the underlying logic of a simple program is not difficult. FORTRAN 90 errors will be deliberately introduced to illustrate what may typically occur during program development.

A recurring task that scientists and engineers encounter is the need to average a list of numbers. There are many examples in science and engineering: averaging the temperatures measured at various points in a process plant (chemical engineering), averaging the measured values of resistances to be used in a circuit design (electrical engineering), averaging the distributed loads on a beam in order to determine its size (mechanical/civil engineering), averaging the number of signals ("pulses") per second being generated by a neuron (neurophysiology), and averaging the amount of energy (gas or electric) produced or consumed during the month (industrial engineering or engineering management). We may specify the problem to be solved by breaking it down into a series of broad tasks and related subtasks to be completed as the program is executed, notably:

1. Permit the user to enter the real numbers to be averaged.
2. Average the numbers.
3. Print the results.

These steps may be restated using the idea of a program pseudocode introduced in Chapter 1. A compact pseudocode description is a good starting point for program development; it improves the chances for successful implementation of a FORTRAN 90 program.

```
PROGRAM CALC_AVG
DISPLAY A SHORT MESSAGE OF EXPLANATION;
        CLEAR PREVIOUS RESULTS;
        SET INITIAL VALUES FOR IMPORTANT UNKNOWNS;
        PROMPT USER FOR THE FIRST NUMBER TO BE INCLUDED IN THE
             AVERAGE;
        ACCEPT THE FIRST NUMBER FROM THE USER;
        PROMPT THE USER FOR THE SECOND NUMBER TO BE INCLUDED IN THE
             AVERAGE;
        ACCEPT THE SECOND NUMBER FROM THE USER;
                * * *
        PROMPT THE USER FOR THE FIFTH NUMBER TO BE INCLUDED IN THE
             AVERAGE;
        ACCEPT THE FIFTH NUMBER FROM THE USER;
        CALCULATE AVERAGE BY DIVIDING THE (RUNNING) SUM BY 5, THE
                NUMBER OF ITEMS ENTERED;
        DISPLAY RESULTANT AVERAGE AND NUMBER OF ITEMS INCLUDED IN
                THE AVERAGE;
END PROGRAM;
```

Figure 2.2 displays a flow diagram that depicts the logic of the pseudocode in an equivalent form. To calculate correct averages, the program must first clear any prior results; namely, the sum of all previously entered values must be set to 0. The user is prompted for the first number to be averaged. The user's response is entered into the computer's memory (READ). The process of prompting the user and storing his or her responses continues until all five numbers to be averaged have been entered.

Once all the numbers are entered and the user signals completion of data entry, the program proceeds to calculate the average. This is accomplished by dividing the running sum, which has been maintained within the computer, by the number of items that have been entered by the user—five in this case. The mathematical representation of this is given by

$$\overline{X} = \frac{n_1 + n_2 \cdots + n_r}{N}$$

where

$\overline{X}$ is the average,

n_i indicates a number to be averaged,

and

N is the number of items included in the average ($N = 5$)

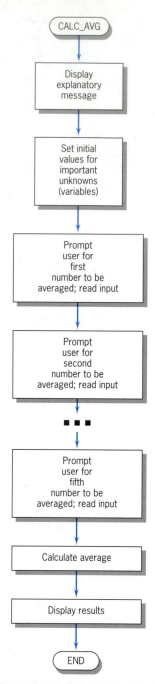

FIGURE 2.2 Flow Diagram for calculating the average of a series of five numbers.

In this case $N = 5$. The results are subsequently displayed on the computer's monitor. The program terminates, and control of the computer is returned to the OS: normally, the OS prompt is visible on the monitor. To invoke the program again, the user simply types the name of the file that contains the executable code—the file whose name includes the ".EXE" extension—when the OS prompt appears on the monitor.

2.2.2 FORTRAN 90 Source Code

Figure 2.3 depicts the source code for the program that averages a sequence of numbers to be entered by a user. Shown in the figure are a series of markers that do not belong to the program itself but identify those elements of the program that are explained below.

Like other high-level languages (HLLs), FORTRAN 90 includes a number of words with special meanings; these are references that the compiler uses when translating the source code. They may signal the start of a section (block) of code (e.g., a DO block that is described in Chapter 5), or they may represent operations that are to be completed

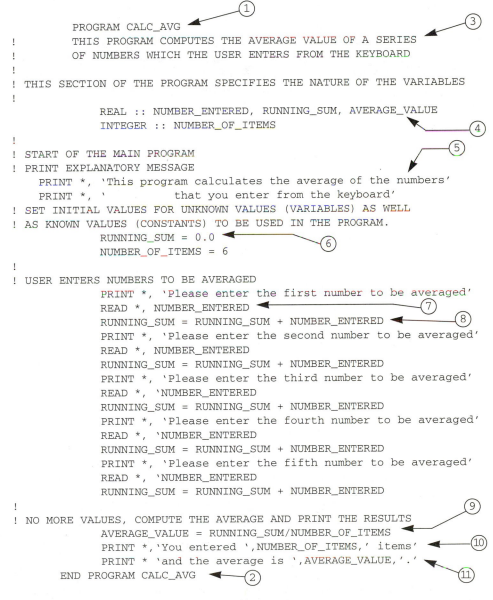

```fortran
        PROGRAM CALC_AVG                                         ①
!       THIS PROGRAM COMPUTES THE AVERAGE VALUE OF A SERIES          ③
!       OF NUMBERS WHICH THE USER ENTERS FROM THE KEYBOARD
!
! THIS SECTION OF THE PROGRAM SPECIFIES THE NATURE OF THE VARIABLES
!
        REAL :: NUMBER_ENTERED, RUNNING_SUM, AVERAGE_VALUE
        INTEGER :: NUMBER_OF_ITEMS                               ④
!
! START OF THE MAIN PROGRAM                                      ⑤
! PRINT EXPLANATORY MESSAGE
    PRINT *, 'This program calculates the average of the numbers'
    PRINT *, '            that you enter from the keyboard'
! SET INITIAL VALUES FOR UNKNOWN VALUES (VARIABLES) AS WELL
! AS KNOWN VALUES (CONSTANTS) TO BE USED IN THE PROGRAM.
        RUNNING_SUM = 0.0
        NUMBER_OF_ITEMS = 6                               ⑥
!
! USER ENTERS NUMBERS TO BE AVERAGED
        PRINT *, 'Please enter the first number to be averaged'
        READ *, NUMBER_ENTERED                             ⑦
        RUNNING_SUM = RUNNING_SUM + NUMBER_ENTERED         ⑧
        PRINT *, 'Please enter the second number to be averaged'
        READ *, NUMBER_ENTERED
        RUNNING_SUM = RUNNING_SUM + NUMBER_ENTERED
        PRINT *, 'Please enter the third number to be averaged'
        READ *, 'NUMBER_ENTERED
        RUNNING_SUM = RUNNING_SUM + NUMBER_ENTERED
        PRINT *, 'Please enter the fourth number to be averaged'
        READ *, 'NUMBER_ENTERED
        RUNNING_SUM = RUNNING_SUM + NUMBER_ENTERED
        PRINT *, 'Please enter the fifth number to be averaged'
        READ *, 'NUMBER_ENTERED
        RUNNING_SUM = RUNNING_SUM + NUMBER_ENTERED
!
! NO MORE VALUES, COMPUTE THE AVERAGE AND PRINT THE RESULTS      ⑨
        AVERAGE_VALUE = RUNNING_SUM/NUMBER_OF_ITEMS
        PRINT *,'You entered ',NUMBER_OF_ITEMS,' items'          ⑩
        PRINT * 'and the average is ',AVERAGE_VALUE,'.'
    END PROGRAM CALC_AVG                          ②                ⑪
```

FIGURE 2.3 Annotated FORTRAN 90 source code for sample program.

(e.g., PRINT in this program). Such words within a program are called *keywords* or *reserved* words. The program in Fig. 2.3 includes a number of such words, for example, PROGRAM, REAL, and PRINT. These words have been reserved for exclusive and specialized use by the compiler and are designated for such purposes within the ISO (International Standards Organization) FORTRAN 90 standard. For the discussions below, refer to the corresponding numbers in the figure.

1 and 2. PROGRAM CALC_AVG and END PROGRAM CALC_AVG

The PROGRAM statement **(1)** defines the start of the source code, and the END statement is the very last physical statement. Although a PROGRAM statement is not required in FORTRAN 90, we strongly recommend its use. When included, it should be followed by the name of the program; in this case we chose CALC_AVG, which helps to remind the reader of the program's purpose. The END statement **(2)** is required even if we do not use a PROGRAM statement. This keyword defines the physical end of the source code for the compiler. In addition, the program stops when it logically encounters the END statement. When a PROGRAM statement is included, the END statement should contain the corresponding name of the program as shown in the example.

3. ! THIS PROGRAM . . . OF A SERIES

The exclamation sign (!) indicates that whatever follows is a comment. Comments are important for a number of reasons: they help someone reading the program to follow the logic or problem solution; they can be used to identify certain parts of the FORTRAN 90 source code, like the section that specifies various features of the data to be encountered; they may be used to make the entire program (physically) easier to read. An example of this latter purpose can be seen when a comment line contains no text as shown in the figure. The effect is to create a visually empty space, known as "white space." A comment statement need not occupy an entire line within the source; it may be included in other FORTRAN 90 statements. Normally, within a statement anything that follows the exclamation is treated as a comment.

4. REAL:: VALUE . . . AVERAGE_VALUE

Data represent one of the most important parts of any program. The compiler, for example, needs to know if the numbers or information to be encountered are integers (whole numbers) or real numbers or even alphabetic characters, among other kinds of data. One reason for this follows from the fact that the compiler adjusts its object code according to the data specified in a calculation. It performs arithmetic (e.g., addition) operations differently for integers and real numbers. In the absence of user-supplied information, the compiler makes its own judgments—*default* conclusions—about the data. It is strongly recommended that the user specify the types of data used in a program instead of relying on default data typing.

Data are most often given a *symbolic name* so that they can be referred to within a FORTRAN 90 statement. This name should reflect the data's purpose and may be quite long—up to 31 characters in length. For example, within the program we have chosen the name NUMBER_OF_ITEMS in order to be able to refer to the number of data items to be included in the average. Another example is RUNNING_SUM, which retains the sum of all numbers entered by the user. Such choices help a reader to readily understand the averaging algorithm.

Because the sum of numbers to be averaged will vary during the course of the program's execution, it is referred to as a *variable*. Numbers whose value remains the same throughout the course of the program are referred to as *constants*.

The program that averages the user-supplied data includes the following variables.

Variable Name	Type
NUMBER_ENTERED	Real-valued
RUNNING_SUM	Real-valued
AVERAGE_VALUE	Real-valued
NUMBER_OF_ITEMS	Integer-valued

The *specification* section (starting at the statement identified as 4 in Fig. 2.3) of a FORTRAN 90 program defines the nature of the data that are found in the program. In this example, there are four *data objects* as indicated in the table above. To identify the real variables, the keyword (or reserved phrase) "REAL::" is followed by a list of all the real variables, separated by commas. (A symbol that separates parts of a program is called a *delimiter*.) The word INTEGER, followed by a list of variables, serves a similar purpose for those objects that will be interpreted as integers. (In this example, there is only one item following INTEGER::.)

5. PRINT*, 'This program calculates. . .the numbers'

Statement 5 is the start of the main portion of the program. All FORTRAN 90 programs have exactly one main program. A program may include references to other programs called *subprograms*. (These will be described in detail in Chapter 7, but they are not required in this example.) The "PRINT*," phrase is a simple FORTRAN 90 command that instructs the computer to display information on its monitor (screen). Information can include text, values of any variables, or a mixture of the two. The information to be displayed is contained in a list using commas as delimiters and follows the PRINT*, keyword. Any text that is to be displayed must be placed between two apostrophes ('). In the case of the statement identified by 5, the user will see

```
This program calculates the average of the numbers
```

on the monitor when the statement is executed. Each PRINT*, command automatically causes the cursor to move to a new line on the monitor by appending *line-feed* and *carriage return* (LFCR) control characters to the text. The PRINT*, statement following 5 will complete the brief explanatory note to a user regarding the nature of the program being executed. This provides a "user-friendly" introduction to someone who does not know what the program is intended to do. The user sees

```
that you enter from the keyboard.
```

just below the previous text. Notice that a series of spaces are included in this PRINT*, statement. Spaces within textual material will be reproduced on the monitor just as any other alphanumeric character.

6. RUNNING_SUM = 0.0

This is the first example of a very important FORTRAN 90 statement known as the *assignment statement*. Such statements form the heart of a computer program. Simply stated, operations listed on the right-hand side of the equal sign (=) are performed, and when complete, the variable on the left-hand side of the equal sign assumes the resulting value. In the case of statement 6, the computer starts by setting the result to "0.0"; since no other computations are shown, the variable RUNNING_SUM assumes the value 0.0. This "initializes" the sum of numbers to be entered to 0.0. A value of 0.0 is deliberately chosen because RUNNING_SUM is a real-valued variable and 0.0 (as opposed to simply 0) explicitly notes this fact. (The program would also work had 0 been used in place of 0.0; this will be explained in Chapter 3.) Wherever possible, we encourage the user to use the same data types on the right-hand side and left-hand side of all assignment statements. This will minimize unexpected side effects that may introduce subtle logical errors. The assignment statement following 6 (NUMBER_OF_ITEMS =6) sets the value of the integer variable equal to 6.

7. READ*, NUMBER_ENTERED

The READ*, command is a complement to the PRINT*, command. PRINT*, displays data on the monitor, and READ*, accepts data from a user that is entered via the keyboard. The list that follows—in this case the variable NUMBER_ENTERED—assumes the value entered by the user. The user "validates" the information by striking the key marked "Enter" on the keyboard. Once this happens, the variable will have the numerical value specified by the user. The number being entered appears on the monitor as it is typed, so that errors (e.g., typing a letter instead of a number) may be corrected by using the "rubout" key on the keyboard, which is often a key marked "←" adjacent to the number keys within the main section of the keyboard. If additional information is to be entered, the READ*, statement may include the names of the variables in the data list separated by commas. The user enters the values on the keyboard similarly separated by commas. Alternatively, a separate READ*, statement may be included for each object. (At this point, separate "READ*" statements are easier to explain; other (formatted) forms of the READ statement provide more flexibility and will be described in Chapter 4.)

8. RUNNING_SUM= RUNNING_SUM+ NUMBER_ENTERED

Statements of this type are fundamental to FORTRAN 90; all high-level programming languages must include provision for statements of this kind. As noted above, it is referred to as an assignment statement. The expression on the right-hand side of the equal sign is evaluated. When it is completed, the variable number on the left-hand side of the equal sign assumes the resultant value; the variable on the left-hand side of the equal sign is "assigned" the results of the calculations indicated on the right-hand side of the equal sign. The word "assignment" is deliberately chosen to distinguish interpretation of this statement from mathematical equality. The two sides of the equation are not "equal." (Some HLLs even use a special symbol such as := to indicate assignment, but FORTRAN 90 retains an equal sign so that the number of reserved words and symbols remains manageable.) Interpretation of the assignment statement that is used here is straightforward. The variable named NUMBER_ENTERED (which has just been entered by the user) is added to the variable RUNNING_SUM, and the result is then assigned to RUNNING_SUM. It is important to note that the value of RUNNING_SUM which is added to NUMBER_ENTERED is the value it had just before the statement was executed—its "current" value. After the assignment operation is completed, RUNNING_SUM will have its newly updated value. The overall result is that RUNNING_SUM always retains the sum of all numbers to be averaged as they are entered. (The assignment statement is repeated after each READ statement.) Notice that this variable (RUNNING_SUM) was initialized to 0 by the statement identified by marker 6. (The reader should recognize that this last statement (marker 8) is also a simple assignment statement.)

9. AVERAGE_VALUE= RUNNING_SUM/NUMBER_OF_ITEMS

This statement follows user entry of the numbers to be averaged. This assignment statement includes a new symbol that was not previously encountered, namely, "/". This is the FORTRAN 90 symbol for division. Thus, the average is computed by dividing the sum of numbers that have been entered by the number of items in the summation. This is in accord with the mathematical formula described in Sec. 2.2.1. The statements that follow statement 9 simply echo the results on the monitor and use PRINT*, as previously described.

10. PRINT*, 'You entered',NUMBER_OF_ITEMS,'items'

Recall that the PRINT*, command displays the values of all items in the list included within the statement and separated (delimited) by commas. In this case, the following sequence occurs:

- The phrase "You entered" appears on the monitor.
- This is followed by the value of the integer variable.

```
NUMBER_OF_ITEMS
```

- The line concludes with the phrase "items."

When the program is executed this line will appear as

```
You entered  6  items
```

11. PRINT* 'and the average is',AVERAGE_VALUE.'.'

At this point, a statement like this should not need further explanation. But observe the statement closely. Instead of "PRINT*," the statement is written as "PRINT*"—the comma following the asterisk (*) has been omitted. This is deliberate and will produce an error message during compilation, as described below. When the error is identified, the editor program must be invoked and the statement corrected by addition of the comma.

To make the program easier to read, some statements within the source code have been indented. These correspond to the indentations shown in the pseudocode above (Sec. 2.2.1). In general, indentations are provided whenever a block of code represents the start of a new logical task. The initialization sequence is one example of where indentation takes place.

2.2.3 Using an Editor Program to Create the Source File

After determining the algorithm to be used in the solution of a problem, the source code is created using some type of editor program. For example, you may use a word processing program. However, such programs insert various commands into the file that is generated—a command to set the margins to a specified value to cite one example. The FORTRAN 90 compiler will not "understand" such information, and numerous errors will result. You may, however, choose to use a word processing program to create the source code. If you do, make sure that the resultant file is saved in what is often called a generic format. The resultant file will be stripped of the word processing command characters, leaving only characters that are readily understood by the compiler. In this section, we describe a simple editor program included with the MS-DOS Operating System (version 6.2), which can be used to create the source file. It is typical of a number of similar editors.

The first step is to invoke (or execute) the editor program. Before invoking the editor, the OS is in control of the computer, and the monitor typically has a prompt awaiting commands from the user. (In some OSs, the user "points" to a picture or an icon that represents the editor program. This is done with a device known as a mouse.) In the case of the DOS, the prompt message might look like:

$$C:\backslash>.\ .\ .$$

where . . . indicates the position of a blinking cursor. The user may type

$$EDIT$$

or

$$EDIT\ FILENAME$$

where filename is the name of the file to be edited, followed by the Enter key in either case. (We could use edit CALC_AVG.F90 for the sample program.) Figure 2.4 is a sketch of the monitor in response to the *edit* command. The area in which textual material will be entered is the large central window. Notice the word "Untitled" at the top of this window. Had we used a specific filename, it would appear in this position.

The editor includes many helpful features; it is therefore considered to be "user-friendly." Only a few keys are needed for the user to be able to manipulate text, particularly those with a modest level of complexity like the source code for CALC_AVG.F90.

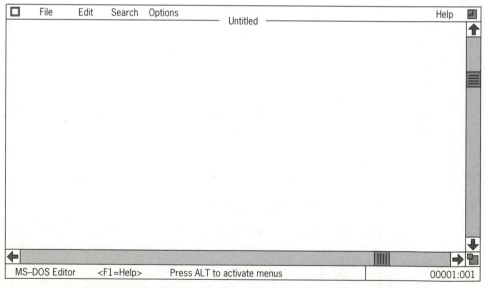

FIGURE 2.4 Sketch of monitor screen after invoking MS-DOS editor.

Extensive help and information about the editor is included within the program itself. To get such help, simply depress the key marked "F1" on the computer's keyboard. (The "F" keys are often referred to as function keys.) A summary of the purpose of the most important keys is included in Appendix B.

Additional aids are found in the messages located at the bottom of the display (Fig. 2.4). The prompt "<F1=Help>" advises the user that the function key marked "F1" on many keyboards will invoke an online help facility, if difficulties or questions arise. (The user should try this key and follow the instructions that are subsequently displayed on the monitor. Most of the features and editor controls are summarized directly on the computer's monitor.) Notice the prompt "Press ALT to activate menus"; this reminds a user of how to obtain the choices available at the top of the display—the menu field of the display. Finally, the numbers at the lower right-hand corner "00001:001" indicate the current position of the cursor. The first number is the line number at which it is located, and the second is its position within the line.

Many computers are equipped with a mouse or "pointing device," a small object that, when rolled around on a flat surface, causes an icon (small, lighted rectangle) to move about on the monitor in a corresponding manner. The presence of a mouse greatly simplifies operation of the editor program. Instead of using the keys, move the mouse so that the mouse-icon is located over the choices that appear at the top of the screen. The mouse contains two or three buttons (switches); when the icon is properly located, depress the button on the left side of the mouse device. For example, Fig. 2.5a shows the (monitor) results when the File option at the top of the screen is selected. A submenu appears, and the mouse is then used to select "Open. . ." (The shaded regions in the figure indicate resulting highlighting or reverse video fields.) When the Enter key is pressed, an image similar to the one shown in Fig. 2.5b appears on the monitor. All the files that may be opened are shown within the text window. In this case only one file is shown, CALC_AVG.F90. (The filename appears because it has been previously edited at an earlier time.) The messages at the bottom of the screen indicate what operational choices are available. By using the Tab key, the highlighted field will move to CALC_AVG.F90, and by depressing the Enter key, the name will appear in the box identifying the "File Name:" to be accessed (opened). Depressing the Enter key once more retrieves this file from the secondary store—in this case drive B:—and displays it within the text area of the editor program. This file is shown in Fig. 2.6; notice that the name of the file— CALC_AVG.F90—appears at the top of the window. The position of the cursor—the point at which text is presently being inserted—is shown as an underscore. (The cursor may be moved to a new position by using the Arrow key, but the mouse is a convenient way to achieve the same result. Simply position the icon over the letter of interest and depress the left mouse key.) The source code for CALC_AVG.F90 is readily created by entering it as shown in Fig. 2.3. It is advisable to store the source code periodically by selecting the File/Save option of the editor program. (In the event of an unexpected power failure, only text that has been entered since the last save operation will be lost.) When finished, choose the File/Exit option; the computer will prompt you to save the source once again before returning the computer to control by the OS.

2.3 TRANSLATING THE PROGRAM: COMPILING AND LINKING

Having created the source code in accordance with the procedures outlined in Sec. 2.1 and depicted in Fig. 2.1, the next step is to translate the English-like instructions into bi-

FIGURE 2.5 Sketch of the monitor screen for the MS-DOS edit program; (a) After a "File," "Open" choice. (b) When the File/Open option is executed.

nary, object code, and ultimately into machine-readable executable code. The familiar prompt will appear when the computer is once again under control of the OS. To invoke the primary translation program—the compiler[1]—the following should be typed:

```
FTN90 filename
```

In the present case, this becomes

---

[1]The FORTRAN 90 compiler used throughout this text is commercially available from Numerical Algorithms Group, Inc. (Nag), 1400 Opus Place, Downers Grove, Illinois, 60515, version 1.21.

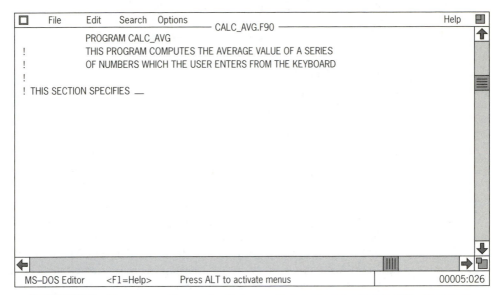

FIGURE 2.6   Appearance of the monitor during an editing session using the MS-DOS edit program.

```
FTN90 B:CALC_AVG
```

The prefix "B:" indicates to the compiler that this file is to be found in the secondary storage system and in particular on drive B, which is a floppy storage device. Notice that the extension ".F90" has been omitted. The compiler assumes that this is the case, and it may be excluded. However, if the programmer has used a different extension (e.g., ".295" to indicate the month and year of its origin), then the extension must be included. The command line shown above for invoking the compiler is its simplest form. A number of options (e.g., "/FIXED," which informs the compiler that the source program conforms to the fixed source code—see Sec. 3.7—which is characteristic of an earlier form of FORTRAN, namely FORTRAN 77) can be added to the command line.

When the compiler is invoked, the following sequence appears on the monitor.

```
[FTN90 Version 1.2 Copyright (c)SALFORD SOFTWARE LTD    &    ]
[                  (c)THE NUMERICAL ALGORITHMS GROUP 1991,1992]
Error: Syntax error at line 41
       ***Malformed statement
[FTN90 terminated—errors found by pass 1]
^C

C:\>
```

A check of the source code at line 41 indicates the erroneous statement with the missing comma. The editor is invoked, the commas are added to the statement, and the compiler is invoked once more. This time the result on the monitor is seen as

```
[FTN90 Version 1.2 Copyright (c)SALFORD SOFTWARE LTD    &    ]
[                  (c)THE NUMERICAL ALGORITHMS GROUP 1991,1992]
     NO ERRORS [FTN90]
```

The first pass in the translation process has been completed. To complete the process, the linker must be executed. This operation is accomplished as follows.

```
C:\>LINK77
[LINK77 Ver 2.66 Copyright (c) University of Salford 1991]
$ LOAD B:CALC_AVG
$ FILE B:CALC_AVG.EXE
Creating run file B:\CALC_AVG.EXE

C:\\>
```

The "$" is the prompt from the linker program which indicates that it is ready to accept user commands. The user responds by typing "LOAD B:CALC_AVG" followed by the Enter key. (Lower case letters may also be used.) When the linking portion of the sequence is complete, the "$" will reappear. The user then informs the linker that the executable file is to be created by entering "FILE B:CALC_AVG.EXE". As before, the B: indicates that these files are to be stored on secondary storage system drive B:. The computer responds with the indicated message, "Creating. . .EXE," and control passes to the OS. The program is now ready for execution at the convenience of the user and as many times as necessary without a need to use the translation procedure outlined above. (This, of course, assumes that there are no logical problems—unforeseen algorithm errors that produce erroneous results.) The program must be tested as much as possible before we can gain complete confidence in its performance.

2.4 RUNNING AND DEBUGGING A PROGRAM

When syntactical errors have been corrected and the translation process is complete, the program is ready to be run. In general, the user simply invokes the name of the file that contains the executable code. The general form of this is

```
C:\> [x:]filename
```

where "C:\>" is the prompt that indicates that the OS is in control of the computer and is ready to accept commands. (Other OSs or enhancements may be used such as Windows, or a "shell" program, which simplifies the user interface. In such cases, the user uses a combination of mouse and keyboard to point and/or drag, and execute the program.) The symbol "x:" designates the path that the OS takes in order to locate the file in question. Square brackets around this path indicate that a path may not be necessary. If, for example, the file to be executed is located in the root directory of the drive "C:", then only the filename will be required. (For student environments, it is recommended that only the compiler and its associated programs be retained on the principal computer system drive and that working disks be created to store FORTRAN 90 programs. Such disks may be easily transported between stations.) In the present case, the sample program was retained on drive B:, thus the execution command appears as

```
C:\> b:calc_avg
```

No extension (".exe") is required. If the file that is invoked is not an executable file, the OS will normally indicate this fact.

Running the number-averaging program produced results on the monitor that are shown below. (User responses are shown in bold typeface.)

```
This program calculates the average of the numbers
              that you enter from the keyboard.
Please enter the first number to be averaged
1
Please enter the second number to be averaged
2
Please enter the third number to be averaged
3
Please enter the fourth number to be averaged
4
Please enter the fifth number to be averaged
5
You entered   6   items
and the average is       2.5000000.
```

Each user response was followed by a carriage return (the Enter key). Notice that the user did not have to enter 1.0 or 2.0 for the test numbers. Recall that the program specifies the variable NUMBER_ENTERED as a real data type. Therefore, upon entering these numbers, they are automatically converted to appropriate form.

The test average is deliberately chosen to be simple so that the results can be confirmed. The average of consecutive numbers from 1 to n is given by:

$$\frac{(n+1)}{2}$$

In this case the result should be 3.0.

For this example, we did not specify the number of decimal places to be included in the answer. The computer thus made its own choices; these are called default decisions. The number of decimal places, the number of digits (as distinct from the number of decimal places), and other qualities of the information to be displayed on the monitor (or stored in a file) are considered to be part of the format of the variables. Formats are discussed at various places in the text, as required, but formal designation of the syntax is included in Chapter 4.

We note that the computer does not produce the correct answer. The example being discussed is a relatively simple FORTRAN 90 program. The test run described above is by no means an exhaustive test of the validity of the program. In fact, program validity is a major concern in all computer calculations and a topic for study in its own right. For example, to completely test the averaging program would take a great deal of time. Consider the task of having to test the average of any number and combination of real values. Because of this fact, logical errors within a program may be difficult to detect. In fact, programs may appear to execute quite successfully for years, only to fail when a specific set of numbers produces an erroneous result. (A typical problem may arise when a program adds numbers that sum to 0 and then uses this as the divisor in an assignment statement; the computer is asked to divide by 0.) In this case we have deliberately introduced a logical (as opposed to syntactical) error into the sample program.

In the sample program, the programmer inadvertently initializes the variable NUMBER_OF_ITEMS to the value 6 instead of the correct value, which should be 5. When the NUMBER_OF_ITEMS is correctly initialized to 5 and the program is recompiled and executed, the computer produces the correct answer.

A FORTRAN 90 program can be terminated at any point during execution. This is accomplished by the Ctrl-C sequence: hold the key marked Ctrl (control), depress the letter C, and release both. The monitor displays "^C" on a new line. (In addition, a sequence of system-related information that reflects the state of a number of related locations at the time of the interruption is also displayed. For the purposes of this text, such information will not be discussed.). Control is returned to the OS where corrections can be made.

2.5 THE GENERAL FORMAT OF A FORTRAN 90 PROGRAM

The statements included in the source code (Fig. 2.3) were written in a particular order. For example, specification statements like "INTEGER:: NUMBER_OF_INTEGERS" appear near the start of the program. This organization follows from the fact that FORTRAN 90 statements fall into several different classifications, one of which is specification statements that should be placed near the beginning of the program. Specification statements provide information to the compiler so that this translation program can set aside the proper number of memory locations. They are not, strictly speaking, calculations to be executed. In formal terms, they must appear before the first "executable" statement. A number of other statements, of varying classification, must appear near the beginning of the source code. (Such statements are described throughout this text.) The general organization of a FORTRAN 90 program is presented in Fig. 2.7; this figure may

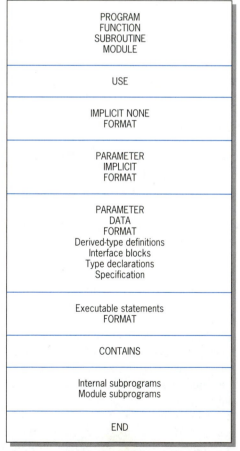

Keywords that appear in more than one place
represent alternative positions within the source program.
Within a box, statements can be in any order.

FIGURE 2.7 General organization of a FORTRAN 90 program.

be referred to as the need arises throughout the book, as well as when solving problems or writing programs.

PROBLEMS

2.1 The source program shown in Fig. 2.3 includes the statement

```
AVERAGE_VALUE = RUNNING_SUM/NO_OF_ITEMS
```

(The right-hand side includes an operation (division) involving a real variable (RUNNING_SUM) and an integer variable (NO_OF_ITEMS). This would seem to be prohibited. Explain why this is allowed. *Hint*: Consult Chapter 3 for the rules regarding mixed-data types in assignment statements.

2.2 Another feature that might be added to the sample program is verification of the numbers entered by a user. This can be accomplished by adding a "PRINT*," statement after the statement READ*,NUMBER_ENTERED in Fig. 2.3, which repeats the number the computer has accepted. The user can then compare this number to the number on the list of numbers to be averaged. Add an appropriate PRINT statement to the program using an editor program; then recompile, link, and execute the program and record the results.

2.3 (a) Using the source program in Fig. 2.3 as a model, write a program that calculates the square root of the number you enter. In order to find the square root of a number in FORTRAN 90, you will need an assignment statement of the form:

```
RESULT = SQRT(X)
```

where X is the number whose square root is to be found and RESULT is the name given to the answer.

(b) Once the program is compiled and linked, run the program using different values for X. In particular, run it once using a negative number.

2.4 Repeat Problem 2.3 but arrange the program to calculate the product of two numbers. The symbol for multiplication in FORTRAN 90 is * (asterisk).

2.5 Repeat Problem 2.3 but arrange the program to calculate the ratio of two numbers. The symbol for division in FORTRAN 90 is / (slash).

2.6 Repeat Problem 2.3 but arrange the program to calculate the difference of two numbers. The symbol for subtraction is − (dash or minus sign).

2.7 Invoke the MS-DOS edit program and using either a mouse or the ALT key,

(a) Select the Edit option and sketch what appears on the monitor. (If the computer system includes a printer, depress the Shift key and, while holding it down momentarily, depress the key marked PrtSc (Print Screen), then release both. The image that appears on the screen will be printed providing a hardcopy result for this problem.) When making the sketch, be sure to indicate which portions of the screen are highlighted (or appear in reverse video).

(b) Repeat part (a) for the Search option.

(c) Repeat part (a) for the Options option.

2.8 With some minor modifications to the sample program, it can be converted into one that adds a series of user-entered numbers. Notice that the averaging algorithm maintains a sum of the numbers that are entered by the user. Therefore, you can modify the program so that it prints the sum of user-entered numbers and not the average. Modify the program so that it calculates and prints a sum of user-entered numbers. Run the program several times to test your solution. In particular, run it once with one number a positive quantity and the second number a negative quantity. The result should be the difference between the two inputs (operands); the program performs subtraction!

3

Data Types and Operations

Before a calculation or operation can be performed on data, the attributes of the data must be known. A major attribute of data is the *data type*. Each data type has a standard name, permissible operations, and rules for performing these operations. We will now discuss these topics.

3.1 INTRINSIC DATA TYPES

When carrying out calculations by use of a computer, we should take note of the way we perform these tasks. In particular, we need to specify the *type of data* involved in calculations; if we fail to do so, there may be surprising results. In FORTRAN 90, operations on data are based on a classification called intrinsic data types. The term *intrinsic* means "defined by the language." The intrinsic data types in FORTRAN 90 are integer, real, character, complex, and logical. The data type double precision used in FORTRAN 77 is achieved in FORTRAN 90 by a statement called *kind,* which will be discussed later in this chapter.

3.2 IMPLICIT-TYPE DECLARATION

In FORTRAN, we assign names to the quantities we use in calculations, and, when feasible, we choose names that designate the significance of the quantity. For example, in a physics problem we might use DISTANCE, TIME, and VELOCITY. This is a useful procedure. However, we should be aware of the following FORTRAN rule: names that begin with one of the letters *I, J, K, L, M,* or *N* are considered to be integer type (*implicitly*). Examples of integer quantities are

```
IOTA, KOUNT, JUMBO, MACHINES, NAME, INDEX, LIST, NUMBER_OF_CITIES
```

Declarations are statements used to specify data type and other attributes of FORTRAN. Using the first letter of a name to establish data type is called an *implicit*-type declaration.

Names that begin with any of the remaining letters of the alphabet are *implicitly real* type. Thus, SAM, ALPHA, XRAY, FAST, and BETA are real (implicitly).

Up to 31 characters may be used to name a variable or constant. The first character of the name must be a letter. The remaining characters may be letters, digits, or underscore. For example, TOTAL_POPULATION and R2D2 are proper names in a FORTRAN program.

At times we may wish to override the implicit-type declaration. This need arises most often when division is performed. The reason is that if an integer number is divided by an integer, *truncation* will occur; that is, the remainder will be discarded, and the quotient will be the next smallest integer.

3.3 EXPLICIT-TYPE DECLARATION

It is possible to eliminate an implicit-type declaration in a program by using the statement IMPLICIT NONE. If this statement is used in a program, then all variables and constants *must* be explicitly typed. Otherwise, an error message will result when the program is compiled. Use of IMPLICIT NONE is considered good programming practice because it helps to detect the misspelled names of variables or constants.

A type declaration *explicitly* defines the mode of the data being stored under a particular name. A type declaration is a nonexecutable statement and must appear in a program before any executable statement. In the present example, we use the following type declarations:

```
IMPLICIT NONE
REAL:: NUMBER_OF_CITIES, TOTPOP, AVERAGE
```

Note that the data type is followed by two colons.

There is no way of implicitly declaring complex and logical data. Therefore, complex data and logical data *must* be declared by a type declaration. For example,

```
COMPLEX:: CURRENT,VOLTAGE,Z
LOGICAL:: SWITCH,A,B
```

COMPLEX and LOGICAL data types are discussed in Sec. 3.10 and Sec. 3.14, respectively.

3.4 INTEGER AND REAL DATA TYPES

Let us provide some simple examples involving integer and real types. Assume that we define a city as a municipality with a population of more than 100,000 people and that we then list the cities in a certain state with their population. City A has a population of 110,341; city B has a population of 314,212; and so on. The point being made here is that the population of each city is an integer; that is, it is a whole number without a decimal point. We will designate the *integer type* by the letter *I*. The designations that we apply to the various data types will be needed when we print their values. Suppose that we have completed the list of cities and find that there are 27 cities in the state. We now wish to calculate the average population of the cities in the state, so we add the populations and divide the total by 27. The answer turns out to be 119,368.751 (rounded to three figures to the right of the decimal point). If we do not wish to discard the fractional part of the average, we must retain the decimal point (and, of course, the three digits shown). In FORTRAN, a number with a decimal point, such as the average just calculated, is called a *real number*. (The data type designation is F. The reason for using the name F is historical; these numbers were called "floating point numbers.")

Now, let us turn to astronomy for a moment in order to demonstrate another way of representing real numbers. We go to a textbook and find that the mass of the earth is approximately 5.98×10^{24} kilograms. The decimal point in this number is not unexpected for it is a real number, but a new feature has been introduced, namely, the presence of 10 raised to a power. This notation is used for convenience: we wish to avoid writing 22 zeros! Designation of real numbers in this form is called exponential representation.

3.4.1 Kind

The term *processor* is used in the discussion below. In the FORTRAN 90 standard, the term signifies the FORTRAN compiler together with the computing system that executes the code.

Each of the intrinsic types of FORTRAN 90 may be specified with a *kind parameter* that selects a processor-dependent representation of variables or constants of the type and kind selected by the programmer. The kind parameter is an integer number that is processor dependent. Thus, kind parameters 1,2,4 might be single, double, or quadruple precision on a particular compiler; other values might be required on other compilers. FORTRAN 90's only requirement is that there be at least two real kinds representing real and double precision. Similarly, there must be at least two complex kinds. Recall that double precision for complex type is not available in FORTRAN 77.

The intrinsic function SELECTED_*type*_KIND(P,R), where *type* is REAL or INT, may be used to select an appropriate kind for a real or an integer variable or constant. For integer variables or constants, *type* is INT, and for real variables or constants, *type* is REAL. The parameters P and R denote precision and range, respectively. P and R are integers and are set as follows.

    a.   For INT, R produces values given by

$$-10^R < \text{value} < 10^R$$

    b.   For Real, P determines the number of decimal digits, and R determines values in the range

$$-10^R < \text{value} < 10^R$$

For example,

```
REAL, PARAMETER::LONG = SELECTED_REAL_KIND(9,60)
```

will produce a kind that has at least nine decimal digits of precision and allows ranges (values) between -10^{60} and $+10^{60}$.

For integer data type, SELECTED_INT_KIND(6) produces an integer type permitting numbers between -10^6 and $+10^6$. As noted above, this intrinsic function has only one argument.

The kind value produced by the SELECTED_*type*_KIND(P,R) statement can be assigned to a variable using a type declaration and PARAMETER. For example, the following statement

```
INTEGER,PARAMETER::LONG = SELECTED_REAL_KIND(9,20)
```

assigns the value 2 to LONG on a particular computer. After this assignment has been made, LONG may be appended to an appropriate variable using an underscore, and the kind value of 2 is assigned to PI. Thus, PI = 3.14159265_LONG will have a precision of nine digits.

3.5 INPUT/OUTPUT

When a program is run, usually data must be supplied for the variables. It is generally *not* desirable to include the values of variables in the program because each time we wished to change their values, the program would have to be edited and compiled. Instead, we provide a means for entering values only when the program is being run.

For entering data, the following elementary forms are available:

```
READ*, V₁, V₂,. . ., Vₙ
READ(unit,*) V₁, V₂,. . ., Vₙ
```

The asterisk relates to the *format* for reading the data. *Format specifications* are symbols that provide information to the computer concerning the *form* in which data are to be read-in or printed. A full discussion of formats is given in Chapter 4; the forms shown here will permit us to communicate effectively with the computer. When an asterisk is used, it denotes *default* or *free format*. This means that the format will be selected by the compiler. The compiler selects a format that will be suitable for most situations. Default format is also called *list-directed format*. We will use default format for READ statements unless it is essential to provide a format. The term *unit* refers to the device from which input is accepted. Very often, unit is replaced by an asterisk; in this case, the input device defaults to the keyboard of a terminal. Thus, the statement READ(*,*) means that data are entered by use of the keyboard and the format is default type. Figure 3.1 shows data entered into the computer by means of a keyboard, displayed on a monitor, stored in the computer on some device such as a disk, and printed.

The word "PRINT" includes hard copy as well as display on the screen of a terminal. For printing the output of a program, the following forms are available:

```
PRINT*, V₁, V₂,. . ., Vₙ
WRITE*, V₁, V₂,. . ., Vₙ
WRITE(unit,*) V₁, V₂,. . ., Vₙ
```

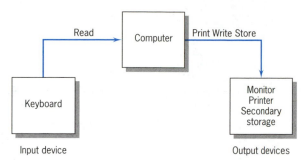

FIGURE 3.1   Input/Output operations.

Again, the asterisk denotes free format. As stated above, the notation "unit" denotes a device number, and, often, the unit number is replaced by an asterisk because the terminal is the standard input or output device. When reading a data file or writing to a data file, a unit number *is required*.

We will use the default format whenever it is feasible and whenever the resulting appearance of the output is satisfactory. One situation in which the default format sometimes produces output with unsatisfactory appearance is in the printing of matrices. For example, suppose that a particular matrix has seven elements in a row and that printing results in an output with six of the elements on a line followed by the seventh on the next line. This would be unsatisfactory, and formatted output would then be used to fit the output on one line. Format specifications and files are discussed in Chapter 4.

3.6 ECHOING INPUT DATA

Although it may seem like a minor point, we should note that it is useful to follow READ statements by WRITE statements that "echo" the input data. Echoing the input data means WRITING the data after having read them. This is particularly important when entering the values of several variables. If not done, it may make the debugging of a program more difficult. We will echo data in all but short programs, that is, programs into which no more than only a few data are to be entered.

3.7 THE FORM OF FORTRAN PROGRAMS

A program is a set of instructions to a computer to carry out a sequence of operations. These operations are defined by statements. *Lexical tokens* are labels, names, operators, keywords, constants, and separators. For example:

```
75 VELOCITY  *  /  ( )  ,  =  =>  :  ::  ;  &  IF  READ
```

A label is a string of digits that precede a statement. A label is used to refer to the statement from other places in the same program unit.

In the expression 1050   IF(PI*FREQUENCY), we see that IF, PI, *, and FRE-

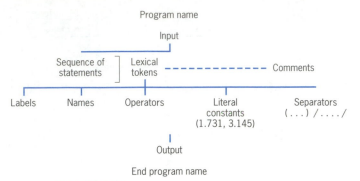

FIGURE 3.2   Structure of a FORTRAN 90 program.

QUENCY are tokens; IF is a keyword, PI and FREQUENCY are names, * is an operator, and 1050 is a label.

Sequences of lexical tokens form statements. A FORTRAN program consists of FORTRAN statements and comments. The statements carry out the problem-solving objectives of the programmer, whereas the comments provide an explanation of the function of the statements or of units of the program. The statements and comments comprise the *source* text. The structure of a FORTRAN 90 program is shown in Fig. 3.2.

In this chapter, we discuss the operations to be carried out using the various intrinsic data types, and we illustrate many of them with FORTRAN programs. Thus, this is a suitable time to discuss the form that will be used in these programs.

A FORTRAN statement may occupy one or more complete or partial lines. If a statement occupies more than one line, the first line of the statement is called the *continued line*. The next and subsequent lines, if any, are called *continuation lines*.

Comment statements are used to explain significant parts of a program; they are *not* involved in the execution of the program.

The source text can be written in one of three forms: Fixed source, free source, and fixed/free source.

3.7.1 Fixed Source Form

In the fixed source form, positions for the components of a program are prescribed. The positions are denoted by column numbers beginning with column 1 at the left. The principal rules and features of the fixed source form are

1. Labels, which are numbers-referencing statements and which consist of one to five digits, must be placed in columns 1 through 5.

2. FORTRAN statements or parts of statements must be positioned in columns 7 to 72.

3. Any character except a blank or zero in column 6 denotes that the line is a continuation line. A statement may have a maximum of 19 continuation lines.

4. An ! in column 1 denotes that the line is a comment. An ! in any column beyond column 6 and not part of a character string indicates that a comment follows. Such comments usually follow FORTRAN statements and are called trailing comments.

5. More than one statement may be placed on a line if separated by semicolons. For example:

```
ALPHA = 7.2; BETA = -17.05; GAMMA = 0.931   !INITIALIZED 3 CONSTANTS
```

6. Extra blanks within a FORTRAN statement are *not* significant. However, they are sometimes used to improve appearance or readability.

For example, the following statements are equivalent.

```
C = SQRT(A**2 + B**2)
C = SQRT ( A**2 + B**2 )
```

SQRT is an intrinsic function in FORTRAN which carries out the calculation of the square root of a real number. (The meaning of the token ** will be explained later in this chapter.)

Extra blanks are significant in character strings. Thus, when printed, the string

```
HAMLET = "PRINCE    OF DENMARK"
```

will have four blank characters between PRINCE and OF.

3.7.2 Free Source Form

In the free source form, there are no rules concerning the positioning of statements. The features of this form are as follows.

1. Each line may contain up to 132 characters. This number of characters is generally too large to fit on a line. In this case, a statement can be continued on subsequent lines. To do this, an ampersand must be placed at the end of the continued line or lines. The maximum number of continuation lines permitted in a FORTRAN statement is 39.

2. The exclamation point (!) indicates a comment. The comment may follow a FORTRAN statement. For example,

```
C**2 = A**2 + B**2   !THIS IS A TRAILING COMMENT
```

3. The continuation symbol is an ampersand at the end of a line to be continued. For example:

```
WRITE(*,*)"In Xanadu did Khubla Khan &
          A stately pleasure dome decree &
          Where Alph, the sacred river, ran &
          Through caverns measureless to man &
          Down to a sunless sea."
```

4. To continue a name, a character constant, or a lexical token consisting of more than one character, which is divided between two lines, *two* ampersands must be used as shown below:

```
CHIEF_EXECUTIVE_OFFICER = "Alexander Graham B&
          &ell
```

The second ampersand (the one on the continuation line) is used and is *adjacent* to the continued text, ell, so that blanks will not be included between B and ell.

5. More than one statement may appear on a line. They must be separated by semicolons.

6. A label may be placed before statements; however, it must be followed by at least one blank.

3.7.3 Example of Program in Free Source Form

```
      PROGRAM FREE                   !FREE SOURCE FORM
  !    CALCULATION OF CRITICAL GAP FOR ENTRY TO TRAFFIC STREAM
   TH = 10.0 ; D = 2.0; S = 0.0
      T = 5.47 + 0.828*TH − 1.043*D + 0.045*D**2 &
      −0.042*TH**2 − 0.847*S
      WRITE(*,*)"CRITICAL GAP = ",T
   END PROGRAM FREE
     CRITICAL GAP = 7.72
```

The statement CRITICAL GAP = 7.72 appears on the screen of the terminal when the program is run. The meaning of the statements in the program will be clear when the remainder of the chapter is read.

3.7.4 Fixed/Free Source Form

It is possible to use a form that is valid for either fixed or free source form. The rules for this mode are

1. **(a)** Labels are limited to columns 1 through 5.

   (b) Statements are limited to columns 7 through 72.

2. Blanks should be treated as significant.

3. The exclamation mark (!) is the only symbol that should be used to denote a comment; however, it should not be used in column 6.

4. For continuation of statements, the ampersand must be used in column 73 of the line to be continued and in column 6 of the continuation line.

3.7.5 Example of Program in Fixed/Free Source Form

An example of a program written in fixed/free source form is

```
      PROGRAM FIXED_FREE          !FIXED/FREE
  !234567                                   |73
              !IN THE LINE ABOVE, | DENOTES COLUMN 72
  !     CALCULATION OF CRITICAL GAP FOR ENTRY INTO TRAFFIC STREAM
      TH = 10.0; D = 2.0 ; S = 0.0
      T = 5.547 + 0.828*TH − 1.043*D + 0.045*D**2               &
      & − 0.042*TH**2 − 0.847*S
      WRITE(*,*)"CRITICAL GAP =,",T
      PROGRAM FIXED_FREE
       CRITICAL GAP = 7.72
```

We believe that a program in fixed source form is *neater in appearance* and *easier to read* than a program in free source form. For this reason, we will generally use the fixed source form.

3.8 OPERATIONS

We begin by discussing operations on the most familiar data types, namely, integers and real. First, we discuss the symbols and their functions and then, we present examples of arithmetic expressions. Finally, we show the order in which operations are carried out.

3.8.1 Arithmetic Operations

The available arithmetic operators and their symbols are

Addition	+
Subtraction	−
Multiplication	*
Division	/
Exponentiation	**

Addition, subtraction, multiplication, and division are *binary* operators; this means that they require two operands. These operands may be constants or variables. Two operators may not be placed side by side. The subtraction operator can also be used as a *unary* opeator; for example,

$$-\text{C**3} \qquad -\text{K}$$

3.8.2 Integer Arithmetic

Addition, subtraction, and multiplication give correct results if the answer is within the range allowed for the integers and the result by the particular computer being used. As shown by the examples in Sec. 3.4, division, unless it is exact, will return the greatest integer value as the answer. Thus,

$$31/10 + 5/9 = 3 + 0 = 3$$

In a typical 32-bit system, the range of integers is from $-2,147,583,647$ to $+2,147,483,648$.

3.8.3 Real Arithmetic

With real numbers, addition, subtraction, multiplication, and division give correct results whose accuracy is dependent on the computer system. In a typical 32-bit system, the range of single-precision real values for negative numbers is from approximately $-3.4028235E+38$ to $-1.17544E-38$, the number zero, and positive numbers from approximately $+1.1756944E-38$ to $3.4028235E+38$.

3.8.4 Exponentiation

Both integers and real numbers can be raised to a power. For *integers*, the exponent must also be an *integer*. For *reals*, the exponent can be either a real number or an integer. If the exponent is a real number, the same number is obtained whether the base number is positive or negative. This means that (+A)**B gives the same results as (−A)**B because the calculation is carried as $|A|$**B using logarithms. If the exponent is an integer number, the computation is accomplished by repeated multiplication. For example, (−4.)**3 = −64 because the computation is (−4.)*(−4.)*(−4.) = −64.

3.8.5 Arithmetic Expressions

An arithmetic expression may be a single variable or a single constant, or it may consist of several constants and/or variables with a number of operations. For example,

```
A**2 + B**2
2.0*PI/CIRCUMFER
5.0*(F−32.0)/9.0
```

3.8.6 Precedence of Arithmetic Operations

When an arithmetic expression involves several arithmetic operations, the normal order in which they are performed regardless of their position in the expression is according to the following order or precedence.

1. Exponentiation   (highest)
2. Multiplication and/or division
3. Arithmetic negation
4. Addition and/or division   (lowest)

It is sometimes necessary to *override* the precedences shown above. This can be done by the use of *parentheses*. Parentheses must always be used in pairs; failure to do so will produce an error during compilation. When parentheses are used, that part of the expression contained within the *innermost* pair of parentheses will be computed first, then the next outermost, and so on.

If there are two or more operations with the same procedure, they are performed sequentially *from left to right*. Consider the following expression.

A/B + C − D**3/9.0

It will be evaluated as follows:

1. **D****3 will be evaluated and stored (exponentiation having the highest precedence).
2. **A** will be divided by **B** and the quotient stored (*first* multiplication or division operation reading from left to right).
3. The result of step 1 will be divided by 9.0 and the result stored (*next* multiplication or division operation).
4. The result of step 2 will be added to **C** and the result stored (*first* addition or subtraction reading from left to right).
5. The result of step 3 will be subtracted from the result of step 4 and the value of the expression stored (*next* addition or subtraction operation).

Now, let us consider the following expression:

$$(A/(B + C) - D**3)/9.0$$

This expression is similar to the expression evaluated above; however, parentheses have been added. It would be evaluated as follows:

1. **C** will be added to **B** and the result stored (*innermost* parentheses).

2. **D****3 will be evaluated and stored (*highest* precedence in the *next* outermost parentheses).

3. **A** will be divided by the result obtained in step 1, and the result stored (*first* multiplication or division within the *outermost* parentheses).

4. The result of step 2 will be subtracted from step 3 (*first* addition or subtraction within the outermost parentheses).

5. The result of step 4 will be divided by 9.0, and the value of the expression will be stored (*highest* precedence and the *only* operation outside of the outermost parentheses).

Parentheses may be used simply for the purpose of making it easier to read an expression. They may also be used to separate operation symbols. For example, "X divided by minus 11" must be written as X/(−11.0) in order to prevent adjacent operation symbols.

3.8.7 Program CABLE1 (*Civil Engineering*)

Let us consider a cable suspended from two towers of equal height. Such a cable might be used for transmission of electrical power. The cable will sag; the maximum sag will occur midway between the two towers. We wish to calculate the amount of the sag. The sag can be calculated from the equation

$$H = \frac{TO}{w}\left[\cosh\left(\frac{(W)(\text{SPAN})}{2TO} - 1\right)\right]$$

where

SPAN = distance between the towers, ft

H = the sag at the midpoint of the span, ft

W = the weight per length of the cable

TO = tension in the cable at the midpoint, lb

The sag of a cable suspended from towers is shown in Fig. 3.3.
Program CABLE1, below, calculates the sag. The run shows that the sag is 200 ft.

```
PROGRAM CABLE1
IMPLICIT NONE
REAL::TO,W,H,SPAN
WRITE(*,*)'ENTER TO,TENSION @ MIDPOINT'
READ(*,*)TO
WRITE(*,*)'ENTER W, WT/UNIT LENGTH OF CABLE'
READ(*,*)W
WRITE(*,*)'ENTER THE SPAN BETWEEN THE TOWERS'
READ(*,*)SPAN
H = (TO/W)*(COSH(W*SPAN/(2*TO))-1)
WRITE(*,*)'THE SAG AT MIDSPAN = ',H
END PROGRAM CABLE1
```

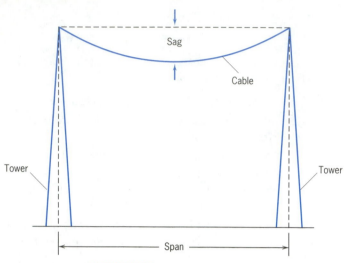

FIGURE 3.3 Calculating cable sag.

The data entered were: SPAN = 800 ft, W = 5 lb/ft, TO = 2140

```
RUN
THE SAG AT MIDSPAN  =  2.0092319 E+02  (FEET)
```

3.8.8 Program PAYMENTS (*Engineering Economics*)

An unanticipated breakdown of a machine in a factory is not an uncommon occurrence. When it happens, the management of the company may decide that it is better to purchase a new machine rather than repair the old machine. Some of the factors that may lead to this decision are:

1. The cost of repair is too high relative to the price for which the machine was purchased.
2. A new model is available with features that management believes would decrease production costs. The new model will cost $61,800.

However, if the decision to buy this machine was not planned, there may not be a provision in the budget for it or the company may not wish to expend its reserve funds. Accordingly, the decision is made to borrow the money for the machine and repay the loan by 24 monthly payments. Each payment will include interest on the loan. This procedure is called *amortizing* a loan. The business manager wants to know how much each monthly payment will be in order to determine if this unanticipated expenditure will be a problem.

The formula shown below calculates the monthly payment, P, for a loan, L, monthly interest rate, R, and N equal payments.

$$P = \frac{LR(1.0 + R)^N}{(1.0 + R)^N - 1.0}$$

Program Payments, which calculates P, and a trial run are shown below. It is seen that the loan of $61,800 can be repaid by 24 monthly payments of $3085.32.

```
      PROGRAM PAYMENTS
!     THIS PROGRAM CALCULATES THE PERIODIC PAYMENT REQUIRED
!     TO REPAY A LOAN,D, TO ZERO IN N EQUAL PAYMENTS, P.
!     THE MONTHLY RATE OF INTEREST IS R.
      IMPLICIT NONE
      REAL:: L,P,R
      INTEGER:: N
      WRITE(*,*)'ENTER THE AMOUNT OF THE LOAN'
      READ(*,*) L
      WRITE(*,*)'THE LOAN IS $',L
      WRITE(*,*)'ENTER THE MONTHLY INTEREST RATE'
      READ(*,*)R
      WRITE(*,*)'THE MONTHLY INTEREST RATE IS ',R,' %'
      WRITE(*,*)' ENTER THE NUMBER OF PAYMENTS TO BE MADE'
      READ(*,*) N
      WRITE(*,*)' THE NUMBER OF PAYMENTS IS ',N
      P = L*R*(1.0 + R)**N/((1.0 + R)**N - 1.0)
      WRITE(*,*)'EACH OF THE N PAYMENTS IS $',P
      WRITE(*,*)' EACH OF THE N PAYMENTS IS $ ',P
      END PROGRAM PAYMENTS
```

RUN

```
 THE LOAN IS $   6.1800000E+04
 THE MONTHLY INTEREST RATE IS   1.5000000E-02 %
  THE NUMBER OF PAYMENTS IS 24

 EACH OF THE N PAYMENTS IS $   3085.32
*      *       *       *       *
```

3.8.9 Vehicle Braking

Braking is a crucial feature of vehicle performance. In the design of vehicle braking systems, it is necessary to distribute the braking forces between the vehicle's front and rear brakes. This may be achieved by the allocation of hydraulic pressure within the braking system. The optimal situation is to favor the front braking force F_{bf}. The proportion of braking force allocated to the front axle is K_{bf}; the proportion of braking force allocated to the rear axle is K_{br}.

Brake force proportions are given by the following formula:

$$\frac{K_{bf}}{K_{br}} = \frac{l_2 + h(\mu + 0.01(1 + 1.47\,V/147))}{l_1 - h(\mu + 0.01(1 + 1.47\,V/147))}$$

where

l_2 = distance from vehicle center of gravity to the rear axle

l_1 = distance from vehicle center of gravity to the front axle

h = height of center of gravity above roadway surface

μ = coefficient of road adhesion

V = vehicle speed feet per second

K_{bf} = proportion of braking force allocated to the front axle

K_{br} = proportion of braking force allocated to the rear axle

Program BRAKE, below, calculates K_{bf} and K_{br} for a vehicle with the following parameters: $l_2 = 64$ in, l_1, $= 36$ in, $h = 24$ in, $\mu = 0.6$, speed $= 80$ mph. In the formula, the speed is converted to feet per second. A RUN is shown using these data. The results show that about 78 percent of the braking force is allocated to the front and 21 percent to the rear brakes.

3.8.10 Program **BRAKE** (*Civil Engineering*)

```
PROGRAM BRAKE
IMPLICIT NONE
REAL::KBF,KBR,L1, L2,H,MU,FR,V,
L2 = 64; L1 = 36; H = 24 ; MU = 0.60; V = 80
!

FR = 0.01*(1. + (V*1.47)/147.)
!

KBF = L2 + H * (MU + FR)
KBR = L1 - H * (MU + FR)
WRITE(*,*)'KBF = ', NUM
WRITE(*,*)'KBR = ', KBR
END PROGRAM BRAKE
```

```
RUN
```

```
KBF =          78.8320007
KBR =          21.1679993
```

3.8.11 Stress in Highway Pavement (*Civil Engineering*)

The function of highway pavement is to support traffic loads. Any pavement has a finite useful life. A rigid pavement is constructed with portland cement concrete and aggregates. The concrete is laid in slabs that may vary in length from about 10 feet to 40 feet. Slab thicknesses on highways vary from 8 to 12 inches. Several parameters may be calculated for the performance of slabs. One of these is calculated by the Westergaard equation for corner stress. This equation is

$$\sigma_c = \frac{3P}{h^2}\left[1 - \left(\frac{a_1}{l}\right)^{0.6}\right]$$

where

σ_c = corner stress, psi

h = slab thickness, in

P = load, lb

a_1 = distance to point of action of load

We will calculate the corner stress using the following values:

$$h = 10; l = 37.06; P = 15000; a_1 = 12$$

Program STRESS, below, calculates the stress.

3.8.12 Program **STRESS** (*Civil Engineering*)

```
PROGRAM STRESS
!

IMPLICIT NONE
REAL::SIGMAC,P,H,A1,L
```

```
P= 15000; A1 = 12; H = 10; L = 37.06
SIGMAC = (3.0*P)/H**2*(1-(A1/L)**0.6)
WRITE(*,*)'SIGMAC = ',SIGMAC,' PSI'
END PROGRAM STRESS
```

RUN

```
SIGMAC = 2.2124112E+02 PSI
```

3.9 CHARACTER DATA

Character data signifies "alphanumeric" data, that is, information that may, in general, consist of alphabetic, numeric, and special characters. A sequence of characters in a word or expression is called a *string*.

One example of the use of character data arises in programs in which the user is asked to select an option. For example, the user may be asked to type BYE in order to terminate a program. The string of characters BYE must be denoted as character data.

The declaration for character variables is of the form

$$\text{CHARACTER*}n \text{ var}_1, \text{var}_2, \ldots \text{var}_n$$

or

$$\text{CHARACTER (LEN} = n)\text{var}_1, \text{var}_2, \ldots \text{var}_n$$

where n indicates the number of characters that may be stored in the variables. LEN is an intrinsic function that indicates the number of characters stored in a variable,

or

$$\text{CHARACTER (LEN} = *) \text{ NAME} = \text{"THOMAS ALVA EDISON"}$$

When the asterisk is used, the length will be determined from the value of the string. It is permissible to have different values of n associated with one character statement. For example,

$$\text{CHARACTER* 15 LAST\_NAME, FIRST\_NAME*8, DEPT*12, AGE*3}$$

Here, LASTNAME may have 15 characters, but FIRSTNAME may have only 8 characters, DEPT 12 characters, and AGE 3 characters.

If no value of n is stated, the default value is 1.

3.9.1 Assigning a String to Character Variables

Strings are assigned to character variables by enclosing the assigned value within quotation marks or within apostrophes.

```
TEAM = "GREEN DEVILS"
CAPTAIN = 'JONES'
```

If the string contains an apostrophe, it should be contained within quotation marks. For example,

```
MESSAGE = "It ain't necessarily so"
```

If the string contains quotation marks, enclose it within apostrophes. For example,

```
MESSAGE = 'He said "EUREKA" and left the room'
```

3.9.2 Concatenation

There is only one character operator, namely, two slashes: //; it produces a *concatenation* of character strings—that is, strings are combined. For example,

```
'THEODORE'//'ROOSEVELT'
```

will be printed as THEODORE ROOSEVELT.

3.9.3 Copying Substrings

A *substring* is a sequential group of characters in a string. Substrings may be copied from strings as shown by the following example. Suppose that a string is stored in character variable G as follows.

```
G = 'IN XANADU DID KHUBLA KHAN A STATELY PLEASURE DOME'
```

We wish to *copy* the characters KHUBLA KHAN and store them in the character variable STRING. The following FORTRAN statement will copy the substring KHUBLA KHAN from G.

```
STRING = G(15:26)
```

This causes the fifteenth through the twenty-sixth character of G to be *copied* to STRING. The substring stored in G remains in G. As a result of this statement, the characters KHUBLA KHAN are stored in STRING.

3.9.4 The Intrinsic Functions LEN and INDEX

The length of a character variable is the length assigned to it in the type declaration. The length of a character constant is the number of characters *between* the apostrophes which delimit the constant.

The intrinsic function LEN determines the length of a character string. For example,

```
K = LEN(XTRA)
```

will store the number of characters in the string XTRA in K.

The intrinsic function INDEX(STRING1,STRING2) returns a number that indicates the position of the first character of STRING1 in STRING2. As an example, consider the character variable M

```
M = 'WOLFGANG AMADEUS MOZART WAS BORN IN 1756 IN SALZBURG'
```

The following statement will store a number that represents the position of the first character of the string AMADEUS within the string stored within the variable M.

```
K = INDEX(M,'AMADEUS')
```

3.9.5 Example   Program CHAR1A, Some Operations on Character Variables

Program CHAR1A, which illustrates some operations involving variables, and a trial run are shown as follows.

```
!     PROGRAM CHAR1A
      IMPLICIT NONE
      CHARACTER TOTNAM*13,STRING*11,G*60,H*20,M*55
      CHARACTER FRSTNAM*6,LSTNAM*8,XTRA*8
      INTEGER:: K,L
      FRSTNAM = 'OMAR'
      LSTNAM = 'KHAYYAM'
!
!     TOTNAM IS DEFINED BY CONCATENATION OF FIRSTNAM & LASTNAM
      TOTNAM = FRSTNAM//LSTNAM
      G = 'IN XANADU DID KHUBLA KHAN A STATELY PLEASURE DOME'
      XTRA = ' DECREES'
!     EXTRACTING PART OF A LINE OF TEXT
!
      STRING = G(15:26)
      H = STRING//XTRA
      M = 'WOLFGANG AMADEUS MOZART WAS BORN in 1756 in SAZLBURG'
      K = LEN(XTRA)
      L = INDEX(M,'AMADEUS')
      WRITE(*,"(///A///A///A///)") TOTNAM,G,H
      WRITE(*,"('LENGTH OF STRING XTRA',I6///)") K
      WRITE(*,*)'LOCATION OF STRING AMADEUS IN STRING M',L
      END PROGRAM CHAR1A
```

RUN

```
OMAR KHAYYAM

IN XANADU DID KHUBLA KHAN A STATELY PLEASURE DOME

KHUBLA KHAN DECREES

LENTH OF STRING XTRA   8

LOCATION OF STRING AMADEUS IN STRING M   10


*     *     *     *     *
```

In the program, the string 'OMAR' is stored in FRSTNAM and 'KHAYYAM' is stored in LSTNAM. The concatenation of FIRSTNAM and LASTNAM is stored in TOTNAM. As a result, OMAR KHAYYAM is printed. A part of a line of poetry is stored in variable

G, and a portion of it is copied by the statement STRING = G(15:26). The string ' DE-CREES' is stored in XTRA. The printout shows that the concatenation of STRING and XTRA produces the string 'KHUBLA KHAN DECREES'. The statement K = LEN(XTRA) assigns a value of 8 to K, because the string consists of a space plus the seven letters of DECREES. The statement L = INDEX(M,'AMADEUS') assigns the value of 10 to L because the string 'AMADEUS' begins at the tenth letter in the string stored in M.

3.9.6 Collating Sequence

Character information is stored in computers by codes that assign numbers to each letter of the alphabet, the digits 0 to 9, and to special characters such as !, %, #, >. Two widely used codes are EBCDIC (Extended Binary Coded Decimal Interchange Code) and ASCII (American Standard Code for Information Interchange). For eample, in the ASCII code, the code, in decimal, for a space is 32, A = 65, B = 66, C = 67,. . ., Z = 90. As may be expected, the codes for lower case letters differ from the codes for upper case letters. Thus,

$$a = 97, \quad b = 98, \quad c = 99, . . ., z = 122$$

The digits have codes ranging from 48 for the digit 0 to 57 for the digit 9. Within the computer, these numbers are stored as binary numbers. There are 128 codes in the ASCII coding system, some of which are nonprinting, for example, line-feed is 10.

Because characters have numeric codes and the codes form a sequence, characters may be compared to determine which is "larger" or "smaller." For this reason, the codes are said to form a *collating sequence*. In carrying out these comparisons, four intrinsic lexical functions may be used. (Lexical means "relating to the vocabulary of a language.") These lexical functions are:

LGE lexically greater than or equal to

LGT lexically greater than

LLE lexically less than or equal to

LLT lexically less than

The form of these functions is:

LGE(string1, string2)

LGT(string1, string2)

LLE(string1, string2)

LLT(string1, string2)

These functions can be used to determine the order of characters in the collating sequence. For example, if string1 contains the character A and string 2 contains B, then LLE(string1, string2) returns a value .TRUE.; that is, the function LLE(string1, string2) is true if string1 precedes string2 in the collating sequence. This means that its numerical code is a smaller number than the code of string2.

When comparing strings of different length, the shorter one is treated as if it were padded at its end with enough spaces to make the lengths equal. When two strings are compared, the first character of one string is compared with the first character of the other. If they are equal (the same), then the second characters are used to determine which is greater and so forth. Because the letters of the alphabet and the digits are stored as numbers and these numbers form a sequence, this is the basis for sorting them.

3.9.7 Two Examples

1. Program CHAR3, Use of Function ICHAR

Program CHAR3, shown below, uses the intrinsic function ICHAR to show the codes corresponding to various characters. The printout shows that the codes for the digits 0,1,2,3 are 48,49,50, and 51; the codes for A,B,C,D are 65,66,67, and 68; and the codes for a,b,c,d are 97,98,99, and 100. These codes correspond to the ASCII (American Standard Code for Information Exchange) codes. Thus, the collating sequence follows the ASCII code.

Note that this program is using a procedure that has not yet been discussed. This is carried out by the statements DO I = 1,12. . . END DO. These statements cause the WRITE statement to be executed repeatedly, with I in the WRITE statement assuming values 1,2, . . . 12. This procedure is called a DO construct and is discussed fully in Chapter 5.

```
      PROGRAM CHAR3
!     USE OF FUNCTION ICHAR TO SHOW CHARACTER CODES
      CHARACTER*1 CHARS(20)
!
      CHARS(1) = '0';CHARS(2) = '1'; CHARS(3) = '2'; CHARS(4) = '3'
      CHARS(5) = 'A';CHARS(6) = 'B'; CHARS(7) = 'C'; CHARS(8) = 'D'
      CHARS(9) = 'a'; CHARS(10) = 'b'; CHARS(11) = 'c'; CHARS(12) =
       'd'
!
      DO I = 1,12
        WRITE(*,*) CHARS(I),"      *",ICHAR(CHARS(I))
      END DO
      END PROGRAM CHAR3
```

RUN
```
0   *   48
1   *   49
2   *   50
3   *   51
A   *   65
B   *   66
C   *   67
D   *   68
a   *   97
b   *   98
c   *   99
d   *   100
```

2. Program CHAR4, Use of Functions LGE, LLT, LGT

Program CHAR4, below, shows the use of the intrinsic functions LGE, LLT, and LGT.

```
      PROGRAM CHAR4
      IMPLICIT NONE
      LOGICAL:: A1,A2,A3
      CHARACTER*8 STR1, STR2, STR3, STR4, STR5, STR6
```

```
!
        STR1 = 'ALPHA'
        STR2 = 'ALBERT'
        STR3 = 'CADAVER'
        STR4 = 'cadaver'
        STR5 = 'HORSE'
        STR6 = 'ZEBRA'
!
        A1 = LGE(STR1,STR2)
        A2 = LLT(STR3,STR4)
        A3 = LGT(STR6,STR5)
        WRITE(*,*)'A1',A1,' A2',A2,' A3 ',A3
        END PROGRAM CHAR4
```

RUN
```
 A1  T   A2  T    A3  T
 *    *    *    *     *
```

In the program, the following character assignments are made

```
        STR1 = 'ALPHA'
        STR2 = 'ALBERT'
        STR3 = 'CADAVER'
        STR4 = 'cadaver'
        STR5 = 'HORSE'
        STR6 = 'ZEBRA'
```

STR1 and STR2 are compared using the statement LGE(STR1,STR2). Because the first two letters of ALPHA and ALBERT are the same, the comparison is made on the basis of the third letter of each word. P is greater than B (comes after in the sequence); therefore, the statement STR1 is lexically greater than or equal to STR2 is true.

STR3 and STR4 are compared using the statement LLT(STR3,STR4); that is, is the statement STR3 is lexically less than STR4 true? From the results of program CHAR3 we see that the code for C is 67 and the code for c is 99. Thus, we expect the result of the run to be T. STR5 and STR6 are compared using the statement LGT(STR6,STR5). Here, we are testing to determine whether STR6 is lexically greater than STR5. Because Z comes after H, we again expect the result to be T. The results of the run confirm our expectations.

3.9.8 Derived Data Type

A derived type is a type that is *not* intrinsic; rather, it is defined by the user. It requires a type definition and a specification of its *components*. The components may be either intrinsic or user-defined types. An object of derived type is called a *structure*.

The derived type definition begins with a statement

TYPE *type-name*

Following the definition, the components are listed in the form of type declarations. The definition is concluded by END TYPE *type-name*. After a derived type has been defined, structures can be created.

As an example, suppose that a psychiatrist is just starting a practice and wants to create a file consisting of

1. An ID number that will be an integer. The first value of ID is 1, indicating the psychiatrist's first patient. The second patient will have an ID number of 2, and so forth.
2. The patient's name.
3. The address of the patient's residence.
4. The city in which the patient resides.
5. The date of the patient's first visit, written in the form mo/day/year.

We will omit the zip code and the patient's telephone number.

The derived type is

```
TYPE PATIENT
      INTEGER::ID
      CHARACTER(LEN = 30) NAME
      CHARACTER(LEN = 28) ADDRESS
      CHARACTER(LEN = 24) CITY
      CHARACTER(LEN = 10) FIRST_VISIT
END TYPE PATIENT
```

There are five components. Now that the derived type is specified, we can create a generic variable PATIENT_DATA:

```
TYPE(PATIENT)::PATIENT_DATA
```

PATIENT_DATA is a structure with components ID, NAME, ADDRESS, CITY, and FIRST_VISIT.

The components of a structure are denoted by writing the name of the structure followed by % and the name of the component. Thus, we can write:

```
PATIENT_DATA % ID
PATIENT_DATA % NAME
PATIENT_DATA % ADDRESS
PATIENT_DATA % CITY
PATIENT_DATA % FIRST_VISIT
```

In a *type declaration,* the name of the type is enclosed in parentheses. For example:

```
TYPE(PATIENT)::PATIENT_DATA
```

In a type definition, the name of the type is not enclosed in parentheses. For simplicity, we will limit the example to only one patient, the psychiatrist's first patient. Program TYPEA illustrates this situation. As noted above, the components of PATIENT_DATA are ID, NAME, ADDRESS, CITY AND FIRST_VISIT. These components are initialized in the program.

```
PROGRAM TYPEA
TYPE PATIENT
      INTEGER::ID
      CHARACTER(LEN = 30)::NAME
      CHARACTER(LEN = 20)::ADDRESS
```

```
                         CHARACTER(LEN = 14)::CITY
                         CHARACTER(LEN = 8)::FIRST_VISIT
                   END TYPE PATIENT
       !
                   TYPE(PATIENT)::PATIENT_DATA
                   PATIENT_DATA % ID = 1
                   PATIENT_DATA % NAME = 'CORDELL BROWN'
                   PATIENT_DATA % ADDRESS = '25 171 AVE'
                   PATIENT_DATA % CITY = 'ALBANY'
                   PATIENT_DATA % FIRST_VISIT = '7/15/93'
                   WRITE(*,*)PATIENT_DATA
                   WRITE(*,*)PATIENT_DATA % NAME
                         END PROGRAM TYPEA
```

A trial run is shown below. Note that the result of the first two WRITE statements is the printing of *all* the components of the structure PATIENT_DATA. However, as the trial run also shows, it is possible to print only a component.

```
        TRIAL RUN
         1 CORDELL BROWN      25 171 AVE    ALBANY    7/15/93
           CORDELL BROWN
        *    *    *    *    *
```

This program is too simple to satisfy the psychiatrist's needs. What is required is a program somewhat like this program but one that creates a file that can accept data concerning additional patients on a continuing basis and that can used to retrieve the data on request by the user of the program. Such a file is called a *database*. Databases are discussed in Chapter 9.

3.10 COMPLEX DATA TYPE

Complex data must be declared by an explicit-type statement. When a complex number is to be printed using a FORMAT statement, *two* specifications must be supplied—one for the real and one for the imaginary part.

3.11 COMPLEX NUMBERS

Now, let us turn to *complex numbers,* which we may recall from algebra. Assume that we wish to solve the equation

$$x^2 = \alpha$$

Here α is a negative number. For example, assume that $\alpha = -36$. We cannot solve for x because there is no real number which when multiplied by itself results in a negative number. To overcome this problem, let us define a quantity j which has the property that $j^2 = -1$. We believe that we now have a solution to the equation, namely, $x = j6$. Let us check this:

$$j^2(6)^2 = (-1)(36) = -36$$

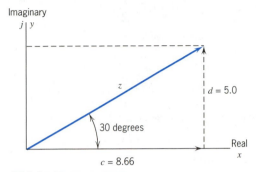

FIGURE 3.4   Representation of a complex number.

Thus, we see that $x = j6$ is a solution. We will find that another solution is $x = -j6$. Let us check this

$$(-1)^2(j^2)(6)^2 = (-1)(36) = -36$$

Now that we have defined the parameter j, we can use it to establish a type of number called *complex number*.

A complex number is a number of the form $c + jd$, where c is called the real part and d is called the imaginary part; j has been defined above. The word "real" comes from mathematics; from the point of view of FORTRAN 90, c and d may be integer or real data type. Although mathematicians use i, we are using the symbol j rather than i because the engineering profession prefers it in order to avoid confusion with i, which denotes current. A complex number in the form $c + jd$ is said to be in *rectangular form*. We can denote this number by a single symbol, say z. That is, $z = c + jd$. The components of a complex number z can be shown as in Fig. 3.4:

From the Pythagorean theorem,

1. $|z| = r = \sqrt{a^2 + b^2}$ r is always positive

   From the drawing, we see that

2. $a = r \cos \varphi$
3. $b = r \sin \varphi$
4. $\tan \varphi = b/a$
5. $\varphi = \arctan b/a$

Using (1), (2), and (3), we see that a complex number can be represented in the form

$$z = r(\cos \varphi + j \sin \varphi)$$

This form is useful when it is necessary to raise a complex number to some power or to find the roots of a complex number. For example,

$$z^n = [r(\cos \varphi + j \sin \varphi)]^n = r^n(\cos n\varphi + j\sin n\varphi)$$

Example

Given $z = (1 + j1)$

Calculate $z^3 = (1 + j1)^3$

Solution

$n = 3$

$$r = \sqrt{1^2 + 1^2} = \sqrt{2}; \quad r^3 = 2\sqrt{2}$$

$$\varphi = \arctan 1/1 = 45°$$

Therefore,

$$z^3 = 2\sqrt{2}[\cos(135°) + j\sin(135°)] \qquad \textbf{Answer}$$

3.11.1 Complex Constants and Variables

A complex constant is an ordered pair of numbers, either real or integer, separated by a comma enclosed within a pair of parentheses. The j operator is not shown; it is implicitly assigned to the second number.

A variable Y of type complex can be made into a constant by the assignment

```
Y = CMPLX(alpha,beta)
```

If $y = 0 + j4.3$, alpha $= 0$ and beta $= 4$; the FORTRAN statement will be

```
Y = CMPLX(0, 4.3)
```

where alpha and beta are either real or integer type and CMPLX is an intrinsic function.

3.11.2 Complex Arithmetic Operations

All of the arithmetic operators that are available for real and integer number arithmetic are used for performing complex number arithmetic.

1. **Complex Conjugate** The complex conjugate or, more briefly, conjugate, of a complex number is a complex number, the real part of which is the same as the real part of the given number and the imaginary part of which is the negative of the imaginary part of the given number. For example, the conjugate of $x + yj$ is $x - yj$.

2. **Addition and Subtraction** The sum of two complex numbers is another complex number, the real part of which is the algebraic sum of the real parts of the real parts and the imaginary part of which is the algebraic sum of the imaginary parts. For example,

$$(9 + j3) + (5 + j6) = 14 + j9$$

The difference of two complex numbers is performed by multiplying the subtrahend by (-1) and then adding the numbers. For example, to determine the difference between $(2 + j5)$ and $(8 + j6)$, multiply the second expression by (-1) and add

$$(2 + j5) + (-8 - j6) = -6 - j1$$

3. **Multiplication** Multiplication of the j operator.

$$j^2 = -1; j^3 = (j^2)(j) = -j; j^4 = (j^2)(j^2) = (-1)(-1) = +1, \text{ and so forth.}$$

Examples

(a) Let $X = a + jb$ and $Y = c + jd$. Then,

$$X*Y = ac + jcb + jad + j^2bd = ac + jcb + jad - bd$$

Grouping the reals and the imaginaries, results in

$$X*Y = (ac - bd) + j(ad + cb)$$

(b) The following example shows that the product of complex conjugates is a real number.

$$(5 + j12)(5 - j12) = 25 - j60 + j60 - j^2 144 = 25 + 144 = 169$$

4. **Division** The quotient of a complex number divided by a complex number is obtained by multiplying the numerator and the denominator by the complex conjugate of the denominator. As a result, the denominator becomes a real number. Example

$$\frac{(6+j10)}{(3+j4)} = \frac{(6+j10)(3-j4)}{(3+j4)(3-j4)} = \frac{18+j30-j24+40}{9+j12-j12+16} = \frac{58+j6}{25}$$

5. **Exponentiation** The form is the same as in the exponentiation of real numbers:

```
Z**n
```

This performs the operation $(a + jb)^n = [(a^2 + b^2)^{1/2}(\cos \theta + j\sin \theta)]^n$ where n is an integer and $\theta = \arctan (b/a)$. Occasionally, the exponent is a complex number. For example, to compute $e^{(-j\pi/4)}$, the intrinsic function CEXP must be used:

$$A = \text{CEXP}(0, \pi/4)$$

Note that, although the real part of the complex exponent is 0, it must be explicitly shown.

6. **Magnitude** The magnitude of a complex number is given by

$$\text{mag} = \sqrt{(RE)^2 + (IM)^2}$$

where RE is the real part and IM is the imaginary part of a complex number. The magnitude is a real number.

3.11.3 Intrinsic Functions Involving Complex Numbers

Some intrinsic functions involving complex numbers are CABS, AIMAG, REAL, and CONJG.

1. **Magnitude** If Z is a complex number, its magnitude is given by

```
ZMAG = CABS(Z)
```

2. **Imaginary Part Of** Assuming that W is a complex number,

```
X = AIMAG(W) will store the imaginary part of W in X
```

3. **Real Part Of**

```
Y = REAL(W) will store the real part of W in Y.
```

4. **Complex Conjugate** The complex conjugate of complex number W is

$$COMC = CONJG(W)$$

where COMC is also a complex number.

3.11.4 Example Program COMP1, Some Operations Involving Complex Numbers

Program COMP1, which illustrates the use of several intrinsic functions involving complex numbers, is shown below with a run.

```
PROGRAM COMP1
IMPLICIT NONE
COMPLEX:: W, WC, WWC, X, EXPON
REAL:: ALPHA, WMAG
REAL, PARAMETER::PI = 3.14159
W = CMPLX(8.0,15.0)
WC = CONJG(W)
WWC = W*WC
!
ALPHA = 57.29578*ATAN(AIMAG(W)/REAL(W))
!
WMAG = CABS(W)
!
EXPON = CMPLX(0, PI/4.0)
X = CEXP(EXPON)
!
WRITE(*,*)" W ",W," CONJ-W",WC
!
WRITE(*,*) "W*WC ",WWC
!
WRITE(*,*)"ATAN,DEGREES", ALPHA," MAG_W ",WMAG
WRITE(*,*) " CEXP ",X
END PROGRAM COMP1
```

```
RUN
 W ( 8.0000000, 15.0000000) CONJ-W ( 8.0000000, -15.0000000)
W*WC     289.00   0.00
ATAN,DEGREES     61.9275131   MAG_W   17.0000000
 CEXP ( 0.7071071, 0.7071063)
```

Notes

1. The complex number W is set to a value $8.0 + j\,15.0$. Then the conjugate of W is assigned to the complex number WC. The printout shows that WC $= 8.0 - j15.0$.

2. W*WC is assigned to WWC, which has been declared to be complex type; the printout shows that WWC $= 289 + j0$. The product is a real number. As previously mentioned, the product of a complex number and its conjugate will always be a real number.

3. The arctangent of the quotient {AIMAG(W)/REAL(W)}) = 15/ 8, was calculated. Note that the result was multiplied by 57.29578 in order to convert radians to degrees.

4. The magnitude of W was calculated using the intrinsic function CABS.

5. The function CEXP was used to calculate e^{jexpon} where $jexpon = 0 + j\pi/4$

where n is an integer,   and $\theta = \arctan(b/a)$

3.12 MIXED MODE

Occasionally, the operands of a numeric operator are not of the same FORTRAN-data type. This is called a *mixed mode* operation. FORTRAN 90 handles this situation in the following way.

If one operand is integer and the other is real, the integer is converted to a real.

If one operand is integer and the other is complex, the integer is converted to a complex value.

If one operand is real and the other is complex, the real is converted to a complex value.

Truncation will occur if the division of an integer by another integer is *not* exact. Some examples of integer division are

$$2/3 = 0 \quad 6/3 = 2 \quad 11/4 = 2$$

As an example of division of a real by an integer, we turn to the calculation of average population. Suppose TOTAL_POPULATION, a real number, is the sum of the populations of 27 cities, and TOTAL_POPULATION = 3222956. and NUMBER_OF_CITIES = 27. Then, letting AVERAGE denote the average,

```
AVERAGE = TOTAL_POPULATION/ NUMBER_OF_CITIES = 3222956./27
                                             = 119368.7407
```

The integer variable NUMBER_OF_CITIES was converted to real type, and, as a result, the quotient displays the correct digits to the right of the decimal point. Of course, in this case, we probably would not wish to retain the digits to the right of the decimal point.

3.13 PARAMETER STATEMENT

A parameter is a named constant. The PARAMETER statement is used to define named constants and can be combined with a type declaration. For example,

```
REAL, PARAMETER::VELOCITY_OF_LIGHT = 2.99796E+08
```

In this application, E means "10 to the power", so that the FORTRAN notation E+08 is equivalent to 10^8 in mathematical notation.

By assigning a value to a constant by means of the PARAMETER statement, the programmer is assured that the value of the variable will not be inadvertently changed: an error message will be given if an attempt is made to change the value of a parameter. As shown by this example, the name used for the parameter can also indicate the nature of the quantity defined, thus making it easier to follow the program.

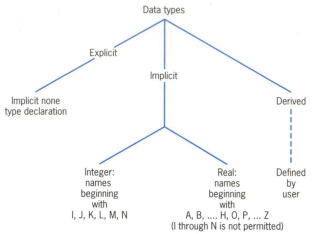

FIGURE 3.5   Data types in FORTRAN 90. Derived data type was not available in earlier versions of FORTRAN

3.14 LOGICAL DATA TYPE

Next, we discuss the data type called "logical." In some circumstances variables are true or false. For example, in the study of logical circuits, such as those used in the construction of computers, logical variables are used to analyze the performance of circuits. These logical variables have only two possible values: .TRUE. or .FALSE. The algebra used in connection with logical variables is called Boolean algebra. The assignment statement used to define them has a particular form. If we initialize logical variable A with the value TRUE and the logical variable B with FALSE, A program segment might be

```
LOGICAL:: A,B,C
A = .TRUE.
B = .FALSE.
C = A.OR.B
```

The first statement is a type declaration that makes A, B, and C logical variables. The next two statements *assign* logical values to A and B. Finally, the Boolean operation OR is performed as indicated by the statement C = A.OR.B. In Boolean algebra, the operation **OR** is denoted by + as shown below.

```
C = A + B = .TRUE. If either A or B is .TRUE. or both are .TRUE.
```

Therefore, in this example, the result will be C = .TRUE.
We will discuss logical operators more fully in Sec. 3.15.3. An overview of the data types discussed in this chapter is shown in Fig. 3.5.

3.15 TYPES OF LOGICAL OPERATORS

3.15.1 Relational Operators

Relational operators are used for making comparisons between the numeric values of arithmetic expressions. The relational operators are as follows.

OPERATOR	Meaning
<	less than
< =	less than or equal to
= =	equals
/ =	is not equal to
> =	greater than or equal to
>	greater than

The result of a relational operation is type *logical* and therefore is either true or false.

3.15.2 Relational Expressions

If *exp*1 and *exp*2 are two arithmetic expressions, a relational expression is formed by placing any one of the relational operators between the two expressions. For example, *exp*1 > = *exp*2 means: "The numeric value of *exp*1 is greater than or equal to the numeric value of *exp*2." If this relation is true, then the relational expression has the value .TRUE.. If this relation is not true, then the relational expression has the value .FALSE.. For this reason, a relational expression is equivalent to a logical variable.

3.15.3 Logical Operations

There are five logical operators: .NOT., .AND., .OR., .EQV., and .NEQV. The significance of the operators is most conveniently shown in the form of a table called a truth table.

Values of the Logical Operators

x_1	x_2	$.NOT.x_2$	$x_1.AND.x_2$	$x_1.OR.x_2$	$x_1.EQV.x_2$	$x_1.NEQV.x_2$
true	true	false	true	true	true	false
true	false	true	false	true	false	true
false	true	false	false	true	false	true
false	false	true	false	false	true	false

The table shows that A.EQV.B is .TRUE. if both A and B are .TRUE., and the expression is also .TRUE. if both are .FALSE.. We also note that A.OR.B is .TRUE. if either A or B are .TRUE. or both are .TRUE..

Note: When the value of a logical variable or expression is displayed or printed as the output of a program, .TRUE. is represented by T and .FALSE. is represented by F.

3.16 OPERATOR PRECEDENCE

Now that we have discussed arithmetic, logical, and relational operators, it is appropriate to discuss the precedence of *all* the operators. This is shown in the table below, which lists the various operators in a column. Each operator has a precedence higher than all of those below it.

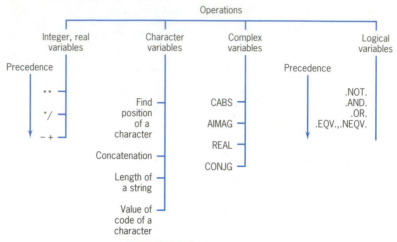

FIGURE 3.6   FORTRAN 90 operations.

```
              OPERATOR
    User defined unary operation
               **
             * or /
          unary + or −
          binary + or −
               //
    ==,   /=,   <,   <=,   >,   >=
              .NOT.
              .AND.
              .OR.
        EQV., or .NEQV.
    User defined binary operation
```

As previously stated, the precedences shown above may be modified by the use of parentheses. A summary of operations on data and the precedence of operations in integer, real and logical variables is shown in Fig. 3.6.

3.16.1 Example   Program RT_TRI

Program RT_TRI, below, shows a logical expression that uses the relational operator = = and the logical operator .OR. in order to illustrate the Pythagorean theorem. According to this theorem, in a right triangle, $A^2 + B^2 = C^2$.

A and B represent two sides of a right triangle and C represents the hypotenuse. In the program, values are assigned for A, B, and C. *A, B and C are then squared,* and the squares are assigned to X, Y, and Z, respectively. Then, $X = A^2$, $Y = B^2$,   and $Z = C^2$. The test to determine whether the Pythagorean theorem is satisfied is performed by the statement

```
        RT_TRI = X + Y ==Z.OR.X + Z==Y.OR.Y + Z==X
```

Thus, there are three expressions in the test:

$$A**2+B**2==C**2$$
$$A**2+C**2==B**2$$
$$B**2+C**2==A**2$$

The logical OR causes the variable RTTRI to be true if *at least one* of the three expressions is satisfied. It will be false *only if none of them is satisfied*.

The test is performed on three sets of values for A, B, and C. The reader will observe that some FORTRAN WRITE statements—for example, WRITE(2,*) RT_TRI1—appear three times in the program. In subsequent chapters, we will learn a more efficient way to write this program.

The first set of data tested was A = 3.0, B = 4.0, C = 5.0. As stated above, each of the data is squared, and it is the squared values that are used in the test. Therefore, the first test really involved A**2 + B**2 = C**2 or 9 + 16 = 25. The other tests are immaterial, and R_TRI1 is TRUE.

In the second test, the input was A = 15.0, B = 20.0, C = 25.0. Now, the test is: 225 + 400 = 625. Therefore, RT_TRI2 = TRUE.

In the third test, A = 6.0, B = 8.0, and C = 11.0. In this case, A**2 + B**3 = 36.0 + 64.0 = 100.0; this is not equal to 11**2 = 121. In fact, none of the other expressions is true, so RT_TRI3 is FALSE.

Note that T represents .TRUE. and F represents .FALSE..

```
      PROGRAM RT_TRI
!     THIS PROGRAM SHOWS USE OF LOGICAL & RELATIONAL
!     OPERATORS DEMONSTRATING THE PYTHAGOREAN THEOREM
      IMPLICIT NONE
      LOGICAL:: RT_TRI1,RT_TRI2,RT_TRI3
      REAL::A,B,C,X,Y,Z
      A = 3.0 ; B = 4.0; C = 5.0
      WRITE(*,*)"A = ", A," B = ",B," C = ",C
      X = A**2 ; Y = B**2; Z = C**2
      RT_TRI1 = (X + Y) == Z .OR. (X + Z) == Y .OR. (Y + Z) == X
      WRITE(*,*)'*      *      *      *'
      WRITE(*,*)RT_TRI1
!
      WRITE(*,*)"
      A = 15.0; B = 20.0; C = 25.0
      WRITE(*,*)"A = ", A," B = ",B," C = ",C
      X = A**2 ; Y = B**2; Z = C**2
      RT_RTI2 = (X + Y) == Z .OR. (X + Z) == Y .OR. (Y + Z) == X
      WRITE(*,*)'*      *      *      *'
      WRITE(*,*)RT_TRI2
      WRITE(*,*)"
!
      A = 6.0; B = 8.0; C = 11.0
      WRITE(*,*)"A = ", A," B = ",B," C = ",C
      X = A**2; Y = B**2, Z = C**2
      RT_TRI3 = (X + Y) == Z .OR. (X + Z) == Y .OR. (Y + Z) == X
      WRITE(*,*)'*      *      *      *'
      WRITE(*,*)RT_TRI3
      END PROGRAM RT_TRI
```

```
RUN
A = 3.   B = 4.   C = 5.
* * * *
T
A = 15. B = 20. C = 25.
* * * *
T
A = 6.   B = 8.   C = 11.
* * * *
F
```

3.17 SUBSCRIPTED VARIABLES

On many occasions it is useful or necessary to use subscripted variables. For example, consider the equations

$$4x + y = 13$$
$$3x + 6y = 36$$

In describing these equations, the names x and y, which are used for the unknowns, are arbitrary. We could have used f and g or any other convenient letters, or we could have used the subscripted variables x_1 and y_1. It is the coefficients of the variables that are important. For this reason, we say that the system of equations shown can be described by the coefficients of the unknowns and the constants in the right-hand column, placed in an *array* as shown

$$
\begin{matrix}
4 & 1 & 13 \\
3 & 6 & 36
\end{matrix}
$$

A rectangular array is called a *matrix*. This particular matrix has two rows and three columns. The numbers in the matrix are called elements and are designated by a_{ij}, where i is the number of the row of the element and j is the column. Thus, in the present example, the element, the numeric value of which is 36, would be represented by a_{23} and the element the numeric value of which is 4 would be represented by a_{11}. A matrix that has two rows and three columns is said to be a 2×3 matrix. Some matrices have only one column; such a matrix is called a column array or a vector. The structure of an array is shown in Fig. 3.7.

3.17.1 Denoting Subscripts

Any FORTRAN variable can have up to a maximum of seven subscripts. A subscript may be an integer variable or expression. The number of subscripts is called the rank. The form of some subscripted variables is shown below

$$\text{name}(k_1) \qquad (\text{rank} = 1)$$

or

$$\text{name}(k_1, k_2) \qquad (\text{rank} = 2)$$

or

$$\text{name}(k_1, k_2, k_3) \qquad (\text{rank} = 3)$$

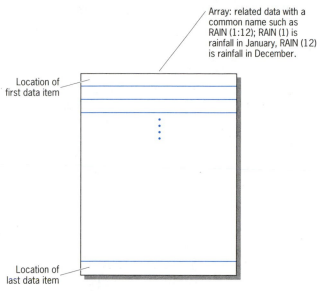

Array: related data with a common name such as RAIN (1:12); RAIN (1) is rainfall in January, RAIN (12) is rainfall in December.

Location of first data item

Location of last data item

FIGURE 3.7   FORTRAN 90 array structure.

where *name* is the FORTRAN name used to designate the array or matrix and k_1, k_2, k_3 may be integer constants, variables, or expressions.

It is customary to denote a matrix or an array by a capital letter. For example, if the elements of the array are denoted a_{ij}, the array or matrix is denoted by **A**. Because it is customary to use capital letters in writing FORTRAN programs, we will use *name* without subscripts to denote the array or matrix.

3.17.2 Dimension Statement

The dimension statement is a nonexecutable statement of the form

$$\text{DIMENSION } name(k_1,\ k_2,\ k_3,\ .\ .\ .)$$

where name is the FORTRAN name of the subscripted variable, array, or matrix. The values k_1, k_2, k_3,... k_n determine the *largest* values that the subscripts can have; these numbers also represent the number of locations in memory which are allocated for storing the data. The number of storage locations allocated is

$$k_1 \times k_2 \times k_3 \times \ldots k_n$$

It is permissible to use smaller, but not larger, numbers than indicated by the DIMENSION statement. This method of reserving storage for arrays is called *static storage allocation*. The programmer sets the value(s) of the subscripts at the largest value which it is anticipated may be needed. In this sense, static storage is wasteful.

As an example, suppose that, in the spring semester, 129 students are enrolled in freshman orientation. The program that stores data concerning these students has a statement DIMENSION NUMBER_ORIENTATION_STUDENTS(250). This allocates 250 storage locations, although only 100 are needed. The number 250 was chosen because the average size of freshman orientation class in the fall semester is usually about 230.

The DIMENSION statement can be combined with a type declaration; one dimension statement can be used for two variables. For example,

```
REAL, DIMENSION(0:99):: ALPHA,BETA
```

As shown by this example, a zero subscript is permitted. Negative subscripts are also permitted. The notation 0:99 indicates that subscripts 0 to 99 can be used with variables ALPHA and BETA. The first subscript is called the lower bound, and the second subscript is called the upper bound. If the lower bound is not specified, the default value is 1. It is possible to use *dynamic storage allocation;* in this method, storage allocation is determined during execution of the program. Instead of a number in the DIMENSION statement, there is a colon. The following program segment illustrates this.

```
INTEGER, DIMENSION(:), ALLOCATABLE::NUMBER_ORIENTATION_STUDENTS
READ(*,*) NUMBER_ORIENTATION_STUDENTS
```

The statement ALLOCATABLE:: ensures that when the program is run, a value for the actual number of freshman students will be entered and storage will be allocated based on that number.

3.17.3 Examples: The DOT Product

1. Program DOT
2. Program DOT2

Given two vectors, **A** and **B**, each of dimension n,

$$\mathbf{A} = [a_1, a_2, a_3, \ldots, a_n]$$
$$\mathbf{B} = [b_1, b_2, b_3, \ldots, b_n]$$

the scalar product (also called dot product) of these vectors is denoted **A·B**. As the name indicates, **A·B** is a scalar.

$$\mathbf{A \cdot B} = \mathbf{P} = a_1 b_1 + a_2 b_2 + a_3 b_3 + \cdots + a_n b_n$$

For example, if vector **A** is {2.0, 3.0, 5.0} and vector **B** is {4.0, 7.0, 6.0}, then

$$\mathbf{A \cdot B} = (2)(4) + (3)(7) + (5)(6) = 59$$

This example will be used in programs DOT and DOT2 below. If the scalar product is zero, the vectors are said to be *orthogonal*.

Program DOT, shown below, calculates the scalar product of **A** and **B**; each vector has three components.

```
      PROGRAM DOT
!     THIS PROGRAM CALCULATES THE DOT PRODUCT OF 2 VECTORS
!     EACH WITH THREE MEMBERS.
      IMPLICIT NONE
      REAL:: A(3),B(3),DOTPRO
      WRITE(*,*)'ENTER THE 3 MEMBERS OF VECTOR A '
      READ(*,*)A(1), A(2), A(3)
      WRITE(*,*)'VECTOR A   ', A(1),A(2),A(3)
      WRITE(*,*)'ENTER THE 3 MEMBERS OF VECTOR B '
```

```
READ(*,*) B(1),B(2),B(3)
WRITE(*,*)'VECTOR B  ', B(1),B(2),B(3)
DOTPRO = 0
DOTPRO = DOTPRO + A(1)*B(1) + A(2)*B(2) + A(3)*B(3)
WRITE(*,*)'THE DOT PRODUCT OF A & B = ',DOTPRO
END PROGRAM DOT
```

It is seen that the computation of the dot product is easily carried out by the statement
DOTPRO = A(1)*B(1) + A(2)*B(2) + A(3)*B(3)

RUN
```
VECTOR A    2.0 3.0 5.0
VECTOR B    4.0 7.0 6.0
THE DOT PRODUCT OF A & B = 59.00
```

The trial run shows that the scalar product is 59.0, confirming our hand calculation.

In program DOT2, below, we have used the intrinsic function DOT_PRODUCT(A,B) to obtain the same result with a little less effort. Using the same data, we found the result to be the same as that obtained by program DOT. This run is not shown.

In the second run, the scalar product was found to be zero. This is because in the second run, the vectors are orthogonal.

```
      PROGRAM DOT2
!     THIS PROGRAM CALCULATES THE DOT PRODUCT OF 2 VECTORS
!     BY USE OF A FORTRAN 90 FUNCTION
      IMPLICIT NONE
      REAL:: A(3), B(3), DOTPROD
      WRITE(*,*)"ENTER THE THREE MEMBERS OF A"
      READ(*,*) A(1), A(2), A(3)
      WRITE(*,*) 'VECTOR A ',A(1), A(2), A(3)
      WRITE(*,*)"ENTER THE THREE MEMBERS OF B"
      READ(*,*) B(1), B(2), B(3)
      WRITE(*,*) 'VECTOR B ' , B(1), B(2), B(3)
      DOTPROD = DOT_PRODUCT(A,B)
      WRITE(*,*)"THE DOT PRODUCT OF A & B = ",DOTPROD
      END PROGRAM DOT2
```

RUN
```
VECTOR A    2.0 3.0  5.0
VECTOR B    7.0 2.0 -4.0
THE DOT PRODUCT OF A & B =  0.00
*    *    *    *    *
```

PROBLEMS

3.1   The heating value of a solid fuel is given by the following formula:

$$HV = 145(C) + 620\left(H - \frac{O}{8}\right) + 40(S)$$

where

HV = heating value, BTU/LB

C = carbon content, %

H = hydrogen content, %

O = oxygen content, %

S = sulphur content, %

Write a FORTRAN program to calculate the heating value of a solid fuel, given the composition as percentages of sulphur, hydrogen, oxygen, and carbon. Typical Pennsylvania bituminous coal has the following composition:

Sulphur = 0.87%

Hydrogen = 5.16%

Oxygen = 9.19%

Carbon = 74.51%

Use these data for your trial run of the program.

3.2   Stokes's law describes the drag on a sphere moving through a fluid in laminar flow:

$$D = 3\pi V d\mu$$

where

D = drag, lb-ft

V = velocity, ft/sec

d = diameter of sphere, ft

μ = viscosity, lb-sec/ft^2

Write a program that will read values of V, d and μ, echo them, and print the drag, D. Data: $V = 0.1$; d $= 0.1$; $\mu = 0.02$ (Glycerin @ 65 °C)

3.3   The Stefan-Boltzmann law is

$$E_b = \sigma T^4$$

where

E_b = energy radiated by a blackbody, BTU/h-ft^2

T = absolute temperature, °R

$\sigma = 0.1714 \times 10^{-8}$

Write a program that will accept a temperature in degrees Fahrenheit and print the energy that is radiated.

Note: °R = °F + 460.0

3.4   In a manufacturing plant where parts are made in large lots, placed in storage, and used as required in assembling the product, a common problem is determining the most economic lot size. The following expression is used to calculate the number of pieces that should be made in a run:

$$X = \sqrt{\frac{2SDU}{(T + R)C + 2A(1 - U/P)}}$$

where

X = lot size, number of pieces

S = setup and takedown cost, $/run

D = number of working days per year

U = rate of usage of parts, pieces per day

P = production rate, pieces/day

T = taxes and insurance, % as a decimal

R = desired rate of return, % as a decimal

C = cost of material and labor, \$/piece

A = annual storage charges, \$/piece

Write a program that will read-in values of the parameters, echo them, and print the economic lot size.

```
Sample Data
S =   400      T = 0.05
D =   243      R = 0.15
U =   300      C = 0.72
P = 1500       A = 0.25
```

3.5 The Grashof number is a dimensionless parameter used in making heat transfer calculations involving free convection. The formula for the Grashof number is

$$GR = \frac{\rho^2 \beta g L^3 (T_s - T_f)}{(\mu^2)}$$

where

GR = Grashof number

ρ = density, lb-m/ft^3

β = coefficient of thermal expansion, 1/°F

g = gravitational acceleration, ft/s^2

L = characterizing length, ft/s^2

T_s = temperature of surface, °F

T_f = temperature of fluid, °F

μ = viscosity, lb-m/ft-s

Write a program to calculate and print the Grashof number for free convection in a pipe (where the inside diameter is the characterizing dimension), given the properties of the fluid and the temperature of the pipe wall:

Fluid	= air
Fluid temperature	= 250 °F
Viscosity	= 1.669 × 10^{-5} lb-m/ft-s
Coefficient of expansion	= 0.00367, 1/°F
Pipe temperature	= 800 °F
Diameter	= 1 ft

3.6 Stirling's formula provides an alternative way of calculating $N!$. The formula is

$$N! \approx \sqrt{2\pi N}\, N^N e^{-N}$$

Write a program that uses Stirling's formula to calculate N factorial using $N = 20$. If you have time, try larger values of N to determine whether your machine will limit you by the size of the numbers generated.

3.7   According to the Richardson-Dushman equation, the current density, J, owing to electrons escaping from a metal surface at temperature T is

$$J = AT^2 e^{-E_w/KT}$$

where

> J = current density, A/m^2
>
> A = a constant for a particular metal, A/m^2 °K^2
>
> T = absolute temperature, °K
>
> E_W = a work function for a particular metal, eV
>
> K = Boltzmann constant = 8.62×10^{-5} eV/°K
>
> e = base of natural logarithms = 2.71828

Write a program that will accept the data given below, echo the data, and calculate J.

```
Sample Data
Set    Material    A              Ew       T
1      Tungsten    60.2 × 10⁻⁴    4.52     300  °K
2      Tungsten    60.2 × 10⁻⁴    4.52     2500 °K
```

3.8   The Venturi meter is one type of flow meter. It is sometimes called a head meter because a head-loss (pressure drop) measurement is used to determine the rate of flow. The water flow through a horizontal Venturi meter is given by

$$Q = \frac{CA_1 A_2}{\sqrt{A_1^2 - A_2^2}} \sqrt{2g(h_1 - h_2)}$$

where

> Q = flow rate, ft^3/s
>
> C = meter coefficient
>
> A_1 = area of pipe cross section, ft^2
>
> A_2 = area of throat cross-section, ft^2
>
> g = gravitational acceleration, ft/s^2
>
> h_1 = pressure in main pipe, ft
>
> h_2 = pressure in throat, ft

The formula given above expresses the rate of flow of water in terms of the differential pressure head between the main pipe and the Venturi throat, $h_1 - h_2$. This pressure drop is usually observed by a differential manometer. Write a program to read-in the pressure drop in feet of water, the meter coefficient, the diameter of the meter inlet pipe, and the diameter of the throat and to calculate and print the value of the flow rate. The input data should be echoed.

```
Sample Data
Pressure drop = h₁ − h₂ = 6 ft of water
Meter coefficient = 0.98
Inlet pipe diameter, D₁ = 8 ft
Throat diameter, D₂ = 3.5 ft
Gravitational constant = 32.16 ft/sec²
```

3.9   The torque transmitted through a drive shaft that is delivering a specified horsepower at constant rotational speed is given by

$$T = (\text{hp})(63000)/N$$

where

T = torsional moment, lb-in

hp = horsepower

N = rotational speed, rev/min

The formula for drive shaft size is

$$D = \sqrt[3]{\frac{16T}{\pi S}}$$

where

D = shaft diameter, in

T = torsional moment, lb-in

S = allowable shear stress, lb-in^2

Write a program that will accept values for the horsepower to be delivered, the shaft speed, and the allowable shear stress of the shaft material, and that will calculate and print the required shaft diameter.

Sample Data
hp = 600
N = 85
S = 6000

3.10 This problem relates to situations in which it is necessary to shield an instrument from a magnetic field by enclosing it in a ferromagnetic shell. The magnetic field intensity H_3 at the center of a ferromagnetic metal of permeability μ is given by

$$H_3 = \frac{9H_0 \dfrac{\mu}{\mu_0}}{K}$$

$$K = \left(1 + \frac{2\mu}{\mu_0}\right)\left(2 + \frac{\mu}{\mu_0}\right) - 2\left(\frac{a}{b}\right)^3\left(\frac{\mu}{\mu_0} - 1\right)^2$$

where

H_3 = magnetic intensity *at the center* of the shell, A/m

H_0 = magnetic intensity *external* to the shell, A/m

μ = permeability of the shell, H/m

μ_0 = permeability of free space, H/m

a = inner radius of the shell, m

b = outer radius of the shell, m

The ratio H_3/H_0 is a measure of the effectiveness of the shell in reducing the effect of the external field on any object, such as an instrument, which is within the shell. Write a program that will read the value of the ratio μ/μ_0 and the ratio a/b, echo them, and calculate and print the value of the ratio H_3/H_0.

3.11 An expansion or compression of a gas in which the quantity pV^n is held constant, where p and V are the pressure and volume and n is a constant, is called a polytropic process.

   The polytrophic expansion of an ideal gas is governed by the following laws:

$$T_2 = T_1 \left(\frac{P_2}{P_1}\right)^{(n-1)/n}$$

$$\text{Work} = \frac{(WT)RT_1}{M(n-1)}\left[1 - \left(\frac{P_2}{P_1}\right)^{(n-1)/n}\right]$$

where the subscripts 1 and 2 refer to the initial and final conditions, respectively, and

$\quad T$ = absolute temperature, °R

$\quad P$ = absolute pressure, lb/in^2

$\quad n$ = polytropic exponent

work = work, ft-lb

$\quad R$ = universal gas constant = 1545.3 ft-lb/lb-mol/°R

$\quad W$ = weight of gas, lb

$\quad M$ = molecular weight of gas

$\quad T_2$ = final gas temperature, °R

Write a program that reads the following input data:

$\quad n$, the polytropic exponent; the molecular weight, M, of the gas;

$\quad W$, the weight of the gas; T_1, the initial temperature of the gas, °R

$\quad P_1$ and P_2, the initial and final pressure, respectively.

Write a program that calculates and prints the final gas temperature and the work done during a slow expansion of w lb of the gas. The input data should also be echoed. The data are as follows:

3.12 Transmission lines are used to convey electrical energy from the point at which it is generated, the "sending end," to a remote point at which it is used, the "receiving or output end." The characteristic impedance is an impedance which when connected to the output end makes the line appear to be infinitely long.

   The characteristic impedance Z_0 is calculated using the parameters of the line:

$$Z_0 = \sqrt{\frac{R + j\omega L}{G + j\omega C}}$$

where

$R = $ ohms/loop-mi

$L = $ h/loop-mi

$G = $ mhos/loop-mi

$C = $ F/loop-mi

Write a program that calculates and prints the characteristic impedance of a transmission line for which the parameters are

$R = 4$ ohms/loop-mi

$G = 1.0E\text{-}06$ mhos/loop-mi

$L = 0.003$ H/loop-mi

$C = 1.5E\text{-}08$ F/loop-mi

$\omega = 5000$ rad/sec

3.13 There are several types of strain gages. A group of strain gages which can be used to calculate the principal stresses and strains from three strain gages is called a rosette.

Consider a rectangular rosette in which the three gage readings are Q_1, Q_2, and Q_3.

The principal stresses are given by

$$S_{max} = A + B$$
$$S_{min} = A - B$$

where

$$A = \frac{E(1 - K)(Q_1 + Q_3)}{2(1 - \mu)}$$

$$B = E(1 + K)\frac{\sqrt{(Q_1 - Q_2)^2 + (Q_2 - Q_3)^2}}{2(1 + \mu)}$$

and

$E = $ modulus of elasticity

$\mu = $ Poisson's ratio

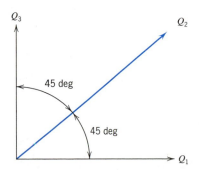

FIGURE P3.13   Strain gage readings Q_1, Q_2, and Q_3 for a rectangular strain rosette.

K = transverse sensitivity of the gage

Write a program that will read-in values for E, μ, K, Q_1, Q_2, and Q_3, echo them, and print the values of the principal stresses.

```
Sample Data
     E          μ        K        Q₁       Q₂       Q₃
  10.1 × 10⁶   0.30     0.03     +140     -55      +765
```

3.14 Around 1905, the noted English electrical engineer Sebastian Ziani de Ferranti was testing an open-circuited transmission line that extended from Deptford to London, England. A generator with an output of 8500 volts was connected to the line. Ferranti made a number of voltage measurements along the line and found (to his surprise) a voltage of 10,000 volts at some distance from the input. This phenomenon is now known as the Ferranti effect.

The voltage along an open-circuited transmission line is given by the formula:

$$VRO = \frac{VS}{\sqrt{\sinh(\alpha S)^2 + \cos(\beta S)^2}}$$

where

    VRO = open-circuited voltage, volts

    VS = input voltage, volts

    S = distance along the line from the input, mi

    α = attenuation factor/loop-mi

    β = phase angle/loop-mi

Write a program which calculates and prints the value of VRO using the following input data.

$$\alpha = 0.0048$$
$$\beta = 0.0275$$
$$VS = 4.0$$

3.15 The inductance of a coil with square cross section is approximately

$$L = 0.000008\left[N^2 S \ln\frac{D}{B} + 0.3794 + 0.4714\frac{B}{D} - 0.0143\left(\frac{B}{D}\right)^2 - 0.029\left(\frac{B}{D}\right)^4 \right]$$

For convenience, let the expression within square brackets be represented by the symbol F. Then the equation above can be represented compactly as

$$L = 0.000008N^2SF$$

The usual engineering problem: Given a specified inductance, solve for N, the required number of turns.

$$N = \sqrt{\frac{L}{0.000008SF}}$$

Write a program that calculates and prints the required number of turns for a specified inductance given the following data.

Specified inductance $\qquad$ = 30 mH

S = Side of square winding form = 32 cm

B = Available winding length $\quad$ = 2.54 cm

D = 1.414

Note that N, the required number of turns, should be an integer, for a fractional number of turns has no physical significance. However, the inductance is usually not an integer, and therefore the variable L should be real.

3.16 A coaxial transmission line consists of two concentric conductors separated by a dielectric and having the same axis. Such a transmission line typically conducts relatively high frequency signals such as television signals.

When the axes of the two conductors are displaced from each other, that is, they are *not* the same, the line is said to be an *eccentric* line. One of the line parameters of interest is the capacitance of the line per unit length.

The capacitance, C, per cm, of an eccentric line is given by

$$C = \frac{2\pi\varepsilon}{\cosh^{-1}\left[a^2 + b^2 - \dfrac{d^2}{2ab}\right]}$$

where

a = radius of the smaller conductor, cm

b = radius of the larger conductor, cm

d = displacement of the axes of the conductor and $d < (b - a)$

ε = permittivity, farads/cm

The function $\cosh^{-1}$ can be calculated as

$$\cosh^{-1} = \ln\left(z + \sqrt{z^2 - 1}\right)$$

$$|z| > 1$$

Write a program that calculates and prints the capacitance per cm of an eccentric line given these parameters.

$a = 2$ cm

$b = 8$ cm

$\varepsilon = 8.854E{-}10$ F/cm

Suggestion:

Let

$$Z = (a^2 + b^2 - d^2)/(2ab)$$

Then, ACOSH = ALOG(Z + SQRT(Z^2 − 1))

3.17 The maximum stress produced in an eccentrically loaded column shown below is given by the formula:

$$\sigma_{max} = \frac{P}{A}\left[1 + \frac{ec}{r^2\cos\left(\dfrac{L}{2r}\sqrt{\dfrac{P}{AE}}\right)}\right]$$

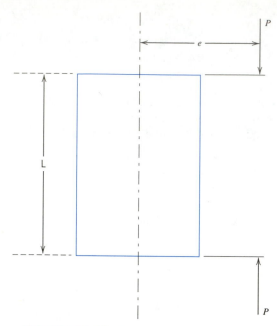

FIGURE P3.17   An eccentrically loaded column.

Write a program that calculates and prints the maximum stress on an eccentrically loaded column. The data to be entered into the program are as follows.

Data

P (applied load)	$= 4000$ lb
A (cross-sectional area of column, in.^{2})	$= 29.43$
e (eccentricity of loading)	$= 15.0$
C (distance from neutral axis to edge of section, in.)	$= 5.56$
R (radius of gyration of the cross section, in.)	$= 4.61$
L (length of column, in.)	$= 120$
E (modulus of elasticity)	$= 3.0E07$

4

How to Make the Computer Communicate with You

A HLL program should contain three important components: prompting and reading data from a user; the control structure specifying the computations to be performed on the data; and reporting results to the user. In previous chapters, we discussed the tools and methods for organizing and preparing a program for execution. We also described the required steps including creation of the source code and translation (compiling) of the program statements into machine-executable code. Many FORTRAN 90 statements that are needed to implement the control structure were described in Chapter 3. However, relatively little has been discussed regarding the means to accept data from a user or to report results to a user. Such operations were left to the computer itself—the default specifications—and input and output were accomplished using "READ *,", "PRINT *,", and simple forms of the WRITE command. These simple statements could be readily explained and understood without detracting from the main points of the discussion. However, complete understanding of such I/O statements is essential for proper solution of many scientific and engineering application programs.

Figure 4.1 includes a sketch of the I/O functions that a HLL must be able to implement. A user must be able to enter data from the keyboard, and the computer must be able to display information on a monitor or a printer; the keyboard and monitor form the computer's *terminal*. Printed, or "hard," copy is obtained from a printer, which the computer controls, to produce a printed record of the calculated results. The computer must be able to accept information from a file that is usually located on the secondary storage system (disk). Similarly, the computer must be able to access a file in order to permanently store information. The source file and destination file can be the same file; files are identified by *filenames* as described in Chapter 1. (The name "EOF" stands for the *end-of-file-mark* and signals the end of the file.) Finally, the computer should be able to communicate with other machines, denoted here by the "external world."

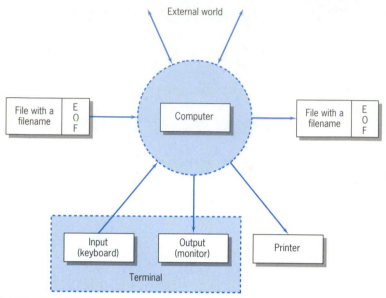

FIGURE 4.1   A HLL should support communication between various components of a computer system.

One of the important distinctions of FORTRAN 90—including its older versions—from other HLLs is the flexibility it provides with regard to the arrangement of data to be used in a program or reported to a user. Specification of data organization is accomplished with a series of *editing controls,* one for each datum or group of data values involved in the communication. Taken together, the editing controls are referred to as the *format*. The format may be contained within the READ, PRINT, or WRITE statement itself, or it may appear within a separate FORMAT statement. Transfer of data under format control is described in Fig. 4.2. The data source normally exists in the form of (coded representations of) alphanumeric characters (e.g., the decimal code for the letter *A* is the number 65). Of course, the user enters data in alphanumeric form; the compiler subsequently encodes it. The computer must store such information within the memory in a form that is compatible with the calculations to be performed on the data (e.g., concatenation, or "joining," of two alphanumeric characters to form a string of such characters). Ultimately, the computer must store the data in one or more memory locations containing binary numbers—numbers containing only 1's and 0's. Therefore, some translation between the external representation of the information and its internal form is necessary. FORTRAN 90 includes the means for such translation; however, proper completion is dependent on the user's specifications. (E.g., the number will contain five digits, or the computer should expect a string of exactly six alphanumeric characters.) A complementary translation occurs when the computer takes the data stored in its memory and produces (e.g., prints) alphanumeric characters that are readily understood by the user.

4.1 AN EXAMPLE IN WHICH A FORMAT SPECIFICATION IS ESSENTIAL

In numerous applications, the data to be presented to the user include a mixture of integers of various types, real variables, as well as alphanumeric information. In addition, the

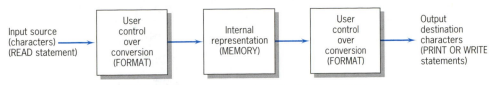

FIGURE 4.2   Format commands control data conversion.

data may have to be in tabular form. In these cases, it is essential to be able to control such things as the position of the variables on the monitor, the number of digits or characters to be included in the display, and the justification of the data.

4.1.1 Using the Computer to Display a Table of Codes

When sending information between two places, it is occasionally useful to be able to send a coded form of the data. The reasons for this include the following

- There is a need for privacy.
- The message must be free of errors.
- The machine (hardware) which is to send the message requires a coded representation of the information. The Morse Code is an example of a code that is compatible with telegraphy, a form of communication that is now largely historical.
- The time it takes to send the message should be minimized, and the most efficient method for sending the message should be provided.

In this example, we describe a coding scheme that is important for coding efficiency. Consider the need to transmit the following stream of (numerical) data: "1,3,5,7,5,7,7,5,7, 7,3,7,7,5,7." When this message is examined, we can observe the following.

Symbol (number)	Number of Times It Appears
1	1
3	2
5	4
7	8

A policy that can be followed when designing a code for this (or any) message is to choose the simplest code for the symbol that appears most frequently. For those symbols appearing less frequently, one can choose the simplest code that uniquely distinguishes it from all other symbols. When sending a coded message with this characteristic, the least time will be spent in transmitting the more frequently encountered symbols because they will have the simplest code. For example, in the case shown above we might choose a binary 1 code for a 7 and a binary sequence 01 for the 5; more complex codes would be needed for 3 and 1. The method for deriving the codes for these numbers in the message stream as well as the general method for coding information according to the policy outlined above will become clear by referring to the diagram shown in Fig. 4.3.

In Fig. 4.3, each symbol to be coded is represented by a circle; within the circle is the symbol, together with the relative frequency with which it appears in the message stream. The square boxes represent sums of the relative frequencies. For any message stream, the top box will always be 1 because the sum of all relative frequencies is 1. The symbols (circles) within the figure are ordered according to their relative frequencies. The least

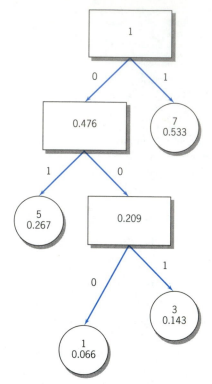

FIGURE 4.3 Diagram for creating an efficient code for a message.

frequent are at the bottom of the diagram, and those that occur most often appear at the top. Directed branches (arrows) connect the squares and circles, and a binary 1 is placed on the arrow leading to the higher frequency symbol, while a binary 0 is associated with the branch leading to the lower frequency element. (In some circumstances, the frequencies may be the same; in such instances, the assignment of 1 or 0 is arbitrary.)

Once such a diagram is complete, assignment of codes to the various symbols is a simple matter. Starting at the box at the top—the root—follow the branches to each symbol noting the sequence of 1's or 0's in each branch as it is traversed. For the example being considered, the symbols (numbers) in the message would be coded as follows:

Symbol	Code
7	1
5	01
3	001
1	000

If an ASCII code is used to transmit the symbol stream in this example, we will require 30 characters because there are 15 numbers and each number is represented by a two-digit ASCII code. However, a sequence of only 25 binary digits is needed when the scheme described above is used (see Problem 4.1).

We are interested in presenting the symbols and their coded forms in a table, and for this purpose we will develop a FORTRAN 90 program. This table will include a variety of data types, including alphanumeric information, integers (for the ASCII equivalents), and binary data for the coded form. A sample table follows.

Symbol	ASCII Value	Code
7	55	1
5	53	01
3	51	001
1	49	000

(Binary data are reserved for use only in DATA statements.)

The first part of the MAIN PROGRAM (see Fig. 4.4) module contains code to prompt the user for the character to be encoded. Notice the READ statement:

```
READ (*, "(A1)") X
```

This statement includes several important factors: the "*" specifies that the device from which to read the information is the default device that translates into the computer's keyboard; the term "(A1)" describes the nature of the expected data—it is the *format*; and the variable "X" specifies that the data will be assigned to the variable named X. In this case, the format "A1" indicates that alphanumeric data are expected and will be composed of a single character (the reason why the number 1 follows the A in the format). The computer expects a single alphanumeric character and will assign a value accordingly. (What happens when the input does not conform to the format will be discussed later in the chapter.)

The user response, X, will be assigned to the (symbol) NAME variable of one of the records of the SYMBOL_TABLE. The DO loop control cycles through each of the four records in the array. In particular, consider the following statement in the program:

```
SYMBOL_TABLE (I) % NAME = X
```

You will recognize this as an assignment statement in which the destination is defined by "SYMBOL_TABLE (I) % NAME." The location to be modified is the (SYMBOL_TABLE) array whose index is I. Because that array element is a record, the user must specify a particular field of that record; this is designated by "% NAME." The percent sign (%) identifies that what follows is one of the fields of the record. Other SYMBOL_TABLE assignments within the DO loop follow directly from this interpretation.

Note the presence of "IACHAR(X)" in the next assignment statement. IACHAR(X) requires the computer to calculate the integer ASCII code (IACHAR) for the symbol X. The computer has such information available to it without intervention by the user, and once this information is accessed, the value is assigned to

```
SYMBOL_TYPE (I) % ASCII_VALUE.
```

Of particular interest in this program are the PRINT statements near the end of program. These are intended to produce the tabular results described above. For each value to be displayed, several parameters are important: what (variable) is to be displayed; where is the information to be located; what is the type of data to be displayed (e.g., integer); how many positions should be set aside for each variable; and other additional refinements. Consider a typical PRINT statement in this part of the program:

```
PRINT "(T13,A,T25,I2,T37,B3.2)", SYMBOL_TABLE (2)
```

Communication statements of this type (I/O), including READ, PRINT, and WRITE, specify two important descriptors for the computer: the list of items involved in the communication; and the format of data, including positional constraints. The format is contained within the parenthetical fragment ("(. . .)"), and the list of variables to be printed follows after the delimiter (e.g., the comma (,)). In this case, the data list is the variable

```
            PROGRAM HUFFMAN_CODING
! THIS PROGRAM ACCEPTS LETTERS OR OTHER SYMBOLS FROM A USER,
! THEN DISPLAYS A TABLE INCLUDING THE CHARACTERS ENTERED, THEIR ASCII
! (DECIMAL) EQUIVALENT VALUES, AND "HUFFMAN" CODES. HUFFMAN CODES
! DEPEND ON THE RELATIVE FREQUENCY OF THE SYMBOL IN THE MESSAGE.
!
! THE VARIABLES TO BE USED INCLUDE:
            IMPLICIT NONE
! A RECORD TYPE FOR EACH CODED SYMBOL
            TYPE SYMBOL
                    CHARACTER (LEN=1) :: NAME
                    INTEGER :: ASCII_VALUE
                    INTEGER :: HUFFMAN_CODE
            END TYPE SYMBOL
!
! AN ARRAY OF SUCH CODED CHARACTERS
            TYPE(SYMBOL), DIMENSION (4) :: SYMBOL_TABLE
!
! AN ARRAY OF HUFFMAN CODES FOR 4 CHARACTERS
            INTEGER, DIMENSION(1:4) :: CODES
            DATA CODES/ B'1',B'10',B'001',B'000' /
! OTHER VARS NEEDED IN THE PROGRAM
            INTEGER :: I
            CHARACTER :: X
!
! START OF THE MAIN PROGRAM
!
! PROMPT THE USER FOR FOUR CHARACTERS: GET THE SYMBOL ITSELF; COMPUTE
! ITS ASCII VALUE, STORE ITS HUFFMAN CODE IN THE SYMBOL_TABLE
            I = 1
            DO
                    PRINT *, 'PLEASE ENTER THE NEXT LEAST FREQUENT &
                    CHARACTER'
                    READ (*, "(A1)") X
                    SYMBOL_TABLE (I) % NAME = X
                    SYMBOL_TABLE (I) % ASCII_VALUE = IACHAR(X)
                    SYMBOL_TABLE (I) % HUFFMAN_CODE = CODES(I)
                        I = I + 1
                    IF (I == 5)EXIT
            END DO
! PRINT THE TABLE OF SYMBOLS, ASCII EQUIVALENTS, AND HUFFMAN CODES
! IN AN ORDERLY MANNER
            PRINT (T10,A,T20,A,T37,A)","SYMBOL","ASCII_VALUE","CODE"
            PRINT *,'    ============================================='
            PRINT "(T13,A,T25,I2,T37,B3.1)", SYMBOL_TABLE(1)
            PRINT "(T13,A,T25,I2,T37,B3.2)", SYMBOL_TABLE(2)
            PRINT "(T13,A,T25,I2,T37,B3.3)", SYMBOL_TABLE(3), SYMBOL_TABLE(4)
            END PROGRAM HUFFMAN_CODING
```

FIGURE 4.4   FORTRAN 90 program for the coding example.

SYMBOL_TABLE (2); recall that this record consists of three fields (NAME, ASCII_VALUE, and HUFFMAN_CODE). Therefore, the format portion of the PRINT statement must specify the format for each of these fields. The format descriptors in this statement are summarized in Table 4.1 together with their meaning. (Consider each line of the monitor to consist of 72 possible positions in which to display information.)

Table 4.1   Summary of Format Specifications for the Coding Example

Specification	Purpose
T13, T20, or T37	The "T" specification is a "tab" or positioning control. The position at which the next information is to be displayed is either 13, 20, or 37, depending on the number that follows T.
A	This signifies that the data to be displayed are alphanumeric or character type. This could be designated as A1 and the descriptor defaults to A1 when the 1 is omitted.
I2	The data to be displayed are of type integer, and two positions should be reserved for the information. The designator "In" would set aside *n* positions.
B3.2	The descriptor "B" signifies that the data are binary (1's or 0's). "B3" would reserve three display positions. "B3.2" not only sets aside three positions but also requires that a minimum of two positions be displayed no matter what the value of the data. For example, if the binary data were 1, the computer would display 01.

Operationally, the computer proceeds to examine each format descriptor. If it finds a control specification (e.g., "T13" format), then it responds accordingly (e.g., prepares to display data in column 13). If it encounters a data descriptor (e.g., "A" format), it retrieves the next item in the variable list (e.g., SYMBOL_TABLE (2) % NAME) and displays what it finds in accordance with the format specification. The computer continues in this fashion (associating format descriptors and items in the variable list) until it exhausts all items in the list. At times the computer exhausts its format list before all data items have been retrieved. This is the case for one of the statements in the program:

```
PRINT "(T13,A,T25,I2,T37,B3.3)",SYMBOL_TABLE(3),SYMBOL_TABLE(4)
```

Having associated the "A," "I2," and "B3.3" with the three fields of SYMBOL_TABLE(3), the computer would have exhausted the format list, yet the variable list includes the three fields of SYMBOL_TABLE(4) which have still to be processed. When this happens, the computer returns to the start of the format list and continues processing in the manner described after moving to the next line on the display. The overall result in this case is to display two lines under the same format. (For the specific statement used here, format control returns to "T13." Other alternatives are possible wherein control is transferred to an intermediate format descriptor; these will be described below.)

For the statement

```
PRINT "(T10,A,T20,A,T37,A)","SYMBOL","ASCII_VALUE","CODE"
```

the following should be noted. The list of variables consists of character constants in the form of a *string* comprising various messages (or in this case titles), namely, SYMBOL, ASCII_VALUE, and CODE. When the computer encounters an "A" format in the specification list, it retrieves one of the variables from the variable list. In this case, it will reference one of the character strings. These strings are thus displayed at the point controlled by the "tab" controls embedded in the format command string.

Once this program is compiled and linked, executing the final code produces the following result.

```
 PLEASE ENTER THE NEXT LEAST FREQUENT CHARACTER
7
 PLEASE ENTER THE NEXT LEAST FREQUENT CHARACTER
5
 PLEASE ENTER THE NEXT LEAST FREQUENT CHARACTER
3
 PLEASE ENTER THE NEXT LEAST FREQUENT CHARACTER
1
```

SYMBOL	ASCII_VALUE	CODE
7	55	1
5	53	10
3	51	001
1	49	000

4.2 DATA FORMATS

As noted in the example discussed above, information must be converted from characters to internal representation during input operations and from an internal form to a string of alphanumeric characters for output uses. A *format specification* furnishes the necessary information; it includes a list of *edit descriptors*, one for each of the list of values being transferred during input or output operations, and they are separated by commas. The edit descriptors control the way in which translation of the data is to be interpreted. Formatting may be accomplished in several ways.

- Included as a string of characters within the I/O statement.
- Included within a separate FORMAT statement.
- List directed or default formatting without specific editing information. Editing or formatting is implicit in such cases.
- Namelist formatting.

The first method is the preferred form of format specification; it is associated with the data transfer statements READ, PRINT, and WRITE. The WRITE statement is an extended form of the PRINT statement and, in particular, includes the means to communicate with flies located in secondary storage. (The WRITE statement is discussed in Sec. 4.3.) I/O operations deal with collections of data generally referred to as *files* which are subdivided into *records*. Records include additional components called *fields*.

The syntax of the READ and PRINT statements is shown in Fig. 4.5. Three components of such statements should be noted: the reserved word (PRINT or READ), the format specification, and the list of data items to be transferred. The format specifications (either as character expressions or within a FORMAT statement) can include combinations of data edit descriptors, control edit descriptors, and character string edit descriptors. The data item(s) include the list of variables to be transferred. If there are several variables—as there might be when transferring an array—then an implicit DO loop (I/O-implied-DO) can be used. (See Chapter 5 for a discussion of DO loops.)

It is sometimes useful to be able to repeat a sequence (string) of edit descriptors without having to explicitly reproduce each descriptor. In such cases, the *repeat factor* is a convenient construction. For example, if the list of data to be transferred consists of five integers, each consisting of two digits, then the format specification can be written as

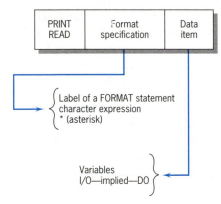

FIGURE 4.5   Syntax diagram for FORTRAN 90 READ and PRINT statements.

$$I2,I2,I2,I2,I2$$

Alternatively, this can be written as

$$5I2$$

which is interpreted to mean, "the next data items in the list consist of five integers, each one of these being composed of two digits"; it is clearly easier to read. When repeated patterns occur, parentheses may be used in conjunction with the repeat factor. A sequence such as

$$I2,I3,I2,I3,I2,I3,I2,I3,I2,I3$$

can be represented as

$$5(I2,I3)$$

4.2.1 Edit Descriptors

The edit descriptors fall into several distinct categories relating to integers, real numbers, character strings, and those that control the positioning of information on the I/O device.

Integer Editing

Integer editing descriptors have the following format:

$$[r]Iw[.m]$$

where the meaning of each symbol is as follows.

- r = the repeat factor
- I = an indication that the descriptor refers to a data item that is assumed to be an integer
- w = referred to as the *width*, indicates the number of digits that is associated with the integer data item. If identified with an output statement (e.g., PRINT), then the computer will reserve w display positions on the monitor (or printer). If the format descriptor is concerned with input operations (e.g., READ) then the computer expects w digits to be received (entered).

m = an optional part of the format descriptor. If included, it is interpreted to mean that a minimum of m digits will be assigned to the data item. On output, if the variable contains more than m digits, the missing digits (normally "leading blanks") will be displayed as zeros. On input, leading blanks are "padded" with zeros.

In the notation shown above, any designation enclosed by square brackets ("[ ]") is an optional part of any descriptor. The letter I may be replaced by B (when the integer is binary); O (when the integer is octal); Z (when the integer is hexadecimal); G may also be used and normally produces the same result as an I format. (The G descriptor is more important when dealing with real or complex numbers and should not be used for integer variables.)

EXAMPLE 4.1   A Simple I Edit Descriptor

If the format includes I7 as the editing descriptor, and the corresponding variable stored within the computer is 149, the output will be bbbb149 where "b" denotes a blank. Notice that the variable is "right justified."

Real Editing

Generic form: $[r]Fw.d$
The symbols are

r = repeat factor

$Fw.d$ = converts to or from a string of w digits with d places after the decimal point; d must not be greater than w. The number may include a sign. For input operations, the value of d has no effect; if there is no decimal point, a decimal point is inserted in front of the rightmost d digits. (The letter F is normally referred to as "floating point" format.)

Important alternatives for real quantities include the E (exponential) or D (double precision) formats.

EXAMPLE 4.2   The Exponential Format

The format descriptor letter is either E or D. Data will have the form

```
{real number} E   or   D {integer exponent}
```

whose numeric value is $\{\text{real number}\}10^{\{\text{integer exponent}\}}$. When D is used, the computer interprets this to mean *double precision,* and the resulting record will provide for a greater number of significant digits. A typical exponential number is 1.234E01 (which is equivalent to 12.34); another example is 1.234E–01 (for .1234). Shown below are examples that include numeric value, E format descriptors, and the resulting record which is generated for output operations:

Numeric Value	E Format Descriptor	Resulting Record
−315.1	E15.4	bbbb−0.3151E+03
−315.1	E15.3	bbbbb−0.315E+03
−3151.521163	D20.10	bbb−0.3151521240D+04

This last example reproduces an incorrect value. This follows from the errors that are introduced when conversion takes place from a real number to a binary number (see Sec. 1.3.5). When dealing with high-precision numbers, the user must carefully check for such anomalies.

When specifying the E or D descriptor in a program, the following important rules should be observed.

- One space must be reserved for the algebraic sign; if it is "+," the position appears as a blank.
- One space must be reserved for a leading zero.
- One space must be reserved for a decimal point.
- Four spaces must be reserved for the exponent (the letter E or D, a sign, and two digits for the integer exponent).
- The number of significant digits that will be printed is d.
- The number will be printed in *normalized form;* the decimal portion will follow the decimal point in the record, and a 0 is assigned to the integer portion of the variable.

EXAMPLE 4.3 The EN Descriptor (ENw.d)

The EN descriptor is referred to as the *Engineering edit* format. When entering information, the effects are exactly the same as the F format; its effect is important for output operations. The resulting output conforms to the following:

- The exponent is divisible by three; this corresponds to various convenient units in engineering problems such as 10^{+6} for mega, 10^{+3} for kilo, 10^{-3} for milli, 10^{-6} for micro, 10^{-9} for nano, 10^{-12} for pico, and so on.
- The absolute value of the mantissa is greater than or equal to 1 and less than 1000, except when the output should be 0.

A simple FORTRAN 90 program for testing this edit descriptor is as follows.

```
PROGRAM TEST_EN_DESCRIPTOR
REAL :: W,X,Y,Z
W = 5987.1
X = 1.234
Y = -0.3
Z = .001
PRINT "(EN12.3)", W,X,Y,Z
END PROGRAM TEST_EN_DESCRIPTOR
```

The results are summarized in the following table.

Initial Value	Output Record
5987.1	5.987E+03
1.234	1.234E+00
−0.3	−300.000E−03
.001	1.000E−03

EXAMPLE 4.4 The ES Descriptor (ESw.d)

Scientific results are often presented in the following format:

$$\pm 0.x_1 x_2 \cdots x_n (10)^{\pm y1y2}$$

where $\pm 0.x_1 x_2 \cdots x_n$ is the mantissa and $\pm y1y2$ is the power to which 10 is raised (or exponent). The ES descriptor is referred to as the *Scientific edit* format and is compatible with the scientific notation. When entering information, the effects are exactly the same as the F format; its effect is important for output operations. The resulting output conforms to the following.

- The absolute value of the mantissa is greater than or equal to 1 and less than 10, except when the output value is 0.

Here are some sample results (see Problem 4.3)

Initial Value	Output Record
5987.1	5.987E+03
1.234	1.234E+00
−0.3	−300.000E−03
.001	1.000E−03

EXAMPLE 4.5 The G Descriptor (Gw.d)

This descriptor may be used when editing complex values as well as real variables. When entering data, simply obey the rules for the F descriptor. Here too, the greatest impact occurs in the output record. The rules follow either the E or F formats depending on the magnitude of the number. (A scale factor may affect those numbers that conform to the E format; scaling is discussed below.) The following illustrates the results when using the G descriptor; data were accepted using F10.1, and the record was displayed on the monitor using G12.4 as the edit descriptor.

Input	Resultant Record on Monitor
123.4	123.4
1234567.8	0.1235E07

Notice that when the number is too large FORTRAN 90 automatically switches to the E format descriptor.

Logic Editing

The L edit descriptor is used when referring to logical data. (The G descriptor may also be used, but, for reasons of clarity, it is not recommended.) The format of this descriptor is

$$Lw$$

where w accounts for the number of positions to be occupied by the data in the record.

When reading data into the computer, the following format may be used for the information being entered. The L descriptor should provide for w positions where w is the total number of characters being entered, including blanks and period, if present.

```
bb. . .b[.][T or F][character string]
```

- Any number of blanks
- An optional period
- Either the letter T for true or F for false, but clearly not both
- Any number of additional characters

EXAMPLE 4.6 Examples of input records under control of the L descriptor

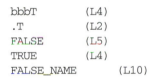

```
bbbT           (L4)
.T             (L2)
FALSE          (L5)
TRUE           (L4)
FALSE_NAME        (L10)
```

When printing or writing logical data to a record, the following rule is to be observed:

- If the format descriptor is Lw, then the output record will consist of $(w-1)$ blanks (b) followed by either the letter T or F, depending on the truth or falsity of the associated data.

Character Editing

The character editing descriptor is

$$A[w]$$

and the following should be noted:

- If the width of the field, w, is omitted, then the number of characters in the record is determined by the datum itself.

EXAMPLE 4.7 Using the A Descriptor

Edit Descriptor	Data to Be Printed	Result
A10	FORTRAN 90 is great	FORTRAN 90
A10	Pressure	bbPressure

Notice the results; when w (10) is less than the number of characters to be printed, only the first w (10) characters are reproduced; when w exceeds the number of characters,

Table 4.2   Summary of Position Descriptors

Descriptor Format	Effect
Tn	Moves the record just before character n; the next character in the record is the nth one.
TLn	Moves n positions to the left.
TRn	Moves n positions to the right.
nX	Moves right n positions.

blanks (b) are added at the left to complete the record. With other edit descriptors, a series of asterisks will be displayed if there is not enough room for the data; this is not the case with the A format.

Position Editing Descriptors

A number of descriptors permit the user to move to arbitrary positions in a record. These are summarized in Table 4.2.

The coding example described in Sec. 4.1.1 includes several instances of the T descriptor; see Fig. 4.4. This descriptor is useful for organizing or tabulating data in a column format.

Additional Edit Descriptors

Several additional useful edit descriptors are described below, including examples of their usage.

EXAMPLE 4.8 Skipping Lines (or Records) Using the Slash (/) Descriptor

If the computer encounters a slash (/) in a list of edit descriptors, it will skip to the next record. When displaying information on the monitor, this has the effect of skipping a line. The fragment

```
print "(A, /)", "one","two","three"
```

will cause the monitor to display

one

two

three

Note that a line has been skipped between each character expression. (The comma between the "A" and the "/" in the PRINT statement above is optional.)

EXAMPLE 4.9 Scale Factors

The scale factor editor descriptor has the format kP where k is an integer constant that may be either negative or positive (e.g., -3, or 5). This edit descriptor establishes a relationship between numbers stored within the computer and their corresponding external values. When it is encountered in a list of descriptors, it establishes the correspondence from that point on, until a new scale factor appears. The scale factor will affect subsequent I, F, E, EN, ES, D, or G descriptors, and it works as follows:

> *When the data are *output,* the following rules are observed:
> - I, F, EN, and ES descriptors are not affected by the scale factor.
> - For E and D descriptors, the nonexponent part of the number is multiplied by 10^k and the exponent is reduced by k.
> - G descriptors will cause data to be displayed in either F or E formats. Scale adjustments therefore follow the rules for these.

EXAMPLE 4.10 Edit Descriptors for Signs

A leading plus sign (+) may be used when printing positive numeric information. The edit descriptors that control this feature of FORTRAN 90 are summarized in Table 4.3. Whenever this descriptor is encountered in a list of edit descriptors, it remains in effect until another one (S, SP, SS) is found.

4.2.2 Examples

The general arrangement of a READ or PRINT statement is shown in Fig. 4.5. Formatted data transfer associates one item in the data list with one item in the list of data edit descriptors, which defines the form of conversion between internal representation and the string of characters representing the information. Recall that it is possible to include a repeat factor for groups of edit descriptors. (When analyzing such descriptor strings, write out the repeated sequence, thereby creating one descriptor for each data item.) Three possibilities exist within FORTRAN 90 programs:

- There is exactly one descriptor for each data item.
- There are more descriptors than items in the data list.
- There are more data items than descriptors in the edit list.

In addition to these conditions, there are three ways to specify where the format edit descriptor list is located, and these are:

- A character expression within the PRINT or READ statement itself.
- A statement label that refers to another statement called a FORMAT statement.

Another form is known as the *namelist* input/output structure, but we will not describe it here because it is not recommended and because the facilities already provided are adequate to handle all data transfer operations.)

Table 4.3 Edit Descriptors for Sign Editing

Descriptor	Effect
S	The printing of the optional plus sign is left up to the processor being used.
SP	The optional plus sign must be printed.
SS	The printing of the optional plus sign should be suppressed.

EXAMPLE 4.11 Associating Edit Descriptors and Data Items

Given the following output statement:

```
PRINT "(I3, 2(F5.2, TR2, F5.3), A2)", I,W,X,Y,Z,"OK"
```

This form of the PRINT statement includes a string of characters ("character expression") that define the edit descriptors as well as the list of data items to be displayed. To analyze this, expand the edit descriptors and associate each one with a data item as shown below:

```
I3   F5.2   TR2   F5.3   F5.2   TR2   F5.3   A2
I    W            X      Y            Z      OK
```

(It is assumed that I is an integer variable, and W, X, Y, and Z are real variables; "OK" is simply an alphanumeric literal.) Notice that TR2 is not associated with any data items because it is a control descriptor and is therefore not related to a data item.

A second form of this PRINT statement makes use of the FORMAT statement. Its syntax would be:

```
      PRINT 15, I, W, X, Y, Z, "OK"
  15  FORMAT (I3, 2(F5.2, TR2, F5.3), A2)
```

In this case the number 15 refers to a statement label (statement number) somewhere within the source program that contains the edit descriptor list. The FORMAT statement may appear anywhere within the source code.

Additional forms of this PRINT statement include:

```
    PRINT (6, 15) I, W, X, Y, Z, "OK"
```

where 15 refers to the FORMAT statement (as above) and 6 refers to a particular I/O unit. This is normally the monitor but might be a printer in some circumstances. The general form would be *PRINT (logical unit number, label or * when list-directed)*.

```
    PRINT (*,15) I, W, X, Y, Z, "OK"
```

where the asterisk indicates the default I/O unit—the monitor—and 15 refers to the FORMAT statement number (label).

In addition to using PRINT as the keyword to specify an output operation, the keyword WRITE may be used; there are numerous alternatives for such commands, and the syntax for WRITE is discussed in Sec. 4.3.

Finally, there is one additional way to display the variables I, W, X, Y, Z, and the constant "OK." This is known as *list-directed* formatting; it is a default specification without specific edit descriptors, and its syntax for this example would be

```
        PRINT *, I,W,X,Y,Z,"OK"
```

The user should observe the following restrictions when using list-directed formatting on input.

1. The actual values associated with READ or PRINT statements must be consistent with the type of data specified in the list. In addition to the intrinsic data types, values can include a null value (e.g., ,, where the commas are item separators or delimiters), a character constant (literal), and a number of repetitions of a constant (e.g., 5*10.3 or repetitions of the null value 5*).

2. Blanks are never considered to be zeros; blank editing (see below) is not allowed.

3. Embedded blanks are not allowed except within a character constant.

4. Complex items include parentheses for a complex constant (e.g., (1.3, − 8.9)).

5. If an input list item has been defined within the program as having a given length ("len =") and fewer characters are entered, blanks are added on the right end. If the field is greater than the length, those characters that exceed the length are ignored.

EXAMPLE 4.12 Implied and Explicit DO Loops in I/O Operations

It would be extremely inconvenient to have to reference each item of an array when accepting input from a user (READ) or displaying results (PRINT, WRITE). Suppose that a mechanical stress test has been performed; a test force is applied to a mechanical member, and its distortion or strain is measured. A table of such results would include the forces applied (stress) and the resultant deformations (strain). Assume that the table includes five rows and two columns. The first column contains the applied forces, and the second contains the resulting strain as

1.0	2.0
2.0	4.0
3.0	6.0
4.0	8.0
5.0	10.0

The values are to be displayed on the monitor, and the following PRINT statement is used:

```
PRINT "(2(F6.1))", stress_test
```

where stress_test is the array identifier. A format of "2(F6.1)" that corresponds to F6.1, F6.1 is used to display the results. There are ten items in the list—the array stress_test consisting of five rows of two columns for a total of ten items. Notice that there are only two edit descriptors for the ten items in the list. When the format descriptor list is exhausted before the list of items, control is returned to the beginning of the task descriptor list, continuing in this fashion until all items in the data list are exhausted. In this case, the sequence of data items, control characters, and edit descriptors is

```
F6.1   stress_test(1,1)
F6.1   stress_test(2,1)
<CR,LF> - carriage return/line feed or cursor moves to a new line.
F6.1   stress_test(3,1)
F6.1   stress_test(4,1)
```

```
<CR,LF>
F6.1   stress_test(5,1)
F6.1   stress_test(1,2)
<CR,LF>
F6.1   stress_test(2,2)
F6.1   stress_test(3,2)
<CR,LF>
F6.1   stress_test(4,2)
F6.1   stress_tests(5,2)
<CR,LF>
```

Unfortunately, the results on the monitor appear as

```
bbb1.0bbb2.0
bbb3.0bbb4.0
bbb5.0bbb2.0
bbb4.0bbb6.0
bbb8.0bb10.0
```

Within the PRINT statement, the order of rows and columns has not been specified. When this happens, the computer defaults according to the following rule: the first dimension is varied most rapidly, and the second index is the next most frequently varied, continuing in this way for all other dimensions. This accounts for the sequence described above. In order to print the results with the column index varying most frequently, we must change the PRINT statement to

```
PRINT "(2(F6.1))", ((stress_test(I,J), J=1,2), I=1,5)
```

The data list designation instructs the computer to carry out an *implied DO loop* with the index J—the one shown first as the "inner loop"—varying the most frequently and the index I varying less frequently. When this statement is executed, the results appear in the desired manner:

```
bbb1.0bbb2.0
bbb2.0bbb4.0
bbb3.0bbb6.0
bbb4.0bbb8.0
bbb5.0bb10.0
```

(DO loops are discussed more fully in Chapter 5, and Sec. 5.9 includes additional illustrations of implied DO loops.)

EXAMPLE 4.13 Blank Editing

When READing data, blanks in a record may be ignored, or they may be treated as zeros. (This does not apply to leading blanks in the record which are ignored; this is also the default case.) Two edit descriptors within a format expression for a READ statement can alter this situation. These descriptors should be considered as switches that are in effect until a new one is encountered. The two descriptors are:

BN, which means ignore blanks in numeric input fields until further notice; the default case.

BZ, which translates blanks in numeric input fields into zeros until the BN switch is again encountered in the format expression.

As an example, the following READ statement,

```
READ (5, "(I3,BZ,I3,BN,I3)") N1,N2,N3
```

will translate the (input) sequence b111b11b1 into 11, 101, and 11 for N1, N2, and N3, respectively (assuming these have been declared to be integer variables).

EXAMPLE 4.14 Editing Complex Data

Two edit descriptors are required for a complex data quantity, one for the real part and one for the imaginary part. (The user may in fact use integer descriptors, but when this happens the computer will convert the integers into real quantities [internally], using the rules of conversion for assignment to complex.) The following fragment provides an example of input and output results:

```
PROGRAM COMPLEX_I/O
IMPLICIT NONE
COMPLEX :: X
READ "(2F7.2)", X
PRINT "(F7.2,A,F7.2)", REAL(X)," + I",AIMAG(X)
END PROGRAM COMPLEX_I/O
```

and when the input is

```
bbb25.1bbb1.21
```

the corresponding output record (on the monitor) is

```
bb25.10b+bIbbb1.21
```

where *b* stands for a blank.

EXAMPLE 4.15 The Presence of a Colon in the Edit Descriptor List

The colon editor descriptor (:) may be used to signal the point where format processing should stop in the event there are no more data items in a list. For example, it is desired to print a list of numbers, each separated by a comma as follows: 1,2,3,4,5. This list might be treated in a direct way by using a format descriptor expression such as 5(I1,"",","). This expression provides for five integers of one digit, each separated by a comma. However, with this descriptor expression, the last digit will also be followed by a comma. To suppress the last comma, a colon is inserted as follows: 5(I1,:,"",""). The colon signals the computer to stop processing edit descriptors at that point if there are no more items in the data list.

EXAMPLE 4.16 Finding Tendencies: A Case of Sign Editing

To find relationships between variables, engineers and scientists often start by searching for trends or tendencies between variables. As a simple example, consider a program that automatically finds the point (on the x axis) where data reach their maximum (or minimum) value. In such cases, the presence of a sign on the output data can improve one's ability to interpret the data. A unimodal function—one with a single maximum within some region of the x axis—is sketched in Fig. 4.6. This could represent, for example, the amount of effluent measured downstream from a point source as a function of time. The algorithm shown below in pseudocode can be used to find the point on the x axis at which the maximum occurs.

```
{FIND DIFFERENCES BETWEEN ADJACENT DATA VALUES}
{PRINT THE RESULT INCLUDING POSITIVE OR NEGATIVE SIGNS}
```

If the output data include the sign even when the result is positive, the user's ability to detect the point at which the differences change sign is enhanced. A FORTRAN 90 program that generates and displays the changes in data along the x axis (including the sign of the change) follows. (The data themselves were produced arbitrarily and stored in the array named Data_Source. That portion of the program is not included.)

```
PROGRAM FIND_MAX
      IMPLICIT NONE
      REAL, DIMENSION (0:99) :: DATA_SOURCE
      INTEGER :: I
!
```

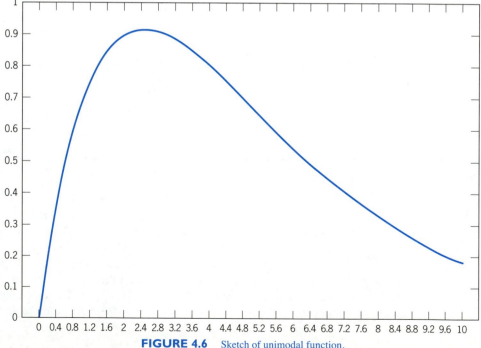

FIGURE 4.6   Sketch of unimodal function.

```
! SOURCE CODE AT THIS POINT FILLS THE ARRAY WITH
! DATA IN ACCORDANCE WITH THE SKETCH IN FIGURE 4.6
!
    DO I = 20,30
        PRINT "(I2,T10,SP,F6.4)", I    &
            (DATA_SOURCE(I)-DATA_SOURCE(I-1))
    END DO
END PROGRAM FIND_MAX
```

The key element of this program is the PRINT statement; it includes the SP edit descriptor that forces the optional plus sign to be printed. Although this descriptor remains enabled once it appears in the edit descriptor list, it does not apply to the integer descriptor because this appears ahead of the SP descriptor, and for each item in the data list, the computer returns to the start of the edit descriptor list where it returns SP to its default mode (suppress sign). (Recall that when the edit descriptor list is exhausted before the data item list is completed, control returns to the start of the edit descriptor list, in general.) Note, too, that only the values close to the maximum are displayed in this case — from I=20 to I=30. (See Problem 4.13 for a program that permits the user to select the region to be displayed. An alternative approach is to store the information in a file, print the file, and study the hard copy before additional analysis.) The results displayed on the monitor in this example are.

20	+.0100
21	+.0079
22	+.0059
23	+.0040
24	+.0023
25	+.0007
26	−.0007
27	−.0020
28	−.0033
29	−.0044
30	−.0056

4.2.3 Format Descriptor Deviations

In some circumstances, mainly on input operations, data may be entered which are at variance with the formats specified by the data descriptors. Deviation from the format specified by the descriptor is not generally recommended; when the user does deviate from the descriptors, the effects can be noted by the results summarized in Table 4.4.

4.3 COMMUNICATING WITH FILES

A *file* is a collection of related data with a common name. They are normally retained on the computer's secondary storage system, although both the keyboard and the monitor are considered to be "file-oriented" devices in that they will generate or receive data from the computer. Such structures serve a variety of purposes:

Table 4.4   Summary of Data Descriptor Deviations

Descriptor or Constraint	Input	Output
Plus signs	May be omitted	
F,E,EN,ES,D,G	Decimal point supersedes placement of decimal point by editor descriptor.	
I,F,E,EN,ES,D,G		Output field is filled with asterisks (*) if the number or exponent is too large for the field width.
Fw.d	• Decimal point may be omitted; a decimal point will then be inserted in front of the rightmost *d* digits. • Input can include E or D indicating an exponent value.	
A[w] len = length of the data object	• w > len: rightmost len characters are read. • w < len: input is padded with blanks on the right.	• w > len: blanks are added on the left. • w < len: leftmost w characters appear in output record.

- They can save large amounts of data generated by programs that would otherwise be difficult to retain.
- One of the ways in which a computer is very useful is for processing large amounts of data. Such quantities of data are not conveniently entered from the keyboard, although sometimes there is no alternative.
- A file is a convenient medium for transferring information between remote sites.
- A file is an efficient way to retain (archive) data in a "relatively permanent" way. Even data in the secondary storage system deteriorates with time as a consequence of environmental effects, causing data bits to "drop out" or be lost and introducing errors.

A functional sketch of the file structure is shown in Fig. 4.7. The file contains the following elements:

- *Header*   This element contains information about the file itself and does not include the user's information.

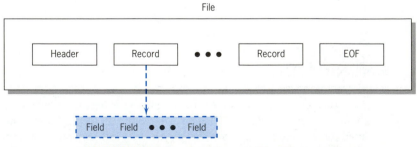

FIGURE 4.7   Functional diagram of the file structure.

- *Record(s)*   This part of the file stores the information to be supplied to or from the computer.
- *Field(s)*   Records are subdivided into fields, the smallest data unit within a file. Fields can contain information of differing (data) types.
- *End-of-File (EOF)*   This is a special type of record that simply signals the end of the file; it does not contain the user's data.

EXAMPLE 4.17 A Sample File

Transportation planning and research is an important engineering function. A program to assist the designer for such applications might include statistical procedures to establish the time patterns of daily traffic flow. The necessary data would include the measuring station identification, date, direction, time, lane, and number of axles passing a test point among other information. A file of such information might have the record/field structure shown below. (Also noted is the type of data for each field, which is not included as part of the file itself but is interpreted as such by a suitable FORTRAN 90 program.)

```
FILENAME—RAW_DATA
EACH RECORD CONSISTING OF THE FOLLOWING FIELDS:
        FIELD 1: STATION_IDENTIFICATION—ALPHANUMERIC
        FIELD 2: DATE—ALPHANUMERIC WITH FORMAT MMDDYY (MONTH, DAY,
           YEAR)
        FIELD 3: TIME_OF_DAY—INTEGER, USING 24 HOUR FORMAT (E.G.,
           1550 HOURS)
        FIELD 4: TRAFFIC_DIRECTION—INTEGER WITH 1 (EAST), 2 (WEST),
           3 (NORTH), 4 (SOUTH)
        FIELD 5: LANE—INTEGER
        FIELD 6: NUMBER_OF_AXLES—INTEGER
```

Notice that each record is a mixture of integer and alphanumeric data types, with the names of each field indicated in boldface type.

From the user's point of view there are two types of files: *sequential access* (SA) or *direct access* (DA). The type depends on how records are accessed for reading or writing.

SA files are read or written in strict sequential order. You cannot "jump over" records when progressing through a file. For some files, the point of access for reading or writing can be selected as needed; these are DA files.

In addition to classifying files according to the way in which information is accessed, other divisions are possible. For example, files may be

- *Unformatted* The values in the file are stored using the same representation used in program memory. Unformatted I/O may be accomplished using sequential or direct access.
- *Formatted*   Data must be converted from/to character strings that form readable representations of information within the program (or memory).

Finally, files may considered to be either internal or external:

External: Data are stored on a peripheral device such as a disk or computer terminal (keyboard/monitor). Allowed access methods include SA or DA, and data may be formatted or unformatted.

Internal: Information is stored in the computer's memory in the form of values of character variables.

In dealing with files, three important operations must be specified by the user within the program:

- The user must establish a communication channel to the file.
- I/O operations on the file in the form of READ or WRITE transmits data from/to the file.
- When the user is finished with the file, communication is terminated by a close operation.

A number of parameters are associated with these operations, and these are explained below. Note, however, that communication does not have to be opened to either the monitor or the keyboard; these are considered to be "preconnected" to the computer. (Unless noted, the discussion below refers to external files.)

4.3.1 Open Communications

The format of the OPEN statement is

```
OPEN (PARAMETER LIST)
```

The list of potential parameters as well as notes about usage are summarized in Table 4.5. In general, the parameter list includes the keywords shown in the table followed by an appropriate expression (e.g., label, integer, character). In some circumstances, the keywords need not be explicit, as indicated in the examples shown below.

EXAMPLE 4.18 File Opening Samples

Open communication to an existing file in which are stored experimental results on the b: drive of the computer; assign the filename "results.exp." It is to be accessed in sequential order and prepared for appending records:

```
open(2,file="b:results.exp",access="sequential",position="append",status
                              ="old")
```

Open a temporary or "scratch" file for use as a temporary buffer (memory) for file operations:

```
open(status="scratch",unit=10)
```

Open a direct access file for writing only; assign status information to the integer variable named ios; call the file "image" on drive c:; the length of the records is to be 32 characters:

```
open(unit=15,file="c:image",access="direct",iostat=ios,action=
"write", recl = 32)
```

Other instances of the open statement as well as file operations will appear in later chapters.

Table 4.5   Summary of Parameters for the Open Statement

Parameter	Notes
unit =	A nonnegative integer designating the logical connection. Subsequent I/O statements reference this number. The keyword "unit=" need not be used, but if it isn't the parameter must appear first in the list.
file =	This indicates the name of the file being connected.
form =	Choices are "formatted" or "unformatted." If omitted, default settings are "unformatted" for direct access files and "formatted" for sequential access files.
access =	This specifies the way in which the file is to be accessed, and the two forms are "direct" and "sequential."
status =	"old" refers to an existing file.
	"new" refers to a file that does not exist.
	response to "unknown" depends on the processor; often it treats an existing file as "old" or creates a "new" file if nonexistent.
	"scratch" creates a temporary file that will cease to exist when the program ends.
	"replace" creates a file with "old" status if it doesn't exist; if already present, the file will be overwritten.
action =	"read" for input operations; "write" for output operations; "readwrite" for input and output operations; default is "readwrite."
position =	"asis"—leave the file position where it is.
	"rewind"—puts file at initial point.
	"append"—puts file just ahead of the EOF record.
iostat =	Must be an integer variable. The computer assigns values as follows:
	<0—EOF condition or end of record condition exists.
	>0—An error has occurred during opening.
	=0—None of the above.
err =	A label must be designated and the program branches to the label if an error occurs.
recl =	An integer that specifies the length of a record if access is direct or the maximum record length if the file is sequential
blank =	May be specified only for files connected for formatted I/O.
	"null"—all blanks in numeric fields are ignored.
	"zero"—all blanks, except leading blanks, are treated as zeros. Default is "null."
delim =	Applicable only to files connected for formatted I/O and is ignored for formatted input.
	"apostrophe"—delimiting symbol for character constants in list directed or namelist formatting is an apostrophe.
	"quote"—delimiting symbol for character constants in list directed of namelist formatting is a quote.
	"none"—character constants will not be delimited.
	Default is "none."
pad =	"yes"—blank padding is used when input list requires more data than the record contains.
	"no"—the input list must contain the data required by formatting.
	Default is "yes."

Table 4.6   Summary of Read/Write Parameters

Parameter	Notes
unit =	Integer specifying the logical unit number (as established in an OPEN statement) to/from which information is to be transferred. An asterisk (*) indicates a processor-dependent external unit such as the keyboard or monitor.
fmt =	A character string that specifies the edit descriptors as described in Sec. 4.2.1. This may also be a label denoting the location of a separate FORMAT statement, which includes the edit descriptor list. An asterisk (*) indicates default format descriptors ("list-directed" format). (An asterisk is incompatible with an advance specification.)
iostat =	An integer variable that is assigned a value dependent on the outcomes of the read or write. (See Table 4.5.)
*err =	A label specifying where to transfer program control should an error occur.
*end =	A label specifying where to transfer program control if the end of the file is encountered.
advance =	"yes"—file is positioned after the end of the last record read or written when I/O is finished.
	"no"—positions the file after the last character read or written rather than skipping to the end of the record.

*Avoid "err=" and "end=" options when possible because these require use of statement labels, and usage of such labels should be minimized in FORTRAN 90 program.

4.3.2 File I/O

Having established communication with the file, it is now possible to read or write data within a program. This is accomplished using a READ or WRITE statement with the following general format.

$$\begin{pmatrix} \text{READ} \\ \text{WRITE} \end{pmatrix} \quad \textit{(list of specifications)} \quad \textit{list of data items}$$

The keyword READ or WRITE is followed by a list of control and/or format specifications for the data items to be transferred; this list is enclosed within parentheses. The list of data items—the I/O list—follows after the parentheses. Parameters are summarized in Table 4.6.

Many examples of I/O have been provided during the description and use of the PRINT statement, demonstrating how to translate data from internal to external form using format edit descriptors. An appropriate WRITE statement may be used wherever a PRINT statement is found; the WRITE statement is essential during I/O operations involving external files.

EXAMPLE 4.19 WRITE to an External File

Samples of the WRITE statement to an external file include the following.

```
WRITE (10,FMT = 100) (X(I),I=1,100)
WRITE (100,"(2F20.5)",IOSTAT=IEND)X,Y
WRITE (*,"(A,F5.3,A)")" THE RESISTANCE IS ",R," OHMS."
```

The first sample specifies logical unit 10, includes a predefined character expression for the format, and shows how an implied DO loop is used to write the values stored in an array. The second sample includes the format (character expression) within the WRITE statement and provides for subsequent testing of the resulting I/O status (e.g., an error occurred). The last example specifies a default unit (e.g., the monitor) and shows how a complete sentence can be formulated with inclusion of a variable result.

EXAMPLE 4.20 "User-Friendly" Interaction on the Monitor

An important part of any program is provided by input from a user and is often accomplished with a WRITE statement followed by a READ statement. The WRITE statement often supplies a prompt to the user. A sample of this sequence is

```
PRINT "(A)", "PLEASE ENTER THE DATA "
READ (*,"(I5)") PROGRAM_DATA
```

When these statements are executed, the prompt message appears on the monitor and the output advances to a "new record." In this case, the "new record" generates a carriage return and line-feed sequence to the monitor. The cursor is moved to the next line where it awaits the user's response to the READ instruction. An alternative approach is to await the user's response on the same line as the prompt message. This can be done using the ADVANCE parameter of the WRITE statement as seen in

```
WRITE (*,"(A)",ADVANCE="NO") "PLEASE ENTER THE DATA "
READ (*,"(I5)") PROGRAM_DATA
```

With this code there will be no advance to a new record (a new line on the monitor), and the cursor awaits input from the user at a point that is visually adjacent to the prompt message. The technique is effective when the user is entering data according to a template in which he or she is to enter several pieces of information on the same line. (Some caution should be noted here: results may not be guaranteed because many systems consider input from a terminal and output to the terminal to involve two different files.)

EXAMPLE 4.21 Unformatted Files

Unformatted files are useful when storing large amounts of data that will be used in subsequent executions of the program with which they are associated. Suppose that a program is to support maintenance of an inventory system for radio frequency interference (RFI) filters. (RFI filter components are important for instruments and equipment that malfunction if used in the presence of electromagnetic radiation produced, for example, by commercial radio or television transmissions; a space vehicle might include a number of such filters in various sensitive instruments.) The following program fragments could be used as part of an inventory system.

To declare an appropriate derived data type:

```
TYPE FILTER_PART
    INTEGER :: KEY_NUMBER, NO_IN_STOCK
    CHARACTER (LEN=20) :: PART_TYPE
    CHARACTER (LEN=40) :: PART_DESCRIPTION
```

```
END TYPE FILTER_PART
INTEGER :: NO_OF_PARTS
TYPE (FILTER_PART), DIMENSION (1000) :: RFI_FILTERS
```

To open the unformatted file for writing (including a typical WRITE statement):

```
OPEN(UNIT=10,FILE="RFIPARTS",FORM="UNFORMATTED",          &
ACCESS="SEQUENTIAL",STATUS="REPLACE",ACTION="WRITE",      &
POSITION="REWIND")
WRITE (10),NO_OF_PARTS,RFI_FILTERS(1:NO_OF_PARTS)
```

The OPEN statement specifies unformatted, sequential access with the file positioned at the starting record and to be overwritten. The WRITE statement presumes that the array has been edited (e.g., an RFI filter description has been added or the number of inventoried units changed). The first record in the file is the number of parts included in the inventory file, which is a convenient way to save this important parameter. The remaining records consist of the array of RFI filters. If a user wished simply to examine the file (that is, "browse"), the following statements are appropriate:

```
OPEN(9,FILE="RFIPARTS",POSITION="REWIND",   &
     FORM="UNFORMATTED",ACTION="READ",STATUS="OLD",   &
     ACCESS="SEQUENTIAL")
READ(9),NO_OF_PARTS,RFI_FILTERS(1:NO_OF_PARTS)
```

4.3.3 The INQUIRE Statement

If a user wants to find out if a file exists, if it is connected, or the status of the other associated parameters, the INQUIRE statement can be used. If, for example, a file system was developed to store information about experimental results or engineering experience (e.g., power was used at different manufacturing stations for each month), a great many files would need to be retained in secondary storage. Part of the software system would provide for the user to name the file into which the records are to be stored. With an extensive file system, it would be difficult to know if the candidate filename had already been assigned. (See Problem 4.15.) The INQUIRE statement is used to test for the prior existence of a file among other parameters. For each parameter of interest, the computer returns the result of the inquiry and assigns this value to a variable designated within the program. The form of the statement is

```
INQUIRE (list_of_parameters)
```

and the list_of_parameters is summarized in Table 4.7. The INQUIRE statement can be used to test for connections to logical units rather than files; results for this case are also included in the table. The INQUIRE statement may be executed before, while, or after a file is connected to a unit.

Many entries in the table provide for considerable flexibility in developing programs. Although the table is provided for completeness, most users will find some specifiers more useful than others. (See Problem 4.16 for a case where the INQUIRE statement is useful.) Notice within the table the existence of "<variable>"; the user must name (define) an appropriate object for each parameter of interest and should make sure that the identifier is defined within the declarations.

Table 4.7   Summary of the INQUIRE Statement Specifiers

Specifier	INQUIRE by File	INQUIRE by Unit
UNIT=<value>	Not applicable	Specifies logical unit number
FILE=<string>	Specifies name of file	Not applicable
IOSTAT=<variable>	I/O status returned	I/O status returned
*ERR=<label>	Xfr to <label> if error	Xfr to <label> if error
EXIST=<variable>	.TRUE. if file exists; .FALSE. otherwise	.TRUE. if unit exists; .FALSE. otherwise
OPENED=<variable>	.TRUE. if connected; else .FALSE.	.TRUE. if connected; else .FALSE.
NUMBER=<variable>	−1 if unconnected; else returns unit number	−1 if unconnected; else returns unit number
NAMED=<variable>	.TRUE. if file is named; otherwise .FALSE.	.TRUE. if unit is named and connected; otherwise returns .FALSE.
NAME=<variable>	Returns filename—not to be confused with FILE=	Returns filename if named and connected; otherwise result is undefined
ACCESS=<variable>	Undefined if file is not opened; otherwise DIRECT or SEQUENTIAL	Undefined if not connected; otherwise DIRECT or SEQUENTIAL
SEQUENTIAL=<variable>	YES, NO if opened and connected for such access; otherwise UNKNOWN	YES, NO if unit is connected for such access; otherwise UNKNOWN
DIRECT=<variable>	Same as SEQUENTIAL=	Same as SEQUENTIAL=
FORM=<variable>	FORMATTED or UNFORMATTED if opened; else undefined	FORMATTED or UNFORMATTED if connected; else undefined
FORMATTED=<variable>	YES, NO, or UNKNOWN, depending on file being opened	YES, NO, or UNKNOWN depending on unit being connected
UNFORMATTED=<variable>	Same as FORMATTED	Sames as FORMATTED
RECL=<variable>	Returns max record length for formatted or unformatted files that are opened; record length for direct access; undefined if not opened	Same results as INQUIRE by file
NEXTREC=<variable>	If opened for direct access, returns next record number; else undefined	Same results as INQUIRE by file
BLANK=<variable>	NULL, ZERO, or UNDEFINED if opened with this parameter specified; else undefined	Same results as INQUIRE by file
POSITION=<variable>	REWIND, APPEND, ASIS, UNDEFINED, depending on state of file	Same results as INQUIRE by file

Table 4.7   *Continued*

Specifier	INQUIRE by File	INQUIRE by Unit
ACTION=<variable>	READ, WRITE, READWRITE, or UNDEFINED, depending on connection	Same results as INQUIRE by file
READ=<variable>	YES, NO, or UNKNOWN, depending on connection	Same results as INQUIRE by file
WRITE=<variable>	Same as READ inquiry	Same as READ inquiry
READWRITE= <variable>	Same as READ inquiry	Same as READ inquiry
DELIM=<variable>	APOSTROPHE, QUOTE, NONE, or UNDEFINED, depending on connection	Same results as INQUIRE by file
PAD=<variable>	YES or NO if opened and the parameter specified; returns YES if file is not opened	Same results as INQUIRE by file

*Avoid "ERR=" if possible; this requires use of statement labels, and usage of such labels should be minimized in a FORTRAN 90 program.

4.3.4 File Positioning Statements

Several file positioning controls may be used within a program in preparation for reading/writing from/to a file. These statements include BACKSPACE, REWIND, and ENDFILE:

- BACKSPACE positions the file one record before the current one.
- REWIND moves the file to the beginning.
- ENDFILE writes a special EOF record and positions the file after this record. If the user wants to write another record, the program must execute a BACKSPACE before attempting a WRITE operation.

The format of such positioning commands includes

```
keyword (BACKSPACE, REWIND, or ENDFILE) (parameter specification
    list)
```

The parameter list may include: "UNIT=", "IOSTAT=", or "ERR=", followed by appropriate variables or labels. Additional rules that must be observed are as follows.

- These statements apply only to external files.
- A file unit number is always required.
- If "UNIT=" is not used, the logical unit number must appear first in the specification list.
- The label for "ERR=" cannot transfer control to outside a subroutine.

EXAMPLE 4.22 Sample Positioning Control Statements

Some positioning control statements include

```
BACKSPACE 9
BACKSPACE (9)
REWIND (IOSTAT=IOS,UNIT=10)
ENDFILE (12)
```

4.3.5 Internal Files

The files that have been described to this point are considered to be *external*—that is, stored on a peripheral device or secondary storage system. In contrast, *internal* files are stored in main memory as values of character variables. These variables can be generated using assignment statements within the program. In addition, I/O statements of the type described in this chapter may also be used. Only formatted, sequential access is permitted on such internal files. In particular, the READ and WRITE commands may be used; however, the list of allowed parameters differs from those permitted for data transfers to external files:

For READ, the parameter list may include

```
(UNIT=<var>,FMT=<format>,IOSTAT=<var>,ERR=<label>,END=<label>)
```

For WRITE, the parameter list is the same except for "END=" which should not appear. ("END=" specifies a transfer point should an EOF record be returned; users are urged to avoid the use of labels in FORTRAN 90 programs.) Internal files are convenient for converting variables into character strings as well as the reverse. In one case, this permits a user to examine a record using character operations and then translate them directly into other types of data (e.g., integer variables).

EXAMPLE 4.23 Writing to an Internal File

The following statement will convert the value of an integer variable *N* into a character string:

```
WRITE (STRING,"(I5)")N
```

If *N* is an integer such as 12, STRING would contain the same information but coded as characters (bbb12 where b is a blank). This utility permits the programmer to carry out arithmetic operations on a variable and then to be able to deal with results (such as in formatted printing) on a character basis where it is conveniently inserted into a string of characters.

4.3.6 CLOSE

The CLOSE operation instructs the computer to terminate connections to external files. The format of such statements follows.

```
CLOSE (specification list)
```

The specifications include:

```
(UNIT=<var>,IOSTAT=<var>,ERR=<label>,STATUS=<var>)
```

The "UNIT=", "IOSTAT=", and "ERR=" parameters have been previously discussed. The attribute "STATUS=" has not yet been explained, although it is used in Example 4.21. This parameter specifies what to do with a file that has been previously opened. The choices are:

- KEEP: This is the default setting, and if it is the user's intention, then it is simply omitted from the specification list. This choice retains the file in the secondary storage system after the program terminates. The one exception to the default status refers to a "scratch" file which, by default, is terminated or DELETED. (You cannot save a scratch file; a run-time error results if you attempt to do so.)
- DELETE: This erases the referenced file.

PROBLEMS

4.1 Show that only 25 binary digits are required to transmit the message in the example described in Sec. 4.1.1 using the coding scheme outlined in the example.

4.2 For the example of Sec. 4.1.1, indicate what program modifications are necessary if there are six characters to be encoded together with their associated codes 10, 00, 111, 110, 011, and 0101.

4.3 Write a program that can be used to test the ES edit descriptor. Arrange the program so that the user enters the values of the variables and the program prints the results. Test your program with the following input values: 6.891, −0.4, .0456, and 9854.2. Use a descriptor that does not truncate any of the input values. Use the F format edit descriptor to accept input values.

4.4 Within a program an EN descriptor appears as "EN12.4." The data item to be displayed is −0.4. The results is "************". This indicates the result could not be printed. Explain why this happens.

4.5 Refer to Example 4.4 in the text. Write a FORTRAN 90 program that will verify the values illustrated in the example.

4.6 You want logical data to consist of the word TRUE (or FALSE). Write a program that uses the L format descriptor for the data but prints the complete word TRUE or FALSE. Arrange the program so that the user enters the truth or falsity of one variable and then print the result. Try the following inputs: t, f, true, false, thursday, friday.

4.7 Write a program to verify the results of Example 4.6.

4.8 Test the scale factor edit descriptor by incorporating the following into a FORTRAN 90 program. Let the variable $X = 10.50$; display X using two different edit descriptors, "(E20.5)" and "(3P,E20.5)."

4.9 Run the following program and note the results:

```
PROGRAM TEST_SIGN_DESCRIPTORS
REAL :: X,Y,Z
X = 10.50
Y = 124.6
Z = 90.65
PRINT "(S,F8.2,SP,F8.2,SS,F8.2)", X,Y,Z
END PROGRAM TEST_SIGN_DESCRIPTORS
```

4.10 Given the following variable values: $I = 55$, $W = -1.24$, $X = 10.50$, $Y = 124.6$, and $Z = 90.65$. What is displayed on the monitor in response to the following instruction:

```
PRINT *, I,W,X,Y,Z,"OK"
```

Hint: Because this is list-directed formatting, the answer is processor dependent; you should generate a short program to obtain the results.

4.11 Determine the output when the following program is executed:

```
PROGRAM F_AND_E
REAL :: X,Y
X = 175.327
Y = 1201.924
PRINT "(F12.4,E12.3)", X,Y
PRINT "(F12.2,E12.1)", X,Y
END PROGRAM F_and_E
```

4.12 Verify the results described in Example 4.15. Write a program that creates an array of five integers; call the array out_list. Initialize the array within the data declaration statement with the numbers 1 through 5 inclusive. Next, write a PRINT statement that displays the array values separated by commas, except for the last digit.

4.13 Modify the program in Example 4.16 as follows:

(a) Add the section of code needed to fill the array data_source with 100 values from 0 to 99 according to the following function:

$$\text{data\_source}(I) = (0.1I)e^{-0.4(.1I)}$$

(b) Modify the source to permit a user to specify what parts of the x axis are to be displayed. Let the user select the starting point and have the program display the next ten differences.

4.14 Determine the result for the following PRINT statement:

```
PRINT"(t10,sp,f6.4)",1.2345
```

4.15 Write a program that allows the user to specify the name of the file to be opened rather than having to supply it at the time the program is compiled (e.g., make the filename a character variable rather than a character constant). Test the program by using an OPEN statement with STATUS="NEW". After the OPEN statement, CLOSE the file and terminate the program; then check secondary storage to see that the file has been created.

4.16 Having opened a file as in Problem 4.15, use the INQUIRE statement to test for the existence of a file with the designated filename. Have the program display the proper answer on the monitor. (Try versions of the INQUIRE statement that will produce both true and false results.)

5

Iterative Processes

Iteration means repeating the same series of processing steps until a predetermined stop or branch condition is reached. In this chapter, we discuss iterative processes. In order to perform iteration in the most efficient way, we will place the main emphasis on the use of the DO loop, a FORTRAN construct for achieving iteration.

A comment concerning terminology is in order. The reader will observe that we are using the term *construct* in this and other sections. By construct we mean a sequence of statements beginning with DO, IF, and other terms to be introduced later and ending with an appropriate terminating statement. For example, the terminating statement of the DO construct is END DO; the terminating statement of the IF construct is END IF.

5.1 THE IF STATEMENT

The general form of an IF statement is

```
IF (logical expression) statement
```

The statement is executed only if the *logical expression* is TRUE. The IF statement is useful for situations in which the outcome of the test IF(X > 0) is only one statement. For example:

```
IF(X > 0) A = 5.0
```

There also is the IF *construct* which has the form

```
IF (logical expression) THEN
        block of statements
        ELSE IF(logical expression)
        ELSE
        block of statements
        END IF
```

The IF. . .THEN construct is discussed in Chapter 6. It will be seen that the IF. . .THEN construct is useful when more than one statement is involved.

5.2 THE GO TO STATEMENT

The general form of the GO TO statement is

```
GO TO n
```

where n is an integer number called the label. The GO TO statement causes the program to branch to the statement with label n. This labeled statement must be in the same main program or in a procedure. We will use the GO TO statement in implementing two algorithms in the next section. However, thereafter, it will be used only occasionally because the IF construct and DO construct, with the EXIT and CYCLE statements, are preferred and usually achieve the same result.

5.3 ITERATIVE PROCESSES

An algorithm is a procedure for solving a problem. To be effective, an algorithm

- must be unambiguous
- must take into consideration all alternatives that may be presented
- must produce an answer in a finite number of steps

In many algorithms, it is necessary to perform a given calculation many times using a different value for one or more variables each time. Executing such an iterative procedure in a computer program is called looping. As an example, the following program segment could be used to evaluate 20!

```
     FACT = 1.0              !Initalize values of FACT and X.
     X = 1.0                 !Initialize values of FACT and X.
40   IF((20.0-X)<=0.0) GO TO 50    !If x = 20, go to 50, print value
                                    !of FACT
     FACT = FACT*X           !Calculate new value for factorial
     X = X + 1.0             !Increment value of X by 1.0
     GO TO 40                !transfer to beginning to the loop
50   WRITE(*,*)' 20 ! = ',FACT    !write output when calculation is
                                   !complete
```

A flow diagram for a segment of a program for calculating a factorial is shown in Fig. 5.1.

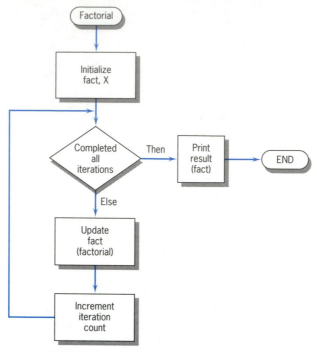

FIGURE 5.1 Flow diagram for factorial segment.

As another example, consider the following algorithm for calculating the square root of a number *A*. We will arbitrarily choose the value of *A* to be 5. The procedure can be programmed as follows.

```
      A = 5.0                                   (a)
      X = A/2.0                                 (b)
100   XNEW = (X + A/X)/2.0                       (c)
      IF(ABS(X-XNEW)< =0.000001 GO TO 200        (d)
      X = XNEW                                   (e)
      GO TO 100                                  (f)
200   WRITE(*,*)'LAST VALUE OF X =',X            (g)
```

Step a Select the number the square root of which is to be found.

Step b Assign the *first estimate* of the square root to *X*.

Step c Calculate a *trial* value of square root and assign it to XNEW.

Step d *Test* the latest estimate of the square root by comparing it to the previous estimate. If successive estimates are within +0.000001 (the allowed tolerance) of each other, the program branches to label 200 and the current (latest) estimate is printed; the program stops.

Step e *Replace* the current value of *X* with the value of the latest estimate. This step is necessary because the algorithm calculates succeeding estimates using the latest estimate.

Step f Return to the beginning of the loop.

Step g Print the result when the test in Step b has been satisified.

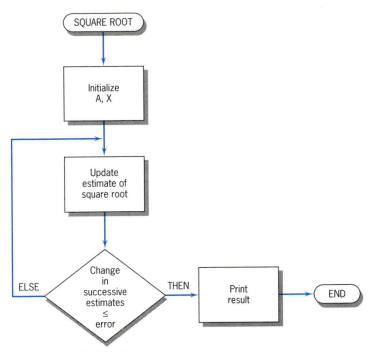

FIGURE 5.2   Flow diagram for square root calculation.

Both of the above examples used the looping process. In the factorial calculation, the loop would be performed exactly 20 times. In the square root calculation, the loop would occur until the test in Step d is satisfied.

A flow diagram for a segment of a program for calculating the square root of a number is shown in Fig. 5.2.

The DO loop is a construct of the FORTRAN language that automatically produces the steps described above. The programs of this chapter illustrate the DO construct and variations of it.

5.4 DO CONSTRUCT

The DO construct makes it possible to execute the same group of statements repeatedly. This is called *looping*. The form of this construct is

```
DO loop control
   group of statements
END DO
```

This form of DO loop is called **BLOCK DO. NONBLOCK DO** has the form

```
      DO label loop control
         group of statements
label    END DO
```

BLOCK DO is the preferred construct. However, FORTRAN 90 supports both BLOCK and NONBLOCK DO.

Two general methods can be used to terminate a loop. One method involves executing the loop a fixed number of times. In the other method, an exit from the loop occurs when some condition has been met.

5.5 DO LOOPS WITH LOOP CONTROL USING A DO VARIABLE

When it is desired to execute a loop a fixed number of times, loop control is achieved by using a DO variable, the value of which changes from a designated initial value to a designated limiting value using designated increments.

The general forms for loop control using a DO variable are

$$DO \ var = e_1, e_2$$

where

    var = variable

    e_1 = initial value

    e_2 = limiting value

and

$$DO \ var = e_1, e_2, e_3$$

where

    e_1 = initial value

    e_2 = limiting value

    e_3 = step size

The phrase "limiting value" indicates the ultimate value reached by the DO variable. The phrase "maximum value" has not been used to emphasize the fact that the ultimate value *may* be less than the initial value. This is possible because step size may be either an *increment* or a *decrement* in the value of the DO variable. When no step size is specified, as in the first case shown, a value of +1 is used. When step size is a decrement, the initial value will be progressively reduced. For example, consider the following loop:

```
DO KOUNT = 16,0,-1
```

KOUNT will assume the values $16, 15, 14, \ldots, 0$.

If the step size is -2:

```
DO KOUNT = 16,0,-2
```

KOUNT will assume the values $16, 14, 12, \ldots, 0$.

It is generally recommended that the DO loop variable *not* be a real variable because of roundoff errors that may occur in the conversion of real to binary. As a result of these errors, the loop may terminate with the DO variable not equal to the limiting value. If it is not essential that the loop terminate exactly at the limiting value, then a real DO loop variable may be used.

When a DO statement is encountered in a program, the following steps are automatically executed:

1. *Initialization* Values for e_1, e_2, and e_3 are obtained from the DO statement. An *iteration count* is obtained from the following computation:

$$\text{maximum of } [(e_2 - e_1 + e_3)/e_3] \quad \text{or} \quad 0$$
$$\text{If } e_1 > e_2 \quad \text{and} \quad e_3 > 0 \quad \text{or} \quad e_1 < e_2 \quad \text{and} \quad e_3 < 0$$

then, the iteration count will be zero.

2. *Computation* Instructions in the range of the DO are executed if the iteration count is not zero.

3. *Incrementation* The present value of var is increased or decreased by e_3.

4. *Testing* The iteration count is decremented by 1. Computation, incrementation, and testing are continued as long as the iteration count remains nonzero.

As mentioned previously, if e_3 is not specified, then the step size is +1. If the value of the DO variable exceeds e_2, the looping is stopped and control passes to the statement immediately following the last statement in the range of the DO.

We will call this a normal exit from the DO.

If exit from a DO is other than normal, the current value of the index at the time of exit is retained and may be used later in the program. If exit from a DO loop is normal, the value of the index will be greater than the test value because the sequence of events after the last statement in a DO is

1. Increment

2. Test

3. Either exit or loop

Now that we have examined the operation of the DO loop in some detail, let us return to the calculation of the factorial discussed in Sec. 5.3 to see how use of the DO loop simplifies the procedure. The following statements could be used:

```
FACT = 1.0
DO KOUNT = 1,20
  X = KOUNT
  FACT = FACT*X
WRITE(*,*) FACT
END DO
```

In this example, the value of the index was used in the calculation. In many cases, the index is used only as a counter. Because the WRITE statement is placed within the loop, each successive value of FACT will be displayed. If this is not desired, then the WRITE statement should be positioned outside of the DO loop.

5.6 RESTRICTIONS ON THE DO STATEMENT

The following rules apply to the DO statement:

1. The range of the DO must not contain any statement that redefines the index.

2. The range of the DO must not contain any statements that redefine the index parameters. This means that e_1, e_2, and e_3 must be "set" (that is, defined) *before* the DO loop is entered.

3. *The first statement in the range of the DO must be an executable statement.*

4. It is possible to *nest* DO loops providing that the *inner* DO is entirely contained within the outer DO. There is no limitation on the number of DOs that may be nested. The names used for the indexes of inner loops must differ from those of the outer loop and from each other. Nesting is discussed in Sec. 5.8.

5. Transfer of control *out* of the range of a DO is permitted.

6. Transfer of control *into* the range of a DO loop is *not* permitted. The only exception to this rule occurs when, within a DO range, a *subprogram is called and the transfer into the loop is the return* from the subprogram.

7. Transfer of control *within* the range of a DO is permitted. In a nest of DOs, it is possible to transfer from an inner loop to an outer loop when the transfer is out of the inner loop and within the outer loop.

5.7 EXAMPLES IN WHICH THE DO LOOP IS USED

EXAMPLE 5.1 Program SQUARE_ROOT

Finding the Square Root

A discrete time system is one in which information in the form of a sequence of numbers (discrete data) is operated on and this generates other discrete data. Computers are an example of a discrete time system. One tool used in the study of discrete time systems is difference equations.

$$y(k) = \frac{1}{2}\left[y(k-1) + \frac{x}{y(k-1)} \right] \qquad k = 0, 1, 2, 3, \ldots \qquad (5.1)$$

The following difference equation will approximate the square root of a number denoted by x. In the program below, we chose $X = 17$.

It is seen that k assumes values $0, 1, 2, \ldots$. When $k = 0$, one of the subscripted variables has the subscript -1. That is, $y(k-1)$ becomes $y(-1)$ when $k = 0$. To solve the equation, a value must be supplied for $y(-1)$. This is known as satisfying an initial condition. We will guess at a value for $y(-1)$. In order to permit the assignment $Y(-1) = 1.0$, the statement DIMENSION $Y(-1:100)$ is used. A poor guess for the assignment will cause a slower convergence toward the "answer"; a good guess will speed it up. The program, SQUARE_ROOT, and a trial run follow.

```
          PROGRAM SQUARE_ROOT
    !
    !     PROGRAM COMPUTES THE SQUARE ROOT OF A NUMBER
          IMPLICIT NONE
          REAL:: Y(-1:100),X
          INTEGER:: K
          X = 17.0
          Y(-1) = 1.0                !AN ESTIMATE FOR Y(-1)
          DO K = 0,8
          Y(K) = 0.5*(Y(K - 1) + X/Y(K - 1))
          WRITE(*,*) 'K', K,' Y (K)', Y(K)
          END DO
          END PROGRAM SQUARE_ROOT
```

```
RUN
K   0 Y(K)  9.0000000
K   1 Y(K)  5.4444447
K   2 Y(K)  4.2834468
K   3 Y(K)  4.1261067
K   4 Y(K)  4.1231065
K   5 Y(K)  4.1231055
K   6 Y(K)  4.1231055
K   7 Y(K)  4.1231055
K   8 Y(K)  4.1231055
```

As noted above, have set $Y(-1) = 1$ and $X = 17.0$. Thus, the square root of 17.0 is being sought. The results of the run showed that convergence toward the final result run revealed that the value 4.1231055 was obtained in six iterations. Note that the lower bound of the DIMENSION statement is -1. This permits us to set $Y(-1)$.

EXAMPLE 5.2 Program GEOMETRIC SERIES

The sum, S, of a geometric series is given by

$$S = \frac{a}{1-r}$$

where

$a =$ the first term of the series

$r =$ the ratio of term $n + 1$ to term n

As an example, in the series

$$1 + 1/3 + 1/9 + 1/27 + \ldots$$

$$a = 1; \qquad r = 1/3$$

Program GEOMETRIC_SERIES and a trial run are shown below.

```
       PROGRAM
!
!      THIS PROGRAM GENERATES A GEOMETRIC SERIES, SUMS N TERMS,
!      AND ALSO CALCULATES THE SUM OF AN INFINITE NUMBER OF
!      TERMS
!
       IMPLICIT NONE
       REAL:: A, R, SUM, SUMSERIES, S(100)
       INTEGER:: NUMBER, N, KOUNT
!
       WRITE(*,*)'ENTER THE NUMBER OF TERMS TO BE SUMMED'
       READ(*,*) N
       WRITE(*,*)N,' TERMS TO BE SUMMED'
       R = 1.0/3.0
       SUM = 0
       A = 1.0
       DO NUMBER = 1,N
         S(NUMBER) = A*R**(NUMBER-1)
       SUM = SUM + S(NUMBER)
```

```
      END DO
      SUMSERIES = A/(1.0 -R)
  !
      WRITE(*,*) "THE FIRST", N," TERMS OF THE SERIES ARE"
      DO KOUNT = 1,N
         WRITE(*,*) S(KOUNT)
      END DO
      WRITE(*,*)' SUM OF', N, 'TERMS = ',SUM
  !   SUMSERIES IS THE SUM OF AN INFINITE NUMBER OF TERMS
         WRITE(*,*)'SUM OF INFINITE NUMBER OF TERMS =', SUMSERIES
      END PROGRAM GEOMETRIC_SERIES
```

The program

    (a) Calculates and prints the first N terms of the series 1, 1/3, 1/9, 1/27 . . . .

    (b) Calculates the sum of the first N terms.

    (c) Calculates the sum of the entire series.

The value of N serves as the maximum value of the index I of the DO loop. In the trial run shown a value of 5 was entered for N. It was found that the sum of five terms was 1.49383. The sum of an infinite number of terms was 1.5. Thus, this series converges rather rapidly.

```
      RUN
       5 TERMS TO BE SUMMED

      THE FIRST 5 TERMS OF THE SERIES ARE

       1.00000
       0.33333
       0.11111
       0.03703
       0.01234
         SUM OF 5 TERMS = 1.49383
      SUM OF INFINITE NUMBER OF TERMS = 1.50000
```

EXAMPLE 5.3 Program PLANCKS_LAW (Physics)

Thermal energy may be transferred from one place to another in three ways: by conduction, by convection, and by radiation. All bodies constantly radiate and absorb heat energy from their surroundings. If the temperature of the body is the same as its surroundings, it radiates heat energy at the same rate that it absorbs heat energy. The radiation is electromagnetic in nature and is governed by Planck's Law, shown below. This radiation occurs in the form of an electromagnetic wave whose wavelength is given by W. As the temperature of a body is changed, the amount of heat energy radiated at a given wavelength will change. If the wavelength is in the band of visible light, then the body will glow with a color that depends on the wavelength.

    Planck's Law is

$$E = \frac{C_1}{W^5[\exp(C_2/WT)-1.0]}$$

where

C_1 and C_2 are constants

T is temperature in degrees Kelvin

W is wavelength in microns (10^6 micron = 1 meter)

E is the monochromatic blackbody emissive power

In the program, PLANCKS_LAW, which is shown below, W is used as the index of the DO loop. The value of W varies from 0.2 to 6.1 microns. The values of C1, C2, and T are provided by the PARAMETER statement. The PARAMETER statement is a method of defining constants and was discussed in Chapter 3.

```
          PROGRAM PLANCKS_LAW
!
!         THIS PROGRAM COMPUTES MONOCHROMATIC BLACK BODY
!         EMISSIVE POWER ACCORDING TO PLANCK'S LAW
!
          IMPLICIT NONE
          REAL:: EM,W
          INTEGER:: N
          REAL, PARAMETER::C1 = 1.187E+08,C2 = 2.5896E+04, T = 3460.0
          W = 0.1
          WRITE(*,*) 'WAVELENGTH    POWER'
          DO N = 1,58
            EM = C1/((W**5)*(EXP(C2/(W*T))-1.0))
            W = W + 0.1
            WRITE(*,*) W, EM
          END DO
          END PROGRAM PLANCKS_LAW
```

RUN

WAVELENGTH	POWER
0.20	0.0000
0.30	0.0000
0.40	0.7146
0.50	86.7109
0.60	1198.7803
0.70	5838.6460
0.80	16050.8643
0.90	31332.8711
1.00	49176.2070
1.10	66721.2656
1.20	81852.6172
1.30	93476.5313
1.40	101339.1484
1.50	105718.2109
1.60	107153.8281
1.70	106264.8047
1.80	103642.7734
1.90	99801.9297
2.00	95162.6484
2.10	90053.9922
2.20	84724.5313

2.30	79356.0625
2.40	74077.1016
2.50	68975.0625
2.60	64106.2070
2.70	59503.7539
2.80	55184.1914
2.90	51152.1563
3.00	47404.0273
3.10	43930.6836
3.20	40719.4844
3.30	37755.7266
3.40	35023.6406
3.50	32507.2090
3.60	30190.5371
3.70	28058.2598
3.80	26095.7520
3.90	24289.2324
4.00	22625.8223
4.10	21093.5625
4.20	19681.4063
4.30	18379.2090
4.40	17177.6426
4.50	16068.1748
4.60	15043.0117
4.70	14095.0420
4.80	13217.7676
4.90	12405.2832
5.00	11652.1973
5.10	10953.6045
5.20	10305.0342
5.30	9702.4141
5.40	9142.0303
5.50	8620.5029
5.60	8134.7427
5.70	7681.9380
5.80	7259.5161
5.90	6865.1279

EXAMPLE 5.4 Program HYPERGEOMETRIC_PROBABILITY

Mathematics: Probability

Now that we are familiar with the calculation of the factorial, we will give an example that makes abundant use of factorials. The hypergeometric probability distribution concerns selection from a population of N objects, M of which are of one type and $N-M$ of which are of another type. For example, N may consist of M men and $N-M$ women. A random sample of size NS is drawn from the population and is not replaced. The problem is to calculate the probability $P(K)$ that there are K of type M in the sample. The formula for P(K) is

$$P(K) = \frac{M!}{K!(M-K)!} \frac{(N-M)!}{(NS-K)!(N-M-NS+K)!} \frac{N!}{NS!(N-NS)!} \qquad (5.2)$$

The program for this calculation, **HYPERGEOMETRIC_PROBABILITY**, is shown below.

```
        PROGRAM HYPERGEOMETRIC_PROBABILITY
!
!   CALCULATION OF HYPERGEOMETRIC PROBABILITIES. N IS THE
!   TOTAL POPULATION; M IS THE NUMBER OF ONE KIND; NM IS THE
!   NUMBER OF OTHER KIND; NS IS SAMPLE SIZE; K IS THE NUMBER
!   OF M IN NS.
!
    IMPLICIT NONE
    REAL:: F(9),P_OF_K,A,B
    INTEGER:: I,N,M,NS,K,MK,NNS,NMSK,NSK,NM,KOUNT1,KOUNT2,KOUNT3
    INTEGER:: KOUNT4,KOUNT5,KOUNT6,KOUNT7,KOUNT8,KOUNT9
    DATA (F(I),I = 1,9)/9*1.0/
    WRITE(*,*)' ENTER VALUES OF N, M, NS, K'
    READ(*,*) N, M, NS, K
    WRITE(*,*)'N =',N,' M =',M,' NS=',NS,' K =',K
!
!   9 DO LOOPS ARE USED IN THE HYPERGEOMETRIC FORMULA
    DO KOUNT1 = 1,M
        F(1) = F(1)*REAL(KOUNT1)
    END DO
    DO KOUNT2 = 1, K
        F(2) = F(2)*REAL(KOUNT2)
    END DO
    MK = M - K
    DO KOUNT3 = 1, MK
        F(3) = F(3)*REAL(KOUNT3)
    END DO
    NM = N - M
    DO KOUNT4 = 1, NM
        F(4) = F(4)*REAL(KOUNT4)
    END DO
    NSK = NS - K
    DO KOUNT5 = 1, NSK
        F(5) = F(5)*REAL(KOUNT5)
    END DO
    NMSK = N - M - NS + K
    DO KOUNT6 = 1, NMSK
        F(6) = F(6)*REAL(KOUNT6)
    END DO
    DO KOUNT7 = 1, N
        F(7) = F(7)*REAL(KOUNT7)
    END DO
    DO KOUNT8 = 1, NS
        F(8) = F(8)*REAL(KOUNT8)
    END DO
    NNS = N - NS
    DO KOUNT9 = 1, NNS
        F(9) = F(9)*REAL(KOUNT9)
    END DO
    A = (F(1)/(F(2)*F(3)))*(F(4)/(F(5)*F(6)))
    B = F(7)/(F(8)*F(9))
```

```
        P_OF_K = A/B
        WRITE(*,*) 'P_OF_K = ',P_OF_K
        END PROGRAM HYPERGEOMETRIC_PROBABILITY
```

RUN
```
 N = 30   M = 20   NS = 5   K = 3
 P_OF_K = 0.35998
```

We observe that the major part of the program involves calculation of the nine factorials required in Eq. (5.2). For convenience, the names F(1), ... F(9) was chosen to represent the various factorials. For example, F(1) represents M! and F(2) represents K!. Also, note that the same name, I, has been used as the index of each of the DO loops. This is permissible because the DO loops are independent of each other. As previously noted, when the DO loops are nested, the labels of the indices must be different. Also note that the variables F(1), ... F(9) are initialized by a DATA statement. Recall that variables of the form $V(n)$, where n is an integer, are called dimensioned variables. The DATA statement is similar to the PARAMETER statement. It is used for initializing variables or for assigning values to constants. However, unlike the PARAMETER statement, the values assigned by the DATA statement can be changed during execution of a program.

This program can be made more compact by use of a function subprogram. (See Problem 7.14.) Function subprograms are discussed in Chapter 7.

EXAMPLE 5.5 Program BIRTH, The Birthday Problem

Mathematics: **Probability**

Another illustration of the use of the DO loop is provided by a program for the solution of the classic "birthday problem." This problem is:

If there are n people in a room, what is the probability that two or more people have the same birthday, assuming 365 days in a year?

Let the probability of the event "no two people have the same birthday" be denoted by $P(E)$. It follows from probability theory that

$$P(E) = \frac{365}{365} \frac{364}{365} \frac{363}{365} \cdots \frac{(365 - n + 1)}{365} \tag{5.3}$$

The solution of the problem is:

$$P(\text{two or more people have the same birthday}) = 1.0 - P(E) \tag{5.4}$$

In Eq. (5.3), the calculation of 365^n may produce very large numbers. For example, for $n = 15$, $365^{15} = 2.7188983 \times 10^{38}$. Thus, for large values of n, there is a possibility of overflow. Eq. (5.3) may be made more convenient for calculation by expressing $P(E)$ as the product of n fractions. The first fraction has a value of 1.0, and the succeeding fractions are progressively smaller. Thus:

$$P(E) = \frac{365}{365} \frac{364}{365} \frac{363}{365} \cdots \frac{(365 - n + 1)}{365} \tag{5.5}$$

Program BIRTHDAY, which calculates the probability, and a sample run follow.

```
     PROGRAM BIRTHDAY
 !
 !    THIS PROGRAM CALCULATES THE PROBABILITY THAT IN A ROOM
 !    WITH N PEOPLE, AT LEAST TWO HAVE THE SAME BIRTHDAY
```

```
!
      IMPLICIT NONE
      REAL:: RATIO, P_OF_E, PROBABILITY
      INTEGER:: ITEMS,N
      WRITE(*,*)'ENTER THE NUMBER OF PEOPLE IN A ROOM'
      READ(*,*)N
!
      P_OF_E = 1.0
      DO ITEMS = 2, N
      RATIO = (365.0 - REAL(ITEMS -1))/365.0
        P_OF_E = P_OF_E*RATIO
      END DO
      PROBABILITY = 1.0 - P_OF_E
      WRITE(*,*)'FOR ',N,' PEOPLE'
      WRITE(*,*)' THE PROBABILITY IS',PROBABILITY
      END PROGRAM BIRTHDAY
```

RUN

```
FOR 12 PEOPLE
THE PROBABILITY IS 0.1670
```

N is the specified number of people in a room. *P(E)* is represented by the name P_OF_E. In the DO loop, the index I is used to generate values of the variable T. T causes RATIO to vary, and P_OF_E is generated by RATIO. For example, when I = 2, T = 1.0, RATIO = 364./365. and P_OF_E = 364./365. Thus, *P(E)* is calculated in accordance with Eq. (5.5). The initial value of I has been set at 2, because a value of I = 1 would result in RATIO = (365./365.) = 1.0. In the trial run, the number 12 was entered as the value of *N*. For this value of *N*, the probability that 2 or more people will have the same birthday was found to be about 0.167. This number may be larger than one might expect, but it has been found to be consistent with statistical data.

EXAMPLE 5.6 Program PERMEABILITY, Specific Permeability of a Porous Medium

Environmental Engineering

Groundwater is water below the surface of the ground. At its lower portion, it is confined by a relatively hard layer of soil. Rainfall is a major factor in maintaining the supply of groundwater. The rain must penetrate the soil to reach the groundwater. Figure 5.3 shows how rain and streams help to maintain the supply of groundwater. Specific permeability, the capacity of a porous rock or soil to transmit rain to the groundwater, is an important factor in maintaining the supply of groundwater. The permeable rock or rocky soil that permits quantities of groundwater to supply wells or streams is called the aquifer. Permeability is a function of the type of soil, the shape and type of rocks within it, the packing (the arrangement of particles within the soil), and the porosity (the ratio of the volume of the pores in a particular formation of rock and soil to the total volume of the formation). Because many obstacles usually prevent rain from reaching groundwater, a significant amount of rain is needed to replenish the groundwater.

As a result of these factors, the specific permeability, *k*, is an important parameter not only in the study of groundwater but also in the design of wells. The following formula is used to calculate specific permeability:

$$k = \frac{1}{m\left[(1-p)^2 / p^3\right]\left[\sum (\theta_j / 100)(P_j / d_j)\right]^2} \tag{5.6}$$

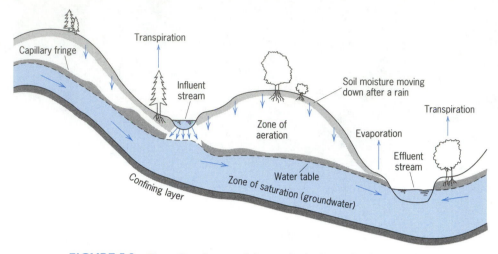

FIGURE 5.3 How rain and streams help to maintain the supply of groundwater.

where

k = specific permeability of mixture, mm^2

m = packing factor

p = porosity

θ_j = particle shape factor

P_j = percent by weight of material j in the medium

d_j = diameter of the particles of material j in the medium, mm

If all the particles of the mixture have the same shape factor, then Eq. (5.6) simplifies to

$$k = \frac{1}{m\left[(1-p)^2 / p^3\right](\theta/100)^2 \left[\sum(P_j/d_j)\right]^2} \tag{5.7}$$

Let us consider the following problem. We have a mixture of two types of sand, type A and type B. How does the specific permeability of the mixture vary as the proportions of A and B in the mixture are varied? The following data concerning the sand are given:

$$d_a = 0.08 \text{ mm} \qquad d_b = 0.40 \text{ mm}$$
$$\theta = 6.5 \qquad p = 0.34 \qquad m = 5$$

Because the particles of each type of sand are assumed to have the same shape factor, Eq. (5.7) is used. Program PERMEABILITY, which carries out the calculation, and a trial run are shown next.

```
    PROGRAM PERMEABILITY
!   THIS PROGRAM CALCULATES THE SPECIFIC PERMEABILITY IN SQ.
!   MM. OF TWO MATERIALS. THE MATERIALS ARE DENOTED "A" &
!   "B". THEIR PROPORTIONS BY WEIGHT IN THE MIXTURE DENOTED
!   BY PWA AND PWB. THE MEAN DIAMETER OF THE PARTICLES OF A
!   IS 0.08 MM.; THE MEAN DIAMETER OF THE PARTICLES OF B IS 0.40
!   MM.
!   THE SHAPE FACTOR OF THE PARTICLES OF EACH MATERIAL IS
```

```
!    ASSUMED TO BE 6.5, AND THE POROSITY IS ASSUMED TO BE
!    0.34.
!    THE PACKING FACTOR IS ASSUMED TO BE 5.0.
     IMPLICIT NONE
     REAL:: THETA, P, M, DA, DB, PWA, PWB, F, K
     INTEGER:: COUNT
     PARAMETER::THETA = 6.5, P = 0.34, M = 5.0, DA = 0.08, DB = 0.4
     PWA = -20.0
     PWB = 120.0
!
     F = M*(1.0-P)**2*(THETA/100.0)**2/P**3
     WRITE(*,"(A/)")' PWA   PWB   SPEC.PERMEABILITY'
     DO COUNT = 1,6
        PWA = PWA + 20.0
        PWB = PWB - 20.0
        K = 1.0/(F*(PWA/DA + PWB/DB)**2)
     WRITE(*,"(F6.0,F8.0,E15.4)") PWA, PWB, K
     END DO
     END PROGRAM PERMEABILITY
```

The following table defines the symbols used.

Formula Symbol	Program Name	Meaning	Units
d_a	DA	Particle diameter, type A	mm
d_b	DB	Particle diameter, type B	mm
θ	THETA	Shape factor	
p	P	Porosity	
m	M	Packing factor	
P_a	PWA	Percentage by weight of type A	
P_b	PWB	Percentage by weight of type B	
k	K	Specific permeability	

```
         RUN
         PWA       PWB      SPEC. PERMEABILITY
          0.      100.          0.6834E-04
         20.       80.          0.2109E-04
         40.       60.          0.1011E-04
         60.       40.          0.5912E-05
         80.       20.          0.3874E-05
        100.        0.          0.2734E-05
```

The variation of the permeability of a composite material consisting of differing proportions of type A and type B is shown in Fig. 5.4. In the program, values are assigned by means of a PARAMETER statement to the shape factor, porosity, packing factor, and diameter of type A and type B particles.

EXAMPLE 5.7 Program OXYGEN_DEFICIT, Oxygen Deficit in a Polluted Stream

Environmental Science

Fish and other aquatic organisms need oxygen to survive, just as land animals do; however, aquatic organisms acquire oxygen from the water in which they live. In recent

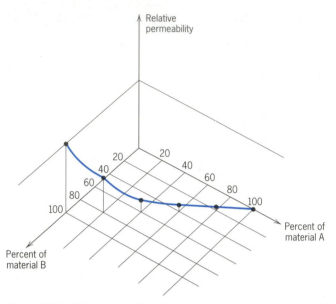

FIGURE 5.4   The variation of the permeability of a composite material consisting of differing proportions of particles of type A and type B.

years, many bodies of water have become polluted, thereby jeopardizing the existence of aquatic life in them, particularly fish. Often, pollutants are *oxygen-demanding wastes,* that is, substances that when added to water cause the dissolved oxygen to decrease. All too frequently, wastes from living organisms, or sewage, are accidentally discharged into bodies of water in which fish and other organisms reside. Bacteria in the water oxidize the wastes, using the oxygen in the water as the oxidizing agent. When this occurs, the oxygen content of the water decreases. If it decreases sufficiently, many fish will die (see Fig. 5.5).

Let us show this change in oxygen by calculating the variation with time of the dissolved oxygen in a polluted stream. To do so, we will summarize a method for calculating D_t, the *oxygen deficit* in a stream.

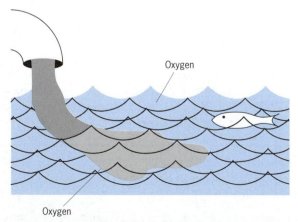

FIGURE 5.5   Oxygen deficiency in a polluted stream results when deoxygenation occurs more rapidly than reoxygenation.

As mentioned above, organic matter in sewage decomposes through chemical and bacterial action. In this process, free oxygen is consumed, and the sewage is deoxygenated. A standard procedure for determining the rate of deoxygenation of sewage involves diluting a sewage sample with water containing a known amount of dissolved oxygen and determining the loss of oxygen after the mixture has been maintained at a temperature of 20°C for a period of five days. This loss is called the biochemical oxygen demand (BOD). The BOD for a period of 20 days at a temperature of 20°C is called the first-stage demand and is denoted Λ_{20}. (The subscript denotes the temperature, 20°C.) For any temperature T, the first-stage demand Λ can be calculated by the formula

$$\Lambda = \Lambda_{20}(0.02T + 0.6) \tag{5.8}$$

As previously noted, when sewage is discharged into a stream, oxygen is consumed in the decomposition of organic matter. At the same time, oxygen is being absorbed from the air. However, in general, deoxygenation and reoxygenation occur at different rates. Usually, reoxygenation lags behind deoxygenation; the dissolved oxygen decreases with time, reaches a minimum, and then increases. As the dissolved oxygen decreases, an oxygen deficit is said to occur. When the dissolved oxygen is at a minimum, the oxygen deficit is at a maximum. The oxygen deficit of the polluted stream is given by

$$D_t = \frac{K_d \Lambda_m}{K_r - K_d}(10^{-K_d t} - 10^{-K_r t}) + D_0 \times 10^{-K_r t} \tag{5.9}$$

where

D_t = oxygen deficit of the stream at time t, mg/liter

K_d = coefficient of deoxygenation

K_r = coefficient of reoxygenation

Λ_m = first-stage BOD of a polluted stream

t = elapsed time, days (when $t = 0$, $D_t = D_0$)

We will calculate D_t by use of Eq. (5.9), and we will assume the following data:

1. The temperature of the mixture of sewage and stream, $T_m = 17.6°C$.
2. $K_r = 0.2$ at T_m
3. $K_{d20} = 0.1$ (the value of K_d at 20°C)
4. The biochemical oxygen demand of the stream $(BOD)_R$ above the point at which the sewage discharges into it is zero.
5. The biochemical oxygen demand of the sewage $(BOD)_S$ is 145 mg/liter.
6. $D_0 = 1.3$ mg/liter.
7. The rate of flow of the stream $Q_R = 23.9$ million gal/day.
8. The rate of flow of the sewage $Q_S = 3.5$ million gal/day.

Before we can calculate D_t, we have to perform the following preliminary calculations:

1. Calculate K_d at T_m from

$$K_d = K_{d20} (1.047)(T_m - 20) \tag{5.10}$$

2. Calculate the BOD of a mixture of sewage and stream, $(BOD)_m$ from

$$(BOD)_m = \frac{(BOD)_s Q_s + (BOD)_R Q_R}{Q_s + Q_R} \tag{5.11}$$

3. Calculate Λ_{20}, the first-stage BOD of the mixture, at 20°C:

$$\Lambda_{20} = \frac{(BOD)_m}{0.68} \tag{5.12}$$

If Λ_{20}, as given by (5.12), is substituted into (5.8), we obtain the first-stage BOD at T_m:

$$\Lambda_{20} = \frac{(BOD)_m}{0.68}(0.02\,T + 0.6) \tag{5.13}$$

With the data assumed above and the use of Eqs. (5.9) to (5.11) and (5.13), we can predict the effect of the sewage on the oxygen content of the stream by calculating D_t as a function of time after the addition of the sewage.

Program OXYGEN_DEFICIT, which carries out these calculations, and a trial run are shown below. In addition, the quantities used in the program are defined. When the program is run, the required data are entered and echoed. The coefficient of deoxygenation at T_m is calculated in accordance with Eq. (5.10). Next, $(BOD)_m$ and Λ_m are calculated in accordance with Eqs. (5.11) and (5.13). The oxygen deficit D_t is calculated as a function of time for a period of 3.5 days by the DO loop. The trial run shows that the maximum deficit is approximately 6.374 mg/liter and occurs at about 2.90 days. A graph of the variation of oxygen deficit as a function of time is shown in Fig. 5.6.

Formula Symbol	Program Name
T_m	TMIX
K_d	KD
K_{d20}	KD20
D_0	D0

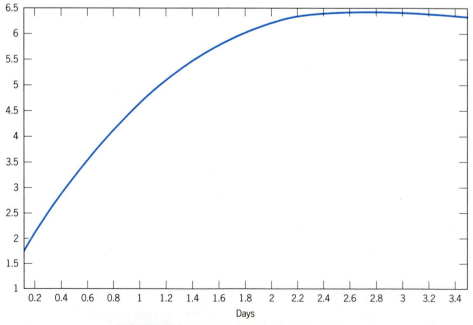

FIGURE 5.6   Oxygen deficit as a function of time.

D_t	DT
Q_S	QSEW
Q_R	QSTR
$(BOD)_S$	BODSEW
$(BOD)_R$	BODSTR
$(BOD)_m$	BODMIX
Λ_{20}	FB

```
      PROGRAM OXYGEN_DEFICIT
!
!     OXYGEN DEFICIT IN A STREAM AS A FUNCTION OF TIME
      IMPLICIT NONE
      REAL:: KR,QSTR,QSEW,KD20,TMIX,BODSTR,BODSEW,D0,KD,BODMIX
      REAL:: FB,Z,A,DT,T
      INTEGER:: INDEX
      WRITE(*,*)'ENTER KR, COEFFICIENT OF REOXYGENATION'
      READ(*,*) KR
      WRITE(*,*)'KR, COEFFICIENT OF REOXYGENATION = ',KR
      WRITE(*,*)'ENTER QSTR,RATE OF FLOW OF STREAM'
      READ(*,*) QSTR
      WRITE(*,*)'QSTR, RATE OF FLOW OF STREAM = ',QSTR
      WRITE(*,*)'ENTER QSEW,RATE OF FLOW OF SEWAGE
      READ(*,*)QSEW
      WRITE(*,*)'QSEW,RATE OF FLOW OF SEWAGE = ',QSEW
      WRITE(*,*)'ENTER KD20, COEFFICIENT OF DEOXYGENATION'KD20
      READ(*,*) KD20
      WRITE(*,*)'KD20, COEFFICIENT OF DEOXYGENATION = ',KD20
      WRITE(*,*)'ENTER TMIX,TEMPERATURE OF SEWAGE-STREAM MIX'
      READ(*,*)TMIX
      WRITE(*,*)'TMIX,TEMPERATURE OF SEWAGE-STREAM MIX = ',TMIX'
      WRITE(*,*)'ENTER BODSTR, OXYGEN DEMAND OF STREAM'
      READ(*,*) BODSTR
      WRITE(*,*)'BODSTR, OXYGEN DEMAND OF STREAM = ',BODSTR
      WRITE(*,*)'ENTER BODSEW, OXYGEN DEMAND OF SEWAGE'
      READ(*,*) BODSEW
      WRITE(*,*)'BODSEW, OXYGEN DEMAND OF SEWAGE = ',BODSEW
      WRITE(*,*)'ENTER D0, INITIAL OXYGEN DEFICIT'
      READ(*,*) D0
      WRITE(*,*)'D0, INITIAL OXYGEN DEFICIT = ', D0
      KD = KD20*1.047**(TMIX - 20.0)
      BODMIX = (BODSTR*QSTR + BODSEW*QSEW)/(QSTR + QSEW)
      FB = BODMIX*(0.02*TMIX + 0.6)/0.68
      WRITE(*,"(//2X,A,5X,A)")"TIME","OXYGEN DEF."
!
      DO INDEX = 1,35,2
        Z = INDEX
        T = Z/10.0
        A = 10.0**(-KR*T)
        DT = ((KD*FB)/(KR-KD))*(10.0**(-KD*T) - A) + D0*A
      WRITE(*,"(F6.1,2X,F12.6)") T,DT
      END DO
      END PROGRAM OXYGEN_DEFICIT
```

```
KR, COEFFICIENT OF REOXYGENATION = 0.2000000
QSTR, RATE OF FLOW OF STREAM = 23.8999996
QSEW,RATE OF FLOW OF SEWAGE = 3.5000000
KD20, COEFFICIENT OF DEOXYGENATION = 0.1000000
TMIX,TEMPERATURE OF SEWAGE-STREAM MIX = 17.6000004
BODSTR, OXYGEN DEMAND OF STREAM = 0.0000000E+00
BODSEW, OXYGEN DEMAND OF SEWAGE = 1.4500000E+02
D0, INITIAL OXYGEN DEFICIT = 1.3000000


TIME      OXYGEN DEF.
0.1        1.758729
0.3        2.584195
0.5        3.297422
0.7        3.909886
0.9        4.431990
1.1        4.873157
1.3        5.241923
1.5        5.546016
1.7        5.792428
1.9        5.987483
2.1        6.136901
2.3        6.245848
2.5        6.318986
2.7        6.360529
2.9        6.374272          < MAXIMUM
3.1        6.363636
3.3        6.331705
3.5        6.281247
```

EXAMPLE 5.8 Program BILINEAR, Bilinear Transformation

Mathematics: Complex Variables

We will illustrate a topic from complex variable theory by discussing a particular relation between two complex variables z and w. In general, complex variables have a real part and an imaginary part (although, occasionally, one of these parts has a value of zero). We can show the complex variables z and w in compact form by denoting the real and imaginary parts of z by (x,y) where x is the real part and y is the imaginary part. Similarly, w can be shown by (u,v) where u and v are the real and imaginary parts of w.

In complex variable theory, when there is a functional relation between variables, $w = f(z)$, information about the functional relationship is displayed graphically by showing separate planes, Z and W, for the two variables z and w. (By convention, the variables are shown in lowercase and the planes in uppercase.) Then, corresponding to each point (xk,yk), in the Z plane, there is a point, (uk,vk), in the W plane. The correspondence between points in the planes is called a transformation. Thus, in the present example, the functional relation between w and z transforms points on the Z plane to points on the W plane. The particular transformation depends on the functional relation. In this case, the functional relation in which we are interested is

$$w = \frac{j-z}{j+z} \tag{5.14}$$

where

$$j = \sqrt{-1}$$

This is called a bilinear transformation. One application of this transformation is in the design of digital filters. The bilinear transformation of Eq. (5.14) has the following properties.

1. Points on the upper half of the Z plane are transformed into points on the interior of a circle of radius one (called a unit circle), centered at the origin on the W plane.

2. Points on the abscissa of the Z plane are transformed into points on the perimeter of a unit circle centered at the origin on the W plane.

Figure 5.7 shows how the bilinear transformation transforms points from the Z plane to the W plane. These properties are shown in program BILINEAR and in the trial run, as shown below. The loop DO I = 1, 9 calculates the transformation of points in the Z plane which are on the abscissa. The results of the trial run show that all values of WMAG (the square root of $u2 + v2$) are equal to 1.0. The loop DO J = 1, 9 calculates the transformation for points in the upper half of the Z plane. The results of the run show that for these points WMAG is less than 1.0.

These data confirm the properties stated above.

```
     PROGRAM BILINEAR
!    THIS PROGRAM DEMONSTRATES THE BILINEAR TRANSFORMATION
!
     IMPLICIT NONE
     REAL:: X, Y, WMAG
     INTEGER:: I,J
     COMPLEX:: Z,W
     X = -5.0
     Y = 0
     WRITE(*,*)'WMAG = 1 IS PERIMETER OF CIRCLE OF UNIT RADIUS!'
     WRITE(*,"(/4X,'X',5X,'Y',15X,'U',10X,'V',9X,'WMAG')")
     DO I = 1,9
```

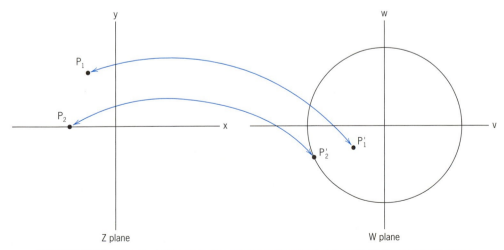

FIGURE 5.7   How the bilinear transformation transforms points from the Z plane to the W plane.

```
            X = X + 1.0
            Z = CMPLX(X,Y)
            W = (−Z + (0,1.0))/(Z + (0,1.0))
            WMAG = CABS(W)
            WRITE(*,*) Z,W, WMAG
            WRITE(*,"(/2F6.2,6X,2F10.4,6X,F10.4)") Z,W, WMAG
         END DO
         WRITE(*,"(/20X,A/)")'  *********'
         WRITE(*,"(/A)")' WMAG<1 IS INTERIOR OF CIRCLE OF UNIT RADIUS'
         WRITE(*,"(/4X,'X',5X,'Y',15X,'U',10X,'V',9X,'WMAG')")
         X = −5.0
         DO J = 1,9
            Y = Y + 0.5
            X = X + 1.0
            Z = CMPLX(X,Y)
            W = (−Z +(0,1.0))/(Z + (0,1.0))
            WMAG = CABS(W)
            WRITE(*,"(/2F6.2,6X,3F12.4)") Z, W, WMAG
         END DO
         END PROGRAM BILINEAR
```

RUN

```
 WMAG = 1 IS PERIMETER OF CIRCLE OF UNIT RADIUS!
    X      Y         U         V        WMAG
 −4.00   0.00    −0.8823   −0.4705    1.0000
 −3.00   0.00    −0.8000   −0.6000    1.0000
 −2.00   0.00    −0.6000   −0.8000    1.0000
 −1.00   0.00     0.0000   −1.0000    1.0000
  0.00   0.00     1.0000    0.0000    1.0000
  1.00   0.00     0.0000    1.0000    1.0000
  2.00   0.00    −0.6000    0.8000    1.0000
  3.00   0.00    −0.8000    0.6000    1.0000
  4.00   0.00    −0.8823    0.4705    1.0000
                   *********

 WMAG<1 IS INTERIOR OF CIRCLE OF UNIT RADIUS
    X      Y         U         V        WMAG
 −4.00   0.50    −0.8356   −0.4383    0.9436
 −3.00   1.00    −0.6923   −0.4615    0.8320
 −2.00   1.50    −0.5121   −0.3902    0.6439
 −1.00   2.00    −0.4000   −0.2000    0.4472
  0.00   2.50    −0.4285    0.0000    0.4285
  1.00   3.00    −0.5294    0.1176    0.5423
  2.00   3.50    −0.6288    0.1649    0.6501
  3.00   4.00    −0.7058    0.1764    0.7276
  4.00   4.50    −0.7621    0.1729    0.7815
```

5.8 NESTED DO LOOPS

We will now illustrate the method of nesting DO loops and the utility of this technique. One of the useful applications of nested DO loops occurs when a formula that is a function of two parameters, *P*1 and *P*2, is to be evaluated. Assume that we wish to vary *P*2 while keeping *P*1 at a fixed value; then we wish to change *P*1 and again vary *P*2, and so on. This type of procedure can be readily carried out by nested DO loops. We will begin with a tutorial example.

EXAMPLE 5.9 Program NESTED, Showing How Nested DO Loops Work

The sole purpose of this program is to show how the nested DO loop works. In this program, one loop is nested within an outer loop. It is possible to have several loops nested within an outer loop.

A program and a trial run are shown below.

```
      PROGRAM NESTED
!
!     THIS PROGRAM SHOWS THE OPERATION OF NESTED DO LOOPS
!
!     THE INDEX OF THE OUTER LOOP REMAINS AT ITS INITIAL VALUE
!     UNTIL THE INDEX OF THE INNER LOOPS IS INCREMENTED TO ITS
!     MAXIMUM VALUE; THEN, THE INDEX OF THE OUTER LOOP IS
!     INCREMENTED ONCE AND REMAINS AT THAT VALUE UNTIL THE
!     INDEX OF THE INNER LOOP IS AGAIN INCREMENTED TO ITS VALUE.
!
!     THE PROCESS CONTINUES UNTIL THE INDEX OF THE OUTER LOOP
!     REACHES ITS MAXIMUM VALUE AND THEN, FOR THE LAST TIME,
!     THE INDEX OF THE INNER LOOP IS AGAIN INCREMENTED TO ITS
!     MAXIMUM VALUE. IN THE PROGRAM, THE TOTAL NUMBER OF
!     LOOPS EXECUTED IS NMAX*JMAX = 12.
!
      IMPLICIT NONE
      INTEGER:: TALLY,NMAX,JMAX,N,J
      TALLY = 0; NMAX = 3; JMAX = 4
      DO N = 1, NMAX
!
        DO J = 1,JMAX
         TALLY = TALLY + 1
         WRITE(*,400) N,JMAX,J
        END DO
      END DO
 400  FORMAT(' N STAYS AT',I2,' TILL J INCREMENTS TO',I3,'. J = ',I5/)
      WRITE(*,*) TALLY
      WRITE(*,"(//A,I3)") 'TALLY = NMAX*JMAX = ', TALLY
      END PROGRAM NESTED
```

RUN
```
N STAYS AT 1 TILL J INCREMENTS TO 4. J = 1
N STAYS AT 1 TILL J INCREMENTS TO 4. J = 2
N STAYS AT 1 TILL J INCREMENTS TO 4. J = 3
N STAYS AT 1 TILL J INCREMENTS TO 4. J = 4
*     *     *     *     *     *
N STAYS AT 2 TILL J INCREMENTS TO 4. J = 1
N STAYS AT 2 TILL J INCREMENTS TO 4. J = 2
N STAYS AT 2 TILL J INCREMENTS TO 4. J = 3
```

```
N STAYS AT 2 TILL J INCREMENTS TO 4. J = 4
*       *       *       *       *       *
N STAYS AT 3 TILL J INCREMENTS TO 4. J = 1
N STAYS AT 3 TILL J INCREMENTS TO 4. J = 2
N STAYS AT 3 TILL J INCREMENTS TO 4. J = 3
N STAYS AT 3 TILL J INCREMENTS TO 4. J = 4

TALLY = NMAX*JMAX = 12
```

The inner DO loop has index J, and the maximum value of J is 4. The outer DO loop has index N, and the maximum value of N is 3. For each index, the increment is 1.

The trial run shows:

N is set to a value of 1; then, J is set to 1.

N remains at 1, and J is incremented to a value of 2.

N remains at 1, and J is incremented to a value of 3.

N remains at 1, and J is incremented to a value of 4.

After J reaches its maximum value of 4, N is then incremented to its next value, 2, and remains at that value until J is again incremented to 4. Finally, N is incremented to its maximum value, which is 3, and J is varied from 1 to 4 for the last time. At the conclusion of this process, there have been a total of 3*4 = 12 iterations.

EXAMPLE 5.10 Program MATEL, Locating Elements of a Matrix

Mathematics

Matrices were discussed in Sec. 3.17 in relation to the subject of subscripted variables. Consider a matrix that has m rows and and n columns. Each number within the matrix is called an element. Using the notation (m, n), we can refer to an element by its position in the matrix. Figure 5.8 illustrates the row-column notation that is used to indicate the position of an element of a matrix.

Consider a matrix that has three rows and four columns. This matrix has $3 \times 4 = 12$ elements. If we refer to element $(1, 1)$, we are referring to the element in the upper left-hand corner of the matrix or in different words, the element in the top row, first column. The element at the bottom right-hand corner in this matrix would be $(3, 4)$. Matrices are useful in a variety of applications, for example, in spreadsheet software. Spreadsheets can be used to simplify calculations in engineering and business applications. They depend

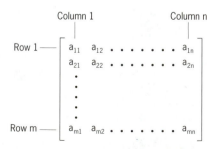

a_{ij} = matrix element in row i, column j

FIGURE 5.8 The row-column notation which is used to indicate the position of an element of a matrix.

on cells that are the equivalent of an element in a particular row and column within the matrix.

Program MATEL numbers the elements of an array, which has three rows and four columns. The numbering is carried out by two nested DO loops that generate the positions of the elements. The outer loop generates the number of the row, and the inner loop generates the number of the column. These positions are stored in the variables ROW and COLM, which have been declared to be INTEGER type.

```
      PROGRAM MATEL
!
!     THIS PROGRAM USES NESTED DO LOOPS TO GENERATE THE
!     POSITION OF THE ELEMENTS OF A MATRIX. THE POSITIONS ARE
!     EXPRESSED IN THE FORM m,n WHERE M DENOTES THE ROW AND
!     N DENOTES THE COLUMN NUMBER
!
      IMPLICIT NONE
      INTEGER, DIMENSION (10,10):: ROW, COLM
      INTEGER:: IROW,JCOL
      DO IROW = 1,3
        DO JCOL = 1,4
          ROW(IROW,JCOL) = IROW
          COLM(IROW,JCOL) = JCOL
        END DO
!
      END DO
      WRITE(*,"(6X,A,//)")'NUMBERED ELEMENTS'
      DO IROW = 1,3
       WRITE(*,"(4(I2,I3,5X)")(ROW(IROW,JCOL),COLM(IROW,JCOL),
          JCOL = 1,4)
      END DO
      END PROGRAM MATEL
```

RUN
```
    NUMBERED ELEMENTS
 1 1   1 2   1 3   1 4
 2 1   2 2   2 3   2 4
 3 1   3 2   3 3   3 4
```

The nested DO loops generate the positions of the elements. These positions are stored in the variables ROW(10,10) and COLM(10,10), which have been declared to be INTEGERS at the beginning of the program. Note that the outer loop DO IROW generates the row number and the inner loop generates the column number. Thus, the element positions are generated row by row.

5.9 IMPLIED DO LOOPS

The technique of implied DO loops is very useful for entering data for the elements of an array or for printing an array. For example, suppose that we have an array that has five elements and these are stored in A(1), A(2), A(3), A(4), A(5). We could write the instruction READ(*,*) A(1),A(2),A(3),A(4),A(5), which would enable us to assign values to the five elements of A. However, a more compact way of doing this is by use of an implied DO loop as follows:

```
READ(*,*)(A(I), I = 1,N)
```

Before using this statement, a *value for N must be supplied*. The implied DO loop can also be used for output. The following example uses the implied DO loop.

EXAMPLE 5.11 Program **ADD_MATRICES**, Adding Two Matrices

Mathematics

Program ADD_MATRICES adds matrices A and B and stores the sum in matrix C. Note that the data entered into the program were echoed and that this was done using an implied DO loop. In addition, the elements of C were printed using an implied DO loop. The *implied DO loop* can be used when there are two subscripts. For example, consider the variable $A(m, n)$. Assuming that the values of m and n have already been assigned, the form of the implied DO loop is

```
READ(*,*) ((A(I,J), J = 1,N), I = 1,M)
```

In the example that follows, the $m \times n$ matrices A and B will be added and the sum stored in C. To add these matrices, they must be conformable. That is, they must have the same number of columns and rows. The rule for calculating each element of C is

$$c_{ij} = a_{ij} + b_{ij}$$

For example, given

$$A = \begin{bmatrix} 2.4 & 1.0 & 6.1 \\ 3.0 & 2.0 & 5.0 \\ 0 & 4.1 & 1.1 \end{bmatrix} \qquad B = \begin{bmatrix} 5.6 & 2.0 & 3.0 \\ 7.1 & 3.0 & 0 \\ 2.0 & 5.0 & 2.3 \end{bmatrix}$$

The sum of A and B is C

$$C = \begin{bmatrix} 8.0 & 3.0 & 9.1 \\ 10.1 & 5.0 & 5.0 \\ 2.0 & 9.1 & 3.4 \end{bmatrix}$$

```
        PROGRAM ADD_MATRICES
!       THIS PROGRAM ADDS TWO CONFORMABLE MATRICES
!
!       IMPLICIT NONE
        REAL, DIMENSION (10,10):: A,B,C
        INTEGER:: I,J,M,N
        WRITE(*,*)'ENTER M (number of rows)'
        READ(*,*) M
        WRITE(*,*)'ENTER N (number of columns)'
        READ(*,*) N
        WRITE(*,*)'ENTER ELEMENTS OF A'
        READ(*,*) ((A(I,J),J = 1,N),I = 1,M)
        WRITE(*,*)' A MATRIX'
        WRITE(*,"(5F9.2,/)")((A(I,J),J = 1,N),I = 1,M)
        WRITE(*,*) ' ENTER ELEMENTS OF B'
```

```
READ(*,*) ((B(I,J),J = 1,N),I = 1,M)
WRITE(*,*)' B MATRIX'
WRITE(*,"(5F9.2,/)") ((B(I,J),J = 1,N),I = 1,M)
DO I = 1,M
 DO J = 1,N
  C(I,J) = A(I,J) + B(I,J)
 END DO
END DO
WRITE(*,*)"SUM OF MATRICES A and B"
DO I = 1,M
  WRITE(*,"(3F9.2/)") (C(I,J), J = 1,N)
END DO
END PROGRAM ADD_MATRICES
```

RUN
```
 A MATRIX
  2.40   1.00   6.10
  3.00   2.00   5.00
  0.00   4.10   1.10
 B MATRIX
  5.60   2.00   3.00
  7.10   3.00   0.00
  2.00   5.00   2.30
SUM OF MATRICES A and B
  8.00   3.00   9.10
 10.10   5.00   5.00
  2.00   9.10   3.40
```

The trial run used the same data as in the example above and produced the same sum. In printing the matrix C, a conventional DO loop was used together with an implied DO loop in order to display the matrix in the usual row array.

5.10 MULTIPLICATION OF MATRICES

The multiplication of matrices arises in many areas of science and engineering, for example, in the study of vibrations and in the study of Markov processes. Before presenting a program, let us review some of the rules concerning matrix multiplication. Two matrices, A and B, are said to be *conformable* for multiplication in the order AB if the number of columns of A is equal to the number of rows of B. Note that the order of the multiplication has been specified. This is because matrix multiplication is not commutative; that is, in general, AB is not equal to BA. As a result, a name has been given to matrix multiplication which indicates the order. For the product AB, A is said to be postmultiplied by B. For BA, B is said to be postmultiplied by A.

Let C be the matrix that is equal to the product AB, where the dimensions of A are $p \times q$ and the dimensions of B are $q \times r$. In all cases, the first dimension is the number of rows and the second the number of columns. Any element c_{ij} of matrix C is given by

$$c_{ij} = \sum_{k=1}^{q} a_{ik} b_{kj} \tag{5.15}$$

To illustrate the multiplication procedure, we will calculate the product AB where

$$A = \begin{bmatrix} 1 & 1 \\ 2 & 4 \\ 3 & 1 \end{bmatrix} \qquad B = \begin{bmatrix} 4 & 2 & 3 \\ 2 & 1 & 2 \end{bmatrix}$$

In this example, $q = 2$, so that k goes from 1 to 2. To calculate the first row of C, $i = 1$, and k is first 1 and then 2.

Thus:

$$c_{11} = a_{11}b_{11} + a_{12}b_{21} = (1)(4) + (1)(2) = 6$$
$$c_{12} = a_{12}b_{12} + a_{12}b_{22} = (1)(2) + (1)(1) = 3$$
$$c_{13} = a_{11}b_{13} + a_{12}b_{23} = (1)(3) + (1)(2) = 5$$

Note that in the calculation of c_{11}, all of the a coefficients are in row 1 and the b coefficients are in column 1; in the calculation of c_{12}, all of the a coefficients are in row 1 and the b coefficients are in column 2; in the calculation of c_{13}, all of the a coefficients are in row 1 and the b coefficients are in column 3. Because of this ordering, matrix multiplication is said to be a row-column procedure. Let us calculate the elements of row 2 of C.

$$c_{21} = a_{21}b_{11} + a_{22}b_{21} = (2)(4) + (4)(2) = 16$$
$$c_{22} = a_{21}b_{12} + a_{22}b_{22} = (2)(2) + (4)(1) = 8$$
$$c_{23} = a_{21}b_{13} + a_{22}b_{23} = (2)(3) + (4)(2) = 14$$

The calculation of row 3 is similar.

The resultant matrix, C, is

$$C = \begin{bmatrix} 6 & 3 & 5 \\ 16 & 8 & 14 \\ 14 & 7 & 11 \end{bmatrix}$$

EXAMPLE 5.12 Program MATRIXMUL

Program MATRIXMUL implements matrix multiplication using the formula (5.15). The user is prompted to enter the number of rows and the number of columns for matrix A and for matrix B. These variables are given descriptive names. For the matrices shown above, which will be used in the first sample run, A is 2×3, so NRA = 2 and NCA = 3. B is 2×3, so NRB = 2 and NCB = 3. Then the elements of each matrix must be entered row by row. Row-by-row entry of the data is a simple and natural way of providing the data. The calculation of the product matrix is carried out by a group of nested loops. These are DO I = 1, NRA; DO J = 1, NCB; and DO K = 1, NCA. Loop DO J is nested within loop DO I, and loop DO K is nested within loop DO J.

To appreciate the operation, let us see how C(1,1) is calculated. When the calculation begins, I = 1 and J = 1. I and J will remain at these values until the innermost loop, which has index K, is satisfied.

```
1) K = 1
C(1,1) = C(1,1) + A(1,1)*B(1,1) = 0 + (1.)(4.) = 4.0

2) K = 2
C(1,1) = C(1,1) + A(1,2)*B(2,1) = 4.0 + (1.)(2.) = 6.0
```

The next element to be calculated is C(1,2). I remains at 1, and J becomes 2.

```
1) K = 1; The initial value of C(1,2) is zero.
C(1,2) = C(1,2) + A(1,1)*B(1,2) = 0 + (1.)(2.) = 2.0
2) K = 2
C(1,2) = C(1,2) + A(1,2)*B(2,2) = 2.0 + (1.)(1.) = 3.
```

With I = 1 and J = 3, C(1,3) is calculated similarly.

```
PROGRAM MATRIXMUL
IMPLICIT NONE
REAL,DIMENSION(20,20):: A,B,C
INTEGER::NRA,NRB,NCA,NCB,I,J,K
WRITE(*,*)'ENTER THE NO. OF ROWS AND COLUMNS OF A'
READ(*,*)NRA,NCA
WRITE(*,"(A,I4)")'NO. ROWS OF A = ', NRA
WRITE(*,"(A,I4/)")'NO. COLUMNS OF A = ', NCA
WRITE(*,*)'ENTER THE ELEMENTS OF MATRIX A'
DO I = 1,NRA
READ(*,*)(A(I,J),J = 1,NCA)
END DO
WRITE(*,*)'ENTER THE NO. OF ROWS AND COLUMNS OF B'
READ(*,*)NRB,NCB
WRITE(*,*)'NO. ROWS OF B = ', NRB
WRITE(*,"(A,I4/)")'NO. COLUMNS OF B = ', NCB
WRITE(*,*)'ENTER THE ELEMENTS OF MATRIX B'
READ(*,*)((B(I,J),J = 1,NCB),I = 1, NRB)
WRITE(*,"(A/)")'A MATRIX'
DO I = 1,NRA
WRITE(*,"(5F11.7)")(A(I,J),J = 1,NCA)
END DO
WRITE(*"(/A/)")'B MATRIX'
DO I = 1,NRB
WRITE(*,"(5F11.7)")(B(I,J),J = 1,NCB)
END DO

DO I = 1,NRA                 ! NOTE THE
 DO J = 1,NCB                 !NESTED
  C(I,J) = 0
   DO K = 1,NCA                    !LOOPS
   C(I,J) = C(I,J) + A(I,K)*B(K,J)
   END DO
 END DO
END DO
WRITE(*,"(//A//)")'PRODUCT MATRIX'
DO I = I,NRA
WRITE(*,"(5F11.7)")(C(I,J),J= 1,NCB)
END PROGRAM MATRIXMUL
```

TRIAL RUNS

RUN 1
NO. ROWS OF A = 1
NO. COLUMNS OF A = 2

```
NO. ROWS OF B = 2
NO. COLUMNS OF B = 2

A MATRIX

 0.7142850   0.2857140
B MATRIX
 0.8000000   0.2000000
 0.5000000   0.5000000


PRODUCT MATRIX

 0.7142850  0.2857140
 *      *       *        *        *        *
RUN 2
 NO. ROWS OF A = 3
 NO. COLUMNS OF A = 2

 NO. ROWS OF B = 2
 NO. COLUMNS OF B = 3
A MATRIX

 1.0000000   1.0000000
 2.0000000   4.0000000
 3.0000000   1.0000000


B MATRIX

 4.0000000   2.0000000   3.0000000
 2.0000000   1.0000000   2.0000000


PRODUCT MATRIX
  6.0000000   3.0000000    5.0000000
 16.0000000   8.0000000   14.0000000
 14.0000000   7.0000000   11.0000000
```

It was stated that matrix multiplication is not commutative. AB has just been calculated. Now, if the product BA is calculated, the result is

$$\begin{bmatrix} 17 & 15 \\ 10 & 8 \end{bmatrix}$$

Thus, it is seen that AB is not equal to BA.

EXAMPLE 5.13. Program MATMULII

Mathematics

We have shown the method by which matrix multiplication can be performed, and we have presented a program that implemented this method. Now that we have shown the method and a program, we can in good conscience provide an easier method. FORTRAN 90 has an intrinsic subprogram that performs matrix multiplication. The multiplication is carried out by a statement of the form

$$C = MATMUL(A,B)$$

where A, B, and C are dimensioned matrices. It is assumed that A and B are conformable and that data have been stored in them prior to the reference to MATMUL.

In program MATMULII, the only additional feature to be noted is the use of the data statement for storing arrays. The first data statement stores matrix $A(p, q)$ where $p = 3$ and $q = 2$. The second data statement stores matrix $B(q, r)$ where $q = 2$ and $r = 3$. The reader will recognize the data as being the same as the data used in program MATRIX-MUL. As before, implied DO loops are used in writing the matrices. In the trial run, matrix A is postmultiplied by B, and the results, shown below, are the same.

```
PROGRAM MATMULII
IMPLICIT NONE
REAL,DIMENSION(10,10)::A,B,C
INTEGER::I,J
DATA A(1,1),A(1,2),A(2,1),A(2,2),A(3,1),A(3,2)/1,1,2,4,3,1/
DATA B(1,1),B(1,2),B(1,3),B(2,1),B(2,2),B(2,3)/4,2,3,2,1,2/
WRITE(*,"(A/)")'A MATRIX'
DO I = 1,3
     WRITE(*,*)(A(I,J),J = 1,2)
END DO
WRITE(*,"( A/)")'B MATRIX'
DO I = 1,2
     WRITE(*,*)(B(I,J),J = 1,3)
END DO
WRITE(*,"(//A/)")'PRODUCT MATRIX'
C = MATMUL(A,B)
DO I + 1,3
     WRITE(*,*)(C(I,J), J = 1,3)
END DO
END PROGRAM MATMULII
```

RUN

A MATRIX

```
  1.0000000   1.0000000
  2.0000000   4.0000000
  3.0000000   1.0000000
```

B MATRIX

```
  4.0000000   2.0000000   3.0000000
  2.0000000   1.0000000   2.0000000
```

PRODUCT MATRIX

```
   6.00   3.00    5.00
  16.00   8.00   14.00
  14.00   7.00   11.00
```

PROBLEMS

5.1   The Fahrenheit (F) and Celsius (C) temperature scales are in common use and are well known to most people. In the Celsius scale, the ice point is 0°; in the

Fahrenheit scale, the ice point is 32°. In the Fahrenheit scale, the steam point is 212°; in the Celsius, it is 100°.

Other temperature scales relate to the triple point of water, the temperature and pressure at which water, water vapor, and ice coexist in equilibrium. This temperature is about −273.15°C. This temperature is also called absolute zero. The Kelvin temperature scale is related to the Celsius scale by

$$1) \quad K = C + 273.15$$

Thus, C = −273.15° is equivalent to K = 0°.
In the Fahrenheit scale, the triple point is at −459.67.
The Rankine temperature scale is related to the Fahrenheit scale by

$$2) \quad R = F + 459.67$$

The relation between C and F is

$$3) \quad C = [5(F − 32)]/9$$

Write a program that prints a table that converts integral values of degrees Fahrenheit to degrees Celsius, degrees Kelvin, and degrees Rankine. The values of Fahrenheit should vary from 30°F to 210°F in steps of 20°.

5.2   It is possible to calculate the sine of an angle when the value of the angle is expressed in radians, using N terms of the series

$$\sin x = \sum_{n=1}^{N} (-1)^{n+1} \frac{x^{2n-1}}{(2n-1)!}$$

Calculate the sine of 30° using $N = 10$. Your program should enter the angle by means of a READ statement so that you can run the program with a variety of angles. The program must convert the angle that has been entered by the user to radians in order to obtain a correct result.

After the program has run, check to determine how closely the answer corresponds to the correct value.

5.3   The Poisson probability distribution solves problems of the following type: If the average number of events of a certain kind that is expected to occur in a unit time is λ, then λt events are expected to occur in time t. The probability that k events will occur in time t is

$$P(k \text{ events per time } t) = e^{-\lambda t} \frac{(\lambda t)}{k!}$$

The Poisson probability distribution is said to be discrete because it deals with outcomes that are expressed by integers.

As an example, suppose there is a gas station that is open 24 hours a day and customers arrive, on the average, at the rate of 30 an hour. What is the probability that no arrivals will occur in an interval of 10 minutes?
Answer: In a 10-minute interval, the expected number of arrivals is

$$\lambda t = (10/60)(30) = 5$$
$$P(0 \text{ arrivals in a 10 minute period}) = e(-\lambda t) = e^{-5} \approx 0.006738$$

Using the formula above, write a program that calculates Poisson probabilities for $k = 0$ to $k = 6$ with $t = 10$ minutes and $\lambda = 0.5$. To make the program more versatile, it should permit the user to enter a value of lambda and a value of t.

5.4   The equation for the velocity of an electron starting from zero velocity and accelerated by a potential difference V is

$$\mu' = c \sqrt{1 - \frac{1}{(1 + \mu^2/2c^2)^2}}$$

where

$$\mu = \sqrt{2eV/m_0}$$

$\mu' = $ velocity with relativistic correction, m/s

$\mu = $ velocity without relativistic correction, m/s

$c = $ speed of light $= 3 \times 10^8$, m/s

$m_0 = $ rest mass of electron $\approx 9.11 \times 10^{-31}$ kg

$V = $ potential difference, volts

Write a program that calculates μ and μ' as V varies from 4000 volts to 30,000 volts in steps of 1000.

5.5   In certain applications such as robotics and automation, it is important or necessary to be able to control the position of the shaft of a motor. This can be achieved by use of a stepper motor. The equation for the torque produced by a stepper motor is

$$T = \frac{0.31 \times 10^{-6} \, tL(r + g/2)F^2}{g}$$

where

$T = $ torque, newton-m

$t = $ number of teeth per phase

$L = $ axial length of rotor, m

$g = $ air gap between rotor and stator, m

$F = $ magnetomotive force across air gaps

Write a program that calculates the torque for $t = 8$, 10, 12, and 14 teeth.

5.6   Purification of water supplies by adsorption of undesirable contaminants to solid adsorbents is one of several methods of water treatment. One of the adsorbents used for this purpose is granular activated carbon. The Freundlich equation quantifies the percentage of contaminants removed as a function of adsorbent concentration.

The Freundlich adsorption equation can be expressed as

$$X = \exp[\ln X_1 + C(\ln Y - \ln Y_1)] \tag{1}$$

where

$X = R/A$

$X_1 = R_1/A_1$

$Y = 1.0 - (R/100.0)$

$Y_1 = 1.0 - (R_1/100.0)$

$A = $ adsorbent concentration, ppm

$R = $ contaminant removed by A, %

and the subscript 1 refers to conditions at a known point.

The constant C in the Freundlich equation can be evaluated by the following formula if conditions at two points are known. These data are shown below.

$$C = \frac{\ln(R_1 A_2)}{\ln(100 - R_1)/(100 - R_2)} \qquad (2)$$

Data for the quantities A_1, R_1, A_2, R_2 in the formula were obtained by treating a sample of water containing suspended material. The water was treated with an adsorbing agent, and the following observations were made:

$$A_1 = 5 \text{ ppm} \qquad R_1 = 70\% \text{ (solids removed)}$$
$$A_2 = 10 \text{ ppm} \qquad R_2 = 93\% \text{ (solids removed)}$$

Write a program that prints a table of A (adsorbent concentration, ppm), versus R (solids removed from suspension, %). First, the program should calculate the value of C using the data for A_1, R_1, A_2, R_2 given the above and Eq. (2).

Then, Eq. (1) should be used with a DO loop to calculate values of A as R varies from 95 to 99.5. For the index of the DO loop, start with $I = 950$ and go to a maximum of $I = 995$ in increments of 5. Generate the required values of R by the statements $R = I$, followed by $R = I/10$. The table should include the values of A versus R given above.

5.7   One method for forming (shaping) sheet metal involves the use of explosives. A tank is placed in the ground with its upper edge at ground level. A die that defines the desired shape is placed in the tank, and the sheet of metal is clamped to the die. The tank is filled with water, and a small amount of explosive is lowered into the tank to a relatively short distance above the surface of the sheet metal. The explosive is connected to the exterior of the tank by wires that are used to detonate the explosive.

Data The peak pressure generated in the water is given by the formula

$$P = K\left(\sqrt[3]{(W/D)^{1.15}}\right)$$

where

P = peak pressure, psi

K = a constant that depends on the explosive used

W = weight of explosive used, lb

D = distance of the explosive from the sheet metal

Write a program that calculates the peak pressure as the distance of the explosive to the sheet metal varies from 0.4 ft to 2.0 ft. Use 0.2 lb of TNT. The program should ask the user to enter the constant, K, which defines the explosive and the weight of the explosive in lb. For TNT, $K = 21600$.

5.8   The following terms used in traffic engineering are relevant to this problem:

Merging   The process by which vehicles in separate traffic streams moving in the same general direction combine to form a single stream.

Headway   The interval of time between successive vehicles moving in the same lane and measured from front of vehicle to front of vehicle as they pass a point on the road.

Gap   A headway that is evaluated by a driver desiring to merge into or to cross the major traffic stream measured in seconds.

The average time for a vehicle waiting on a ramp before attempting to merge is called the merging delay $U(a)$, where a is a parameter in a probability distribution that is used to derive the formula below. $U(a)$ is in seconds. For $a = 2$, the formula is

$$U(2) = \frac{e^{2qT} - 1 - 2qT - 2(qT)^2}{q(1 + 2qT)}$$

In this formula, T is the critical gap. The critical gap is defined as one in which all time intervals less than it are rejected and all longer intervals are accepted; q is the traffic volume in number of vehicles per hour.

Write a program that will calculate the merging delay, $U(2)$, in seconds as q varies from 400 to 800 vehicles per hour in steps of 200 and $T = 2, 4, 5, 6$ (seconds). In the program, be sure to convert q to vehicles per second.

5.9 In the conventional analysis of a parallel plate capacitor, it is assumed that equipotentials and lines of force are uniform between the plates and furthermore that the electric field is confined to the region between the plates. When the size of the plates is not large relative to the spacing, the electric field of the capacitor will extend significantly beyond the edge of the plates. This is called fringing. The total field of the parallel plate capacitor was calculated by the physicist James Clerk Maxwell (1831–1879) in the nineteenth century using a method called conformal transformation. Briefly, this method involves solving a problem in a complex plane where the variables are usually named u and v and then transferring the result to the customary x-y plane.

The solution to this problem in terms of x and y coordinates is

$$x = (1/\pi)(u + 1.0 + \exp(u)\sin(v))$$
$$y = (1/\pi)(v + \exp(u)\sin(v))$$

The geometry of the solution is based on positioning the capacitor so that its plates are parallel to the x axis and the x axis runs through the center of the capacitor.

If these relations are used to plot x and y as a function of u and v, the total field of the parallel capacitor including the fringe field will be displayed. We are asking you to perform a more modest task.

Write a program that calculates x and y for each pair of values of u and v:

(a) $u = 0$ $v = 0$ (x, y) is on the central axis, near the right edge of the capacitor

(b) $u = 0.6\pi$ $v = 0.8\pi$ (x, y) is above the upper plate of the capacitor

(c) $u = -\pi$ $v = 0$ (x, y) is in the interior of the capacitor

5.10 A diode is a nonlinear device that conducts readily when a positive voltage is applied to its input and conducts poorly when a negative voltage is applied. For this reason, the diode is often used as a rectifier—that is, a device that is used to convert alternating current to direct current. When the resistance of the diode material and the resistance of the contacts are ignored, the diode is said to be ideal. The ideal diode equation is

$$I = I_s \exp(qV_j/nkT) \qquad \text{(amperes)}$$

where

I_s = reverse saturation current $\approx .01 \times 10^{-6}$ for a silicon diode

q = electron charge = 1.6×10^{-19} coulomb

V_j = voltage applied to the diode

$n = 2$ for silicon

k = Boltzman constant = 1.38×10^{-23} J/°K

T = 300 degrees Kelvin

Write a program that calculates I for a silicon diode when V_j varies from −0.20 to 0.55 volt in steps of 0.05 volt.

5.11 When wire is wrapped around a cylindrical form and the device is used to produce a magnetic field, the device is called a solenoid. In this problem there is a solenoid of length L. The axis of the solenoid lies along the x axis. The left end of the solenoid is at $x = x_2$ where $x_2 = -L/2$. The right end of the solenoid is at x_1 where $x_1 = +L/2$. The magnetic field B at any point on the x axis is given by

$$B = (0.5nI)(\cos \theta_1 + \cos \theta_2) \qquad \text{teslas}$$

where

L = total length of the solenoid

$$\cos \theta_1 = \frac{0.5L + x}{\sqrt{R^2 + (0.5L + x)^2}} \qquad \cos \theta_2 = \frac{0.5L - x}{\sqrt{R^2 + (0.5L + x)^2}}$$

R = radius of the solenoid

I = current flowing through the wire of the solenoid

x = distance along the x axis (also the axis of the solenoid)

n = turns per meter

In these formulas all dimensions are to be in meters. For this particular solenoid, L = 20 cm, R = 0.5 cm, n = 1500 turns/m, and I = 4 amperes. Calculate B as x varies from $x = 0$ to $x = 0.2$ m in steps of 0.01 m.

5.12 Consider a situation in which a number of women check their hats as they enter a restaurant. The checkroom attendant is disorganized and, as a result, gives each woman as she leaves a hat selected at random. What is the probability no person receives her own hat?

If N hats are checked and A is the event "All hats returned are wrong," the probability of A is

$$P(A) = 1.0 - \sum_{k=1}^{N} \frac{(-1)^{k+1}}{k}!$$

Write a program that calculates $P(A)$ for $N = 2, 3, 4, 5, 6$.

5.13 In the study of complex variables, a symbol such as z can denote any member of a set of complex numbers. Then, z is called a complex variable. If to each value which z can assume there corresponds a complex variable w, then w is called a function of z.

Let us denote z as $z = x + jy$ and w as $w = u + jv$. For each point $P = (x, y)$ in the Z plane, there corresponds a point $P' = (u, v)$ in the W plane. This is called a mapping of P to P'. There is a large literature concerning the mappings of various figures from the Z plane to the W plane. This problem concerns one of these mappings.

Let us consider a rectangle two units wide and one unit high in the Z plane. The perimeter of the rectangle is defined by $x = 0$; $x = 2$; $y = 0$; $y = 1$. Thus, the rectangle is positioned so that the lower part of its wide dimension lies on the x axis and its lower left-hand corner, $x = 0, y = 0$, coincides with the origin.

The mapping

$$W = \sqrt{2}\, e^{\pi j/4} z$$

produces a rectangle in the W plane such that the same corner remains at the origin but the rectangle is rotated $\pi/4 = 45°$ counterclockwise around the origin. Thus, the side $x = 0$ on the Z plane is defined by $u = -v$ on the W plane; the side $x = 2$ on the Z plane is defined by $u + v = 4$ on the W plane.

Write a FORTRAN program that maps the side $x = 0$ and the side $x = 2$ to the W plane using the mapping function given above. Print the output in four columns captioned X, Y, U, V. From the data in these columns you should observe that when $x = 0$, then $u = -v$ and when $x = 2$, $u + v = 4$.

Suggestion: the complex exponential can be written as

```
CEXP((0,1.0)*PI/4.0)
```

6

Control Procedures

In the examples discussed up to now, the DO loop was used to carry out a prescribed number of iterations. The loop was terminated when the number of iterations was completed. Let us call this case a normal exit. Under some circumstances, it is not convenient or possible to specify the desired number of iterations in advance. Instead, iteration is halted when a condition specified in a test statement has been satisfied. In this case, exit from a DO loop occurs before the specified number of iterations has been executed. We will call this a condition-terminated exit to distinguish it from the normal exit. Use of a condition-terminated exit is very useful in obtaining approximate solutions of nonlinear equations.

6.1 THE EXIT STATEMENT

The EXIT statement causes termination of the DO loop. EXIT occurs when some specified condition is met. When it is met, a DO loop and all loops *nested* (contained) within it are terminated.

A generic flow diagram of a program with a condition-terminated exit from a DO loop is shown in Figure 6.1.

6.2 THE CYCLE STATEMENT

The CYCLE statement causes the termination of one iteration of a loop. After the CYCLE statement is executed, control is transferred to the beginning of the group of statements that constitute the DO construct.

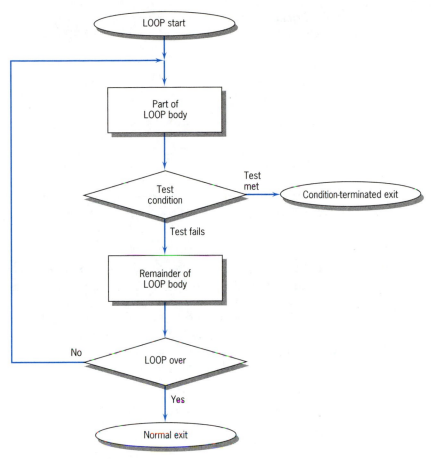

FIGURE 6.1   Flow diagram for condition-terminated exit.

6.3   IF (*LOGICAL EXPRESSION*) THEN

The IF. . .THEN construct makes it possible to select one of several alternatives or statements. Its basic form is

```
IF(logical expression)THEN
    statements
END IF
```

An example is

```
IF(X >= 0 .AND.(Y > = 0.) THEN
    FXY = (1.0 - EXP(-X))*Y**3
END IF
```

An exit from a DO loop could be achieved by the following:

```
IF(TEMPERATURE >= 212.0) THEN
    EXIT
END IF
```

The IF construct must always be terminated by END IF.

Alternative choices are made available by use of the ELSE IF and ELSE statements. For example,

```
IF(X < 0 .OR. Y < 0) THEN
    FXY = 0
    ELSE IF(X > 0)
    FXY = X*EXP(-Y)
    ELSE
    FXY = X*SQRT(Y)
END IF
```

EXAMPLE 6.1 Program **TRIANGLE**, Use of **EXIT** and **CYCLE**

Mathematics

Program TRIANGLE, shown below, illustrates use of the EXIT and CYCLE statements. The user enters values for A(I),B(I) and for HYP(I), all of which are integral numbers. If the values entered do *not* form a right triangle, then CYCLE causes the program to return to the beginning of the DO loop and a new set of values is entered. If these values form a right triangle, then the variable NUMBER_RTTRIS is increased by 1. See Fig. 6.2. The program continues until a negative value is entered for A(I). The results of the run show that there were six trials, five of which indicated right triangles.

```
    PROGRAM TRIANGLE
!   THIS PROGRAM IDENTIFIES RIGHT TRIANGLES WITH SIDES OF
!   INTEGRAL LENGTH AND COUNTS THE NUMBER OF TRIANGLES
!   IDENTIFIED. USER ENTERS A NO. FOR SIDE A, SIDE B AND
!   THE HYPOTENUSE.
    IMPLICIT NONE
    INTEGER:: A(20), B(20), HYP(20), I, NUMBER_RTTRIS
    NUMBER_RTTRIS = 0
    DO I = 1,20
     WRITE(*,*)"ENTER A,B, & HYP IN THAT ORDER"
     READ(*,*) A(I), B(I), HYP(I)
    IF(A(I) <= 0.0) THEN
```

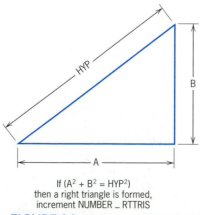

If ($A^2 + B^2 = HYP^2$)
then a right triangle is formed,
increment NUMBER _ RTTRIS

FIGURE 6.2 Test for a right triangle.

```
        EXIT
      ELSE IF(A(I)**2 + B(I)**2 == HYP(I)**2) THEN
        NUMBER_RTTRIS = NUMBER_RTTRIS + 1
        WRITE(*,"(3(I10))") A(I), B(I), HYP(I)
        CYCLE
      ELSE
        WRITE(*,"(A )")'INPUT DOES NOT MAKE A RIGHT TRIANGLE'
      END IF
    END DO
    WRITE(*,"(A,I6//)") "# OF RT. TRIANGLES FOUND = ",NUMBER_RTTRIS
    END PROGRAM TRIANGLE
```

RUNS

```
    5    12    13
    6     8    10
    8    15    17
   20    21    29
   27    36    45
```

```
INPUT DOES NOT MAKE A RIGHT TRIANGLE
# OF RT. TRIANGLES FOUND = 5
```

6.3.1 DO Loops Without Loop Control

Often, a DO loop is used to carry out repetitive calculations until some condition is met. At this point, it is desired that the loop be terminated. Sometimes the index of the loop serves only as a loop counter; that is, it is not explicitly used in a FORTRAN statement. In this case, a DO construct can be used with no loop control. Looping will continue until the EXIT statement terminates the loop. For example:

EXAMPLE 6.2 Program CUBIC

```
              PROGRAM CUBIC
              IMPLICIT NONE
              INTEGER:: CUBE, CUBEPOWER
              CUBE = 1
                DO
                  CUBEPOWER = CUBE**3
                  WRITE(*,"(I5,3X,I8)") CUBE, CUBEPOWER
                  IF(CUBEPOWER > 2000) EXIT
                  CUBE = CUBE + 1
                END DO
              END PROGRAM CUBIC
```

When the program is run, the output is:

```
        1        1
        2        8
        3       27
        4       64
        5      125
```

6	221
7	343
8	512
9	729
10	1000
11	1331
12	1728
13	2197

6.3.2 DO WHILE

The DO WHILE construct provides an alternative method of providing an exit from the DO loop. Its form is

```
DO WHILE(logical expression)
```

As an example:

```
DO WHILE (14.7> TEST)
    .
    .
    .
END DO
```

In this example, iteration continues as long as TEST is less than 14.7. For a complete example, see Example 6.8.

EXAMPLE 6.3 Reliability of a System of Parallel Components

Reliability Engineering

Reliability is defined as the probability that a component or system of components will perform successfully.

Let us consider a system of n identical, parallel parts. Such a system might consist of n thin cables forming a thick cable.

We will use the following notation:

REL = the desired value of reliability, entered when the program runs. R = the calculated reliability of the system

q = the probability that one of the thin cables will *not* perform successfully

Each of the thin cables has the same value of q. The reliability of the system of n thin cables, in parallel, is given by

$$R = 1 - q^{**n}$$

Program RELIABLY, shown below, calculates R. In the program, the value of q has been fixed at 0.2. The user enters a value for REL, the desired reliability. The value of REL will usually be a number between 0.9 and 0.999999. The selected value of REL is constant throughout the run. The user then enters a value for NUMBER. R is calculated, and both R and N are printed. Then the program CYCLEs back to the beginning of the loop. If the result is satisfactory, then a negative value should be entered for N and an EXIT is executed. By observing the resultant reliability for a particular value of N, the engineer can decide if N should be increased to obtain a greater safety factor in reliability. Note that the simple form of IF was used here: IF(logical statement) EXIT

```
        PROGRAM RELIABLY
!       CALCULATIONS OF THE RELIABILITY OF A SYSTEM OF N
!       COMPONENTS IN PARALLEL. USER MAKES AS MANY SELECTIONS
!       OF N AS DESIRED. NEGATIVE N PRODUCES EXIT.
        IMPLICIT NONE
        INTEGER:: NUMBER,COUNT
        REAL:: Q,REL,R
        WRITE(*,*)'ENTER THE DESIRED VALUE OF RELIABILITY'
        READ(*,*) REL
        WRITE(*,*)'THE DESIRED RELIABILITY = ',REL
        Q = 0.2                 !THE UNRELIABILITY OF A COMPONENT
        DO COUNT = 1,1000
            WRITE(*,*)'TO EXIT, TYPE A NEGATIVE NUMBER'
            WRITE(*,*)'OTHERWISE, ENTER A VALUE FOR NUMBER
            READ(*,*)NUMBER
        IF(NUMBER<0) EXIT
        R = 1 - Q**NUMBER
!       WRITE(*,*)'NO. OF PARALLEL COMPONENTS =',NUMBER
        WRITE(*,*)'NO. OF PARALLEL COMPONENTS = ',NUMBER
        WRITE(*,*)' CALCULATED RELIABILITY = ',R
        WRITE(*,"(A,3X,F12.7/)")' CALCULATED RELIABILITY = ',R
        IF(R > = REL) THEN
            EXIT
            ELSE
            CYCLE
            END IF
        END DO
        END PROGRAM RELIABLY
```

RUN

```
THE DESIRED RELIABILITY =  0.9999989
NO. OF PARALLEL COMPONENTS =        5
CALCULATED RELIABILITY =  0.9996799

NO. OF PARALLEL COMPONENTS =        7
CALCULATED RELIABILITY =  0.9999871

NO. OF PARALLEL COMPONENTS =        9
CALCULATED RELIABILITY =  0.9999994
```

In the trial run, the selected value of REL was 0.9999989. The first choice of NUMBER was NUMBER = 5, yielding a value of 0.9996799. The last choice was NUMBER = 9, and this yielded a reliability of 0.9999994. This is only slightly more than the requested reliability. Depending on the nature of the use for which the cable is intended, the designer may accept this result or else increase the number of thin cables in order to provide a greater safety factor.

EXAMPLE 6.4 Program OUTSTANDING_PRINCIPAL

 Engineering Economics

(Uses *selective printing of output* by means of MOD function.)

In Chapter 3, Example 3.8.8, we considered a situation in which a company was considering taking a loan in order to purchase a machine. In that example, the manager wished to know the amount that the company would have to pay each month to repay a loan of $61,800 if the interest was 1.5 percent per month (rate = 0.015) and 24 monthly payments were to be made. The business manager found that a monthly payment of $3085.32 would suffice. Suppose the business manager wanted to determine how much money was owed as the payments were made. This would help management to decide if the company could afford to pay the remainder of the debt in one payment. This calculation is performed by program OUTSTANDING_PRINCIPAL shown below.

The data to be provided by the user of the program are: the amount of the loan; the monthly interest rate; the monthly payment; and the number of payments to be made. In order to keep the printout to a reasonable length, the results are shown only for even-numbered payments. This "selective" printing is achieved by the statement IF(MOD(K,2)==0) THEN. . . . The intrinsic function MOD(m, n) returns the *remainder* that results from dividing m by n. In this case, K, the index of the DO loop, is divided by two. If K is an even number, then the remainder is zero.

```fortran
      PROGRAM OUTSTANDING_PRINCIPAL
!
!     THIS PROGRAM CALCULATES THE OUTSTANDING PRINCIPAL AFTER
!     EACH PAYMENT OF A LOAN. Y(K) IS THE OUTSTANDING PRINCIPAL
!     AFTER THE K'th PAYMENT;P IS THE PERIODIC PAYMENT; L IS
!     THE AMOUNT OF THE LOAN; R IS THE MONTHLY INTEREST RATE.
!
      IMPLICIT NONE
      REAL:: Y(50), R, L, P, TOTAL_PAID, INTEREST_PAID
      INTEGER:: N,K,J
      WRITE(*,*)'ENTER THE AMOUNT OF THE LOAN'
      READ(*,*) L
      WRITE(*,*)'THE AMOUNT OF THE LOAN IS $',L
      WRITE(*,*)'ENTER THE MONTHLY PAYMENT'
      READ(*,*)P
      WRITE(*,"(A,F12.2)")'THE MONTHLY PAYMENT IS $',P
      WRITE(*,*)'ENTER THE MONTHLY INTEREST RATE'
      READ(*,*) R
      WRITE(*,"(A,F12.3)")'THE MONTHLY INTEREST RATE IS', R
      WRITE(*,*)'ENTER THE NUMBER OF EQUAL PAYMENTS TO BE MADE'
      READ(*,*)N
      WRITE(*,*)'THE NUMBER OF EQUAL PAYMENTS TO BE MADE IS',N
      WRITE(*,*)'        ***'
!
      DO K = 1,N
        Y(K) = (1.0 + R)**K*L - P*((1.0 + R)**K - 1.0)/R
        IF(MOD(K,2) == 0) THEN
          WRITE(*,"(A,I4,A,F12.2/)")'PRINCIPAL OWED AFTER PAYMENT',    &
     &K,' IS $', Y(K)
          WRITE(*,"(A,I4,A,F12.2/)")'PRINCIPAL OWED AFTER PAYMENT',    &
     &K,' IS $', Y(K)
```

```
   ELSE
     CYCLE
    END IF
   END DO
   TOTAL_PAID = 0
   DO J = 1,N
   TOTAL_PAID = TOTAL_PAID + P
   END DO
   WRITE(*,"(A,F12.2)")'TOTAL AMOUNT PAID = $',TOTAL_PAID
     INTEREST_PAID = TOTAL_PAID - L
   WRITE(*,"(A,F12.2)")'INTEREST PAID = $',INTEREST_PAID
   END PROGRAM OUTSTANDING_PRINCIPAL
```

RUN

```
THE AMOUNT OF THE LOAN IS $   6.1800000E+04
THE MONTHLY PAYMENT IS $    3075.00
THE MONTHLY INTEREST RATE IS      0.015
THE NUMBER OF EQUAL PAYMENTS TO BE MADE IS 24
  ***
PRINCIPAL OWED AFTER PAYMENT  2 IS $   57471.79
PRINCIPAL OWED AFTER PAYMENT  4 IS $   53012.77
PRINCIPAL OWED AFTER PAYMENT  6 IS $   48418.97
PRINCIPAL OWED AFTER PAYMENT  8 IS $   43686.32
PRINCIPAL OWED AFTER PAYMENT 10 IS $   38810.64
PRINCIPAL OWED AFTER PAYMENT 12 IS $   33787.58
PRINCIPAL OWED AFTER PAYMENT 14 IS $   28612.70
PRINCIPAL OWED AFTER PAYMENT 16 IS $   23281.41
PRINCIPAL OWED AFTER PAYMENT 18 IS $   17788.97
PRINCIPAL OWED AFTER PAYMENT 20 IS $   12130.54
PRINCIPAL OWED AFTER PAYMENT 22 IS $    6301.10
PRINCIPAL OWED AFTER PAYMENT 24 IS $     295.43

TOTAL AMOUNT PAID = $    73800.00
INTEREST PAID = $  12000.00
```

The data here differ from the data in example 3.8.8 in that the monthly payment is $3075 rather than $3085.32.

The debt = $61,800; monthly interest rate = 0.015; number of equal payments = 24; the payment to be made each month = $3075. Of course, from the previous example we already know that the monthly payment should be $3085.32. Therefore, each monthly payment is too small by $13.32, and we are not surprised that the run shows that 24 payments do not quite remove the debt.

The principal owed after payment 24 is $295.43. The printout also shows that $73,800 will have been paid. The sum of $295.43 is required to clear the debt. The printout also shows that $12,000 of the payment was for payment of interest.

EXAMPLE 6.5 BEAM2, Beam Deflection at Several Points

Civil and Mechanical Engineering

In this example, we discuss a program that calculates the deflection, at several equally spaced points, along the length of a simple beam. It is assumed that the cross section of

Table 6.1

Formula Symbol	Program Name	Meaning	Units
y	Y	Deflection at x	in
x	X	Position on beam measured from origin	in
P	P	Applied load	lb
L	L	Length of beam	in
a	A	Distance to load from left end	in
b	B	Distance to load from right end	in
E	E	Modulus of elasticity	lb/in^2
I	XI	Second moment of cross section	in^4
—	N	Number of points at which deflection is to be determined	—
—	SECTS	Number of segments into which beam is divided by the N points	—
—	J	DO loop index	—
—	POINT	Real equivalent of J	—

the beam is uniform and that the beam is loaded by single concentrated load of P lb. The length of the beam is L in, and the number of points at which the deflection is to be calculated is N.

The deflection y of the beam at an arbitrary position x is given by Eqs. (6.1) and (6.2):

$$y = \frac{-Pbx}{6EIL}[2L(L-x) - b^2 - (L-x)^2] \qquad 0 \leq x \leq a \tag{6.1}$$

$$y = \frac{-Pa(L-x)}{6EIL}[2Lb - b^2 - (L-x)^2] \qquad a \leq x \leq L \tag{6.2}$$

The program, BEAM2, is shown below. The symbols in the formulas and the symbols used in the program are defined as shown in the Table 6.1. Where a symbol appears only in the program, there is a dash in the table.

```
      PROGRAM BEAM2
!
!     PROGRAM CALCULATES SIMPLE BEAM DEFLECTION AT SEVERAL
!     POINTS, PRODUCED BY A SINGLE CONCENTRATED LOAD.
!
      IMPLICIT NONE
      REAL:: P ,A ,L ,E ,XI ,B ,SECTS ,POINT, X, FAC, Y
      INTEGER:: N, COUNT
      WRITE(*,*)' ENTER VALUE OF APPLIED LOAD, IN LB'
      READ(*,*) P
      WRITE(*,*)'ENTER BEAM LENGTH (IN.)'
      READ(*,*) L
      WRITE(*,*)' ENTER DISTANCE TO LOAD FROM LEFT END OF BEAM'
      READ(*,*) A
      WRITE(*,*)'ENTER MOD.OF ELASTICITY & SEC.MOMENT OF X-SECT.'
      READ(*,*) E, XI
      WRITE(*,*)'NO. OF PTS. @ WHICH DEFLECTION IS TO BE FOUND ?'
      READ(*,*) N
      WRITE(*,"(A,F15.2)")' APPLIED LOAD', P
```

```
        WRITE(*,50) L,A
50      FORMAT(' BEAM LENGTH & DIST TO LOAD FROM LEFT END',2F12.1)
        WRITE(*,60) E,XI
60      FORMAT(' MOD. OF ELASTICITY & SEC MOMENT OF X-SEC',2E10.2)
        WRITE(*,*)'NO. OF PTS. AT WHICH DEFLECTION IS TO BE FOUND',N
        B = L - A
        SECTS = N + 1
        FAC = -P/(6.0*E*XI*L)
        DO COUNT = 1,N
         POINT = COUNT
         X = POINT*L/SECTS
         IF((A - X)< 0.0) THEN
          Y = FAC*A*(L - X)*((2.0*L - B)*B - (L - X)**2)
          GO TO 25
         ELSE
          Y = FAC*B*X*(2.0*L*(L - X) - B**2 - (L - X)**2)
         END IF
25       WRITE(*,"(/A,F10.4,A,F10.4)")' AT X = ', X,' ; Y = ',Y
        END DO
        END PROGRAM BEAM2
```

RUN

```
        APPLIED LOAD    500.00
        BEAM LTH. & DIST TO LOAD FROM LFT END   154.00    65.00
        MOD OF ELAST & SEC MOMENT OF X-SEC  0.30E+08  0.25E+01

NO. OF PTS. AT WHICH DEFLECTION IS TO BE FOUND 15

AT X =     9.6250 ;  Y =  -0.0970

AT X =    19.2500 ;  Y =  -0.1906

AT X =    28.8750 ;  Y =  -0.2774

AT X =    38.5000 ;  Y =  -0.3538

AT X =    48.1250 ;  Y =  -0.4165

AT X =    57.7500 ;  Y =  -0.4620

AT X =    67.3750 ;  Y =  -0.4869

AT X =    77.0000 ;  Y =  -0.4897

AT X =    86.6250 ;  Y =  -0.4724

AT X =    96.2500 ;  Y =  -0.4375

AT X =   105.8750 ;  Y =  -0.3876

AT X =   115.5000 ;  Y =  -0.3251

AT X =   125.1250 ;  Y =  -0.2526

AT X =   134.7500 ;  Y =  -0.1726

AT X =   144.3750 ;  Y =  -0.0875
```

In the trial run, a beam length of 154 inches and 15 points was selected. Note that the values of the various parameters that were entered at the time of the run are "echoed" in the printout. As previously mentioned, this procedure is very useful when several data are to be entered. The deflections are negative values as the beam is assumed to be coincident with the x axis and the deflected portions of the beam lie below the x axis.

EXAMPLE 6.6 Van der Waals's Equation

Chemistry

In 1662 Robert Boyle (1627–1691) performed experiments on the relation between the volume of a confined gas and the pressure applied to it. His conclusion, known as Boyle's Law, can be expressed as follows: At a constant temperature, the pressure P of a given quantity of gas is given by:

$$PV = k$$

where k is a constant. This is now called Boyle's "ideal gas law."

The ideal gas law does not take into account the volume of gas molecules. Although the volume occupied by a gas molecule is very small compared to the distance between molecules, it does occupy some space. As the volume of the container decreases, the volume of the molecules occupies a significant proportion of the volume of the container. Another important factor not accounted for by the ideal gas law is the force of attraction and repulsion between the gas molecules. When the molecules are relatively far apart, these forces are negligible; however, when the volume of the enclosure is smaller, these forces are sufficiently large to make the ideal gas law inaccurate. In 1873 Johannes van der Waals (1837–1923) modified the ideal gas law in order to take into account the attractive and repulsive forces between gas molecules. We will discuss a program that solves van der Waals's equation for the volume of a gas when the temperature and pressure are known. For one mole of gas, van der Waals's equation is given by Eq. 6.3:

$$\left(P + \frac{A}{V^2} \right)(V - B) - RT \tag{6.3}$$

where

P = pressure, atm

A = constant for a particular gas

V = vol, liters

B = constant for a particular gas

R = ideal gas constant = 0.08205 liter·atm/mole·°K

T = absolute temperature, °K

In the program, we seek to find the volume of a mole of CO_2, in liters, at a specified temperature in degrees Celsius and at a specified pressure in atmospheres. For CO_2, the values of the parameters A and B are

$$A = 3.59 \text{ liter}^2 \cdot \text{atm/mole}^2$$

$$B = 0.0427 \text{ liter/mole}$$

```
      PROGRAM VAN_DER_WAALS
!
!     THIS PROGRAM CALCULATES GAS VOLUME BY VAN DER WAALS'S
!     EQUATION. IN THE PROGRAM, CONSTANTS ARE FOR CO2. C IS IN
```

```
!     DEGREES CELSIUS; P IS ATMOSPHERES. T IS DEGREES KELVIN.
!     TO TERMINATE THE PROGRAM ENTER A NEGATIVE VALUE FOR P.
!
      IMPLICIT NONE
      INTEGER:: J
      REAL:: C,P,T,X,F1,F2,F3,VOL,PROD
      REAL, PARAMETER:: A = 3.59, B = 0.0427, R = 0.08205
      C = 20.0
      DO
          WRITE(*,"(A/)")'ENTER A VALUE FOR THE PRESSURE'
          READ(*,*) P
          IF(P <= 0.0) EXIT
          WRITE(*,*) P
          T = 273.0 + C
          F3 = R*T
!
          DO J = 1,10000
           X = J
           VOL = X/1000.0
           F1 = P + A/VOL**2
           F2 = VOL - B
           PROD = F1*F2
           IF((PROD - F3) >=0.0) THEN
           WRITE(*,"(A,F8.4,A,I8)")' VOL = ',VOL,'  NO. ITERATIONS',J
           GO TO 90
           END IF
          END DO
         WRITE(*,*)'NO CONVERGENCE, NO VOLUME CALCULATED'
         WRITE(*,"(A,F15.4,A,F15.4)")'PROD = ',PROD,'   F3 = ',F3
        WRITE(*,*)' NUMBER OF ITERATIONS = ',J
 90     CYCLE
       END DO
       END PROGRAM VAN_DER_WAALS
```

A flow diagram for program VAN_DER_WAALS is shown in Fig. 6.3. In the program, the variables F1, F2, and F3 are used and are defined as

$$F1 = P + \frac{A}{(VOL)^2}$$

$$F2 = VOL - B$$

$$F3 = RT$$

The temperature, C, is set at a value of 20 degrees Celsius. Therefore, $F3 = RT$ is a constant. When the program is run, a value of P, the pressure, is entered. A value for VOL, the volume, is calculated using the index J which is incremented from 1 to 10,000 in steps of 1. X is set equal to J. Then, VOL = X/1000. Thus, VOL is incremented from an initial value of 0.001 liter. The variable PROD, which is equal to F1*F2, increases as VOL increases. In each iteration, the quantity (PROD − F3) is tested. When PROD is equal to or greater than F3, a solution has been found using the particular value of P that was chosen and the values of VOL and J are printed. Then the program branches to statement 90. If, for a particular value of P, (PROD − F3) *always remains negative*, a solution is *not* obtained. In this event, 10,000 iterations are performed, and a normal exit from the loop occurs. Then the message "No convergence; no volume calculated" is printed; in addition, the values of J, *PROD*, and *F3* are printed.

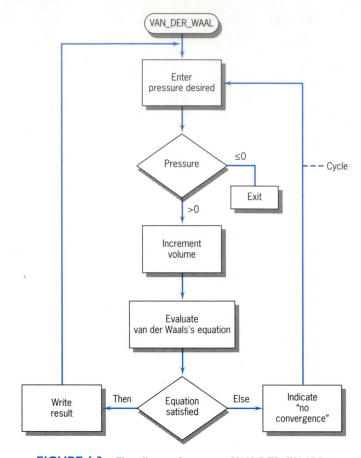

FIGURE 6.3 Flow diagram for program VAN_DER_WAALS.

```
RUN


ENTER A VALUE FOR THE PRESSURE


   2.0000000
 NO CONVERGENCE, NO VOLUME CALCULATED
PROD =     20.2721   F3 =     24.0407
  NUMBER OF ITERATIONS = 10001


ENTER A VALUE FOR THE PRESSURE
 10.0000000
VOL =  2.2940   NO. ITERATIONS   2294


ENTER A VALUE FOR THE PRESSURE
 50.0000000

  VOL =  0.3380   NO. ITERATIONS    338
```

```
ENTER A VALUE FOR THE PRESSURE


  80.0000000

  VOL =   0.0820   NO ITERATIONS      82

ENTER A VALUE FOR THE PRESSURE

   1.0000000E+02

VOL =   0.0770   NO ITERATIONS      77
```

Several runs are shown above. Values of P ranging from 2 to 100 atmospheres were entered. For P = 2, there was no convergence, so no solution was obtained. Note that the
printout indicated that J, the index, attained a value of 10001. Then P was increased to a
value of 3, and the result was a volume of 7.906 liters. (This run is not shown.) Several
additional values of P were used, the last being P = 100. At that pressure, the volume was
found to have decreased to 0.0770 liter.

EXAMPLE 6.7 Program REFORMING, Re-forming of Cyclohexane

 Chemical Engineering

In calculating mass balances of chemical reactions, the engineer often encounters equations that are difficult or perhaps impossible to solve analytically. The conversion of hydrocarbons to other hydrocarbons of higher octane number is called re-forming. Let us
consider the re-forming of cyclohexane to produce benzene. An analysis on a pound-
mole basis of the reaction for the re-forming of cyclohexane results in Eq. (6.4)

$$\frac{(4+3n_B)^3 n_B}{[(1-n_B)/13](5+3n_B)} = 14.7 \tag{6.4}$$

where n_B = benzene produced, lb-mol

Shown below are Program REFORMING, which calculates the number of lb-mol
produced, and a sample run. In the program, the name B is used to denote the number of
lb-mol of benzene produced, and TEST denotes the left side of Eq. (6.4). The desired solution is obtained by means of a DO loop and an IF statement. For each iteration of the
DO loop, the value of B is increased by 0.01. Iteration continues until the difference between TEST and 14.7 is equal to or less than zero. When this condition is attained, an
EXIT from the DO loop occurs, and the program prints the current value of B, thus providing an approximate solution to Eq. (6.4). Then the program stops. A flow diagram for
program REFORMING is shown in Fig. 6.4.

```
     PROGRAM REFORMING
!
!     PROGRAM CALCULATES THE NUMBER OF LB-MOLES OF BENZENE
!     PRODUCED IN THE REFORMING OF CYCLOHEXANE
!
     IMPLICIT NONE
     INTEGER:: K
```

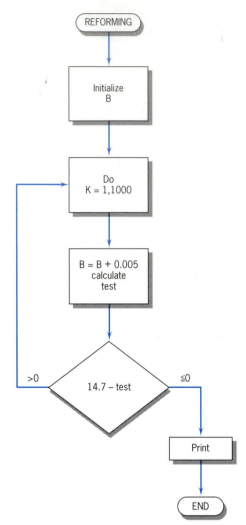

FIGURE 6.4 Flow diagram for program REFORMING.

```
REAL:: B,TEST
B = 0
DO K = 1,1000
B = B + 0.005
 TEST =((4.0 + 3.0*B)**3*B)/((1. - B)/13.0)/(5.0 + 3.0*B)**3
  IF((14.7 - TEST)<= 0.0) THEN
    EXIT
 END IF
END DO
!
WRITE(*,*)'NO. OF ITERATIONS AT EXIT = ',K,' TEST = ',TEST
WRITE(*,"(/A,F9.4)")' NO. OF LB-MOLE OF BENZENE PRODUCED = ',B
END PROGRAM REFORMING

RUN
NO. OF ITERATIONS AT EXIT = 129  TEST =  14.8045988
NO. OF LB-MOLE OF BENZENE PRODUCED =      0.6450
```

EXAMPLE 6.8 Program REFORM2

Program REFORM2 is an alternative solution to the problem of calculating the amount of benzene. Here, the DO WHILE construct is used. The program and a run are shown below. The results are essentially the same as those found previously.

```
PROGRAM REFORM2
!
!    CALCULATION OF N0. OF LB-MOLES OF BENZENE
!    PRODUCED IN THE REFORMING OF CYCLOHEXANE
!
IMPLICIT NONE
INTEGER::K
REAL::B,TEST
B = 0
DO WHILE(14.7>TEST)
K = K + 1
B = B + 0.005
TEST = ((4.0 + 3.0*B)**3*B)/ ((1.-B)/13.0)/(5.0 + 3.0*B)**3
END DO
WRITE(*,*)'TEST =',TEST
WRITE(*,*)'NO. OF ITERATIONS AT EXIT = ',K
WRITE(*,*)'NO. OF LB-MOLE OF BENZENE PRODUCED = ',B
END PROGRAM REFORM2
```

RUN

```
TEST = 14.8045988
NO. OF ITERATIONS AT EXIT = 129
NO. OF LB-MOLE OF BENZENE PRODUCED = 0.6449995
```

EXAMPLE 6.9 Program MAXIMUM-OXYGEN-DEFICIT, Maximum Oxygen Deficit in a Stream

Environmental Science

In Example 5.7, we discussed a program that calculates the oxygen deficit, D_t, as a function of time. In that program, the time was increased in steps of 0.1 day. The trial run showed that the maximum oxygen deficit was about 6.3743 and occurred at about 2.9 days after the discharge of sewage began. Let us assume that we now wish to determine *only* the maximum oxygen deficit and the time at which it occurs. The revised program, MAXIMUM_OXYGEN_DEFICIT, is shown below.

```
PROGRAM MAXIMUM_OXYGEN_DEFICIT
!
!    THIS PROGRAM CALCULATES THE MAXIMUM OXYGEN DEFICIT IN A

!    STREAM AS A FUNCTION OF TIME.
!
IMPLICIT NONE
REAL: KR,QSTR,QSEW,KD20,TMIX,BODSTR,BODSEW,D0,KD,BODMIX
```

```
REAL:: FB,A,DT,T,DTOLD
INTEGER:: I
WRITE(*,*)'ENTER KR, THE COEFFICIENT OF REOXYGENATION'
READ(*,*)KR
WRITE(*,*)'KR, THE COEFFICIENT OF REOXYGENATION = ',KR
WRITE(*,*)'ENTER QSTR, THE RATE OF FLOW OF THE STREAM'
READ(*,*) QSTR
WRITE(*,*)'QSTR,THE RATE OF FLOW OF THE STREAM = ',QSTR
WRITE(*,*)'ENTER QSEW,THE RATE OF FLOW OF SEWAGE'
READ(*,*)QSEW
WRITE(*,*)'QSEW, THE RATE OF FLOW OF SEWAGE = ',QSEW
WRITE(*,*)'ENTER KD20,THE COEFFICIENT OF DEOXYGENATION'
READ(*,*)KD20
WRITE(*,*)'KD20,THE COEFFICIENT OF DEOXYGENATION = ',KD20
WRITE(*,*)'ENTER TMIX,TEMPERATURE OF SEWAGE-STREAM MIX'
READ(*,*)TMIX
WRITE(*,*)'TMIX,TEMPERATURE OF SEWAGE-STREAM MIX = ',TMIX
WRITE(*,*)'ENTER BODSTR,THE OXYGEN DEMAND OF STREAM'
READ(*,*)BODSTR
WRITE(*,*)'BODSTR,THE OXYGEN DEMAND OF STREAM = ',BODSTR
WRITE(*,*)'ENTER BODSEW,OXYGEN DEMAND OF SEWAGE'
READ(*,*)BODSEW
WRITE(*,*)'BODSEW,OXYGEN DEMAND OF SEWAGE = ',BODSEW
WRITE(*,*)'ENTER D0, INITIAL OXYGEN DEFICIT'
READ(*,*) D0
WRITE(*,*)'D0,THE INITIAL OXYGEN DEFICIT = ',D0
 KD = KD20*1.047**(TMIX - 20.0)
 BODMIX = (BODSTR*QSTR + BODSEW*QSEW)/(QSTR + QSEW)
 FB = BODMIX*(0.02*TMIX + 0.6)/0.68
!
DTOLD = D0
DO I = 2700,3100
 T = I/1000.0
 A = 10.0**(-KR*T)
 DT = ((KD*FB)/(KR - KD))*(10.0**(-KD*T) - A) + D0*A
 IF((DT - DTOLD) < = 0) THEN
  EXIT
 END IF
 DTOLD = DT
END DO
WRITE(*,"(A//)")'*************************************************'
WRITE(*,"(//A,F9.4,A,F9.4)")' MAXIMUM DEFICIT AT ',T,' DAYS IS',DT
END PROGRAM MAXIMUM_OXYGEN_DEFICIT
```

To achieve greater accuracy, time was incremented in steps of 0.001 day (rather than 0.1 day). The approximate value of the maximum oxygen deficit is found by means of the IF statement. Note that the initial value of the DO loop was set at 2.7 (days) and the maximum value at 3.1, for it was known from the previous program that the answer would lie in this range. The results of the run are as follows.

RUN

KR,THE COEFFICIENT OF REOXYGENATION =   0.2000000

```
QSTR,THE RATE OF FLOW OF THE STREAM =   23.8999996
QSEW, THE RATE OF FLOW OF SEWAGE =    3.5000000
KD20,THE COEFFICIENT OF DEOXYGENATION =    0.1000000
TMIX,TEMPERATURE OF SEWAGE-STREAM MIX =  17.6000004
BODSTR,THE OXYGEN DEMAND OF STREAM =   0.0000000E+00
BODSEW,OXYGEN DEMAND OF SEWAGE =    1.4500000E+02
DO,THE INITIAL OXYGEN DEFICIT =   1.3000000


**************************************************
   MAXIMUM DEFICT AT   2.9090 DAYS IS   6.3743
```

EXAMPLE 6.10 Program TIME_OF_FLIGHT, Time of Flight of an Electron

Physics

We now discuss a program for calculating the time of flight of an electron from the cathode to the anode of a vacuum diode. The electrodes (cathode and anode) are parallel planes, and the electron is assumed to begin its flight with zero velocity. The cathode emits electrons, and, if the anode is positve with respect to the cathode, electrons will be attracted to the anode. A generator, $V_m \sin \omega t$, is connected to the electrodes. The parameters are so chosen that the time of flight is less than a half period of the generator voltage. As a result, the applied voltage is positive during one half period and negative during the next half period. Therefore, the applied voltage is positive during a half period, and while this positive voltage is being applied to the anode, electrons will be attracted to it. See Fig. 6.5.

The instantaneous distance y of the electron from the cathode is

$$y = \frac{eV_m}{m\omega^2 D}(\theta - \sin \theta) \qquad (6.5)$$

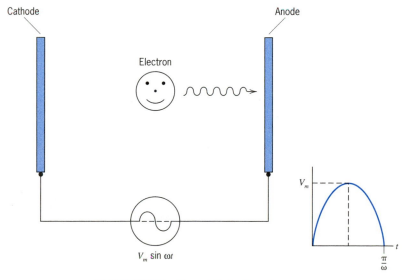

FIGURE 6.5   Time of flight of an electron.

where

e/m = electron charge to mass ratio

D = the distance from cathode to anode

$\theta = \omega t$

We then replace $\sin\theta$ by the first three terms of its Taylor series representation about the origin, and we obtain

$$y = \frac{eV_m}{m\omega^2 D}\left[\theta - \left(\theta - \frac{\theta^3}{3!} + \frac{\theta^5}{5!}\right)\right] = \frac{eV_m}{\omega^2 D}\left(\frac{\theta^3}{6} + \frac{\theta^5}{120}\right)$$

Let $P = (e/m)(V_m/\omega^2 D)$, then write the equation as

$$\frac{y}{P} - \left(\frac{\theta^3}{6} - \frac{\theta^5}{120}\right) = 0 \tag{6.6}$$

If y is set equal to the distance D from cathode to anode, the quantity D/P is a constant. By substituting successively increasing values of θ, we can find a value that satisfies the equation. This is accomplished by the DO loop and the IF statement within it. In the program, TIME_OF_FLIGHT, shown below, the angle θ is represented by TH, D/P by Z, the radian frequency ω by W, and the quantity within parentheses in Eq. (6.6) by THETFUN. The quantity e/m has a value of 1.759E11 in the MKS system and is used in defining P.

```
      PROGRAM TIME_OF_FLIGHT
!
!     THIS PROGRAM CALCULATES THE TIME OF FLIGHT OF AN
!     ELECTRON RELEASED WITH ZERO INITIAL VELOCITY AT THE
!     CATHODE OF A PARALLEL PLATE DIODE. A HALF PERIOD OF A
!     SINUSOIDAL VOLTAGE IS APPLIED TO THE PLATES.
!
      IMPLICIT NONE
      REAL:: W,VMAX,D,P,Z,B,THETA,THETAFUN,T,HALFPERIOD
      INTEGER:: I
      WRITE(*,*)'ENTER THE FREQUENCY (RAD/SEC) OF THE VOLTAGE'
      READ(*,*)W
      WRITE(*,*)'THE FREQUENCY OF THE VOLTAGE = ',W
      WRITE(*,*)'ENTER THE MAXIMUM VOLTAGE APPLIED'
      READ(*,*)VMAX
      WRITE(*,*)'THE MAXIMUM VOLTAGE APPLIED = ',VMAX
      WRITE(*,*)'ENTER THE SPACING BETWEEN PLATES (METERS)'
      READ(*,*)D
      WRITE(*,*)'THE SPACING BETWEEN PLATES (METERS) = ',D
!
      P = (1.759E11)*VMAX/((W**2)*D)
      Z = D/P
      DO I = 1,10000
        B = I
        THETA = B/1.0E08
      THETAFUN = (THETA**3)/6.0 -(THETA**5)/120.0
        IF((Z - THETAFUN) <= 0.0) THEN
         EXIT
        END IF
```

```
       END DO
       T = THETA/W
!
       WRITE(*,"(//A,E15.8//)" ) 'THE TIME OF FLIGHT IN SECONDS = ',T
       WRITE(*,*)'THE NUMBER OF ITERATIONS = ',B
       HALFPERIOD = 3.14159/W
       WRITE(*,"(A,E15.7)")'HALFPERIOD OF VOLTAGE(SEC.) = ',HALFPERIOD
       END PROGRAM TIME_OF_FLIGHT
```

The trial run is shown below. Note that it took 7856 iterations to obtain a solution. This is a fairly large number of iterations and is a good reason for evaluating constants such as P and Z *before* the loop so that they are evaluated *only once*. This practice significantly reduces the time required to execute this and similar loops.

```
       RUN

       THE FREQUENCY OF THE VOLTAGE =    3.7700000E+02
       THE MAXIMUM VOLTAGE APPLIED =    1.0000000E+03
       THE SPACING BETWEEN PLATES (METERS) =    9.9999998E-03

       THE TIME OF FLIGHT IN SECONDS = 0.20838196E-06

       THE NUMBER OF ITERATIONS =    7.8560000E+03
       HALFPERIOD OF VOLTAGE(SEC.) =    0.833313E-02
```

EXAMPLE 6.11 Program BEAM3, Maximum Beam Deflection

Civil and Mechanical Engineering

In this example, a simple beam deflection problem involving a single concentrated load will be used to illustrate the use of several IF statements in an iterative solution. The equations for simple beam deflection were given in Example 6.4. The method we will use here is not needed for so elementary a problem. However, it provides an opportunity to discuss a particular *maximum-seeking* procedure that has application in optimization design.

The optimum-seeking method to be discussed is applicable to any unimodal function—that is, any function that has only one maximum or one minimum in the region being investigated. The elastic curve of the simple beam that we are considering falls into this category. The region involved is in the entire length of the beam, and the function the maximum of which is sought is actually the *two* functions that describe the elastic curve—one in effect to the *left* of the applied load, and the other in effect to the *right* of the load.

The search method itself is a simple process for reducing the size of the *region of uncertainty* in which the maximum is located. The procedure depends on successive *pairs* of simultaneous "experiments" being used to section the region and reduce its size. Figure 6.6 shows the elastic curve of a simple beam on which two experiments, that is, function evaluations, have been made at points $P1$ and $P2$. These points were chosen, according to the plan described below, within the region of uncertainty contained between

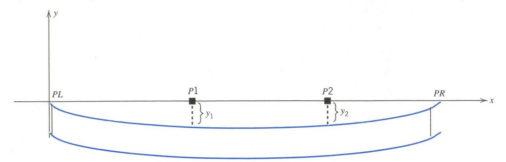

FIGURE 6.6 Elastic curve of a simple beam.

the points PL and PR. Now, as the beam curve is the graph of a unimodal function, we can state that

1. If $|y_1| > |y_2|$

   then y_{max} must lie between PL and $P2$.

2. If $|y_1| < |y_2|$

   then y_{max} must lie between $P1$ and PR.

3. If $|y_1| = |y_2|$

   the y_{max} must lie between $P1$ and $P2$.

Therefore, for any of the three cases, part of the beam can be eliminated from the search. With the knowledge obtained from the above analysis, the region of uncertainty can be reduced, and two new experiments can be made which will lead to a further reduction. The process can be repeated until the region has been reduced to some acceptable size and no further significant improvement can be made.

In applying this procedure to our beam problem, we are defining the bounds of the region of uncertainty as PL and PR. The points within the region at which the experiments are to be made are taken as the one-third points so that for *any* region of uncertainty the X locations of these points are

$$P1 = PL + (1/3)(PR - PL)$$

and

$$P2 = PL + (2/3)(PR - PL)$$

The *original* region of uncertainty is defined as the entire beam, with $PL = 0$, and $PR = XL$, where XL is the entire beam length. After the results of the first pair of experiments have been analyzed, the bounds of the region are redefined and two more experiments are made. Each time the bounds of the region are redefined, a test must be made to determine whether the region has been reduced to the specified size. In writing this program, the acceptable size of the region of uncertainty was set at some fractional part of the beam length. The fraction used is specified by the value of the variable D, which is entered by the user of the program. The program, BEAM3, is as follows, and a flow diagram is shown in Fig. 6.7.

```
        PROGRAM BEAM3
    !
    !     THIS PROGRAM CALCULATES THE MAXIMUM DEFLECTION
```

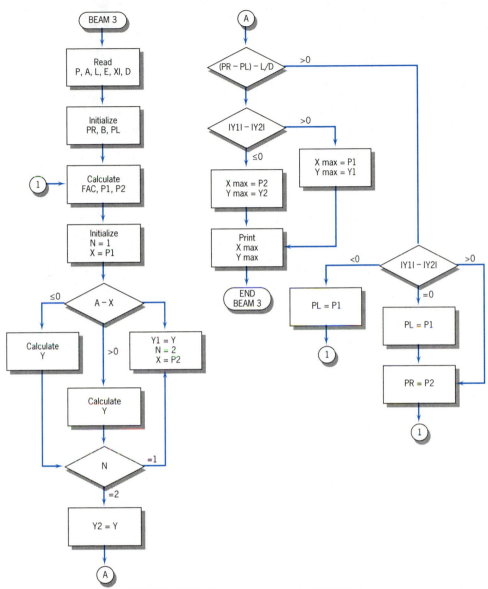

FIGURE 6.7 Flow diagram for program BEAM3.

```
!     PRODUCED BY A SINGLE CONCENTRATED LOAD ACTING ON A
!     SIMPLE BEAM.
!
      IMPLICIT NONE
      REAL:: P,A,L,E,XI,D,PR,PL,FAC,B,Y,Y1,Y2,P1,P2,X,XMAX,YMAX,TEST
      INTEGER:: N
      WRITE(*,*)' ENTER VALUE OF APPLIED LOAD, IN LB'
      READ(*,*) P
      WRITE(*,"(A,F15.2)")' APPLIED LOAD = ', P
      WRITE(*,*)'ENTER BEAM LENGTH (IN.)'
      READ(*,*) L
      WRITE(*,*)' ENTER DISTANCE TO LOAD FROM LEFT END OF BEAM'
      READ(*,*) A
```

```
          WRITE(*,400) L,A
400    FORMAT(' BEAM LENGTH & DIST TO LOAD FROM LEFT END',2F12.1)
          WRITE(*,*)' ENTER MOD.OF ELAST & SEC.MOMENT OF X-SECTION'
          READ(*,*) E, XI
          WRITE(*,"(A,2E10.2)")'MOD ELASTICITY & SEC MOMENT OF   &
             X-SEC',E,XI
          WRITE(*,*)
          WRITE(*,*)'ENTER THE DIVISOR FOR BEAM LENGTH'
          READ(*,*) D
          WRITE(*,"(A,F12.2)")' DIVISOR FOR BEAM LENGTH = ',D
          WRITE(*,"(A//)")' ******************************'
          B = L - A
          PL = 0
          PR = L
          FAC = -P/(6.0*E*XI*L)
40     P1 = (2.0*PL + PR)/3.0
          P2 = (PL + 2.0*PR)/3.0
          N = 1
          X = P1
100    IF(A - X) >= 0.0) THEN
             Y = FAC*B*X*(2.0*L*(L - X) - B**2 - (L - X)**2)
          ELSE
             Y = FAC*A*(L - X)*((2.0*L-B)*B - (L - X)**2)
          END IF
          TEST = (PR - PL) - (L/D)
          IF(N == 1) THEN
           Y1 = Y
           N = 2
           X = P2
           GO TO 100
            ELSE
             Y2 = Y
           END IF
             IF( TEST > 0.AND.ABS(Y1) - ABS(Y2) < 0) THEN
               PL = P1
               GO TO 40
             END IF
              IF ( TEST > 0 .AND.(ABS(Y1)-ABS(Y2)) == 0) THEN
               PL = P1
               PR = P2
               GO TO 40
              END IF
              IF( TEST > 0 .AND.(ABS(Y1)-ABS(Y2)) > 0) THEN
               PR = P2
               GO TO 40
              END IF
               IF (TEST <= 0.AND.ABS(Y1)-ABS(Y2) <= 0) THEN
                 YMAX = Y2
                XMAX = P2
                 GO to 90
               ELSE IF(TEST<= 0.AND.ABS(Y1) - ABS(Y2) >0) THEN
                 YMAX = Y1
                 XMAX = P1
                 END IF
90     WRITE(*,"(A,F10.4,5X,A,F15.8)")'XMAX = ',XMAX,' YMAX =', YMAX
```

```
END PROGRAM BEAM3

RUN

    APPLIED LOAD =      500.00
    BEAM LENGTH & DIST TO LOAD FROM LEFT END     154.0     65.0
    MOD ELASTICITY & SEC MOMENT OF X-SEC   0.30E+08 0.25E+01
    DIVISOR FOR BEAM LENGTH =   100000.00


*******************************


XMAX =   73.3951     YMAX =   -0.49118989
```

The run uses the same data for the beam length, load, load position, modulus of elasticity, and second moment as in Example 6.4. The parameter D was entered as 1.0E05, and as the beam length is set at 154, the fraction of the beam length used in testing is 154/100000. The run shows the maximum deflection to be −0.491189484 in. and it occurs at X = 73.3923 in. In the program of Example 6.4, the deflection for the same beam parameters was calculated at 15 points along the beam. Comparison of the results of the two programs shows that the present result is consistent with the previous results. In Example 6.4, the deflection was calculated at 15 points, two of which were

$$x = 67.375, \qquad y = -0.4870; \qquad x = 77.0, \qquad y = -0.4897$$

In the present example, the result is $x = 73.97$, y = −0.49118984.

EXAMPLE 6.12 Program **OVERSHOOT**, First Overshoot and First Undershoot of a Network

Electrical Engineering

The time response of an electrical or mechanical network to a unit step function is of interest in many areas of engineering because it is important to know how long it takes for the response to reach a steady state. After the time response over some time interval has been calculated by an appropriate method, it is relatively easy to write a program that will calculate the time response for a specified set of times. It is somewhat more difficult to write a program that locates only particular points of a function such as maxima or minima. In this example, we will consider the problem of calculating the first overshoot (maximum) and the first undershoot (minimum) of the response of a certain network. Let us assume the following response function

$$e(t) - 1.0 - [(\cos(0.975t) + 0.216 \sin(0.975t)]e^{-1.21t} \tag{6.7}$$

The program for calculating the overshoot and undershoot and a trial run are as follows.

```
        PROGRAM OVERSHOOT
!       THIS PROGRAM CALCULATES THE TIME AND AMPLITUDE OF THE
!       FIRST OVERSHOOT AND THE FIRST UNDERSHOOT OF A NETWORK
!       RESPONSE TO A STEP FUNCTION
        IMPLICIT NONE
        REAL:: E,E_OLD,T,T_OLD
        INTEGER:: I
        E_OLD = 0
```

```
            T_OLD = 0
            T = 0
            DO I = 1,2000
              E = 1.0 -(COS(0.975*T)+0.216*SIN(0.975*T))/EXP(1.21*T)
                IF((E_OLD - E) <= 0) THEN
                  E_OLD = E
                  T_OLD = T
                   ELSE
                   WRITE(*,*)'T_OLD =',T_OLD, E_OLD
                   WRITE(*,600) T_OLD, E_OLD
                   EXIT
                     END IF
              T = T + 0.005
            END DO
     !
     600    FORMAT(1X,'OVERSHOOT AT ',F8.4,' SEC., AMPLITUDE IS ',F11.7//)
              DO I = I, 2000
              T = T + 0.005
            E = 1.0 -(COS(0.975*T)+0.216*SIN(0.975*T))/EXP(1.21*T)
                IF((E - E_OLD).LE.0.0) THEN
                  E_OLD = E
                  T_OLD = T
                  ELSE
            WRITE(*,650) T_OLD, E_OLD
            EXIT
                END IF
            END DO
     650    FORMAT(1X,'UNDERSHOOT AT', F8.4,' SEC., AMPLITUDE IS =
                ',F11.7//)
            END PROGRAM OVERSHOOT
```

In this program, values of time are generated by incrementing T, the time, by 0.005 sec at each pass through each of the two DO loops. At the first pass through the DO loop, T = 0 sec. The voltage $e(t)$ is calculated at T = 0 sec, and the value is stored in E. This value of E is compared with E_OLD, which has been set at a value of zero. E exceeds E_OLD, so the current value of E is assigned to E_OLD, and the current value of T is assigned to T_OLD. Iteration continues until E_OLD exceeds E. At this point, the maximum overshoot has been reached or exceeded (see Fig. 6.8), and the program branches out of the DO loop to statement 70.

The values of T_OLD, E_OLD, T, and E are printed.

Calculation of the approximate value of the undershoot is accomplished by the second DO loop. Note that the index of the second DO loop has been set equal to the final value of the index of the first DO loop.

In this example, the time increment was 0.005. The smaller the value of the time increment, the more closely the true values of the maximum and minimum will be approached. However, the use of smaller time increments increases computation time, and, therefore, judgment must be exercised as to whether the increased time is justified. A trial run is shown below.

RUN

```
OVERSHOOT AT  2.5250 SEC., AMPLITUDE IS   1.0302442
UNDERSHOOT AT   5.7551 SEC., AMPLITUDE IS =   0.9993870
```

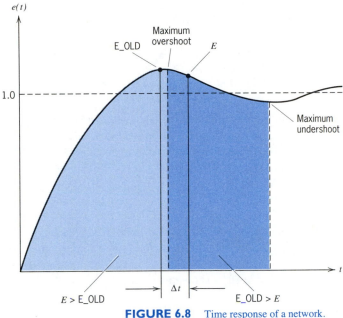

FIGURE 6.8 Time response of a network.

EXAMPLE 6.13 Program FRICTION, Effect of Friction on Velocity

Physics

If a body of constant mass is acted upon by a constant force, a constant acceleration is produced. However, if the mass is also acted upon by a friction force, the magnitude of which is a function of the velocity of the body, the velocity will tend to approach a limiting value in certain cases. One case producing such a result occurs when the functional relationship between the coefficient of friction and the velocity is given by

$$\mu = 0.1857(v)^{0.09} \tag{6.8}$$

where

μ = coefficient of kinetic friction

v = velocity of body, cm/sec

In this example, we will examine a case of sliding friction in which Eq. (6.8) describes the coefficient of the friction. A free-body diagram for the problem is shown in Fig. 6.9. The equation governing the motion is

$$F - \mu N = ma \tag{6.9}$$

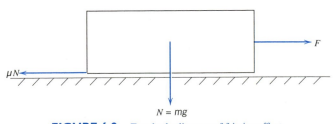

FIGURE 6.9 Free body diagram of friction effect.

and the normal force is

$$N = mg \tag{6.10}$$

If Eq. (6.9) is solved for a and then N is replaced using Eq. (6.10), the result is

$$a = \frac{F}{m} - \mu g \tag{6.11}$$

We will solve this problem by assuming that the friction effect (and therefore the acceleration) remains constant over small increments of time, and then calculating the change in velocity as the product of the constant acceleration and the magnitude of the time increment. At the *end* of each time interval, we will calculate the coefficient of friction to be used in the *next* time interval. The velocity at the end of a time interval, v_f, can be found from

$$v_{\text{final}} = v_{\text{init}} + a(\Delta t) \tag{6.12}$$

where v_i is the initial velocity and Δt is the magnitude of a time increment. The actual time at which a particular velocity occurs can be found by summing the time increments. The program for solving this problem, FRICTION, and a trial run are shown below.

The variable names are defined as shown in Table 6.2.

```
        PROGRAM FRICTION
   !
   !    CALCULATION OF THE VELOCITY OF A MASS AT TIME T
   !    RESULTING FROM A CONSTANT FORCE WITH THE EFFECT OF
   !    SLIDING FRICTION TAKEN INTO ACCOUNT.
   !
        IMPLICIT NONE
        REAL:: F,M,VELOCITY,T_INC,T,G,MU,A
        INTEGER:: K,N,LINES
        WRITE(*,*)'ENTER THE APPLIED FORCE (DYNES)'
        READ(*,*)F
        WRITE(*,*)'THE APPLIED FORCE = ',F
        WRITE(*,*)'ENTER THE MASS (grams)'
        READ(*,*)M
        WRITE(*,*)'THE MASS = ', M
        WRITE(*,*)'ENTER THE INITIAL VELOCITY (CM/SEC)'
        READ(*,*)VELOCITY
```

Table 6.2

Symbol	Name	Meaning	Units
F	F	Applied force	dynes
m	M	Mass of the body	g
v	V	Velocity	cm/sec
Δt	TINC	Time increment	sec
...	N	Number of printed lines of results	
g	G	Gravitational acceleration	cm/s^2
...	KPRINT	Counter controlling printing	
	K	DO loop index	
	T	Current time	sec
μ	MU	Coefficient of kinetic friction	
a	A	Acceleration of body	cm/s^2

```
       WRITE(*,"(/A,F10.1//)")' INITIAL VELOCITY (CM/SEC) = ',    &
          VELOCITY
       WRITE(*,*)'ENTER NUMBER OF LINES OF RESULTS TO BE PRINTED'
       READ(*,*)N
       LINES = 1; T_INC = 0.125; G = 980.0
       DO K = 1, 50000
        T = K*T_INC
          IF(VELOCITY == 0) THEN
            MU = 0.1758
            ELSE
            MU = 0.1758*VELOCITY**0.09
           END IF
          A = F/M - MU*G
          VELOCITY = VELOCITY + A*T_INC
          IF((LINES - K) <= 0) THEN
             WRITE(*,"(F14.4,F14.4)") T,VELOCITY
          LINES = 2*LINES
             ELSE IF((LINES - 2**(N-1)) > 0) THEN
             EXIT
            END IF
       END DO
       WRITE(*,"(///A,I16)") 'VALUE OF K AFTER EXIT FROM DO = ',K
       END PROGRAM FRICTION
```

RUN

```
    THE APPLIED FORCE =    2.9400000E+03
    THE MASS =  10.0000000

    INITIAL VELOCITY (CM/SEC) =       0.0


 NUMBER OF LINES TO BE PRINTED =   15

        0.1250      15.2145
        0.2500      24.4502
        0.5000      39.7775
        1.0000      64.4986
        2.0000     102.5358
        4.0000     156.9712
        8.0000     226.4939
       16.0000     299.9421
       32.0000     355.1125
       64.0000     376.7454
      128.0000     379.2130
      256.0000     379.2394
      512.0000     379.2394
     1024.0000     379.2394
     2048.0000     379.2394

   VALUE OF K AFTER EXIT FROM DO =      16385
```

The program used a DO construct to produce iteration. To permit the user to control the duration of the calculation, the loop is terminated when K exceeds $2^{(N-1)} + 1$. In the trial run, N was given a value of 15. The run shows that exit from the DO loop occurred when

K had a value of 16,385, which equals $2^{(N-1)} + 1$. The index of the DO was given a maximum value of 50,000, which provided a more than adequate number of iterations to produce the desired number of printed results.

Because the velocity changes rapidly during the early stages of the motion and changes slowly during the later stages, the results were printed at geometrically increasing intervals. The first result was printed after one time increment, the second after two more time increments, the third after four more additional time increments, and so on. The results show that after about 256 seconds, the velocity does not change.

6.4 THE CASE CONSTRUCT

We have seen that the IF construct when used with the ELSE and ELSE IF statements provides a method of selecting among several options. FORTRAN 90 provides an additional method of selection among options. This method is the CASE construct. The form of this construct is

```
SELECT CASE(expression)
 CASE(selector)
 selection
 CASE(selector)
 selection
        .
        .
END SELECT
```

Expression is called the CASE *index*. The *value* of expression must be of the type integer, character, or logical.

Selector may be either a single value or a range. A range is indicated by a colon(:). The colon form may be used in the construct only for the type integer and the type character. It may not be used for the type logical.

Thus, assuming that TIME_STEP is equal to 20, the message 'SIGNAL IS ZERO', shown below, will be printed:

```
TIME_STEP = 20
SELECT CASE(TIME_STEP)
    CASE(12:20)
    WRITE(*,*)'SIGNAL IS ZERO'
        .
        .
END SELECT
```

In fact, any value of TIME_STEP from 12 to 20 will cause SIGNAL IS ZERO to be printed. Then, the CASE construct is terminated, and the next executable statement after END SELECT is executed.

6.5 MODULES, PART I

The module is a program unit that contains information relevant to other program units such as the main program. For example, the module may contain DIMENSION statements, type declarations, and PARAMETER statements. Other program units gain access to this information by containing the statement USE *module name*. We will use the module and the CASE construct in program BUTTERA, Example 6.14 below. Additional examples of the module that illustrate its versatility are discussed in Sec. 7.8.

EXAMPLE 6.14 Program BUTTERA, An Introduction to Butterworth Filter Design

Electrical Engineering

Electric filters are very important in many branches of electrical engineering. Analog and digital filters are two broad categories of filter. We will briefly discuss *analog* filters and show a use of nested DO loops in demonstrating the performance of filters. An electric filter is a device to the input of which is applied the output of a source of voltage such as an amplifier in a music system or the voltage obtained by connecting electrodes to the scalp of a human. We will call the voltages from these, and similar sources, *signals*. The filter attenuates signals. That is, the amplitude of the signals is reduced. However, the attenuation is selective: signals of certain frequencies are transmitted by the filter with little or no attenuation, and signals of other frequencies are attenuated significantly. The word *analog,* when describing signals as well as filters, signifies "continuous with respect to time." The voltage from a household electrical outlet is an analog voltage. An analog filter is a filter that processes analog signals. An *analog filter* is one that accepts signals that are continuous functions of time.

One way of classifying filters is by the frequency range of those signals that are transmitted with little attenuation and the frequency range of those that are attenuated. A *low-pass* filter is one that transmits signals from zero frequency to a frequency of ω_c radians per second with little attenuation and signals of higher frequency with "appreciable attenuation." How much attenuation is considered to be appreciable depends on the specifications required by the application. In general, the greater the attenuation required, the more components are required to construct the filter. The frequency range from 0 to ω_c is called the *passband,* and the frequency band beyond ω_c is called the *stopband.* The term *stopband* signifies only that it is the frequency range wherein signals are attenuated appreciably; they are not literally stopped. The frequency ω_c is called the *cutoff* frequency. Let us denote the signal that is applied to the input of a filter V_i and the signal that appears at the output V_o. The function $H(\omega) = V_o/V_i$ is called the *transfer function:* $H(\omega)$ is a complex quantity; however, here we are concerned only with its magnitude,

$$H(\omega) = \frac{V_0}{V_i} \tag{6.13}$$

namely, $|H(\omega)|$, a real number. If $|H(\omega)| = 1$, then $V_o = V_i$, and there is no attenuation.

There are many design methods for filters; one of these is called *Butterworth* (after its inventor). If the transfer function has a cutoff frequency of 1 radian per second, it is said to be *normalized*. For a Butterworth filter, the magnitude of its *normalized* transfer function is and as it normalized, the cutoff frequency, ω_c, is 1 radian per second. If necessary, the

$$|H(\omega)| = \frac{1}{\sqrt{1+\omega^{2n}}} \tag{6.14}$$

transfer function can be *denormalized* so that the cutoff frequency is higher.

The integer variable n in Eq. (6.14) is called the *order* of the filter. For the Butterworth type of filter, the magnitude of the transfer function has a value of 0.707 at

ω_c. At frequencies higher than ω_c, the magnitude of the transfer function declines; thus, the filter is attenuating these frequencies. The larger the value of n, the greater the *rate* of decline of the magnitude, that is, the greater the rate of attenuation.

Program BUTTERA, shown below, calculates the magnitude of the transfer function for Butterworth filters of order 4, 6, and 8 over the frequency range

$$0 \le \omega \le 2.0$$

Note that a module, BUTFILTER, precedes the main program. The main program accesses the data of the module by means of the statement USE BUTFILTER. The CASE construct is used to choose the appropriate variable H4, H6, or H8 as n assumes the value 4, 6, or 8, respectively.

```
      MODULE BUTFILTER
      REAL,DIMENSION(50)::H4,H6,H8
      REAL::W,HMAG
      INTEGER::N,K,KK
      END MODULE BUTFILTER
!
      PROGRAM BUTTERA
      USE BUTFILTER
      DO N = 4,8,2
      W = 0
      DO K = 1,21
        HMAG = 1.0/SQRT(1.0 + W**(2*N))
        W = W + 0.1
      SELECT CASE(N)
          CASE(4)
            H4(K) = HMAG
          CASE(6)
            H6(K) = HMAG
          CASE(8)
            H8(K) = HMAG
      END SELECT
      END DO
      END DO
      WRITE(*,"(2X,3(A,7X),A)")'W','4th ORDER','6th ORDER','8th    &
          ORDER'
      W = 0
      DO KK = 1,21
      WRITE(*,"(F4.2,3F15.4)")W, H4(KK),H6(KK),H8(KK)
      W = W + 0.1
      END DO
      END PROGRAM BUTTERA
```

A trial run is shown below.

W	4th ORDER	6th ORDER	8th ORDER
0.00	1.0000	1.0000	1.0000
0.10	1.0000	1.0000	1.0000
0.20	0.9999	1.0000	1.0000
0.30	0.9999	1.0000	1.0000
0.40	0.9996	0.9999	1.0000
0.50	0.9980	0.9998	0.9999

0.60	0.9917	0.9989	0.9998
0.70	0.9723	0.9931	0.9983
0.80	0.9253	0.9673	0.9862
0.90	0.8361	0.8830	0.9185
1.00	0.7071	0.7071	0.7071
1.10	0.5640	0.4915	0.4227
1.20	0.4343	0.3175	0.2265
1.30	0.3304	0.2028	0.1216
1.40	0.2519	0.1316	0.0676
1.50	0.1937	0.0874	0.0389
1.60	0.1508	0.0594	0.0232
1.70	0.1188	0.0413	0.0143
1.80	0.0948	0.0293	0.0090
1.90	0.0765	0.0212	0.0058
2.00	0.0623	0.0156	0.0039

The results show the following:

1. For all three filter transfer functions, the response is 0.707 at $\omega = 1.0$; that is, they have the same passband.

2. The attenuation in the stopband is greater for larger values of n. For example, at $\omega = 2.0$,

The response of the fourth-order filter is 0.0623.

The response of the sixth-order filter is 0.0156.

The response of the eighth-order filter is 0.0039.

Thus, the higher the order of the filter, the greater the attenuation at any given frequency. Figure 6.10 is a graph which shows the magnitude frequency response of low-pass Butterworth filters of orders 4, 6, and 8.

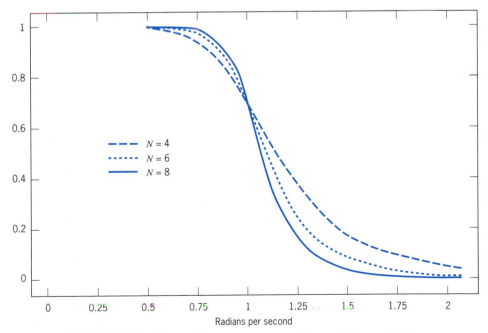

FIGURE 6.10   Magnitude frequency response of low-pass Butterworth filters.

For example, if a signal of 1 volt amplitude and frequency 2.0 radians per second were applied to the input of an eighth-order filter, at the output there would be a signal of amplitude 0.0039 and frequency of 2.0 radians per second. For the fourth-order filter, if a signal of 1 volt amplitude and frequency of 2.0 radians per second were applied, the output would be 0.0624 volt. Thus, the signal of 2.0 radians per second has been significantly attenuated by both filters, but more so by the eighth-order filter.

PROBLEMS

6.1   The transfer function of a network is defined as the ratio of the output voltage to the input voltage. A normalized transfer function is one in which the radian frequency or frequency in Hz is divided by some particular frequency. As a result, the frequency range involves smaller numbers. These numbers are dimensionless.

   The square of the magnitude of the normalized transfer function of a certain network is

$$|F(x)|^2 = \frac{1 + 0.144x^2 + 0.0386x^4}{1 + 0.144x^2 + 0.0386x^4 + 0.0386x^6}$$

The three-decibel frequency x is of importance in network design. At this frequency, the magnitude of the transfer function is equal to 0.707, and the square of the magnitude of the transfer function is equal to fi. We set the function above equal to fi, cross-multiply, collect terms, and set the result equal to zero. We obtain:

$$x^6 - x^4 - 3.73x^2 - 25.9 = 0$$

   (a)   Write a program to compute the value of x. This is essentially a problem in finding a positive root. Because the value of x is known to be between 1.8 and 2.0, it can be found by the methods of this chapter.

   (b)   Write a program to find the root of the equation above by writing a DO loop in which x varies from 1.8 to 2.0 in steps of 0.0001. The current value of the polynomial varies with x; the polynomial is assigned to the variable THREEDB. Let an EXIT occur from the loop when the absolute value of THREEDB is equal to or less than 0.01. This procedure will provide a satisfactory solution for x.

6.2   There are two broad classifications of electric filters: analog and digital. The input to analog filters is an analog voltage, that is, a voltage that is continuously variable. The input to digital filters is a sampled or discrete voltage. This voltage is defined by samples that occur at uniformly spaced time intervals 1T, 2T, 3T. . . . The duration of these samples is very short, so that the samples are simply a sequence of numbers. The sequence of numbers is the input to the digital filter. The filter operates on this sequence and produces another sequence at its output.

   (a)   The transfer function of a high-pass digital filter is given below. A high-pass filter attenuates frequencies from 0 to some specified frequency v_c. Beyond v_c, frequencies are virtually unattenuated.

$$H = \frac{0.067455(1 - 2e^{-j\pi v} + e^{-j2\pi v})}{1 + 1.14298e^{-j\pi v} \quad 0.412802e^{-j2\pi v}}$$

(b) Write a program that calculates the value of the transfer function in decibels as nu varies. Set the DO loop so that nu can vary from 0.001 to 1.051 in steps of 0.050. An EXIT should occur when the decibel value of the transfer function is equal to or greater than 0. To obtain the transfer function in decibels, the program must calculate 20 $\log_{10}$ (magnitude of the transfer function). Note that the quantity $e^{-j(\pi v)}$ is defined by the intrinsic function CEXP(a, b) where in this case $a = 0$. When you examine the output of the program, you will find that the three-decibel frequency occurs at about $v = 0.8$.

6.3 A twin T network has the property that it will eliminate a signal the frequency of which is f_0. That is, if signals of varying frequency are applied to its input, the output at frequency f_0 is almost zero volts (ideally zero). The transfer function of the twin T network is

$$\frac{V_{out}}{V_{input}} = \frac{1}{1 - \left[j2\left(\sqrt{n} + 1/\sqrt{n}\right)\right] / \left(R - R^{-1}\right)}$$

where

$R = f/f_0$

n = an integer parameter equal to the ratio of two of the components of the network

Write a program that calculates the *magnitude* of V_{out}/V_{input} as R varies from 0.4 to 0.95 for $n = 1, 3$, and 5. We are limiting R to a maximum of 0.95 to avoid the possibility of overflow.

6.4 A manufacturer purchases resistors in lots of 100,000. A lot is rejected (or accepted) based on the following procedure. A sample of 100 resistors is drawn at random. If any are defective, the whole lot is rejected. The probability of 0.95 of acceptance is stated as

$$P(accept) = 0.95$$

Therefore, we want to find q given the relation below:

$$0.95 = (1.0 - q)^{100}$$

The variable q is the probability that a resistor is defective.

Write a program to calculate the value of q. Use a DO loop that increases q from 0 in steps of 0.000001. Note that when $q = 0$, the right side of the relation is equal to 1, so that 0.95 $(1.0 - q)^{100}$ is negative. Therefore, we wish to test for the condition that 0.95 >= $(1.0 - q)^{100}$. The program should print the value of q and the number of iterations required to obtain the solution.

6.5 We are familiar with the calculation of the average; the average is also called the mean. A less familiar calculation is the harmonic mean, which is defined as

$$x_h = \frac{n}{\sum\limits_{i}^{n} \frac{1}{x_i}}$$

You may wonder whether there is any application for this calculation. The following example may be helpful. Imagine that a pilot flies an airplane around a square, each side of which is 100 miles long. The pilot varies his speed so that it is

100 mph for the first side, 200 mph for the second side, 300 mph for the third side, and 400 mph for the fourth side. What is the average speed for the flight? Let us calculate the arithmetic average of the four speeds.

$$\text{Average} = (100 + 200 + 300 + 400)/4 = 1000/4 = 250 \text{ mph}$$

We can check this result by calculating the total time of flight.

$$
\begin{aligned}
\text{Time to travel along the first side} \quad &= 100/100 = 1 \text{ hour} \\
\text{Time to travel along the second side} &= 100/200 = 1/2 \text{ hour} \\
\text{Time to travel along the third side} \quad &= 100/300 = 1/3 \text{ hour} \\
\text{Time to travel along the fourth side} \; &= 100/400 = 1/4 \text{ hour} \\
\text{Total} &= 25/12 \text{ hours}
\end{aligned}
$$

Based on the total time used to complete the flight, the average speed is given by distance traveled divided by elapsed time

$$= 400 \text{ miles divided by } 25/12 \text{ hours} = 192 \text{ mph}$$

There is a discrepancy between the two calculations because the speeds were not maintained for the same length of time. The correct answer is given by the harmonic mean:

$$\text{Harmonic mean} = \frac{4}{(1/100 + 1/200 + 1/300 + 1/400)}$$

$$= \frac{4 \times 1200}{25} = 192 \text{ mph}$$

Now that you are convinced of the utility of the harmonic mean, write a program to calculate the harmonic mean of the first n integers to result in a value as close as possible to 2.699.

The program should print the value of n and the calculated value of the mean.

6.6 The catalyzed reaction of ethylene and water vapor forms ethyl alcohol. This reaction has the following equilibrium expression:

$$\frac{n_a(1.6 - n_a)}{(1 - n_a)(0.6 - n_a)} = 0.156$$

where n_a = number of moles of alcohol.

Write a program that calculates and prints the value of n_a. In addition, the number of iterations should be printed.

6.7 The Bessel's function of the first kind and order zero can be closely approximated by

$$J_0(x) = 1 - 2.24999X3^2 + 1.26562X3^4 - 0.31638X3^6 + 0.04444X3^8$$
$$- 0.00394X3^{10} + 0.00021X3^{12}$$

where

$x = $ the argument

and

$X3 = x/3$

Write a program that calculates $J_0(x)$ as x varies from $x = -3$ through $x = 4$ in steps of 1. Use a format such that the answers appear in the form

$$J_0(x) = \text{value}$$

where x is printed to the specification F4.0 and value to the specification F14.8.

6.8 The Manning equation is used to analyze fluid flow through a channel. For a certain channel, after substitution of the appropriate values for the variables, the following equation is obtained.

$$[Y(10 + Y)]^{2.5} - 1750Y = 7800$$

where

$$Y = \text{the depth, in ft, of the fluid}$$

Write a program that calculates Y, the depth of the fluid. Let the program begin with an estimate of $Y = 2.0$ ft and increment Y in steps of 0.001. Note that as a result of this estimate, the quantity $(Y(10 + Y))^{2.5}$ is less than the quantity $1750Y$. Take this fact into account when testing for a halt to the iteration. Let ALPHA = $[Y(10 + Y)]^{2.5} - 1750Y$. The program should print the value of Y which has been calculated, and should also print the value of ALPHA to see how close the answer is to the exact value.

6.9 A body starts from the origin at $t = 0$ sec and moves to the right along the x axis. Its position at time t is given by the equation

$$x = 12t^2 - (1/6)t^3 - (1/2)t^4 + 4t$$

where x is in feet.

Write a program that will determine the time t at which x is equal to or greater than 70 ft. In your program set the initial value of t at $t = 0$ and increment t in steps of 0.1 sec.

6.10 In Example 5.1, we discussed program SQUARE_ROOT. In that example, the square root of 17 was calculated. In the program, Y(K) was computed, and the results showed that Y(5) through Y(8) had the same value, namely, 4.1231055. Obviously, the calculation could have been terminated before K reached a value of 8. Revise the program by placing a test in the loop:

```
IF(ABS(OLD - Y(K)) <= 0.001) THEN
EXIT
```

The value of OLD should be set before the DO loop by OLD = Y(-1). If the test is not satisfied, then OLD = Y(K) and looping continues. Use the program to calculate the square root of 21.0.

7

Amplifying the Power of a Program by Use of Subprograms

In this chapter, we discuss programming tools called statement functions, function subprograms, and subroutine subprograms. Function subprograms and subroutine subprograms are separate programs that are added to main programs, whereas statement functions reside within the main program. These tools are very valuable for several reasons. One reason becomes apparent when a calculation must be repeated in a program. For example, in Chapter 5 we computed a probability using the hypergeometric distribution. This computation involved calculating nine factorials and required nine DO loops. If we had written a function subprogram and specified it nine times *within the formula* for the probability calculation, we would have eliminated the need to write the nine factorial calculations. That is, the program would have "called" the function subprogram nine times, and each call would have required a statement of the form FACT(K). This would have shortened the program and made it easier to write, understand, and debug.

Subroutine subprograms are more flexible than function subprograms in that they can "return" more than one value to a main program. It will be apparent that the use of subroutines can greatly enhance the utility of a program. For example, a program that designs one type of electrical filter can be expanded to design other types by adding one or more subroutines as required. Thus, subroutines extend the versatility of a program. Moreover, because they are distinct modules, they make it easier to understand the program. In addition to function subprograms and subroutine subprograms, in this chapter we discuss library functions and statement functions. We begin by examining statement functions.

7.1 FORTRAN INTRINSIC FUNCTIONS AND STATEMENT FUNCTIONS

Fortran provides more than one hundred compiler-supplied functions; these are called *intrinsic* or *library* functions. We have already encountered several of these functions in Chapter 5. In Example 5.3 involving Planck's Law, we used the function exp(arg), where exp is the exponential function. In Example 5.15, Time of Flight of an Electron, we used sin(θ). (Some intrinsic functions are listed at the end of this chapter.) Although FORTRAN has a plentiful supply of intrinsic functions, sometimes we must create our own. These are called *statement functions*.

The form of a statement function is

$$\text{name } (\mu_1, \mu_2, \ldots, \mu_n) = \text{expression}$$

where the programmer assigns the name and $\mu_1, \mu_2, \ldots \mu_n$ are dummy arguments used in defining the arithmetic expression. When the function is used, the actual arguments are supplied in place of the dummy arguments. The name must not be the same as a library function. The actual arguments may be expressions, variables, subscripted variables, or intrinsic functions.

Statement functions must appear in a program *after* all declaration statements but *before* all executable statements. (See Fig. 7.1.)

Consider the following program segment containing the statement function ARSCH:

```
REAL :: X,ARSCH,Z,T
ARSCH(X) = ALOG(ABS(X) + SQRT(ABS(X)**2 + 1.0))
Z = 9.0
T = ARSCH(Z)
```

In this case, the statement function uses the intrinsic functions ALOG, ABS, and SQRT. The dummy argument X is replaced by Z when the function is referenced. The statement function shown above calculates the inverse of the sinh function for a *positive* argument. If we needed the inverse for both positive and negative arguments, we would need to use a function subprogram because it provides more programming flexibility.

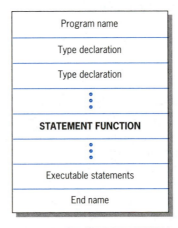

FIGURE 7.1 Position of the STATEMENT FUNCTION in a FORTRAN 90 program.

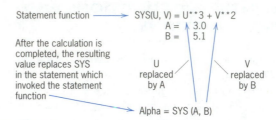

FIGURE 7.2   How the STATEMENT FUNCTION operates.

As a second example, consider the program segment containing the function SYS (Fig. 7.2):

```
REAL :: U,V,SYS,A,B
SYS(U,V) = U**3 + V**2
PI = 3.14159
A = 3.0
B = 5.1
ALPHA = PI*SYS(A,B)
```

Here, ALPHA is assigned the value of PI*(A**3 + B**2).

7.2 THE RETURN STATEMENT

The RETURN statement is an executable statement that terminates a subprogram and returns control to the calling program. It is not usually needed because END produces the same result. However, it may be used anywhere in the procedure to provide an alternative point of return. A subprogram must be concluded by an END statement.

7.3 THE FUNCTION SUBPROGRAM

The FUNCTION subprogram is a statement of form

$$\text{FUNCTION name } (\mu_1, \mu_2, \ldots, \mu_n)$$

Name is assigned to the function by the programmer and must not be the same as that of any intrinsic function or variable used in the program. Name must appear at least once in the subprogram on the left side of an assignment statement. The mode of the value to be returned by the function is implicitly assigned, or it can be explicitly declared by the defining statement. For example, the statement

```
REAL FUNCTION DECIMAL(HN,N)
```

explicitly declares the mode of DECIMAL to be real.

7.3.1 The Gamma Function (*Mathematics*)

The gamma function, which is a generalization of the factorial, permits calculation of the factorial of numbers that are not integers. It also includes negative numbers.

Program GAMMA1, shown here, calculates the gamma function of *positive* numbers.

```
      PROGRAM GAMMA1
!     THIS PROGRAM COMPUTES GAMMA(x). ENTER ARGUMENTS EQUAL
!     TO OR GREATER THAN 1.0. ARGUMENTS ARE STORED IN T, AND
!     X = T -1.
      CHARACTER*3 ACTION
      WRITE(*,*)'TYPE BYE TO EXIT OR ELSE TYPE YES TO CONTINUE'
      READ(*,50) ACTION
50    FORMAT(A3)
      IF(ACTION == 'BYE') THEN
         EXIT
      ELSE
      WRITE(*,*)'ENTER THE ARGUMENT OF THE GAMMA FUNCTION'
      END IF
      READ(*,*)T
      TT = T
!
      ANS = GAMMA(T)
      WRITE(*,"(A,F5.2,A,F12.4/)")'GAMMA(',TT,')',ANS
      END DO
      END PROGRAM GAMMA1
      FUNCTION GAMMA(T)
      DIMENSION A(5)
      DATA A/-0.5748646,0.9512363,-0.6998588,0.4245549,-0.1010678/
!     NEXT STATEMENT IS ARITHMETIC STATEMENT FUNCTION WHICH
!     COMPUTES GAMMA(x) TO ACCURACY OF BETTER THAN 0.2%.
      G(X) = 1.0+ X*(A(1) + A(2)*X + A(3)*X**2 + A(4)*X**3 + &
A(5)*X**4)
!
      GAMMA = 1.0
      IF(T == 1.0.OR. T ==2.) EXIT
      IF(T > 1.0.AND.T <2.0) THEN
          XX = T -1.0
          GAMMA = GAMMA*G(XX)
          EXIT
            ELSE IF(T > = 2.0) THEN
            GAMMA = 1.0
            END IF
          DO J = 1,10
           T = T - 1.10
           GAMMA = GAMMA*T
           IF(T <= 2.0) EXIT
          END DO
!
      IF(T <= 1.0.AND.T>>=0) THEN
      GAMMA = GAMMA*G(T)
```

```
ELSE
    T = T - 1.0
    GAMMA = GAMMA*G(T)
END IF
END
```

This program contains function subprogram GAMMA, which calculates the GAMMA function for positive arguments T, where T ≥ 1. The function subprogram contains the statement function $G(x)$, which consists of a power series that calculates

$$\Gamma(x + 1) = x! \qquad 0 \leq x \leq 1$$

to better than 0.05 percent accuracy.

We want the program to be capable of calculating the gamma function for positive arguments equal to or greater than one. (See Fig. 7.3.) To achieve this capability, a variable T is introduced, where $T = x + 1.0$. If the user enters a value of T that lies within the limits $1 \leq T \leq 2$, then the program calculates $x = T - 1.0$, and the gammma function is given by GAMMA = GAMMA*G(x) = 1.0*G(x) where G(x) is the statement function referred to above. If T exceeds 2.0, the recursion formula $\Gamma(n + 1) = n\Gamma(n)$ is used repeatedly, together with $T = T - 1.0$, to reduce T to less than 2.0; then, as before, the statement function G(x) is used. These operations are carried out by the loop DO J. For example, suppose that a value of 3.6 is entered for T. The sequence of calculations is

```
T = T - 1.0 = 2.6
GAMMA = GAMMA*T = GAMMA*2.6
T = T - 1.0 = 1.6
GAMMA = (1.6)*(2.6)*GAMMA
```

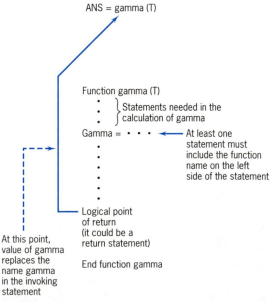

FIGURE 7.3   Operation of the FUNCTION SUBPROGRAM.

Because *T* is now less than 2.0, the statement

```
IF(T<2.0) EXIT
```

is executed, and then:

```
X = T - 1.0 = 0.6
GAMMA = (1.6)*(2.6)*G(0.6) = 3.717
```

This example, and several others, are shown in the trial runs that follow.

```
RUN

GAMMA( 1.00)      1.0000

GAMMA( 5.00)      24.0000

GAMMA( 6.00)     120.0000

GAMMA( 1.50)       0.8862

GAMMA( 1.60)       0.8935

GAMMA( 3.60)       3.7170

    *    *    *    *    *
```

7.4 THE SUBROUTINE SUBPROGRAM

The SUBROUTINE statement is a nonexecutable statement of the form

$$\text{SUBROUTINE name}(v_1, v_2, v_3, \ldots v_m)$$

where name is the name of the subroutine and $v_1, v_2, \ldots v_m$ are the names of the dummy arguments used in defining the subroutine. The arguments can be: nonsubscripted variables; names of arrays; and names of other functions.

A subroutine program does not necessarily have a list of arguments because values of the arguments may be transmitted by means of the COMMON statement (discussed in Sec. 7.7).

7.4.1 The INTENT Statement

It is often useful to indicate the intended use of the *dummy* arguments that appear in a subroutine or function statement. This is done by use of an attribute called *intent*. Intent may be IN, OUT, or INOUT. If a dummy argument is INTENT(IN), it may not be changed within the procedure. If intent is OUT, the argument must be given a value by the procedure. If it is INOUT, the dummy argument receives a value and returns a value to the main program.

This chapter presents several examples of INTENT. For example, see SORTING in Sec. 7.9.2 and MATRIXPOWER in Sec. 7.10.1.

7.4.2 The RESULT Clause

As previously noted, a function subprogram must provide a value that is returned to the program which references it, and the name assigned to the function must appear at least once in the subprogram on the *left side* of an assignment statement. For example:

```
FUNCTION FEX(X)
REAL:: X
FEX = SQRT(X**2*EXP(X))
RETURN
END FUNCTION FEX
```

The main program might call this function

```
ANSWER = 2.0*FEX(Q)
```

Suppose that we do not wish to use the name FEX to obtain the result of this function. To achieve this objective, the *RESULT* clause is used. Its form is RESULT(*name*) where *name* differs from the name of the function. Thus, in this example, the revised function might be

```
FUNCTION FEX(X)   RESULT(FEXPO)
REAL::X, FEXPO
FEXPO = SQRT(X**2*EXP(X))
RETURN
END FUNCTION FEX
```

Upon return to the main program from the function, the value of the function FEX is the last value given to FEXPO. In this example, use of the RESULT clause is optional.

We now consider a situation called *recursion*—an operation in which a subprogram calls itself. This operation is valid only if the subprogram is designated recursive. For example,

```
RECURSIVE FUNCTION FACTORIAL(N)
```

In a recursive subprogram, the RESULT clause is essential to distinguish the use of the function name from the function result. For example,

```
RECURSIVE FUNCTION FACTORIAL(N) RESULT(ALPHA)
INTEGER:: ALPHA, N
IF(N==1) THEN
     ALPHA = 1
ELSE
     ALPHA = N*FACTORIAL(N-1)
END IF
END FUNCTION FACTORIAL
```

Recursion is again illustrated later in this chapter in Sec. 7.4.7. For the present, we are concerned only with the RESULT clause.

The program CONVERT2 below illustrates use of the RESULT clause. In this program, it is not essential to use it. This program converts positive integer numbers from hexadecimal to decimal. Before discussing the program further, however, we should review some facts about number systems, and we begin with the decimal system.

7.4.3 Conversion of Octal and Hexadecimal Numbers to Decimal

The decimal number 5369 can be expressed as

$$5(10^3) + 3(10^2) + 6(10^1) + 9(10^0) = 5000 + 300 + 60 + 9 = 5369$$

We see that the number 5369 is expressed by multiplying each of its digits by an appropriate power of 10. The number 10 is the *base* of the decimal system; the quantities within parentheses are called weights, and for the decimal number system, the weight is a power of 10. The rightmost weight is 10 to the zero power; moving from right to left, the power increases in steps of 1. The available digits in the decimal system are 0, 1, 2, 3, 4, 5, 6, 7, 8, 9.

Next, we turn to the octal system in which the base is 8. We will use the subscript 8 to remind ourselves that a given number is octal. The octal number 26741_8 can be expressed as

$$26741_8 = 2(8^4) + 6(8^3) + 7(8^2) + 4(8^1) + 1(8^0) = 8192 + 3072 + 448 + 32 + 1 = 11745$$

In the octal system, the weights consist of powers of 8; the available digits are 0, 1, 2, 3, 4, 5, 6, 7.

Finally, let us give an example of the conversion of a hexadecimal number. In the hexadecimal number system, the base is 16 and the digits are 0, 1, 2, 3, 4, 5, 6, 7, 8, 9, *A, B, C, D, E, F*. The letters *A,B,C,D,E,* and *F* denote 10, 11, 12, 13, 14, and 15, respectively. As an example of converting a hexadecimal number to decimal, we convert F8E6:

$$F8E6 = 15(16^3) + 8(16^2) + E(16^1) + 6(16^0) = 63718$$

We are now prepared to discuss program CONVERT2.

7.4.4 Program **CONVERT2** (*Computer Science*)

Program CONVERT2, shown below, uses the RESULT clause in FUNCTION HEXTO. The RESULT clause is RESULT(HEXTODEC). In the subprogram, HEXTODEC appears on the left side of an assignment statement.

```
        PROGRAM CONVERT2
!       CONVERTING HEXADECIMAL NUMBER TO DECIMAL NUMBER
        IMPLICIT NONE
        INTEGER:: N,I
        REAL:: DEC,HEXTO
        CHARACTER HN(8), ACTION*3
        DO
        WRITE(*,*)'TYPE BYE TO EXIT'
        WRITE(*,*)'TYPE HEX for HEX TO DECIMAL CONVERSION'
        READ(*,"(A)") ACTION
        IF(ACTION=='HEX') THEN
        WRITE(*,*)'ENTER N,THE NUMBER OF DIGITS IN THE HEXADEC. NO.'
        READ(*,*)N
        WRITE(*,*)'TYPE THE HEXADECIMAL NUMBER'
        READ(*,"(8A1)") (HN(I),I = 1,N)
        WRITE(*,"(8A1)") (HN(I),I = 1,N)
        DEC = HEXTO(HN, N)
```

```
      WRITE(*,*)'THE DECIMAL EQUIVALENT IS:'
      WRITE(*,*) INT(DEC)
      WRITE(*,"(A/A)")' * * *'
      ELSE
          EXIT
      ENDIF
      END DO
      END PROGRAM CONVERT2
!     NOTE USE OF RESULT CLAUSE
      FUNCTION HEXTO(HN,N)    RESULT(HEXTODEC)
      INTEGER:: VAL(0:15), EXP(8)
      REAL::HEXTODEC
      CHARACTER:: X(0:15),HN(8)
      DATA X/'0','1','2','3','4','5','6','7','8','9',&
    'A','B','C','D','E','F'/
!
      HEXTODEC = 0
      DO J = 1,N
       DO I = 0,15
         IF(HN(J)==X(I)) THEN
              VAL(J) = I
              EXP(J) = N - J
         ENDIF
      END DO
       END DO
      DO J = 1,N
       HEXTODEC = HEXTODEC + VAL(J)*16**EXP(J)
      END DO
      END FUNCTION HEXTO
```

RUN

```
TYPE THE HEXADECIMAL NUMBER
B7
THE DECIMAL EQUIVALENT IS:
183
   * * *
   * * *
 TYPE THE HEXADECIMAL NUMBER
 F8E6
 THE DECIMAL EQUIVALENT IS:
 63718
   * * *
   * * *
TYPE THE HEXADECIMAL NUMBER
A3CDF
THE DECIMAL EQUIVALENT IS:
670943
```

7.4.5 Fibonacci Numbers

The Italian mathematician Leonardo Fibonacci (c.1170–c.1250) discovered a sequence of numbers. Now called the Fibonacci sequence, it is defined by

$$F(1) = 1; \qquad F(2) = 1$$
$$F(n) = F(n-1) + F(n-2) \qquad n > 2$$

One application of this sequence is in modeling the growth of rabbit populations. Characteristically, the ratio of two sequential Fibonacci numbers approaches a specific number as the number of terms becomes sufficiently large. This ratio is called the *golden mean*. Roman architecture followed the belief that the ratio of length to the width of a building was most pleasing aesthetically if it was about 1.618. This value is very close to the golden mean.

7.4.6 Program FIBONACCI (*Mathematics*)

In Program FIBONACCI shown below, function FIB calculates as many terms of the sequence as are requested by the main program. In this case, the number is 13. This number is determined by the index, MAX, of the loop DO K in the main program. The initial value of the loop is 3, so that the first two terms of the sequence, each of which is equal to 1, are not included in the count. The ratio of successive terms is also calculated and printed.

```
         PROGRAM FIBONACCI
   !
         IMPLICIT NONE
         INTEGER::K, MAX, ANSWER, FIB
         REAL:: RATIO
         MAX = 15
         WRITE(*,"(4X,A/)")'FIBONACCI SEQUENCE, FROM TERM 3'
         WRITE(*,"(12X,A,8X,A/)")'SERIES','RATIO'
         RATIO = 2.0
         DO K = 3, MAX
           ANSWER = FIB(K)
              RATIO = REAL(FIB(K))/REAL(FIB(K-1))
            WRITE(*,"(10X,I6, 7X, F9.4)") ANSWER, RATIO
         END DO
         END PROGRAM FIBONACCI
         FUNCTION FIB(LIMIT)     RESULT(FIBON)
         INTEGER,INTENT(IN)::LIMIT
         INTEGER,DIMENSION(100):FS
         INTEGER:: J, FIBON
         FS(1) = 1
         FS(2) = 1
         DO J = 3, LIMIT
          FS(J) = FS(J -1) + FS(J -2)
          FIBON = FS(J)
         END DO
         END FUNCTION FIB
```

The results of the run are as follows. Note that the ratio reaches a value of 1.6180.

```
    OUTPUT of RUN

 FIBONACCI SEQUENCE, FROM TERM 3

     SERIES     RATIO

        2       1.0000
        3       1.5000
        5       1.6667
```

```
   8       1.6000
  13       1.6250
  21       1.6154
  34       1.6190
  55       1.6176
  89       1.6182
 144       1.6180
 233       1.6181
 377       1.6180
 610       1.6180
```

7.4.7 Recursion

We now present program FIBONN2 which computes the Fibonacci series using a recursive function. Note the RESULT clause. Within the function the results are stored in FIBON, but on return from the function the results are assigned to the function FIB. The run shows that the Fibonacci series has been correctly calculated.

7.4.8 Program FIBONN2

```
      PROGRAM FIBONN2
!
      INTEGER:: ANSWER,FIB,K
      WRITE(*,"(4X,A/)")'FIBONNACI SERIES'
      DO K=1,15
         ANSWER = FIB(K)
         WRITE(*,"(16X,I6)") ANSWER
      END DO
      END PROGRAM FIBONN2
      RECURSIVE FUNCTION FIB(LIMIT)   RESULT(FIBON)
      IMPLICIT NONE
      INTEGER, INTENT(IN)::LIMIT
      INTEGER:: FIBON
       IF(LIMIT<=2)THEN
         FIBON = 1
       ELSE
         FIBON = FIB(LIMIT -1) + FIB(LIMIT -2)
       END IF
!
      END FUNCTION FIB
```

RUN

```
 FIBONNACI SERIES

           1
           1
           2
           3
           5
           8
```

```
       13
       21
       34
       55
       89
      144
      233
      377
      610
```

7.5 THE CALL STATEMENT

The CALL statement is an executable statement of the form:

$$\text{CALL name}(\alpha_1, \ \alpha_2, \ \alpha_3, \ . \ . \ .)$$

where name is the name of a SUBROUTINE SUBPROGRAM and $\alpha_1, \alpha_2, \alpha_3, \ldots$ is the list of arguments to be used in the subroutine. The CALL statement causes the computer to transfer control to the start of the called program, and execution begins.

7.6 THE EXTERNAL STATEMENT

As stated above, the list of arguments in the subroutine defining statement could include other function or subroutine subprograms. When this is done, the function or subroutine subprograms must be specified in an EXTERNAL statement. The form of the EXTERNAL statement is

$$\text{EXTERNAL name1, name2, . . .}$$

where name1, name2, . . . are user-written function or subroutine subprograms. By this means, the compiler can distinguish between variables and the subprograms.

7.7 THE COMMON STATEMENT

7.7.1 Blank COMMON

One method of transmitting data between main programs and subprograms is by means of the lists in the subprogram defining statements. When a COMMON statement is used, the variables named in it are assigned to storage locations called the common block. The same COMMON statement is placed in the main program and in one or more subprograms. When the COMMON statement is used, then the values of the variables listed in the COMMON statement are available to both the main program and those subprograms that contain the COMMON statement. The variables listed in the COMMON statement are *not* listed in the subroutine defining statement or in the call to the subroutine.

The COMMON statement is a nonexecutable statement of the form

$$\text{COMMON } \mu_1, \ \mu_2, \ \mu_3, \ \ldots$$

where $\mu_1, \mu_2, \mu_3, \ldots$ is a list of variable names and/or array names. This form of COMMON statement is called *blank* common. As an example, consider the following program segment:

```
!    THIS IS THE MAIN PROGRAM

     COMMON A(10,10), B(10,10),C(10,10), INDEX

                            •

                            •

                            •

     CALL MATRIX

                            •

                            •

                            •

     END

     SUBROUTINE MATRIX

     COMMON X(10,10),Y(10,10),Z(10,10),KOUNT

                            •

                            •

                            •

     END
```

The COMMON statement in the main program reserves 301 storage locations. As a result of the COMMON statement in the subroutine, X shares 100 locations with A, Y shares 100 locations with B, Z shares 100 locations with C; and INDEX and KOUNT share one location. Because of the COMMON statement, neither the subroutine defining statement nor the CALL to it requires a list of variables. A DIMENSION statement is not needed because the arrays are dimensioned by the COMMON statement. If the COMMON statement did not dimension the arrays, then the subroutine would appear as follows:

```
          DIMENSION X(10,10),Y(10,10), Z(10,10)
          COMMON X,Y,Z,KOUNT
```

and the main program

```
          DIMENSION A(10,10), B(10,10), C(10,10)
          COMMON A,B,C,INDEX
```

7.7.2 Labeled **COMMON**

Labeled COMMON, which is also called named COMMON, is a feature of COMMON that makes it possible to designate portions of the common storage. This feature is useful when a particular subroutine needs to share only particular areas of COMMON storage.

The form of labeled COMMON is

```
COMMON label1/ δ₁, δ₂, . . . , δₘ /label2/μ₁, μ₂, . . . , μₙ/
```

where $\delta_1, \delta_2, \ldots$ and $\mu_1, \mu_2, \ldots$ are variables or arrays.

A COMMON statement can designate labeled as well as blank COMMON by using a pair of slashes before the blank COMMON. Thus:

```
COMMON //X(10,10),Y(10,10)/ZEBRA/Z(10,10), INDEX
```

Here, X(10,10) and Y(10,10) are blank COMMON, and Z(10,10) and INDEX are labeled COMMON: Z(10,10) and INDEX are in the COMMON area labeled ZEBRA.

As another example, consider the following program segment:

```
!MAIN PROGRAM

COMMON //X(10,10),Y(10,10)/ZEBRA/Z(10,10), INDEX

                      .

                      .

                      .


END MAIN PROGRAM

SUBROUTINE SWITCH

COMMON ALPHA(10,10),BETA(10,10)
                      .

                      .

                      .

END SUBROUTINE SWITCH

SUBROUTINE GAUSS

COMMON/ZEBRA/DELTA(10,10),KOUNT

                      .

                      .

                      .


END SUBROUTINE GAUSS
```

In this example, arrays ALPHA(10,10) and X(10,10) in SUBROUTINE SWITCH share memory locations with arrays X(10,10) and Y(10,10), respectively, in the main program.

Array DELTA(10,10) in subroutine GAUSS shares memory locations with Z(10,10) in the main program; also, KOUNT in GAUSS and INDEX in the main program share the same memory location.

7.7.3 Program **COMMONS**

An example involving both blank and named COMMON is given in program COMMONS, shown as follows.

```
    PROGRAM COMMONS
!
    INTEGER :: HITS,N
    REAL :: PERCENT
    CHARACTER*15, DIMENSION(10) :: TEAM,PLAYERS
    COMMON//PERCENT(10),AVG,N/TOTL/HITS(10), M
    WRITE(*,"(A/)") 'DATA FOR SUBROUTINE AVERAGE'
    WRITE(*,*)' ENTER THE NUMBER OF TEAMS'
    READ(*,*)N
    WRITE(*,*)'ENTER THE NAMES OF THE TEAMS'
    READ(*,"(9A)")(TEAM(I),I = 1,N)
    WRITE(*,*)'ENTER THE PERCENTAGES OF THE TEAMS'
    READ(*,*)(PERCENT(I),I = 1,N)
    CALL AVERAGE
    WRITE(*,"(A/)") 'AMERICAN LEAGUE,EASTERN DIVISION'
    WRITE(*,*) (TEAM(I),I = 1,N)
    CALL AVERAGE
    WRITE(*,*)'AVERAGE OF THE PERCENTAGES OF AMERICAN LEAGUE&
    EAST'
    WRITE(*,"(A/F8.31)")'AVERAGE = ', AVG
    WRITE(*,"(A/A)")' * * *','   * * *'
    WRITE(*,"(A/)") 'DATA FOR SUBROUTINE TOTALHITS'
    WRITE(*,*)'ENTER THE NUMBER OF PLAYERS TO BE INCLUDED'
    READ(*,*) M
    WRITE(*,*)'ENTER THE NAMES OF PLAYERS'
    READ(*,*)(PLAYERS(I),I = 1,M)
    WRITE(*,"(/A)")'ENTER THE TOTAL NUMBER OF HITS OF EACH PLAYER'
    WRITE(*,"(/A/)") 'TOTAL NUMBER OF HITS OF EACH PLAYER'
    READ(*,*)(HITS(I),I = 1,M)
    CALL TOTALHITS
    DO I = 1,M
     WRITE(*,*) HITS(I)
    END DO
    WRITE(*,"(/A)") 'SOME OF THE BEST HITTERS'
    WRITE(*,"(/A/)")'CAN YOU MATCH PLAYERS WITH TOTAL HITS?'
    DO J = 1,M
     WRITE(*,"(A)") PLAYERS(J)
    END DO
    END PROGRAM COMMONS
    SUBROUTINE AVERAGE
    COMMON//X(10),AVG, N
    AVG = 0
```

```
       DO I = 1,N
        AVG = AVG + X(I)
       END DO
       AVG = AVG/N
       RETURN
       END
       SUBROUTINE TOTALHITS
       INTEGER HITS,M,TEMP
       COMMON/TOTL/HITS(10),M
       DO I = 1, M-1
        MAX = M - I
         DO J = 1, MAX
           IF(HITS(J) > HITS(J + 1)) THEN
             TEMP = HITS(J)
             HITS(J) = HITS(J + 1)
             HITS(J + 1) = TEMP
              ELSE
              CYCLE
           END IF
        END DO
       END DO
       END
```

In the main program, blank COMMON consists of array PERCENT(10) and variables N and AVG. The blank common is shared by array SCORE(10) and variables N and AVG in subroutine AVERAGE. In the main program there is TOTL, a named COMMON containing HITS(10) and M; these variables are used in subroutine TOTALHITS.

Subroutine AVERAGE computes the average of the percentages of American League teams, Eastern Division, as of the first week of September 1992. (The percentages denote {number games won/total games played} × 100%.) The subroutine also lists the teams in the Eastern Division of the American League.

Subroutine TOTALHITS accepts the total number of hits scored by nine leading players and sorts them in ascending order. It also prints the names of the players associated with these hits. As a modest challenge, the reader is asked to associate the players with the number of hits.

RUN

DATA FOR SUBROUTINE AVERAGE

AMERICAN LEAGUE,EAST DIVISION

TORONTO,BALTIMORE,MILWAUKEE,DETROIT,YANKEES,BOSTON,CLEVELAND

AVERAGE OF THE PERCENTAGES OF AMERICAN LEAGUE EAST

AVERAGE = 0.502

* * *

* * *

DATA USED IN SUBROUTINE TOTALHITS

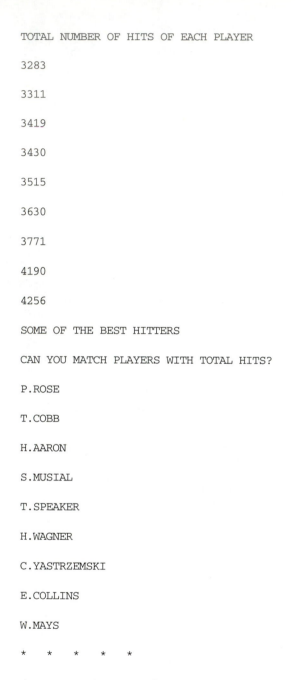

```
TOTAL NUMBER OF HITS OF EACH PLAYER

3283

3311

3419

3430

3515

3630

3771

4190

4256

SOME OF THE BEST HITTERS

CAN YOU MATCH PLAYERS WITH TOTAL HITS?

P.ROSE

T.COBB

H.AARON

S.MUSIAL

T.SPEAKER

H.WAGNER

C.YASTRZEMSKI

E.COLLINS

W.MAYS

*    *    *    *    *
```

A summary of data transfer methods is shown in Fig. 7.4.

7.8 MODULES, PART II

We began our discussion of modules in Chapter 6. Now that we have introduced subroutines, our discussion of modules can be extended. We have shown how the COMMON statement can be used to transfer data between a main program and subroutines. In cer-

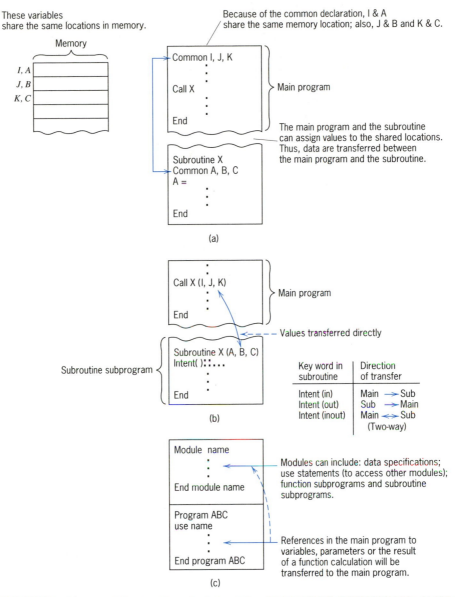

These variables share the same locations in memory.

Because of the common declaration, I & A share the same memory location; also, J & B and K & C.

Memory

I, A
J, B
K, C

Common I, J, K
Call X
End

Main program

Subroutine X
Common A, B, C
A =
End

The main program and the subroutine can assign values to the shared locations. Thus, data are transferred between the main program and the subroutine.

(a)

Call X (I, J, K)
End

Main program

Values transferred directly

Subroutine subprogram

Subroutine X (A, B, C)
Intent( ):
End

(b)

Key word in subroutine	Direction of transfer
Intent (in)	Main ⟶ Sub
Intent (out)	Sub ⟶ Main
Intent (inout)	Main ⟷ Sub (Two-way)

Module name
End module name

Program ABC
use name
End program ABC

(c)

Modules can include: data specifications; use statements (to access other modules); function subprograms and subroutine subprograms.

References in the main program to variables, parameters or the result of a function calculation will be transferred to the main program.

FIGURE 7.4   Summary of data transfer methods to and from SUBROUTINE SUBPROGRAMs: (a) Using COMMON data declaration; (b) Using direct communication: CALL statement specifying the arguments to be used; (c) Using a MODULE unit.

tain cases, when several variables and parameters are involved, the COMMON statement can be quite long. There is a possibility of error, for example, in the list of arguments. When data are to be shared among several subroutines, modules are a very convenient alternative to the COMMON statement.

Modules can also include FUNCTION subprograms (see Program SELECT in Sec. 7.12.1.).

First, we consider a simple program to calculate forces on charges by means of Coulomb's Law. The program uses a module. A trial run is shown.

7.8.1 Program MODPI

```
         MODULE DATAPI
         REAL::PI = 3.1415927
         REAL::E0 = 8.854E-12
         REAL :: QT = 1.0E-08
         END MODULE DATAPI
         PROGRAM MODPI
   !     COULOMB'S LAW
         USE DATAPI
         WRITE(*,*)'ENTER THE VALUE OF CHARGE Q1'
         READ(*,*)Q1
         WRITE(*,"(A,E12.2/)")'Q1 = ',Q1
         WRITE(*,*)'ENTER X2 on LINE 1, X1 on LINE 2'
         READ(*,*)X2
         READ(*,*)X1
         WRITE(*,"(A,F12.7,4X,A,F12.7)")'X1 = ',X1,'X2 = ',X2
         F1X = Q1*QT/(4.*PI*E0*(X2 - X1)**2)
         WRITE(*,*)'F1X = ', F1X
         END PROGRAM MODPI


   TRIAL RUN

   Q1 =      0.10E-07

   X1 =     0.0000000    X2 =     1.0000000
   F1X =       8.9877420E-07
```

Note that the module DATAPI precedes the program MODPI. The program accesses the module by means of the statement USE NAME where name is the name of the module. In this example, the module is named DATAPI and provides the values of PI, E0, and QT to program MODPI.

7.8.2 Highway Traffic Flow

One concern involved in traffic analysis has to do with estimating the number of vehicles that might arrive in an interval of time t at some point on a highway. A realistic model of this situation assumes that vehicles are not uniformly spaced and that their arrival is a *random* process. Therefore, a probability distribution must be chosen. One probability distribution that gives a reasonable estimate of traffic flow is the Poisson distribution. The formula for the Poisson distribution is

$$P(n) = \frac{(\lambda t)^n e^{-\lambda t}}{n!} S$$

where

$P(n)$ = the probability that n vehicles arrive in time t

λ = the average arrival rate of vehicles at some point on a highway in vehicles/sec

t = the number of seconds during which the vehicles arrive

n = the number of vehicles for which the probability of arrival is desired

It has been found by traffic engineers that about 720 vehicles per hour pass the point chosen for study. In the program TRAFFIC below, we calculate $P(n)$ for $n = 0,1,2,3,4,5,6$ with $t = 20$ sec and $\lambda = 720/3600 = 0.2$ vehicle per second.

7.8.3 Program **TRAFFIC** (*Civil Engineering*)

```
MODULE FACTOR
IMPLICIT NONE
REAL::P,T,LAMBDA
INTEGER::I,L,N
CONTAINS
INTEGER FUNCTION FACT(K)
INTEGER,INTENT(IN)::K
FACT = 1
IF(K>0)THEN
DO L = 1,K
      FACT = L* FACT
END DO
END IF
END FUNCTION FACT
END MODULE FACTOR
PROGRAM TRAFFIC
!   POISSON DISTRIBUTION USED FOR TRAFFIC FLOW
USE FACTOR
LAMBDA = 0.2
T = 20
DO N = 0,6
WRITE(*,*)'  FACT = ', FACT(n)
P = (LAMBDA*T)**N*EXP(-LAMBDA*T)/FACT(N)
WRITE(*,*)'N = ',N,'  P = ',P
END DO
END PROGRAM TRAFFIC
```

RUN

```
N = 0    P =  1.8315639E-02
N = 1    P = 7.3262557E-02
N = 2    P = 0.1465251
N = 3    P = 0.1953668
N = 4    P = 0.1953668
N = 5    P = 0.1562934
N = 6    P = 0.1041956
```

Fig. 7.5 is a graph of the results.

7.8.4 Program **BUTTERWORTH** (*Electrical Engineering*)

In Example 6.13, we discussed the frequency response of Butterworth filters. The program shown in Example 6.13 has been rewritten here, and the version of the program shown below uses a module called BUTFILTER.

Use of a module is effective because the main program and subroutines OUTPUT and RESPONSE employ this module. Note that the module assigns dimensions to arrays H4, H6, and H8 by the statement REAL,DIMENSION(50):: H4,H6,H8. Each subroutine uses these arrays. Because of the module, a COMMON statement is not needed inasmuch as the data within the module are available to the main program and the subroutines. Subroutine RESPONSE also uses the CASE construct.

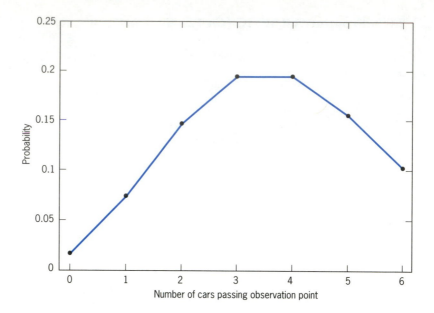

FIGURE 7.5 A graph of the results of PROGRAM TRAFFIC.

No run is shown because the results are identical to those found in Example 6.13.

```
MODULE BUTFILTER
REAL,DIMENSION(50)::H4,H6,H8
REAL::W,HMAG
INTEGER::N,K
END MODULE BUTFILTER
!
PROGRAM BUTTERWORTH
USE BUTFILTER
DO
WRITE(*,*)'ENTER N,EITHER 4,6 OR 8'
READ(*,*)N
IF(N==4.OR.N==6.OR.N==8) THEN
CALL RESPONSE
ELSE
EXIT
END IF
END DO
CALL OUTPUT
END PROGRAM BUTTERWORTH
SUBROUTINE OUTPUT
USE BUTFILTER
WRITE(*,"(2X,3(A,8X),A)") 'W','4th ORDER','6th ORDER','8th &
ORDER'
W = 0
DO K = 1,21
WRITE(*,"(F4.2,3F15.4)") W,H4(K),H6(K),H8(K)
 W = W + 0.1
END DO
END SUBROUTINE OUTPUT
```

```
SUBROUTINE RESPONSE
USE BUTFILTER
W = 0
WRITE(*,*)
DO K = 1,21
  HMAG = 1.0/SQRT(1.0 + W**(2*N))
  W = W + 0.1
SELECT CASE(N)
     CASE(4)
       H4(K)  = HMAG
     CASE(6)
       H6(K)  = HMAG
     CASE(8)
       H8(K)  = HMAG
END SELECT
END DO
END SUBROUTINE RESPONSE
```

7.9 RANDOM NUMBERS

We will use random numbers in Chapter 9 when discussing simulation. For now, however, we will introduce the topic of random numbers while illustrating the use of subroutines in order to extend the versatility of a program.

We define a random number as one that belongs to a class of numbers such that each member is equally probable. Imagine a stack of 10,000 cards numbered 0.0001, 0.0002, 0.0003, . . . 0.9999. If a card is drawn, and the number on it is, say, 0.3004, we asssign a probability of 1/10,000 to that event. The card is returned to the deck and another card is drawn, say, 0.7002; the probability of that event is also 1/10,000. In fact, the probability of any of the numbers on the cards is the same, namely, 1/10,000.

Of course, this is not a practical method for generating random numbers. Over the years, many algorithms have been devised for random number generators (RNG). Today, most FORTRAN compilers contain a subroutine that users can access for this purpose. These provide random numbers, r, such that $0 < r < 1.0$. The numbers are uniformly distributed. In probability theory, a uniform distribution is one in which the probability of a number in the range $(b - a)$ is equal to the probability of a number in the range $(d - c)$, where $(b - a) = (d - c)$.

In addition to the uniform distribution, many other probability distributions are available, including the standard normal (also called Gaussian), Poisson, Bernouilli, hypergeometric, and exponential. Methods have been devised that allow the conversion of uniformly distributed random numbers to random numbers that obey other probability distributions such as standard normal. We will illustrate two of these methods. In addition, we will illustrate scaling uniformly distributed random numbers. Scaling means changing the minimum and/or the maximum of the range of the numbers and the numbers between.

Program RANDOMB, shown in Sec. 7.9.1, uses random numbers and MODULE RANDATA. Note that all the subroutines of the program use the module RANDATA, thereby eliminating the need for COMMON declarations.

The compiler-supplied subroutine for generating random numbers is accessed in loop DO K = 1, N by the statement CALL RANDOM_NUMBER(U(K)). The random numbers are stored in U(K). Before the RNG is called, the statement CALL RANDOM_SEED is executed. A seed is a number that initializes the RNG. By using the same seed on different occasions, the user can replicate a sequence of random numbers. In the trial runs, 500 random numbers have been stored; thousands of random numbers may be required in some simulations, but for our purposes 500 will suffice. The 500 random numbers, which are stored, are uniformly distributed from 0 to 1. The mean (average) of the 500 numbers is computed and is found to be 0.508574, which is quite close to the theoretical value of 0.5.

The program contains several subroutines: SCALUNIFORM (for scaling uniformly distributed random numbers) and STDNORMAL (for generating standard normal numbers from uniform random numbers). The trial run shows samples of standard normal random numbers and the average of 500 standard normal numbers, which is found to be −0.082368. The theoretical value is 0. The formula for generating standard normal numbers was developed by the mathematicians G.E. Box and M.E. Muller. It yields a very good approximation to the standard normal distribution.

7.9.1 Program **RANDOMB**

```
      MODULE RANDATA
      REAL,DIMENSION(5000)::U,GAUSS,USC
      REAL::MEAN,MAX,MIN,AVG,SDEV
      INTEGER::N,K,JI,J
      CHARACTER (LEN=3):: ANS
      END MODULE RANDATA
      PROGRAM RANDOMB
!     THE UNIFORM, UNSCALED AND SCALED, DISTRIBUTION; THE
!     STANDARD NORMAL DISTRIBUTION
!     NOTATION: UNI = UNIFORM; NOR = NORMAL
!     SCA = SCALED; NAY = DON'T SCALE
      USE RANDATA
!
      DO
      WRITE(*,"(A/)")'TYPE UNI, NOR, OR BYE'
      READ(*,"(A)")ANS
      IF(ANS == 'UNI') THEN
      CALL UNIFORM_RANDOM
        ELSE IF (ANS =='NOR') THEN
      CALL NORMAL_RANDOM
      ELSE
        EXIT
      END IF
      END DO
       END PROGRAM RANDOMB
       SUBROUTINE UNIFORM_RANDOM
       USE RANDATA
      WRITE(*,*)'UNIFORM DISTRIBUTION,UNSCALED'
      WRITE(*,*)'ENTER DESIRED NUMBER OF RANDOM NOS.(5000 MAX)'
      READ(*,*) N
       WRITE(*,"(A,I6/)")'SELECTED NUMBER OF RANDOM NUMBERS ',N
       CALL RANDOM_SEED
!
       MEAN = 0
```

```
      DO K = 1,N
       CALL RANDOM_NUMBER(U(K))
       MEAN = MEAN + U(K)
      END DO
      MEAN = MEAN/N
      WRITE(*,"(A/)")' * * *'
      WRITE(*,*)'THE MEAN OF ',N,' UNIFORMLY DISTD. R.N. IS ',MEAN
      WRITE(*,"(A/)")' * * *'
      WRITE(*,*)'SAMPLES OF UNIFORMLY DISTD. RANDOM NUMBERS'
      DO K = 1,15
       WRITE(*,"(F12.6)") U(K)
      END DO
      WRITE(*,"(A/)")' * * *'
      WRITE(*,*)'FOR SCALED UNIFORMLY DISTD. NOS. TYPE SCA'
      WRITE(*,*)'OTHERWISE WRITE NAY'
      READ(*,"(A)")ANS
      IF(ANS =='SCA') THEN
       WRITE(*,"(A/)")' * * *'
       WRITE(*,*)'SCALED UNIFORM DISTRIBUTION'
       WRITE(*,*)'ENTER THE DESIRED MAXIMUM'
       READ(*,*) MAX
       WRITE(*,*)'THE DESIRED MAXIMUM IS ',MAX
       WRITE(*,*)'ENTER THE DESIRED MINIMUM'
       READ(*,*)MIN
      WRITE(*,*)'THE DESIRED MINIMUM IS ',MIN
!
      CALL SCALUNIFORM
      WRITE(*,"(A/)")' * * *'
      WRITE(*,"(A/)")' * * *'
      WRITE(*,*)'THE AVG. OF ',N,'SCALED UNIFORMLY DISTD. NOS. &
IS',AVG
        END IF
     END SUBROUTINE UNIFORM_RANDOM
!
      SUBROUTINE SCALUNIFORM
       USE RANDATA
      AVG = 0
      DO J = 1,N
       USC(J) = (MAX − MIN)*U(J) + MIN
       AVG = AVG + USC(J)
      END DO
      AVG = AVG/N
      END SUBROUTINE SCALUNIFORM
       SUBROUTINE NORMAL_RANDOM
          USE RANDATA
       CALL STDNORMAL
      WRITE(*,"(A/)")' * * *'
      WRITE(*,*)'THE AVG.OF ',N,'STD. NORMAL RANDOM NOS.IS. ',AVG
      WRITE(*,"(A/)")' * * *'
      WRITE(*,*)'STD DEV. OF ',N,'STD. NORMAL RANDOM NOS.IS ',SDEV
     END SUBROUTINE NORMAL_RANDOM
!
      SUBROUTINE STDNORMAL
          USE RANDATA
      AVG = 0
```

```
SDEV = 0
DO M = 1,N
 U(M) = 0
END DO
DO MM = 1,N
    CALL RANDOM_NUMBER(U(MM))
END DO
DO L = 1,N
 M = L + 1
 GAUSS(L) = SQRT(-2.0*ALOG(U(L)))*COS(6.283*U(M))
 AVG = AVG + GAUSS(L)
END DO
AVG = AVG/N
DO KK = 1,N
 SDEV = SDEV + (GAUSS(KK) - AVG)**2
END DO
SDEV = SQRT(SDEV/N)
END SUBROUTINE STDNORMAL
RUN
UNIFORM DISTRIBUTION,UNSCALED
ENTER THE DESIRED NUMBER OF RANDOM NOS. (5000 MAX)
SELECTED NO. OF RANDOM NOS. 500
  * * *
THE MEAN OF 500 UNIFORMLY DISTD. R.N. IS 0.5085743
  * * *
THE AVG.OF 500 STD. NORMAL RANDOM NOS.IS -8.2326867E-02
  * * *
STD. DEV. OF 500 STD. NORMAL RANDOM NOS.IS 1.0355474
```

7.9.2 Program SORTING

Program SORTING generates 50 random numbers, U(J), multiplies each by 10, and then uses CALL SORT(U,N,UMAX,UMIN) to call subroutine SORT.SORT arranges the random numbers in ascending order, so that U(50) contains the largest and U(1) the smallest. Within the subroutine the dummy variables RANDOMS and NN receive data from U and N, respectively, in the main program. However, RANDOMS also returns the sorted data to the main program; in addition, RMAX and RMIN are sent to the main program and stored in UMAX and UMIN, respectively. Therefore, in the subroutine, NN has intent IN and RANDOMS has intent INOUT. Because RMAX and RMIN are given values within subroutine SORT, they have intent OUT.

The function $MOD(n, k)$ divides integer n by integer k and returns the remainder. In the program, in loop DO I = 1, N, if MOD(I, 2) returns a value of zero, then U(I) is printed; otherwise it is not. By this means, alternate values of U(I) are printed.

```
PROGRAM SORTING
IMPLICIT NONE
REAL:: U(100),UMAX,UMIN
INTEGER:: I,J,N
CALL RANDOM_SEED
N = 50
DO J = 1,N
 CALL RANDOM_NUMBER(U(J))
 U(J) = 10.0*U(J)
END DO
```

```fortran
CALL SORT(U,N,UMAX,UMIN)
WRITE(*,"(A,F8.3,A,F8.3/)")'UMAX = ', UMAX,' UMIN = ', UMIN
DO I = 1,N
  IF(MOD(I,2)==0) THEN
  WRITE(*,"(F8.3)") U(I)
  ELSE
    CYCLE
  END IF
END DO
END PROGRAM SORTING
SUBROUTINE SORT(RANDOMS,NN,RMAX,RMIN)
IMPLICIT NONE
REAL, INTENT(INOUT)::RANDOMS(100)
REAL, INTENT(OUT)::RMAX,RMIN
INTEGER, INTENT(IN)::NN
REAL:: TEMP
INTEGER:: I,MAXI,L
MAXI = NN
    DO I = 1, MAXI
    MAXI = MAXI-1
    DO L = 1,MAXI
            IF(RANDOMS(L)>RANDOMS(L+1)) THEN
          TEMP = RANDOMS(L)
          RANDOMS(L) = RANDOMS(L+1)
                RANDOMS(L+1) = TEMP
                ELSE
                  CYCLE
        END IF
        END DO
    END DO
 RMAX = RANDOMS(NN)
 RMIN = RANDOMS(1)
RETURN
 END SUBROUTINE SORT
```

The trial run follows. As previously noted, the random number generator produces numbers between 0 and 1. However, we multiplied by 10 all the random numbers that were generated. Therefore, it is not surprising that we found that UMAX = 9.785 and UMIN = 0.107.

RUN

```
UMAX =    9.785  UMIN =   0.107

 0.208
 0.713
 0.823
 1.034
 1.411
 1.718
 1.727
 2.363
 2.417
 3.710
```

```
3.972
4.464
5.068
5.216
5.467
5.772
5.848
6.058
6.205
6.585
7.610
7.967
8.782
9.634
9.785
 *    *    *    *
```

7.10 MATRIX EXPONENTIATION

Certain types of network analysis require that a matrix be raised to a positive integer power. Matrix exponentiation is also needed in some branches of probability theory, for example, in Markov processes.

Our discussion of matrix multiplication in Chapter 5 and the program we used there will be useful in this chapter. To perform matrix exponentiation, we will successively multiply a matrix by itself.

7.10.1 Program **MATRIXPOWER**

Program MATRIXPOWER performs matrix exponentiation.

```
        PROGRAM MATRIXPOWER
!       THIS PROGRAM RAISES AN N × N MATRIX TO THE M'th POWER
        IMPLICIT NONE
        REAL, DIMENSION(10:10):: A,B,W
        INTEGER::POWER,P1,N,I,J,L,K,KJ
        CHARACTER*3: ACTION
        DO
        WRITE(*,*)' TO EXIT TYPE BYE; TO PROCEED, TYPE YES'
        READ(*,"(A)") ACTION
        IF(ACTION=='YES')THEN
        WRITE(*,*)'ENTER THE NUMBER OF ROWS OF THE MATRIX'
        READ(*,*)N
        DO I = 1,N
         DO J = 1,N
          A(I,J) = 0
         END DO
        END DO
        WRITE(*,*)'ENTER THE ELEMENTS OF THE MATRIX'
        DO I = 1,N
         READ(*,*)(A(I,J), J = 1,N)
```

```
END DO
DO K = 1,N
  WRITE(*,"(5F11.7)")(A(K,KJ), KJ = 1,N)
END DO
WRITE(*,*)'ENTER THE POWER TO RAISE MATRIX TO'
READ(*,*) POWER
CALL COPY(B,A,N)           !A IS COPIED TO B
P1 = POWER - 1
DO L = 1,P1
CALL MULTIPLY(A,B,W,N)
  CALL COPY(A,W,N)
END DO
WRITE(*,"(/A,I3,A/)")'MATRIX RAISED TO',POWER,' POWER'
DO I = 1,N
  WRITE(*,"(5F11.7)")(W(I,J), J = 1,N)
END DO
WRITE(*,"(//)")
ELSE
EXIT
END IF
END DO
END PROGRAM MATRIXPOWER
SUBROUTINE MULTIPLY(U,V,WM,NM)
REAL, DIMENSION(10,10), INTENT(IN):: U,V
REAL, DIMENSION(10,10), INTENT(OUT):: WM
INTEGER,INTENT(IN) :: NM
DO I = 1, NM
  DO J = 1, NM
    WM(I,J) = 0
      DO K = 1, NM
        WM(I,J) = WM(I,J) + U(I,K)*V(K,J)
      END DO
  END DO
END DO
END SUBROUTINE MULTIPLY
SUBROUTINE COPY(X, WC, NC)
REAL, DIMENSION(10,10),INTENT(OUT):: X
REAL, DIMENSION(10,10),INTENT(IN):: WC
INTEGER, INTENT(IN):: NC
DO I = 1,NC
  DO J = 1,NC
  X(I,J) = WC(I,J)
  END DO
END DO
END SUBROUTINE COPY
```

Let us identify the key parts of the program.

1. The elements of matrix **A** are entered by use of loop DO I and an implied DO loop within it. In this way, the elements of **A** are entered row by row.
2. Subroutine COPY(X,W,NC) is used to copy matrix **W** to matrix **X**.
3. Subroutine MULTIPLY(U,V,W,NM) calculates the matrix product **UV** (**V** post-multiples **U**), and the product is stored in **W**.

A copy of **A** is made *before* **A** is multiplied by itself, so that **A** will be available for repeated multiplication by itself. Therefore, subroutine COPY is called before multiplication is performed. As a result of the call, matrix **A** is copied to matrix **B**. **A** is unaffected by this procedure. After the copying operation, the program proceeds to loop DO L, where subroutine MULTIPLY is called. As a result, the product **AB** = **AA** is stored in matrix **W**. Then, subroutine copy is called again. This time matrix **W** is stored in matrix **A**. Matrix **B** continues to be identical to the original value of matrix **A**. Subroutine multiply is called again; **A** is postmultiplied by **B**, and the result, **A****3, is stored in **W**. Subroutine COPY is called one last time, and matrix **W** is copied to **A**. Because the index of the loop now has a value of 2, an exit occurs. Now both **A** and **W** contain the result of the calculation, **A****3.

The program is written so that the user has the opportunity to raise a particular matrix to a power and then, later, to raise it to another power. This opportunity continues until the user types BYE. BYE terminates the run.

Note that the INTENT attribute is used in both subroutines. For example, in COPY, dummy argument WC receives arrays from the main program; these arrays are transferred to dummy argument X, which returns them to the main program. Initially, **WC** receives **A**, and it is copied to **B** via **X**. Because it is **X** that returns the copied matrix, **X** has INTENT(OUT).

```
RUN

    0.8000000 0.2000000

    0.5000000 0.5000000

MATRIX RAISED TO 21   POWER

    0.7142858 0.2857143
    0.7142859 0.2857143


    0.8000000 0.2000000

    0.5000000 0.5000000


MATRIX RAISED TO 19   POWER


    0.7142858 0.2857143

    0.7142859 0.2857143


    0.8000000 0.2000000

    0.5000000 0.5000000


MATRIX RAISED TO 10   POWER
```

```
0.7142874 0.2857126

0.7142816 0.2857185
```

                *   *   *   *   *

7.11 THE CONTAINS STATEMENT

We have seen that modules make it possible for subprograms to share data and variables. Now we show another method we can use to achieve this objective. A subroutine or function is called a *procedure*. A CONTAINS statement is used within a main program in order to give procedures access to the data of the main program. The CONTAINS statement can be followed by one or more procedures. In this case, the procedures are said to be *internal*. The main program is called the *host*. The data of the host are available to the internal procedures. Thus, a call to the subroutine does not require any arguments.

Note that the END PROGRAM statement follows the end of the last procedure. Program OPERATE shown below provides a simple example using CONTAINS.

7.11.1 Program OPERATE

```
PROGRAM OPERATE
IMPLICIT NONE
REAL::W,X,Y
INTEGER::N
N = 3
X = 5; Y = 7
CALL EXPON
CALL SQUARE
WRITE(*,*)'X = ',X
WRITE(*,*)'W = ',W
     CONTAINS
SUBROUTINE EXPON
     X = X**N
END SUBROUTINE EXPON
SUBROUTINE SQUARE
     W = X**N + Y**N
END SUBROUTINE SQUARE
END PROGRAM OPERATE   !Note position of END PROGRAM
```

```
RUN
X =    1.2500000E+02
W =    1.9534680E+06
```

The next example illustrating the use of CONTAINS is program CONVERTB, which gives the user the option of converting either a hexadecimal or an octal number to a decimal number. Again, observe that there is no COMMON declaration. Use of the CONTAINS statement achieves the sharing of variables and data.

Note that the statement END PROGRAM CONVERTB occurs after the end of the last subroutine.

7.11.2 Program CONVERTB

```
PROGRAM CONVERTB
!    THIS PROGRAM CONVERTS AN OCTAL OR HEXADECIMAL NUMBER
!    TO A DECIMAL NUMBER
     INTEGER:: N,I
     REAL ::DEC,OCDEC,HEXDEC
     CHARACTER::HN(8), OCN(8),X(0:15),Y(0:7), ACTION*3
     INTEGER VAL(0:15), EXP(8),VALUE(0:7)
     DATA X/'0','1','2','3','4','5','6','7','8','9',&
'A','B','C','D','E','F'/
     DATA Y/'0','1','2','3','4','5','6','7'/
     DO
     WRITE(*,*)'TYPE BYE TO EXIT'
     WRITE(*,*)'TYPE HEX for HEX TO DEC; OCT FOR OCT TO DEC'
     READ(*,"(A)") ACTION
     IF(ACTION=='HEX') THEN
     WRITE(*,*)'ENTER N,THE NUMBER OF DIGITS IN THE HEXADEC. NO.'
     READ(*,*)N
     WRITE(*,*)'ENTER THE HEXADECIMAL NUMBER'
     READ(*,"(8A1)") (HN(I),I = 1,N)
         CALL HEXTODEC
         WRITE(*,*)'THE DECIMAL EQUIVALENT IS:'
         WRITE(*,*) INT(HEXDEC)
     WRITE(*,"(A/A)")'  * * *','  * * *'
     ELSE IF(ACTION=='OCT') THEN
     WRITE(*,*)'ENTER N,THE NUMBER OF DIGITS IN THE OCTAL NO.'
     READ(*,*)N
     WRITE(*,*)'ENTER THE OCTAL NUMBER'
     READ(*,"(8A1)") (OCN(I),I = 1,N)
     CALL OCTODEC
     WRITE(*,*)'THE DECIMAL EQUIVALENT IS:'
     WRITE(*,*) INT(OCDEC)
     WRITE(*,"(A/A)")'  * * *','  * * *'
     ELSE
     EXIT
     END IF
     END DO
!
     CONTAINS
     SUBROUTINE HEXTODEC
     HEXDEC = 0
!
     DO J = 1,N
      DO I = 0,15
        IF(HN(J) == X(I)) THEN
            VAL(J) = I
            EXP(J) = N - J
        ENDIF
     END DO
      END DO
!
     DO J = 1,N
      HEXDEC = HEXDEC + VAL(J)*16**EXP(J)
     END DO
```

```
        END SUBROUTINE HEXTODEC
!
        SUBROUTINE OCTODEC
        OCDEC = 0
        DO J = 1, N
         DO I = 0, 7
           IF(OCN(J) == Y(I)) THEN
           VALUE(J) = I
           EXP(J) = N - J
            END IF
         END DO
        END DO
        DO J = 1, N
         OCDEC = OCDEC + VALUE(J)*8**EXP(J)
        END DO
        END SUBROUTINE OCTODEC
        END PROGRAM CONVERTB
```

RUN

```
ENTER THE HEXADECIMAL NUMBER
A3CDF
THE DECIMAL EQUIVALENT IS:
670943
  * * *
  * * *
ENTER THE OCTAL NUMBER
26741
THE DECIMAL EQUIVALENT IS:
11745
  * * *
  * * *
```

7.12 COMBINATIONS AND PERMUTATIONS

A *combination* of different items is a group of these items without regard to the order in which they were taken. For example, suppose that we have five cards labeled *A,B,C,D,E*. If we randomly draw three of these cards, the possible combinations are *ABC*, *ABD*, *ABE*, *ACD*, *ACE*, *ADE*, *BCD*, *BCE*, *BDE*, and *CDE*. Note that neither *ACB* nor *BDC* is on this list because from the viewpoint of combinations, *ACB* is the same as *ABC* and *BDC* is the same as *BCD* because order does not count. The number of combinations of *n* different items taken *k* at a time is

$$_nC_k = n!/[(k!)(n-k)!]$$

For the example presented above, in which we drew three cards from five cards, $n = 5$ and $k = 3$, so that

$$_5C_3 = 5!/[(3!)(2!)] = 120/[(6)(2)] = 10$$

We listed these combinations above.

A *permutation* of n different items is an arrangement of these items taking order into account. Using cards A, B, C the permutations are ABC, ACB, BAC, BCA, CAB, and CBA. As we can observe, there are six permutations.

In general, the number of permutations, P, of n different objects is given by

$$P = n!$$

If we have n items, of which k are alike, then the number of permutations is

$$_nP_k = n!/k!$$

With $n = 5$ *and* $k = 3$, we have $P = 5!/3! = 120/6 = 20$. For example, consider the word SASSY. Here, $n = 5$ and $k = 3$, and, as just calculated, there are 20 permutations, including SSSAY, SSAYS, SAYSS, and AYSSS.

Figure 7.6 shows the difference between combinations and permutations as applied to the selection of balls.

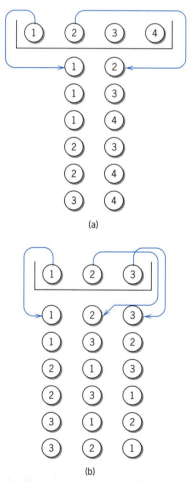

(a)

(b)

FIGURE 7.6   (a) Selections of two balls from a group of four balls (*combinations*). (b)Selections of three balls from a group of three balls (*permutations*): Each arrangement is considered to be a permutation.

7.12.1 Program **SELECT** (*Mathematics*)

Program SELECT, which calculates combinations and permutations using the formulas given in Sec. 7.12 is shown below. The program gives the user three choices: (1) Enter COM to calculate the number of combinations; (2) enter PER to calculate permutations; or (3) enter BYE to end the program. If PER is selected, the user is prompted to enter a value of 0 if all *n* items are different; otherwise, the user should enter a nonzero value for *k*.

Note that module CHOICE includes the statement CONTAINS followed by the function subprogram FACT(N). Because the subroutines include the statement USE CHOICE, the function FACT(N) is available to the subroutines.

```
        MODULE CHOICE
        CHARACTER*3 OPTION
        INTEGER::N,COMBS,K,PERM,L
        CONTAINS
        INTEGER FUNCTION FACT(N)
        INTEGER::N,L
        FACT = 1
        IF(N>0) THEN
        DO L = 1,N
             FACT = L*FACT
        END DO
        END IF
        END FUNCTION FACT
        END MODULE CHOICE
        PROGRAM SELECT
!       THIS PROGRAM COMPUTES COMBINATIONS & PERMUTATIONS OF
!       N DISTINCT ITEMS;ALSO,PERMUTATIONS IF K ITEMS ARE ALIKE
        USE CHOICE
        DO
        WRITE(*,*)'IF YOU WANT COMBINATIONS,TYPE COM'
        WRITE(*,*)'IF YOU WANT PERMUTATIONS,TYPE PER'
        WRITE(*,*)'IF YOU WANT TO END THIS SESSION,TYPE BYE'
        READ(*,*) OPTION
        IF(OPTION == 'COM') THEN
        WRITE(*,*)'CALCULATION OF NUMBER OF COMBINATIONS'
        WRITE(*,*) 'ENTER THE NUMBER OF DISTINCT ITEMS'
        READ(*,*) N
            WRITE(*,*)'ENTER THE NUMBER OF ITEMS SELECTED'
        READ(*,*)K
         CALL COMBIN
        WRITE(*,*)'THE NO. OF COMBINATIONS OF 'K,'ITEMS OUT OF ',N
        WRITE(*,*)'IS ',COMBS
        WRITE(*,*)'     *    *    *'
         ELSE IF(OPTION =='PER') THEN
        WRITE(*,*)'PERMUTATIONS OF N ITEMS; ENTER THE VALUE OF N'
        READ(*,*) N
        WRITE(*,*)'IF THE N ITEMS ARE ALL DIFFERENT,ENTER 0; IF K OF '
        WRITE(*,*)'THE ITEMS ARE ALIKE, ENTER THE VALUE OF K'
        READ(*,*) K
         CALL PERMUT
        WRITE(*,*)'THE NUMBER OF PERMUTATIONS OF',N,' ITEMS = ',PERM
        WRITE(*,*)K,' OF THE ITEMS ARE ALIKE'
```

```
      WRITE(*,*)'      *     *     *'
       ELSE
       EXIT
       END IF
      END DO
      END PROGRAM SELECT
!
      SUBROUTINE COMBIN
      USE CHOICE
       COMBS = FACT(N)/(FACT(K)*FACT(N - K))
      END
!
      SUBROUTINE PERMUT
      USE CHOICE
      DO
      IF(K == 0) THEN
        PERM = FACT(N)
       EXIT
        ELSE
        PERM = FACT(N)/FACT(K)
          EXIT
        END IF
          END DO
      END
```

Trial runs are shown below.

RUN

```
CALCULATION OF NUMBER OF COMBINATIONS
THE NO. OF COMBINATIONS OF 4 ITEMS OUT OF 7
IS 35
* * *
THE NUMBER OF PERMUTATIONS OF 8 ITEMS = 40320
0 OF THE ITEMS ARE ALIKE
* * *
THE NUMBER OF PERMUTATIONS OF 6 ITEMS = 360
2 OF THE ITEMS ARE ALIKE
* * *
```

7.13 INTRODUCTION TO FILTER DESIGN (*ELECTRICAL ENGINEERING*)

In this section, we discuss a program that enables the user to design one type of analog electrical filter. First, we discuss a unit called the decibel, which is used in specifying the filter performance.

7.13.1 The Decibel

In studying devices such as amplifiers, telephone lines, and various control systems, one characteristic of interest is the magnitude of the ratio of two quantities, the output and input voltage. This ratio is plotted as a function of frequency. The frequency scale, generally the x-axis, is usually logarithmic. This makes it possible to include a wider frequency range on the axis.

When calculating the magnitude of the ratio of the output to input voltage, it has become standard procedure to use a unit called the decibel (dB) to characterize it. The calculation is

$$dB = 20\log_{10} |H(j(\omega)|$$

where $|H(j\omega)|$ is the magnitude of the ratio (output voltage)/(input voltage) and both voltages are functions of radian frequency (ω).

The quantity $H(j\omega)$ is usually called the *transfer function* because it is an indicator of how the voltage applied to the input of the device is "transferred" to the output. When the device is an amplifier, the output voltage usually exceeds the input voltage, and so the magnitude of the transfer function is greater than one. When the device is a filter, the output voltage in the frequency region where filtering occurs is less than the input voltage; thus, the magnitude of the transfer function in that frequency region is less than 1.0. When $|H(j\omega)|$ is less than 1.0, the decibel value is negative. Hence, if $|H(j\omega)| = 0.707$, this is equivalent to -3.0116 decibels. When transfer functions are plotted in terms of dB, significant portions of the graph are straight lines; this makes it easy to sketch them.

We are particularly interested in the decibel because the performance of filters is almost universally specified in terms of decibels. Thus, a typical filter may be specified as having, for example, 18 dB of attenuation at a frequency of 2000 Hz (hertz). The word *attenuation* means that the output voltage is less than the input voltage and that the magnitude of the transfer function is less than 1.0. For example, if the magnitude of the transfer function of the filter is 0.125, then $20\log_{10} (0.125) = -18.06$ dB.

7.13.2 Chebychev Filters

In Example 6.12, we introduced the subject of electric filters and exemplified it with the Butterworth type. In this section we discuss a program that designs another type of electrical filter, Chebychev type I. (The Chebychev type II filter has a monotonic response in the passband and a ripple in the "stop" or attenuation band.)

To keep the program reasonably short, it is limited to low-pass filters with either 1 dB or 3 dB ripple.

Let us discuss the basic difference between Butterworth and Chebychev filters. As shown in Example 6.12, the magnitude of the transfer function of a Butterworth filter is a smooth curve. Such a smooth curve is called monotonic. The transfer function of a type I Chebychev filter has a *ripple* in the passband, the frequency band where no or little attenuation is desired. The ripple consists of maxima and minima of equal amplitudes (see Fig. 7.7). The drawing shows the magnitude of the transfer function as a function of radian frequency. The passband ends at the cutoff frequency. The transfer function is normalized; that is, its cutoff frequency is 1.0 radian per second. In the drawing, the peak of the ripple is at a magnitude of about 1.122, and the trough is at 1.0. In dB, the ratio 1.122/1.00 is $20\log_{10}(1.122/1.00) = 1.0$ dB. For this reason, this particular Chebychev filter is said to have a 1 dB ripple. The most widely used values of ripple are 0.5, 1.0, 2.0, and 3 dB. The advantage of the Chebychev filter is that, for a particular order, it produces a greater increase of attenuation beyond the cutoff frequency than the Butterworth. Its disadvantage is the ripple in the passband.

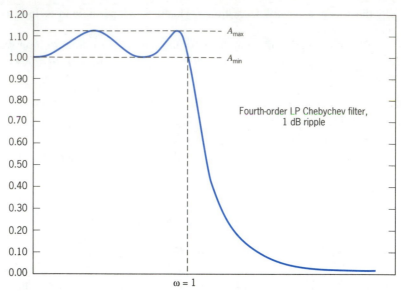

FIGURE 7.7   Plot of the frequency response of a fourth order low pass (LP) Chebychev filter with 1 decibel (dB) of ripple.

Program FILMENUG and trial runs follow.

```
      PROGRAM FILMENUG
!      PROGRAM ENABLES THE USER TO DESIGN LOW PASS ANALOG
!         CHEBYCHEV TYPE FILTERS WITH RIPPLE OF 1 OR 3 dB.
!
      CHARACTER*3 FILTYPE
      DO
      WRITE(*,*) 'CHOOSE CHEBYCHEV FILTER BY TYPING CH'
      WRITE(*,*)' TO END THIS SESSION, TYPE BYE'
      READ(*,"(A3)") FILTYPE
              IF(FILTYPE =='BYE') THEN
              EXIT
         ELSE IF(FILTYPE == 'CH ') THEN
      WRITE(*,*)' LOWPASS CHEBYCHEV DESIGN'
      WRITE(*,*)' ENTER THE CUTOFF FREQUENCY IN HZ'
      READ(*,*) COFF
      WRITE(*,*)' ENTER THE PASSBAND RIPPLE (1 or 3)'
      READ(*,*) R
      WRITE(*,*)' THE SELECTED RIPPLE (dB) IS ',R
      WRITE(*,*)' ENTER THE DESIRED ATTEN.,DB,& THE FREQU. IN HZ'
      READ(*,*) DB, FRA
      WRITE(*,*)'DESIRED ATTEN.: ',DB,' AT ',FRA,' HZ'
!
      CALL CHEBORDER(COFF, R, DB, FRA, CORDER, N)
!
      WRITE(*,*)' THE VALUE OF ORDER IS',CORDER
      WRITE(*,*)' THE ROUNDED-UP,INTEGER VALUE OF ORDER IS ',N
      END IF
```

```
      IF(R == 1.0) THEN
          CALL CHEB1TRAN(N,COFF)
      ELSE IF(R == 3.0) THEN
          CALL CHEB3TRAN(N,COFF)
      END IF
      END DO
!

      CONTAINS
!     SUBROUTINE CHEBORDER CALCULATES THE ORDER
      SUBROUTINE CHEBORDER(COFF, R, DB, FRA, CORDER, N)
      EPS = SQRT(10**(R/10.)-1.0)
      Q = FRA/COFF
      CORDER = (DB-20.0*LOG10(EPS) + 6.0)/(20.0*LOG10(Q) + 6.0)
      N = CORDER + 1
      END SUBROUTINE CHEBORDER
!     SUBROUTINE DESINGS FILTER BASED ON RIPPLE & ORDER
      SUBROUTINE CHEB1TRAN(N,COFF)
!     RIPPLE = 1 dB
      REAL :: C1(0:1),C2(0:2),C3(0:3),C4(0:4),C5(0:5),NUMER
      REAL :: CH1(0:1),CH2(0:2),CH3(0:3),CH4(0:4),CH5(0:5)
      DATA CH1/1.9652,1.0/,CH2/1.1025,1.0977,1.0/
      DATA CH3/0.4913,1.2384,0.9883,1.0/
      DATA CH4/0.2756,0.7426,1.4539,0.9528,1.0/
      DATA CH5/0.1228,0.5805,0.9744,1.6888,0.9368,1.0/
      TUBO = (6.2831*COFF)
      IF(N == 1) THEN
       NUMER = (TUBO**N)*CH1(0)
       WRITE(*,*)'THE NUMERATOR OF THE TRANSFER FN.IS',NUMER
       WRITE(*,*)'THE DENOMINATOR OF THE TRANSFER FN.IS'
       DO I = 0,N
         C1(I) = CH1(I)*(TUBO**(N-I))
       END DO
      WRITE(*,"(E9.4,A//)") C1(0),' + s'
      ELSE IF(N == 2) THEN
      NUMER = (TUBO**N)*CH2(0)
      WRITE(*,*)'THE NUMERATOR OF THE TRANSFER FN. IS',NUMER
      WRITE(*,*)'THE DENOMINATOR OF THE TRANSFER FN.IS'
       DO I = 0,N
       C2(I) = CH2(I)*(TUBO**(N-I))
       END DO
      WRITE(*,155) (C2(I),I = 0,1)
155   FORMAT(1X,E9.4,'+',E9.4,'s + s**2',//)
      ELSE IF (N == 3) THEN
       NUMER = (TUBO**N)*CH3(0)
      WRITE(*,*)'THE NUMERATOR OF THE TRANSFER FN.IS',NUMER
      WRITE(*,*)'THE DENOMINATOR OF THE TRANSFER FN. IS'
       DO I = 0,N
         C3(I) = CH3(I)*(TUBO**(N-I))
       END DO
      WRITE(*,160) (C3(I),I = 0,2)
160   FORMAT(1x,E9.4,'+ ',E9.4,'s +',E9.4,'s**2 + s**3',//)
      ELSE IF(N == 4) THEN
      NUMER = (TUBO**N)*CH4(0)
```

```
          WRITE(*,*)'THE NUMERATOR OF THE TRANSFER FN. IS',NUMER
          WRITE(*,*)'THE DENOMINATOR OF THE TRANSFER FN. IS'
          DO I = 0,N
            C4(I) = CH4(I)*(TUBO**(N-I))
          END DO
          WRITE(*,165) (C4(I),I = 0,3)
165   FORMAT(1x,E9.4,'+ ',E9.4,'s +',E9.4,'s**2+',E9.4,'s**3 + s**4',//)
          ELSE IF(N == 5) THEN
          NUMER = (TUBO**N)*CH5(0)
          WRITE(*,*)'THE NUMERATOR OF THE TRANSFER FN. IS',NUMER
          WRITE(*,*)'THE DENOMINATOR OF THE TRANSFER FN. IS'
          DO I = 0,N
           C5(I) = CH5(I)*(TUBO**(N-I))
          END DO
          WRITE(*,170) (C5(I),I = 0,4)
          END IF
170   FORMAT(1X,E9.4,' + ',E9.4,'s + ',E9.4,'s**2 + ',E9.4,'s**3 + ', &
      E9.4,'s**4 + s**5',//)
          END SUBROUTINE CHEB1TRAN
!
          SUBROUTINE CHEB3TRAN(N,COFF)
!     RIPPLE = 3dB
          REAL:: CE1(0:1),CE2(0:2),CE3(0:3),CE4(0:4),CE5(0:5),NUMER
          REAL:: EH1(0:1),EH2(0:2),EH3(0:3),EH4(0:4),EH5(0:5)
          DATA EH1/1.0023,1.0/,EH2/0.7079,0.6449,1.0/,EH3/0.2506,0.9283, &
0.5972,1.0/
          DATA EH4/0.177,0.4048,1.1691,0.5816,1.0/
          DATA EH5/0.06264, 0.4079, 0.5489, 1.415,0.5744,1.0/
          TUBO = (6.2831*COFF)
          IF(N== 1) THEN
          NUMER = (TUBO**N)*EH1(0)
          DO I = 0,N
           CE1(I) = EH1(I)*(TUBO**(N-I))
          END DO
          WRITE(*,*)'THE NUMERATOR OF THE TRANSFER FUNCTION IS',NUMER
          WRITE(*,*)'THE DENOMINATOR OF THE TRANSFER FUNCTION IS'
          WRITE(*,210) (CE1(I),I = 0,0)
210   FORMAT(1X,E9.4,' + s',//)
          ELSE IF(N == 2) THEN
          NUMER =(TUBO**N)*EH2(0)
          DO I = 0,N
           CE2(I) = EH2(I)*(TUBO**(N-I))
             END DO
!
          WRITE(*,*)'THE NUMERATOR OF THE TRANSFER FN. IS,'NUMER
          WRITE(*,*)'THE DENOMINATOR OF THE TRANSFER FUNCTION IS'
          WRITE(*,220) (CE2(I),I = 0,1)
220   FORMAT(1x,E9.4,'+',E9.4,'s + s**2',//)
          ELSE IF(N == 3) THEN
          NUMER = (TUBO**N)*EH3(0)
          WRITE(*,*)' THE NUMERATOR OF THE TRANSFER FN. IS ',NUMER
          DO I = 0,N
           CE3(I) = EH3(I)*(TUBO**(N-I))
          END DO
```

```
         WRITE(*,*)' THE DENOMINATOR OF THE TRANSFER FN. IS'
         WRITE(*,230) (CE3(I),I = 0,2)
230      FORMAT(1x,E9.4,' + ',E9.4,'s + ',E9.4,'s**2 + s**3',//)
         ELSE IF (N ==4) THEN
         NUMER = (TUBO**N)*EH4(0)
         WRITE(*,*)' THE NUMERATOR OF THE TRANSFER FN. IS',NUMER
         DO I = 0,N
           CE4(I) = EH4(I)*(TUBO**(N-I))
         END DO
!
         WRITE(*,*)' THE DENOMINATOR OF THE TRANSFER FUNCTION IS'
         WRITE(*,240) (CE4(I),I = 0,3
240      FORMAT(1x,E9.4,' + ',E9.4,'s + ',E9.4,'s**2 +',E9.4,'s**3 + s**4',//)
         ELSE IF (N == 5) THEN
           NUMER = (TUBO**N)*EH5(0)
         WRITE(*,*)'THE NUMERATOR OF THE TRANSFER FN. IS',NUMER
         WRITE(*,*)'THE DENOMINATOR OF THE TRANSFER FN. IS'
           DO I = 0,N
             CE5(I) = EH5(I)*(TUBO**(N-I))
           END DO
         WRITE(*,250) (CE5(I), I = 0,4)
         END IF
250      FORMAT(1x,E9.4,' + ',E9.4,'s + ',E9.4,'s**2 + ',E9.4,'s**3 + ', &
         E9.4,'s**4 + s**5',//)
         END SUBROUTINE CHEB3TRAN
         END PROGRAM FILMENUG
```

The user enters CH and is then prompted to enter the cutoff frequency (Hz), the desired ripple (1 or 3 dB), the desired attenuation (decibels), and the frequency (Hz) at which that attenuation is desired. Based on the desired attenuation, the necessary order of the transfer function is computed by

```
         SUBROUTINE CHEBORDER(COFF, R, DB, FRA, CORDER,N)
```

where

COFF = the cuttoff frequency

R = the ripple (dB)

DB = the specified attenuation

FRA = the frequency at which the attenuation is specified

CORDER = the calculated order of the filter

N = CORDER + 1

Recall that the order of the filter, N, must be an integer. Note that N equals 1 plus the calculated order; that is, N = CORDER + 1. For example, in one of the trial runs, we see that CORDER = 2.809, but N = 2.809 + 1 = 3. Thus, a third-order filter is used; a second-order filter would not meet the attenuation specification. After the return from CHEBOR-DER, an IF statement is used to call either subroutine CHEB1TRAN (1 dB ripple) or CHEB3TRAN (3 dB ripple). Within this subroutine, the normalized CHEBYCHEV transfer functions are stored in DATA statements. Recall that a normalized transfer function has a cutoff frequency of 1 radian per second. Based on the value of N, an appropriate transfer function is selected. Then this (normalized) transfer function is *scaled*, and its numerator and denominator are printed.

TRIAL RUNS OF FILMENUG

Design 1:

TEST of DESIGN (see Program CHEB03R3, Sec. 7.13.3)

```
LOWPASS CHEBYCHEV DESIGN
THE SELECTED CUTOFF FREQUENCY IS  5.0000000E+03
THE SELECTED RIPPLE (dB) IS  3.0000000
DESIRED ATTEN.: 37.0000000  AT  1.5000000E+04 HZ
THE VALUE OF ORDER IS  2.7679479
THE ROUNDED-UP,INTEGER VALUE OF ORDER IS 3
THE NUMERATOR OF THE TRANSFER FN. IS  7.7698569E+12
THE DENOMINATOR OF THE TRANSFER FN. IS
.7770E+13 +  .9162E+09s +  .1876E+05s**2 +  s**3
                  * * *
```

Design 2:

TEST of DESIGN (see Program CHEBO4R3, Sec. 7.13.3)

```
LOWPASS CHEBYCHEV DESIGN
THE SELECTED CUTOFF FREQUENCY IS  10.0000000
THE SELECTED RIPPLE (dB) IS  3.0000000
DESIRED ATTEN.: 36.5000000  AT  20.0000000 HZ
THE VALUE OF ORDER IS  3.5789082
THE ROUNDED-UP,INTEGER VALUE OF ORDER IS 4
THE NUMERATOR OF THE TRANSFER FN. IS  2.7584758E+06
THE DENOMINATOR OF THE TRANSFER FN. IS
.2758E+07+ .1004E+06s +  .4615E+04s**2 + 3.654E+02s**3 + s**4
                  * * *
```

Design 3:

TEST of DESIGN (see Program CHEBO3R1, Sec. 7.13.3)

```
LOWPASS CHEBYCHEV DESIGN
THE SELECTED CUTOFF FREQUENCY IS  10.0000000
THE SELECTED RIPPLE (dB) IS  1.0000000
DESIRED ATTEN.: 20.0000000  AT  20.0000000 HZ
```

```
THE VALUE OF ORDER IS  2.6511366
THE ROUNDED-UP,INTEGER VALUE OF ORDER IS 3
THE NUMERATOR OF THE TRANSFER FN. IS  1.2186211E+05
THE DENOMINATOR OF THE TRANSFER FN. IS
.1219E+06+ .4889E+04s +.6210E+02s**2 + s**3
                * * *
```

Design 4:

TEST of DESIGN (see Program CHEBO4R1, Sec. 7.13.3)

```
LOWPASS CHEBYCHEV DESIGN
THE SELECTED CUTOFF FREQUENCY IS  10.0000000
THE SELECTED RIPPLE (dB) IS  1.0000000
DESIRED ATTEN.: 31.0000000  AT  20.0000000 HZ
THE VALUE OF ORDER IS  3.5662324
THE ROUNDED-UP,INTEGER VALUE OF ORDER IS 4
THE NUMERATOR OF THE TRANSFER FN. IS  4.2951180E+06
THE DENOMINATOR OF THE TRANSFER FN. IS
.4295E+07+ .1842E+06s + .5740E+04s**2+.5987E+02s**3 + s**4
                * * *
```

Design 5:

TEST of DESIGN (see Program CHEB5R1B, Sec. 7.13.3)

```
LOWPASS CHEBYCHEV DESIGN
THE SELECTED CUTOFF FREQUENCY IS  1.0000000E+02
THE SELECTED RIPPLE (dB) IS  1.0000000
DESIRED ATTEN.: 41.0000000  AT  2.0000000+02 HZ
THE VALUE OF ORDER IS  4.3981376
THE ROUNDED-UP,INTEGER VALUE OF ORDER IS 5
THE NUMERATOR OF THE TRANSFER FN. IS  1.2024532E+13
THE DENOMINATOR OF THE TRANSFER FN. IS
.1202E+14 + .9047E+11s + .2417E+09s**2 + .6667E+06s**3 + &
.5886E+03s**4 + s**5
                * * *
```

7.13.3 Checking the Designs

Before constructing a device, it is important to check the design, particularly if the device is expensive. For filters, we can write a program that calculates the variation with frequency of the magnitude of the transfer function. This procedure validates the filter designs. This is equivalent to impressing a signal of 1 volt constant amplitude at the input, varying the frequency of the signal, and determining the output of the filter.

The procedure is as follows.

1. In the transfer functions, shown in the designs above, replace each s by $j\omega$, replace s^2 by $(j\omega)^2 = -\omega^2$; replace s^3 by $-j\omega^3$; replace s^4 by $(j\omega)^4 = \omega^4$.
2. Calculate the magnitude of the transfer function using the intrinsic function CABS. Express the magnitude in decibels.
3. Calculate the variation of decibels as a function of frequency (hertz) over the frequency range of interest.

When examining the trial runs, the main points of interest are (1) the actual attenuation at the specified frequency versus the attenuation specified; and (2) variations of attenuation in the passband. For example, in Design 1, an attenuation of 37 dB was specified at 15,000 Hz. The trial run indicates 39.89 dB was attained. The specified passband ripple is 3 dB.

In the passband, the attenuation is zero at frequency zero. (The output is 1.0 and 1.0 produces 0 dB.) The attenuation is 3 dB at 2500 Hz and, also, at 5000 Hz, the cutoff frequency.

In Design 5, attenuation of 41 dB was specified at 200 Hz. The trial run indicates that an attenuation of about 45 dB was attained. The specified passband ripple is 1 dB. The trial run shows 0 dB at zero frequency and 1 dB attenuation at 32 Hz, 80 Hz, and 100 Hz (the cutoff frequency).

```
      PROGRAM CHEBO3R3
!     CHEBYCHEV; ORDER 3, R 3 db; CUTOFF 5K; -37db @ 15K
      IMPLICIT NONE
      REAL:: Y, W, A, B
      COMPLEX:: HDEN
      INTEGER :: F
      REAL, PARAMETER:: PI = 3.1415927
       WRITE(*,"(A,5X,A/)")'FREQUENCY   DECIBELS'
      DO F = 0, 15000, 500
       W = 2.0*PI*F
       A = 7.77E12 -1.8763E04*W**2
       HDEN = A + CMPLX(0.0, 9.162E08*W - W**3)
       Y = 20.0*LOG10(CABS(7.77E12/HDEN))
       WRITE(*,"(1X,I6,4X,F8.2)") F,Y
      END DO
      END PROGRAM CHEBO3R3
```

TRIAL RUN

FREQUENCY	DECIBELS
0	0.00
500	-0.36
1000	-1.21
1500	-2.11
2000	-2.76
2500	-3.00
3000	-2.72
3500	-1.84
4000	-0.50
4500	-0.19
5000	-3.00

```
     5500        −7.06
     6000       −10.76
     6500       −13.94
     7000       −16.69
     7500       −19.12
     8000       −21.29
     8500       −23.26
     9000       −25.06
     9500       −26.73
    10000       −28.29
    10500       −29.74
    11000       −31.11
    11500       −32.40
    12000       −33.62
    12500       −34.79
    13000       −35.90
    13500       −36.96
    14000       −37.98
    14500       −38.95
    15000       −39.89
  *      *      *      *      *
```

```fortran
      PROGRAM CHEBO4R4
!     CHEBYCHEV; ORDER 3, R 3 db; CUTOFF 10HZ; −37db @ 20HZ
      IMPLICIT NONE
      REAL:: Y, W, A
      COMPLEX:: HDEN
      INTEGER :: F
      REAL, PARAMETER:: PI = 3.1415927
      WRITE(*,"(A,5X,A/)")'FREQUENCY  DECIBELS'
      DO F = 0, 21, 1
       W = 2.0*PI*F
       A = 2.758E06 − 4615*W**2 + W**4
       HDEN = A + CMPLX(0.0,1.004E05*W − 36.54*W**3)
       Y = 20.0*LOG10(CABS(2.758E06/HDEN))
       WRITE(*,"(1X,I6,4X,F8.2)") F,Y
      END DO
      END PROGRAM CHEBO4R3
```

```
FREQUENCY   DECIBELS
      0        0.00
      1        0.34
      2        1.30
      3        2.51
      4        2.97
      5        2.03
      6        0.67
      7        0.00
      8        0.67
      9        2.78
     10        0.00
     11       −7.07
     12      −12.76
     13      −17.30
```

```
    14          −21.11
    15          −24.41
    16          −27.34
    17          −29.99
    18          −32.41
    19          −34.64
    20          −36.72
    21          −38.66
*     *     *     *     *
```

```
    PROGRAM CHEBO3R1
!   CHEBYCHEV; ORDER 3, R 1 db; CUTOFF 10 HZ; −20db @ 20 hZ
    IMPLICIT NONE
    REAL:: Y, W, A, B
    COMPLEX:: HDEN
    INTEGER :: F
    REAL, PARAMETER:: PI = 3.1415927
    WRITE(*,"(A,5X,A/)")'FREQUENCY  DECIBELS'
    DO F = 0, 21
     W = 2.0*PI*F
     A = 1.2186E05 −62.1*W**2
     HDEN = A + CMPLX(0.0, 4889*W − W**3)
     Y = 20.0*LOG10(CABS(1.2186E05/HDEN))
     WRITE(*,"(1X,I6,4X,F8.2)") F,Y
    END DO
    END PROGRAM CHEBO3R1
```

TRIAL RUN

```
FREQUENCY    DECIBELS
    0            0.00
    1           −0.09
    2           −0.34
    3           −0.65
    4           −0.90
    5           −1.00
    6           −0.88
    7           −0.55
    8           −0.13
    9           −0.05
   10           −1.00
   11           −3.14
   12           −5.84
   13           −8.57
   14          −11.10
   15          −13.42
   16          −15.53
   17          −17.47
   18          −19.25
   19          −20.91
   20          −22.46
   21          −23.91
*     *     *     *     *
```

```
    PROGRAM CHEBO4R1
!   CHEBYCHEV; ORDER 3, R 1 db; CUTOFF 10 HZ; -31db @ 20 HZ
    IMPLICIT NONE
    REAL:: Y, W, A
    COMPLEX:: HDEN
    INTEGER :: F
    REAL, PARAMETER:: PI = 3.1415927
    WRITE(*,"(A,5X,A/)")'FREQUENCY  DECIBELS'
    DO F = 0, 21, 1
     W = 2.0*PI*F
     A = 4.295E06 - 0.574E04*W**2 + W**4
     HDEN = A + CMPLX(0.0, 0.1842E06*W - 59.87*W**3)
     Y = 20.0*LOG10(CABS(4.295E06/HDEN))
     WRITE(*,"(1X,I6,4X,F8.2)") F,Y
    END DO
    END PROGRAM CHEBO4R1
*    *    *    *    *
```

TRIAL RUN

FREQUENCY	DECIBELS
0	0.00
1	0.13
2	0.49
3	0.86
4	0.99
5	0.72
6	0.26
7	0.00
8	0.26
9	0.93
10	0.00
11	-4.29
12	-9.23
13	-13.57
14	-17.31
15	-20.59
16	-23.51
17	-26.15
18	-28.56
19	-30.80
20	-32.87
21	-34.81

```
*    *    *    *    *
```

```
    PROGRAM CHEB5R1B
!   CHEBYCHEV; ORDER 5, R 1 db; CUTOFF 100 HZ; -41db @ 200 HZ
    IMPLICIT NONE
    REAL:: Y, W, A
    COMPLEX:: HDEN
    INTEGER :: F
    REAL, PARAMETER:: PI = 3.1415927
    WRITE(*,"(A,5X,A/)")'FREQUENCY  DECIBELS'
```

```
DO F = 0, 200, 4
 W = 2.0*PI*F
 A = 1.202E13 − 0.2417E09*W**2 + 588.6*W**4
 HDEN = A + CMPLX(0.0, 0.9047E11*W − 0.6667E06*W**3 + W**5)
 Y = 20.0*LOG10(CABS(1.202E13/HDEN))
 WRITE(*,"(1X,I6,4X,F8.2)") F,Y
END DO
END PROGRAM CHEB5R1B
```

TRIAL RUN

FREQUENCY	DECIBELS
0	0.00
4	−0.04
8	−0.16
12	−0.34
16	−0.54
20	−0.73
24	−0.89
28	−0.98
32	−1.00
36	−0.93
40	−0.80
44	−0.61
48	−0.38
52	−0.18
56	−0.04
60	−0.01
64	−0.12
68	−0.35
72	−0.63
76	−0.87
80	−1.01
84	−0.94
88	−0.65
92	−0.21
96	−0.03
100	−1.00
104	−3.46
108	−6.60
112	−9.74
116	−12.64
120	−15.29
124	−17.72
128	−19.95
132	−22.03
136	−23.96
140	−25.78
144	−27.50
148	−29.13
152	−30.69
156	−32.17
160	−33.59
164	−34.95

```
168        -36.26
172        -37.53
176        -38.75
180        -39.92
184        -41.07
188        -42.17
192        -43.25
196        -44.30
200        -45.31
 *     *     *     *     *
```

Once the design is complete, a Chebychev filter can be constructed using electronic elements as shown in Fig. 7.8.

7.13.4 Use of the INCLUDE Statement

When we examine the subroutines CHEB1TRAN and CHEB3TRAN, we observe that the statements

```
'THE NUMERATOR OF THE TRANSFER FN. IS ',NUMER
'THE DENOMINATOR OF THE TRANSFER FUNCTION IS'
```

appear 10 times requiring 20 lines in the program. Because this situation occurs sufficiently often, it is worth providing a remedy. A possible solution involves using the INCLUDE statement, which is called a *metacommand*. To illustrate its use, we show program DEMOINCL, which, though resembling the filter design program we have discussed, is much shorter.

```
PROGRAM DEMOINCL
OPEN(2,FILE = 'C:\FOR90\INCL.DAT')
CALL BUTTERWORTH
NUMER = 1.58E06
INCLUDE 'C:\FOR90\TRANSFER.DAT'
A1 = 1.58E06
A2 = 1.777E03
A3 = 1.0
```

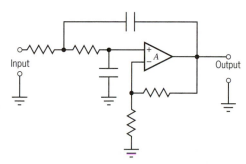

FIGURE 7.8   A Chebychev filter can be realized using appropriate combinations of electronic components including high gain amplifiers, resistors and capacitors. Here, *A* is an electronic amplifier with a very high amplification.

```
WRITE(*,*)A1,'+',A2,'s','+',A3,'s**2'
WRITE(2,*)A1,'+',A2,'s','+',A3,'s**2'
RETURN
END SUBROUTINE BUTTERWORTH
```

Program DEMOINCL opens logical unit 2 and file INCL.DAT, which will contain the results of WRITE statements that reference logical unit 2. Note that the statement IN-CLUDE:'C:\FOR90\TRANSFER.DAT' provides the location of TRANSFER.DAT, namely, the subdirectory FOR90.

The file TRANSFER.DAT consists of the statements

```
!     TRANSFER.DAT
      WRITE(*,*)'NUMERATOR OF THE TRANSFER FUNCTION IS ',NUMER
      WRITE(2,*)'NUMERATOR OF THE TRANSFER FUNCTION IS ',NUMER
      WRITE(*,*)'THE DENOMINATOR OF THE TRANSFER FUNCTION IS'
      WRITE(2,*)'THE DENOMINATOR OF THE TRANSFER FUNCTION IS'
```

After program DEMOINC has been compiled and run, the file INCL.DAT appears as follows.

```
NUMERATOR OF THE TRANSFER FUNCTION IS 1580000
THE DENOMINATOR OF THE TRANSFER FUNCTION IS
  1.5800000E+06 + 1.777E+03 s+ 1.0000000 s**2
```

If we had used the INCLUDE statement in program FILMENUG, we could have shortened the program by 10 lines.

Some Intrinsic Functions	
ABS(y)	The absolute value of y; if y is integer or real, the result is $\|y\|$; if y is complex (w,z), the result is $\sqrt{w^2 + z^2}$.
AIMAG(w)	The imaginary part of complex number w.
AINT(x)	Produces the truncation of real number x to a whole number. For example, if $x = 3.14159$, the result of AINT(x) is 3.0.
ASIN(x)	The arcsin, in radians, of the real number x.
ATAN(y)	The arctangent, in radians, of the real number y.
CABS(w)	The absolute value of the complex number w.
CMPLX(a,b)	Convert the arguments to complex number $a + jb$
COS(z)	The cosine, in radians, of z.
COSH(z)	The hyperbolic cosine of z.
DOT_PRODUCT(**A**,**B**)	Given vectors **A** and **B**, this function computes their dot product.
EXP(y)	The exponential function e^y.
FLOOR(r)	Returns the greatest integer less than or equal to the real number r. For example, FLOOR(7.4) has the value 7.
INT(d)	Converts d to integer type. If $\|d\|, < 0$, then INT(d) = 0. If $\|d\| \geq 1$, then INT(d) is the largest integer that does not exceed the magnitude of d and the sign of which is the same as the sign of d.
ICHAR(D)	This function returns a number which is the ASCII code (collating sequence) for a character enclosed within the apostrophes. Thus, ICHAR('C') returns the number 67, ICHAR('D') returns 68, ICHAR('c') returns 98 and ICHAR('d') returns 99.
LEN(STRING)	Determines the length of a character string. For example, if COMPOSER is declared by the statement CHARACTER*6 COMPOSER

	Some Intrinsic Functions
	Then, K = LEN('MOZART') will assign the value 6 to K.
LOG(x)	Calculates the natural logarithm of x: e^x
LOG10(x)	Calculates $\log_{10}(x)$
LLT(A,B)	This function tests whether the character A precedes character B in the ASCII collating sequence. A and B must be of character type. A and B may be single characters or they may be character strings. If A precedes B in the collating sequence, the result of the test is the value true.
MATMUL(**A,B**)	This function performs multiplication of matrices **A** and **B** in the order **AB**. The matrices must be conformable; that is, the number of columns of A must be equal to the number of rows of **B**.
MAX(X1,X2, . . .)	Returns the largest argument.
MIN(X1,X2, . . .)	Returns the smallest argument.
MOD(n,k)	This function divides the integer n by the integer k and returns the value of the remainder.
NINT(x)	For x real, this function returns the nearest integer. For example, NINT(7.6) has the value 8.
SQRT(x)	Approximates the square root of x.
TAN(x)	With x in radians, the result is an approximation to $\tan(x)$
TANH(x)	The result is an approximation to the hyperbolic tangent of x.

▶ **PROBLEMS**

In some of the problems below, more than one set of data are provided for testing the program. To use these data, you can run the program several times. However, a better method is to begin by including a statement similar to:

```
WRITE(*,*)'ENTER BYE TO END THE PROGRAM, ELSE ENTER YES'.
```

If the user enters BYE, an IF statement will cause GO TO 1000 to be executed, where 1000 is the label at the end of the program. The program will branch there and terminate. At the previous line there should be a GO TO 900, where 900 is a label at the statement WRITE(*,*)'ENTER BYE . . .' . The program will branch to the beginning of the program, and the user can then enter additional data and peform another trial run. These steps can be repeated until BYE is entered.

We will refer to the above procedure by the comment, "Include statements in your program for running the program repeatedly."

7.1 A normalized vector $\bar{a}$ is a vector of unit magnitude that is obtained from another vector $\bar{A}$ by dividing each component of $\bar{A}$ by the magnitude of $\bar{A}$. For example, if

$$\bar{A} - [1, -1, 3, 2]$$
$$\text{then, } |\bar{A}| - \sqrt{15}$$
$$\bar{a} = \left[\frac{1}{\sqrt{15}}, \frac{-1}{\sqrt{15}}, \frac{3}{\sqrt{15}}, \frac{2}{\sqrt{15}} \right]$$

Write a program that contains a subprogram UNIT which receives the components of a vector from a main program and returns the components of the unit vector, as in the example above, to the main program. Include statements in your program for running the program repeatedly.

```
Sample Data

Set    N                  Ā

 1     4         [1, − 1, 3, 2]

 2     6         [2, 3, 6, −5, 4, −7]
```

Sample data are not part of the program; they are data which the user enters, *when the program* is *run*, in order to test the program; this comment applies to all programs.

7.2   Occasionally, it is necessary to convert a binary number (a number in base 2) to the base 10. When the binary number has only a few digits, this task is easy. However, as the number of digits increase, it becomes desirable to allow the computer to do the work.

Let the digits of the binary number be $b_1, b_2, \ldots b_n$ where b_n is the least significant digit. The decimal equivalent is generated step by step and stored in D_n, $D_{n-1}, \ldots, D_1$. D_1 contains the answer. The algorithm is

$$D_n = b_n$$
$$D_{n-1} = b_{n-1} + 2D_n$$
$$D_{n-2} = b_{n-2} + 2D_{n-1}$$
$$\cdots\cdots\cdots$$
$$D_1 = b_1 + 2D_2$$

As an example, we convert 110011_2 to its decimal equivalent.

$$D_6 = b_6 \qquad\quad = 1$$
$$D_5 = b_5 + 2D_6 = 3$$
$$D_4 = b_4 + 2D_5 = 6$$
$$D_3 = b_3 + 2D_4 = 12$$
$$D_2 = b_2 + 2D_3 = 25$$
$$D_1 = b_1 + 2D_2 = 51 \qquad \textbf{Answer}$$

Write a program that contains a subroutine whose input is the number of digits and the binary number. The subroutine should return the decimal number to the main program. Include statements in your program for running the program repeatedly.

```
            Sample Data

      1     110011₂
      2     1101011₂
```

7.3   In many branches of engineering, it is necessary to calculate the variation of a transfer function over a relatively wide range of frequencies. In this case, it is customary to use a logarithmic frequency scale. For example, the first frequency band might be: 1, 2, ... , 8, 9; the second, 10, 11, ... , 80, 90; the third 100, 200, ... , 900, 1000; and so forth. We will call the frequency bands cycles.

Write a program that prompts the user to enter the number of cycles. The frequencies should be generated and *printed* by a DO loop such as

```
DO I = MIN, MAX, INC
```

Initially, the values of these variables should be

```
MIN = 1;   MAX = 9;   INC = 1
```

After each cycle, a subroutine CHANGE should be called, which multiplies each of the variables by 10. Test the program by using at least three cycles.

7.4   The Belleville washer spring is used for carrying heavy loads with relatively small deflections (See Fig. P7.4).

The design equations for the Belleville washer spring are:

$$P = \frac{4E\delta}{(1-v^2)K_1D_0^2}[(h-\delta)(h-\delta/2)t + t^3]$$

$$\sigma = \frac{4E\delta}{(1-v^2)K_1D_0^2}[K_2(h-\delta/2) + K_3t]$$

with

$$K_1 = \frac{6(\alpha-1)^2}{(\pi \ln\alpha)\alpha^2}$$

$$K_2 = \frac{6}{\pi \ln\alpha}\left[\frac{(\alpha-1)}{\ln\alpha} - 1\right]$$

$$K_3 = \frac{6}{\pi \ln\alpha}\frac{\alpha-1}{2}$$

$$\alpha = \frac{D_0}{D_i}$$

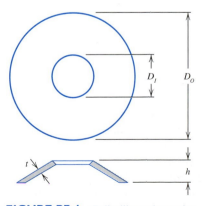

FIGURE P7.4   Belleville washer spring.

where

P = applied load, lb

E = modulus of elasticity, lb/in^2

δ = deflection, in

v = Poisson's ratio

h = inside height of spring, in

t = thickness of spring, in

D^o = outside diameter, in

D^i = inside diameter, in

σ = maximum tensile strength, lb/in^2

Write a FORTRAN program that will accept the physical dimensions of the spring (outer and inner diameters, inside height, and thickness) and the physical properties of the material (modulus of elasticity, Poisson's ratio, and maximum allowable stress) and that will print a table. The table should have the deflection, load, and stress. Start with a deflection of 0.001 in. and increase the deflection in steps of 0.001 until the maximum allowable load is exceeded. At that point, the message ALLOWABLE STRESS EXCEEDED, DEFLECTION = *value* should be printed. Include statements in your program for running the program repeatedly.

Sample Data

Set	D_0	D_i	h	t	E	v	σ
1	2.	1.	0.125	0.05	3×10^7	0.3	2×10^5
2	3.	1.25	0.100	0.06	3×10^7	0.3	2×10^5

7.5 When the dimensions and material of a Belleville spring are known, it is relatively simple to analyze the spring to find its load-deflection characteristics and the stresses produced at different loads. This was accomplished in the solution to the previous problem. However, if the spring must be *designed* to meet a particular set of load-deflection specifications, the required dimensions for the spring cannot be found directly. Instead, an iterative method of solution must be used.

Using the design equations given in the preceding problem, write a program to design a Belleville spring given the following data.

1. Outside and inside diameter of the washer.

2. Maximum deflection (δ) at a specified load.

3. Physical properties (modulus of elasticity and Poisson's ratio) of the material used.

The program should calculate and print the values for the required thickness and height.

Suggestion: The program should produce successive values of thickness, beginning with $t = 0.001$, and calculate the load required to produce maximum deflection. It should compare this load with the specified design load and continue until a satisfactory design has been obtained. It may not be possible to obtain an *exact* solution because uniform increments of thickness are used. Therefore, the user should print the required thickness and height for the calculated loads immediately above and below the specified load.

7.6   In many engineering applications, the joint probability of two continuous random variables X and Y is of importance. For example, one might be interested in the hardness and tensile strength of a metal. A typical probability calculation involving two random variables is, "Find the probability that $X \leq x$ and $Y \leq y$." This can be expressed by the notation $P(X \leq x$ and $Y \leq y)$.

A probability of this type can be calculated from the *joint distribution function* $F(x, y)$. That is, $P(X \leq x$ and $Y \leq y) = F(x, y)$.

Consider a particular joint distribution function:

$$F(x, y) = \begin{array}{ll} 0 & x < 0 \quad \text{or} \quad y > 0 \\ (1 - e^{-x})y^3 & 0 \leq x, 0 \leq y \leq 1 \\ (1 - e^{-x}) & 0 \leq x, 1 < y \end{array}$$

Note that the distribution function assumes *different values* as the *range* of the random variables changes. For the present case, we illustrate this by the following examples:

$$P(X \leq 0.1 \text{ and } Y \leq -0.1) = F(0.1, -0.1) = 0$$
$$P(X \leq -0.1 \text{ and } Y \leq 0.1) = F(-0.1, 0.1) = 0$$
$$P(0 < X \leq 1 \text{ and } 0 < Y \leq 0.5) = (F(1, 0.5)$$
$$= (1 - e^{-1})(0.5)^3 = 0.0790$$
$$P(0 < X \leq 1 \text{ and } 1 < Y) = F(1, Y > 1) = (1 - e^{-1}) = 0.632$$

Write a program that carries out probability calculations using the distribution function shown above and calculates probabilities for the four examples given. Include statements in your program for running the program repeatedly. Use the data in the four examples for your trial runs.

7.7   Relative humidity can be determined from dry- and wet-bulb temperatures by using a psychrometric chart. One of the difficulties associated with using the chart is that it must be constructed for a particular barometric pressure. Correction of the chart readings to elevation and atmospheric conditions is tedious.

This problem indicates a method for calculating the relative humidity without use of a chart. If the saturated vapor conditions at the wet- and dry-bulb temperatures can be found, the Carrier equation makes it possible to find the actual vapor pressure for the existing atmospheric pressure, and from this value the relative humidity can be calculated. It is possible to calculate the saturation pressure using Eq. (1):

$$p_s = p_c \exp[(0.01)(t_c - t) \sum_{i=1}^{8} F_i (0.65 - 0.01t)^{i-1} (C + 273.15)] \qquad (1)$$

where

p_s = saturation pressure, lb/in^2

p_c = critical pressure = 3246.0525 lb/in^2

t_c = critical temperature = 374.136 °C

t = saturation temperature, °C

C = either the dry-bulb or the wet-bulb temperature converted from degrees Fahrenheit to degrees Kelvin

The function coefficients, F_i, are

$F_1 = -741.924$

$F_2 = -29.721$

$F_3 = -11.55286$

$F_4 = -0.868564$

$F_5 = 0.10941$

$F_6 = 0.439993$

$F_7 = 0.25207$

$F_8 = 0.0521868$

The saturation pressure at the wet-bulb temperature determined from Eq. (1) can be used with a Carrier equation, Eq. (2), to find the vapor pressure:

$$p_v = p_{wb} - \frac{(p_a - p_{wb})(t_d - t_w)}{(2831. - 1.43t_w)}$$

(2)

where

p_v = actual vapor pressure, lb/in^2 absolute

p_{wb} = saturation pressure at the wet-bulb temperature, lb/in^2 absolute

p_a = atmospheric pressure, lb/in^2 absolute

t_d = dry-bulb temperature, °F

t_w = wet-bulb temperature, °F

With the vapor pressure from Eq. (2) and the saturation pressure from Eq. (1), the relative humidity is calculated from Eq. (3):

$$R = (p_v/p_{db})100$$

(3)

where R = relative humidity, %, P_{db} = saturation pressure at the dry bulb temperature, lb/in^2 abs.

Write a FORTRAN program that calculates the relative humidity, R. The data to be entered are:

Atmospheric pressure, psia (AP)

Dry-bulb temperature, °F (DBT)

Wet-bulb temperature, °F (WBT)

In order to calculate the relative humidity, R, the saturation pressure at the dry-bulb temperature, PDB, and the saturation pressure at the wet-bulb temperature, PWB are needed.

Your program should use a SUBROUTINE PRESSURE (PS, T) which should contain Eq. (2). The main program should contain Eq. (1) and Eq. (3). Note that the subroutine statement has two dummy arguments, namely PS and T.

When the subroutine is called by the main program, the call will transmit either a value of DBT or a value of WBT to the dummy argument T. If DBT is transmitted, then the subroutine will return the value of PDB to the main program. If the WBT is transmitted to the subroutine, the subroutine will return the value of PWB. In summary, the two calls in the main program are

```
CALL PRESSURE(PDB, DBT) (First call; the value of PDB is returned)
CALL PRESSURE(PWB, WBT) (Second call; the value of PWB is returned)
```

After the calls have been executed, the main program has the values of PWB and PDB. Then, using the acquired value of PWB and the other data already available, Eq. (2) should be used to calculate PV, the vapor pressure. Finally, PV and PDB are used in Eq. (3) to calculate R, the relative humidity.

As stated above, the input to the subroutine is either a dry-bulb temperature DBT or a wet-bulb temperature WBT. Each of these is in °F. Because Eq. (2) requires temperature in °C, t should be converted within the subroutine from F to C. The term $(C + 273.15)$ in the denominator of (1) converts to °K.

Within the subroutine, use a DATA statement to store the values of the coefficients F_i. In addition, set the value of the critical temperature, TC, and the critical pressure, PC, as follows:

$$TC = 374.136; \quad PC = 3246.053$$

Include statements in your program for running the program repeatedly. The program should use the following data for the trial runs

```
1. ATMOSPHERIC PRESSURE 14.3
   DRY-BULB TEMPERATURE 80.0
   WET-BULB TEMPERATURE 60.0

2. ATMOSPHERIC PRESSURE 14.7
   DRY-BULB TEMPERATURE 80.0
   WET-BULB TEMPERATURE 60.0

3. ATMOSPHERIC PRESSURE 14.7
   DRY-BULB TEMPERATURE 80.0
   WET-BULB TEMPERATURE 60.0
```

7.8 In certain scientific or engineering problems, it is necessary to evaluate integrals of the form

$$K(k) = \int_0^{\pi/2} \frac{d\phi}{\sqrt{1 - k^2 \sin^2 \phi}}$$

This integral is known as the complete elliptic integral of the first kind, and it is usually denoted, as indicated above, by $K(k)$. The parameter k is determined by the particulars of the problem, often the geometry. Some of these applications are shown in the problems at the end of this chapter.

One method of evaluating $K(k)$ is to use the polynomial approximation

$K(k) = 1.38629 + U*(0.111972 + 0.0725296*U) - \ln(U)*(0.5 + U*(0.1213478 + 0.0288729*U)$

where $U = 1.0 - k^2$.

Write a program that contains a function subprogram that evaluates $K(k)$ for $k = 0.1, 0.3, 0.5, 0.7$ and 0.9.

7.9 The scalar electric potential, V, at any point (r, ϕ, z) owing to a filamentary ring of charge of radius R in the plane $z = 0$ and centered at the origin is

$$V = \frac{\rho R}{\pi \epsilon_0 \epsilon_r \sqrt{(r + R)^2 + z^2}} K(k)$$

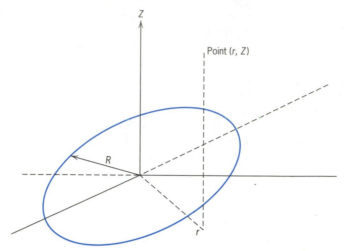

FIGURE P7.9   Filamentary ring of charge.

where

$$k = \frac{2\sqrt{rR}}{\sqrt{(r+R)^2 + z^2}}$$

where

V = scalar electric potential, V

ϵ_0 = permittivity of vacuum = 8.85×10^{-12} F/m

ϵ_r = relative permittivity

r, z = coordinates of field point in circular coordinate system, m

R = radius of ring charge, m

ρ = charge density, C/m

$K(k)$ = complete elliptic integral of the first kind

Note that V is independent of the angular coordinate ϕ; therefore, ϕ does not appear in the equation for the scalar electric potential.

Write a FORTRAN program that calculates and prints the value of the electric potential V. The program should use the function subprogram developed in Problem 7.8.

```
Sample Data
R = 0.2 m
r = 0.2 m
z = 0.3 m
εr = 1.0
ρ = 27.8 × 10⁻¹²
```

7.10   The permutation symbol ϵ_{ijk} is defined by the following rules:

$\epsilon_{ijk} = 0$ if two or more subscripts are equal

$\epsilon_{ijk} = +1$ if ijk are in cyclic order clockwise

$\epsilon_{ijk} = -1$ otherwise

For example,

$$\epsilon_{112} = \epsilon_{122} = 0$$
$$\epsilon_{123} = \epsilon_{231} = \epsilon_{312} = +1$$
$$\epsilon_{321} = \epsilon_{132} = \epsilon_{213} = -1$$

Write a FORTRAN program that contains a subprogram that receives the values of i, j, and k from a main program and returns the value of ϵ_{ijk} to the main program. The main program should print a table of the values the permutation symbol assumes as i, j, and k are varied. The table will contain 27 rows.

7.11 The cross product of two three-dimensional vectors

$$\bar{A} = [A_1, A_2, A_3]$$
$$\bar{B} = [B_1, B_2, B_3]$$

is defined by

$$\bar{A} \times \bar{B} = \sum_{i=1}^{3} \sum_{j=1}^{3} \sum_{k=1}^{3} \epsilon_{ijk} A_j B_k \bar{a}_i$$

where the three components of the cross product are

$$(A_2 B_3 - A_3 B_2)$$
$$(A_3 B_1 - A_1 B_3)$$
$$(A_1 B_2 - A_2 B_1)$$

and a_i is a unit vector.

Write a program that calculates the three components of the cross products of $\bar{A}$ and $\bar{B}$. Use the subroutine written for Problem 7.10 to return the value of the permutation symbol.

Sample Data

Set	$\bar{A}$	$\bar{B}$
1	[1, 4, −2]	[2, −3, −1]
2	[27, 16, 95]	[43, −9, −4]

7.12 The capacitance between flat conductors lying on a substrate of high dielectric constant is of interest in the design and analysis of microelectronic circuits. A small section of a circuit is shown in Fig. P7.12 on the next page.

The capacitance C is

$$C = \frac{0.1125 \epsilon_r K(k_1)}{K(k_2)} \quad pF/inch$$

where

$$k_1 = \sqrt{1 - \frac{a}{b^2}}$$
$$k_2 = (a/b)^2$$

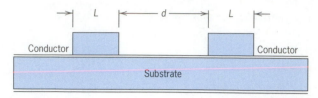

FIGURE P7.12 Capacitance between flat conductors on a substrate.

Where

$$a = \frac{\pi}{2t} \tanh \frac{\pi d}{4t}$$

$$b = \frac{\pi}{2t} \tanh \left(\frac{\pi L}{2t} + \frac{\pi d}{4t} \right)$$

ϵ_r = relative permittivity

$K(k_1), K(k_2)$ = complete elliptic integrals of the first kind with arguments k_1 and k_2, respectively:

Write a FORTRAN program that calculates C. The program should use the function subprogram developed in Problem 7.8.

Sample Data

$$\varepsilon_r = 1773$$
$$t = 0.001 \text{ in.}$$
$$L = 0.001 \text{ in.}$$
$$d = 0.002 \text{ in.}$$

7.13 Write a program that consists of

(a) MODULE ASSIST

(b) Main program ALGEBRA

(c) SUBROUTINE CALC1

(d) SUBROUTINE CALC2

MODULE ASSIST should contain a declaration for real variables W, X, Y, Z, which gives each of them DIMENSION(10). ASSIST should be used by ALGEBRA, CALC1 and CALC2.

CALC1 should assign: $Y(1) = 12; Z(1) = 14$
and $W(1) = Y(1)**2 + Z(1)**2$
CALC2 should assign: $Y(2) = 7; Z(2) = 22$
and $X(2) = SQRT(2*Y(2) + 4*Z(2))$

Main program ALGEBRA should print the value of $W(1)$ and the value of $X(2)$.

7.14 A program for calculating hypergeometric probabilities was shown in Example 5.4. In that program there were nine DO loops for calculating the factorial. Now that we have studied subprograms, we can shorten the program by using one function subprogram. Rewrite the program using a function subprogram and test it using the data of Example 5.4.

8

Program Testing
and Debugging

8.1 PRINCIPLES

Development of successful FORTRAN 90 programs involves several important steps: determining and specifying the engineering or scientific problem to be solved; designing the algorithm (method of solution) to be used; generating, compiling, and linking the code needed to produce an executable version; and finally, debugging and testing the resultant code. The debugging and testing phase often requires the most time. Many logical errors in a program do not appear until well after the program has been in use for a considerable period of time. This delay occurs because it is virtually impossible to test a program for all possible combinations of input data. A particular set of input numbers that causes program failure may not occur until many users have had extensive experience with the software. Testing and debugging a program is further complicated by the possibility that a given algorithm does not have a single correct answer.

Once a number of difficulties are detected, the software developer will resolve these problems, resulting in a new version of the program. Thus, a user will notice that his or her program will have an accompanying "version number." (A typical version number has a format such as "$x.y$" where y represents the percentage of change since the last revision and x is the number of complete revisions; version 2.1 would signify that the program is in its second complete revision and has already undergone a 10% change since this new improvement was introduced.) The process of correcting errors may in itself introduce additional errors of a subtle nature, problems that were not present when the task of revising the program began. Normally, a manufacturer will decided that a complete revision is necessary once the current one has been changed by only 30 percent. This is because programs may become extremely fragmented and disorganized after undergoing revisions, even modest ones. Maintaining a well-structured program becomes increasingly difficult when various "exceptions" (necessary to provide for errors) must be added to the code. Removing errors is the purpose served by *debugging*. Debugging and upkeep of programs are generally referred to as *program maintenance*. These processes often account for 80 percent (or more) of the cost of a software product, with design and development of the original code making up only 20 percent of the cost.

Debugging begins with the design and structure of the program itself. A well-organized program makes extended use of subroutines to implement the tasks required to achieve the software goals.

EXAMPLE 8.1 Organization of a Transportation Planning and Research Program

In a number of instances, engineers rely on programs for proper planning of transportation systems. (Transportation in its broadest meaning includes a variety of "traffic." Some applications such as roadway systems established to handle automobile and truck traffic are familiar ones; telephone systems, systems to transmit computer data over local area networks [LANs], and systems that transmit television images can also be considered "transportation systems.") Software in support of planning is designed to process, store, and apply traffic volume data over appropriate networks (e.g., highways or LANs). A modular approach to the design of a transportation planning (and research) program could include subroutines for statistical analysis of traffic; estimation of daily traffic from small samples; Database (DB) file maintenance subroutines; various traffic-modeling algorithms; and queuing simulation for the planning of transportation gateways. Each of these elements of the program can be developed as a subprogram, which greatly eases the problems associated with program debugging and maintenance.

Some advantages of modular software include:

- Isolation of logical errors is simplified when subprograms are tested independently.
- Only minimum interference between different subroutines occurs when debugging.
- Ease of modification of subprograms without undue interaction with other subroutines is possible as long as a well-defined data structure is part of the design.

The first consideration in the course of program development is to successfully compile the source code. This step will eliminate most, but not all, syntactical errors. (One instance in which a syntactical error is detected during program execution is described below.) Once the source code is compiled, the program may be executed and any immediate ("gross") logical errors will be disclosed and will appear as *run-time* errors when the program is aborted.

The process of testing the program can proceed once it is free of syntactical errors. If convenient, data should be classified according to their characteristics and one sample from each classification used to test the program. For example, if the objects (variables) are records with different data types composing each field, then test samples should include cases that test the program for each data field. There is no objective rule regarding how many test samples should be included. Rather, it will depend on a number of factors, including practical estimates of how many unique data points the program must be able to accept; the economics of testing many points; and the complexity for each test. In the case of test complexity, for example, it may be necessary to create a file using an editor program that may require considerable time. It may be useful to write yet a second program to test the first program. For example, a program that supplies data to the target program in a systematic way may provide a thorough test. This approach, however, is limited by the necessity to develop (test and debug) an additional program that itself may include logical errors. The target program may not therefore be tested in accordance with the plan.

In addition to the factors discussed above, it is extremely important to observe that the user should examine the results closely. A program may execute properly, produce a numerically correct result, and yet be totally incorrect and make no sense whatsoever.

Finally, many examples do not have a (single) correct answer for a given set of input data. A program that suggests the number of trunk lines required for a telephone network may depend on the estimates of traffic which the program generates, and these estimates can vary from run to run even if the same input data are used each time. (Trunk lines are those that carry messages between substations of a telephone system; individual customers are connected to substations. Substation architectures eliminate the need to connect every customer to every other customer—an approach that is prohibitively expensive and complicated.) How, then, can we concude that such a program is functioning properly? (See Problem 8.1.)

Detailed debugging begins when the test samples reveal errors. Program debugging parallels testing a mechanical or an electrical system; "meters" are inserted at critical points, and the measured results are used to detect deviations from the design. In a program, such "meters" are temporary PRINT statements that are inserted to display the values of appropriate variables at critical junctions in the code. One way to start is to insert such "probes" at points that are well-defined boundaries of the pseudocode (or flow diagram), particularly if it is unclear at which point the error is introduced. Once the point(s) at which the program results deviate from expected answers is (are) established, additional PRINT statements may be added to localize the error within the offending block of code.

We now discuss a number of specific examples that are representative of those described in a general way in Sec. 8.1. They contain samples of how to test as well as debug programs, and they will include a case where a syntactical error occurs at run time; an instance of the occurrence of a gross logical error; at least one case in which "intelligent" interpretation of computer results detects a subtle logical error; a way to test programs for which a range of answers is possible; and a case in which the process of testing and debugging a program proceeds in a systematic manner.

EXAMPLE 8.2 A Case in Which a Syntactical Error Is Revealed at Run Time

A short program is shown below, and it is described by the following pseudocode:

```
program run_time_syntax_error
{initialize array values}
{display the array on the monitor}
end program run_time_syntax_error
```

The FORTRAN 90 source code for this program is

```
PROGRAM RUN_TIME_SYNTAX_ERROR
!
! DECLARATIONS
```

```
          IMPLICIT NONE
          REAL, DIMENSION(1:8), PARAMETER :: &
                SAMPLE_DATA = (/0.1,0.2,0.3,0.4,0.5,0.6,0.7,0.8/)
    !
    ! START OF MAIN PROGRAM
    !
                PRINT "(A,8F6,3)",                               &
                        "   THE ARRAY VALUES ARE ",              &
                        SAMPLE_DATA
    END PROGRAM RUN_TIME_SYNTAX_ERROR
```

The values of the variables in array SAMPLE_DATA are defined using the PARAMETER option within a type declaration. The array contains eight real valued items from 0.1 to 0.8. The main portion of the program consists of a simple PRINT statement. The first portion of the statement should display the phrase "THE ARRAY VALUES ARE" on the monitor, and this phrase should be followed immediately (on the same line) with the values for the array SAMPLE_DATA. However, a syntactical error has been deliberately introduced, namely, the edit descriptor "8F6,4." Notice the presence of the comma; this should have been a decimal point ("8F6.4"—the offending phrase is shaded). The program compiles, links and loads successfully. However, during execution the program aborts with the following message displayed on the monitor:

```
          Expected decimal point in format specification
          Program terminated by fatal I/O error
          ^C
```

The symbol "^C indicates that a *control-C* command was issued to the PC, which means that control was returned to the operating system. Once the error is corrected, the program successfully displays the results:

```
    THE ARRAY VALUES ARE 0.100 0.200 0.300 0.400 0.500 0.600 0.700 0.800
```

This example demonstrates that an error in syntax may escape detection during compilation. Such errors depend on the FORTRAN 90 compiler that is being used, but all compilers may produce code with one or more syntactical errors of this type.

Detection of the error within this program is relatively easy. Only one statement includes a format specification, and there the error is immediately noticed. In more complex programs, detection of this kind of error is significantly more difficult, for many more format specifications would likely be present. However, those portions of the program that precede the erroneous specification would execute properly and thus provide some clues to its location.

EXAMPLE 8.3 A Numerical Bug

Logarithmic functions occur frequently in the solution of scientific and engineering problems. Examples include relationships between voltage and current flow in electronic devices (e.g., transistors) and the human ear's response to sound intensity as well as the human eye's response to light intensity. The short program that follows might appear as part of a larger program; it is intended to demonstrate how numeric failures can be introduced into software.

```
PROGRAM NUMBER_BUG
!
! DECLARATIONS
        IMPLICIT NONE
        REAL :: LOG_RESULT,H
        INTEGER I
!
! START OF MAIN PROGRAM
!
        DO I=1,100
            H = 0.01*REAL(I)
            LOG_RESULT = LOG10(1.0-H)
        END DO
END PROGRAM NUMBER_BUG
```

The program was aborted during execution, with the following message (shown in abbreviated form):

```
Coprocessor fault (status=58A8 ,instruction address = 000000F4)
Overflow at User/000000F7
```

Without further investigation, the exact location of the failure may not be apparent. As noted in Sec. 8.1, one of the general measurement tools is the use of the temporary PRINT statement to detect where a failure occurs. These PRINT statements should normally use the simplest format (in order to minimize the potential to introduce unexpected errors because of edit descriptor failures). In the present example, a PRINT statement,

```
PRINT *, H,LOG_RESULT
```

is introduced just after assignment statement

```
LOG_RESULT = LOG10(1.0-H)
```

The last few samples shown on the monitor are

```
    0.9499999    -1.3010299
    0.9599999    -1.3979398
    0.9699999    -1.5228783
    0.9799999    -1.6989691
    0.9899999    -1.9999979
Coprocessor fault (status =68A8 ,instruction address = 000000F4)
Overflow at User/000000F7
---
```

It is now clear that as *H* approaches 1, the result (LOG10[1.0–H]) is increasingly negative until the coprocessor that carries out the arithmetic operations within the computer can no longer handle the size of the numbers generated by the implicit function (the logarithm [log] taken to the base 10). The programmer has asked the computer to find the logarithm of a number that eventually becomes 0 (1.0–H = 0 when H = 1.0), and we know that the logarithm of 0 is $-\infty$, a number that the computer clearly cannot reproduce.

EXAMPLE 8.4 A Logical Error in Control Structure

 Sorting a group of items into either ascending or descending order is a useful function that can be carried out by a computer; arranging objects in alphabetical order is one application of the sorting procedure. Because it is so useful, considerable study has been devoted to sorting algorithms, particularly with regard to the time it takes to sort a group of data items completely. Although the procedure described here is not the fastest method of sorting, the FORTRAN 90 program used to realize it is relatively simple. It is called a *bubble* sort, and a pseudocode description follows, assuming that the items to be sorted are found in an array (list):

```
program ascending_sort
do {for all items in the list addressed sequentially by the index
     (pointer)}
     do {for all items in the list starting with the one after
          pointer target}
              {compare pointer target with next item in the list}
              {If item is less than pointer target, interchange the
                  two items}
     end do
end do
end program ascending_sort
```

A *pointer* is an identifier (name) that can be used to refer to different objects during execution of a program. (The index in a DO loop or the index of an array may be "interpreted" to be pointer variables. However, FORTRAN 90 provides a more formal definition of pointer variables as distinct data types. In the sorting pseudocode, the term *pointer* refers to the DO loop index.)

The inner DO loop of the program places the smallest value in the array at the "top of the list." Assume that the top of the list is the first location of the array. The inner loop sequentially compares the value of each item in the array to the one stored in the top of the list. If an item is smaller, the two are interchanged. When the inner loop is complete, the smallest item will be stored at the top of the list.

The outer DO loop sequences the "top of the list pointer" through the array. After the smallest item has been placed in the first location of the array, the index of the outer loop is incremented so that it points (addresses) the second location of the array. The inner loop is repeated and when complete will have placed the next largest item in this location.

Continuing in this manner will result in a completely ordered list when the outer DO loop is terminated. The program used in this example will place the sorting algorithm within a subprogram (subroutine). The main program will open communication to a file in secondary storage, read the array values, call the subroutine, display the results, and finally close the communications channel. (The file and array will consist of a small number of integers because a logical error has been deliberately introduced into the control structure in the program shown below and a large file will only distract from the discussion.) The FORTRAN 90 source code is shown below:

```
        PROGRAM ASCENDING_SORT
  !
  ! DATA DECLARATIONS
  !
        IMPLICIT NONE
```

```
        INTEGER, DIMENSION(10) :: LIST_TO_BE_SORTED
!
! THE MAIN PROGRAM
!
        OPEN (2, FILE="B:DATALIST",ACTION="READ",STATUS="OLD")
        READ (2,"(I2)") LIST_TO_BE_SORTED
        PRINT "(T10,A)","THE UNSORTED LIST IS"
        PRINT "(I2)",LIST_TO_BE_SORTED
        CALL SORT
        PRINT "(T10,A)","THE SORTED LIST IS"
        PRINT "(I2)",LIST_TO_BE_SORTED
        CLOSE (2)
!
        CONTAINS
!
! SUBROUTINE SORT FOLLOWS
!
        SUBROUTINE SORT
        IMPLICIT NONE
        INTEGER :: TEMP,I,J,J1
        DO I = 1,10
          J1=I+1
              DO J=J1,9
                IF (LIST_TO_BE_SORTED(J) & LIST_TO_BE_SORTED(I)) THEN
                    TEMP = LIST_TO_BE_SORTED(I)
                    LIST_TO_BE_SORTED(I)=LIST_TO_BE_SORTED(J)
                    LIST_TO_BE_SORTED(J)=TEMP
                END IF
              END DO
        END DO
        END SUBROUTINE SORT
        END PROGRAM ASCENDING_SORT
```

Notice that within the subroutine it is not necessary to declare the array "LIST_TO_BE_SORTED" because it is already declared in the main program and the subroutine is internal to the program. In such cases, the CONTAINS statement is used. However, the variables TEMP, I, J, and J1 are local to the subroutine and therefore should be declared to be within the body of the subroutine. The main portion of the program follows the design of the algorithm. The file "DATALIST" located on drive "B:" is opened; it has been created "off-line" using an editor program. The data in the file are read and displayed on the monitor for demonstration purposes. Next, the subroutine SORT is called. The data list is once again displayed in order for us to verify that the list has indeed been sorted. Finally, the logical communication channel is closed.

The subroutine SORT cycles through the data list in the manner described in the pseudocode described above. We should note the way an interchange is accomplished; the relevant code is:

```
IF (LIST_TO_BE_SORTED(J) < LIST_TO_BE_SORTED(I)) THEN
        TEMP = LIST_TO_BE_SORTED(I)
        LIST_TO_BE_SORTED(I)=LIST_TO_BE_SORTED(J)
        LIST_TO_BE_SORTED(J)=TEMP
END IF
```

Important here is the need for the separate location, TEMP, which temporarily retains the data to be moved. If this location is not used, the data to be moved will invariably be lost. Once the smaller value is stored in TEMP, its location can be overwritten with the larger number that has been identified.

The file "B:DATALIST" contains the following sequence of numbers:

$$(25,6,12,8,26,15,10,33,2,35)$$

When the program is executed, the screen displays the following:

```
                              THE UNSORTED LIST IS
          25
          6
          12
          8
          26
          15
          10
          33
          2
          35

                              THE SORTED LIST IS
          2
          6
          8
          10
          12
          15
          25
          26
          33
          35
```

These results suggest that the program is reliable. Consider, however, that a second user runs the program and observes the following results. (Notice that the original list is different from the one used above.)

```
                              THE UNSORTED LIST IS
          25
          6
          12
          8
          26
          15
          10
          33
          5
          2

                              THE SORTED LIST IS
          5
          6
          8
          10
```

12
15
25
26
33
2

Table 8.1   Sample Walkthrough Tabulation

I	J1	J	list(J)	list(I)	Interchange
1	2	2	6	25	yes
1	2	3	12	6	no
...	...	...	...	...	...
1	2	7	10	6	no
1	2	8	33	6	no
1	2	9	5	6	yes

Clearly, the program has failed because the particular set of data that were used for this run revealed the malfunction. It remains to debug the problem in order to find the problem. The general approach proposed in Sec. 8.1.—the insertion of temporary PRINT statements within the code—would work in the present case but would require considerable time. (This extra time is needed because the error actually occurs at the end of the nested DO loops.) In particular, debugging nested DO loops as required here may be better served using a procedure known as a *walkthrough*. A walkthrough requires a step-by-step analysis of all variables in the order in which they are encountered in the program just as the computer sees them during execution. This procedure is carried out for the subroutine (SORT) shown in the accompanying table (see Table 8.1). (We have limited table entries to the few that highlight the logical control error within the program.) The walkthrough table reveals that the last entry in the list (2) has not been tested because the pointer J fails to reach 10, the last location in the list, and therefore it is never sampled. Simply changing a single line in the program eliminates this logical control error:

$$DO\ J=J1,10$$

With this change the program runs correctly.

EXAMPLE 8.5 Interpreting Program Results in an "Intelligent" Manner

A program designed to calculate the weight of a steel door is to be developed. A sketch of the door is shown in Fig. 8.1. The FORTRAN 90 source code for this calculation as originally developed is as follows.

```
PROGRAM CALCULATE_WEIGHT
!
! DECLARATIONS
        IMPLICIT NONE
        REAL :: DEPTH, LENGTH, WIDTH, DENSITY, WEIGHT
!
! START OF MAIN PROGRAM
```

```
! SET VALUES
        WIDTH = 3.0        ! FEET
        LENGTH = 6.0       ! FEET
        DEPTH = 2.0        ! INCHES
        DENSITY = 0.25     ! POUNDS/CUBIC INCH
! CALCULATE WEIGHT
        WEIGHT = WIDTH*LENGTH*DEPTH*DENSITY
! DISPLAY THE RESULTS
        PRINT "(A,F4.2)", " THE WIDTH OF THE DOOR IS ",WIDTH
        PRINT "(A,F4.2)", " THE LENGTH OF THE DOOR IS ",LENGTH
        PRINT "(A,F4.2)", " THE DEPTH OF THE DOOR IS ",DEPTH
        PRINT "(A,F6.2)", " THE WEIGHT OF THE DOOR IS ",WEIGHT
        END PROGRAM CALCULATE_WEIGHT
```

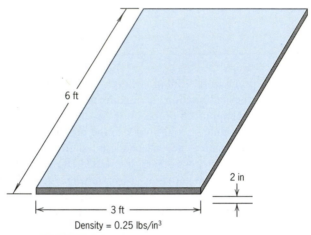

6 ft

2 in

3 ft

Density = 0.25 lbs/in^3

FIGURE 8.1 The steel door used in Example 8.5.

Values for the width, length, depth (thickness), and density of the door are defined within the program. The weight is calculated as a simple product of these variables, and all results are displayed on the monitor as shown by reading the PRINT statements. The results of the program appear as follows.

```
THE WIDTH OF THE DOOR IS 3.00
THE LENGTH OF THE DOOR IS 6.00
THE DEPTH OF THE DOOR IS 2.00
THE WEIGHT OF THE DOOR IS   9.00
```

From a superficial reading of the results, the uncritical observer would conclude that the steel door weighs 9 pounds. However, a perceptive user would question the answer; a steel door whose dimensions are 6 feet long by 3 feet wide is very likely to weigh considerably more than 9 pounds. Our experience tells us that the door should weigh considerably more. This example seeks to reinforce the idea that *computer results should be examined closely* before using the answers to make decisions. This program, though without syntactical error and without gross logical errors, produces results that are quite unreasonable. The logical error should be clear to the reader—the failure to convert all dimensions to a consistent set of units. If density is provided in pounds per cubic inch, then all dimensions must be converted to inches before assigning a value to weight. Once the program is changed, the resulting weight is displayed as

```
THE WEIGHT OF THE DOOR IS    1296.00
```

This is a more reasonable result. A variety of ways can be used to effect the necessary changes within the program. However, in addition to alterations of appropriate assignment statements, the format edit descriptor for the variable WEIGHT must be changed, or it will be incompatible with the result and the monitor will display a series of asterisks instead of the answer. (In this example, the format edit descriptor for weight was changed to F10.2, but others would work equally well.)

Although the original program produced answers that were clearly suspicious, some errors might be quite subtle, and the results might not be questioned in a critical way. Suppose that the value for the variable DENSITY was given in terms of pounds per cubic foot (and set to a value of 10.). In this case the answer turns out to be:

```
THE WEIGHT OF THE DOOR IS     360.00
```

Here the error is much less obvious, and the user might be tempted to accept this result and conclude that the program is reliable. *Computer results must always be carefully reviewed.* (In Problem 8.2 the reader is asked to develop a FORTRAN 90 program that will calculate the weight of the door correctly.)

EXAMPLE 8.6 Comparing Results to the "Real World"

One of the most powerful computer applications is simulation of real-world events; the results of such programs permit the engineer or scientist to gain insights, draw conclusions, test the validity of a theory, or make decisions. However, real-world events may vary with time or other circumstances; this variation introduces a problem for developing confidence in the proper operation of the program (or the underlying model). How do we test the reliability of the code? The programs shown below illustrate two checks that can be applied to such "nondeterministic" applications:

- Compare results to the real world.
- Use known constraints or rules that must be satisfied when the program is working correctly.

The first application refers to a program designed to test a theory about the way visual systems in animals work, including human vision. The results of this model might be used to design and develop improved robotic vision systems. (Refer to Fig. 8.2 for the discussion that follows.) A light is projected onto a screen and the cross section of the intensity is shown in Fig. 8.2a. The intended image is a band of bright light adjacent to a band of dim (or dark) light. We consider the visual system to be made up of a series of devices capable of detecting the intensity. Simplified representations of such detectors are shown in the figure. (Although only a few are shown for clarity, imagine a great many of such detectors arranged close together.) Each detector produces a number that is proportional to the average light that falls on it. If each detector "sees" the intensity directly in front of it, the ideal result is to exactly reproduce the light/dark transition (Fig. 8.2a). Unfortunately, practical optical detectors have a field of vision that is more closely depicted in Fig. 8.2b. When this is the case, the detectors near the light/dark boundary receive some high-intensity and some low-intensity information. The resultant "image" is more gradual and not sharp like the original stimulus (input). Therefore, the image that the system reports is a "blurred" edge. Animals (including humans) do not see this way: our vision is not blurred.

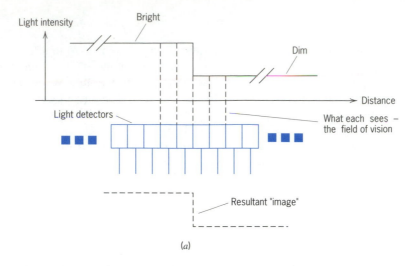

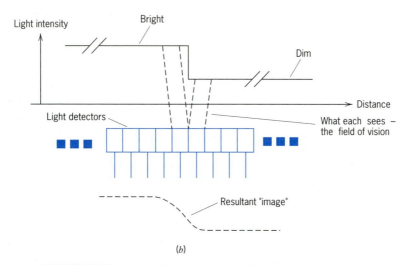

FIGURE 8.2 Model of a visual system. (a) Ideal; (b) System with practical components.

This model is inaccurate and the FORTRAN 90 program shown below is intended to represent animal visual systems. In this model, each detector subtracts a portion of the signal that adjacent detectors receive. (A schematic of the detector model is shown in Fig. 8.3.)

```
        PROGRAM VISION_SYSTEM
! THIS PROGRAM SIMULATES A VISION SYSTEM. THE INPUT INTENSITY CONSISTS
!
! OF AN ARRAY OF 10 VALUES, HALF = 1.0 AND HALF = 0.5 TO SIMULATE A
!
! LIGHT/DARK TRANSITION. A CORRESPONDING ARRAY OF 10 DETECTORS GENERATES
!
! NUMBERS ACCORDING TO THE FOLLOWING FORMULA:
!
!   [STIM(I-1) + STIM(I) + STIM(I+1)]/3 - 0.25*STIM(I-1) - 0.25*STIM(I+1)
!
```

```
!
! DECLARATIONS
      IMPLICIT NONE
      REAL,DIMENSION(10),PARAMETER :: &
            STIMULUS = (/1.0,1.0,1.0,1.0,1.0,0.5,0.5,0.5,0.5,0.5/)
      REAL,DIMENSION(10) :: DETECTOR
      INTEGER I
!
! START OF MAIN PROGRAM
!
      OPEN(2,FILE="B:JUNK.DAT",STATUS="UNKNOWN")
      DO I=2,9
        DETECTOR(I) = (STIMULUS(I-1)+STIMULUS(I)+STIMULUS(I+1))/3.0 - &
            0.25*STIMULUS(I-1) - 0.25*STIMULUS(I+1)
      END DO
        PRINT "(F6.3)",DETECTOR
        WRITE(2,"(F6.3)")DETECTOR
        CLOSE(2)
      END PROGRAM VISION_SYSTEM
```

The program contains no syntactical or logical errors. The key statement in the simulation is

```
DETECTOR(I) = (STIMULUS(I-1)+STIMULUS(I)+STIMULUS(I+1))/3.0 -      &
        0.25*STIMULUS(I-1) - 0.25*STIMULUS(I+1)
```

Each detector averages three stimulus inputs: its own, the stimulus to the right, and the stimulus to the left. This average represents the "field of vision" as seen in Figure 8.2b. This average is further modified by subtracting portions of the stimulus intensity to the

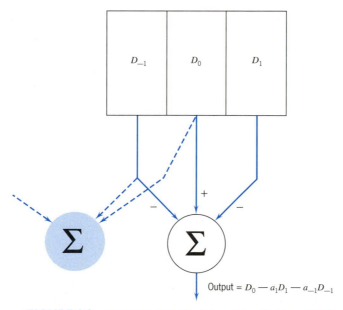

FIGURE 8.3   Schematic of the visual detector used in Example 8.6.

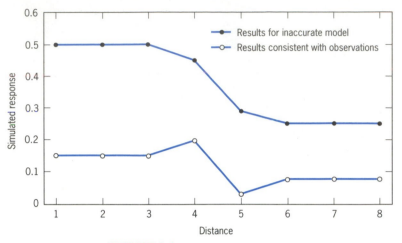

FIGURE 8.4 Simulated vision system.

left and the right as indicated in Fig. 8.3. The program results are displayed on the monitor and stored in a file in order to plot the results. The results are shown in Fig. 8.4. In particular, the upper trace represents the results generated by the program shown above. In this case, the results do not agree with observations that are gathered from experiments in the animal world. Therefore, we do not have confidence in the program and/or the underlying model.

A simple change in the model serves to rectify the inaccuracy. When the statement shown above is replaced with

```
DETECTOR(I) = (STIMULUS(I-1)+STIMULUS(I)+STIMULUS(I+1))/3.0 -    &
        0.425*STIMULUS(I-1) - 0.425*STIMULUS(I+1)
```

the results are consistent with experimental observations. (Note that the coefficients for the amounts to be subtracted from adjacent detectors have been changed from 0.25 to 0.425.) The results are plotted in the lower trace of the graph in Fig. 8.4. The results indicate that the light/dark transition is "exaggerated." In fact, animals (like frogs) see images in this way because it helps them to detect the presence of food. (The boundaries of a fly in their field of vision can easily be detected.) In humans, the phenomenon is called *Mach Bands*; at transitions of the kind described above, we "see" a bright band and a dark band adjacent to the light/dark transition where it really does not exist.

The second application is a short program intended to simulate street traffic. We are interested in simulating the number of cars that can be expected to pass a given point in a street every hour for a period of eight hours. The array CARS_PER_HOUR (with eight locations) stores the number of (simulated) cars passing the given point each hour.

```
        PROGRAM STREET_TRAFFIC
! THIS PROGRAM IS INTENDED TO REPRODUCE TRAFFIC FLOW ON A STREET.
! ULTIMATELY, IT MIGHT BE CONVERTED INTO A SUBROUTINE AND USED IN
! PROGRAMS TO STUDY DESIGN OF A TRAFFIC CONTROL SYSTEM.
!
! DECLARATIONS
        IMPLICIT NONE
        REAL :: X,Y
        INTEGER,DIMENSION(8) :: CARS_PER_HOUR
```

```
        INTEGER :: I,J
!
! START OF MAIN PROGRAM
!
        CARS_PER_HOUR = (/0,0,0,0,0,0,0,0/)
        CALL RANDOM_SEED
        DO I = 1,1000
                CALL RANDOM_NUMBER(Y)
                X = -(1.0/2.0)*LOG(1.0 - Y)
                J = INT(6.0*X+1)
                CARS_PER_HOUR(J) = CARS_PER_HOUR(J)+1
        END DO
        PRINT *,"THE NUMBER OF CARS PER HOUR IS"
        PRINT *, CARS_PER_HOUR
        END PROGRAM STREET_TRAFFIC
```

All locations within the array are initialized to 0 by

```
        CARS_PER_HOUR = (/0,0,0,0,0,0,0,0/)
```

As explained in Chapter 7, the subroutine RANDOM_SEED is used by the random number generator. The call returns a random number Y from the subroutine RANDOM_NUMBER(Y). Random numbers generated within the computer are evenly distributed (*uniformly distributed*) between 0 and 1. The statement

```
        X = -(1.0/2.0)*LOG(1.0 - Y)
```

converts the uniformly distributed number Y to a new number X whose distribution is exponentially distributed. In this example, traffic flow is considered to follow this pattern; the number of cars passing the given point falls exponentially with time. (In this example, we assume that this is an accurate model for traffic flow.) By computing J according to the assignment statement

```
        J = INT(6.0*X+1)
```

the computer determines which bin (location) of the array CARS_PER_HOUR to increment. In this statement, the real variable X—a scaled random number—is first multiplied by 6.0, and 1 is subsequently added. This result becomes the operand of the intrinsic FORTRAN 90 function INT. The INT function converts the real result into an integer quantity, which is then assigned to the integer variable J, which is the bin number. Each bin stores the number of cars passing the given point at hour J where J is the array index. The program compiles, links, and executes without error. The monitor displays the following:

```
        THE NUMBER OF CARS PER HOUR IS
        274 189 176 106 73 48 42 21
```

The results of the simulation are plotted in Fig. 8.5 along with the theoretical values for an exponentially decaying function. Although the data appear to be reasonable, a subtle problem still exists. Notice in the program DO loop that 1000 repetitions are required. Therefore, the total number of (simulated) cars passing the given point during the entire

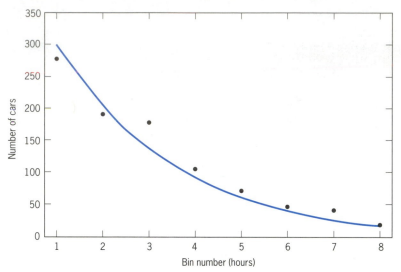

FIGURE 8.5 Exponential model for street traffic.

eight-hour period should total 1000. Adding the numbers produced by the computer (274, ... , 21) yields only 929 outcomes. (*In this instance, we have applied a known constraint to the results which must be satisfied in order have confidence in the program;* this rule is equivalent to concluding that the sum of the probability of all possible outcomes must add to 1.) The constraint has not been satisfied.

In order to debug the program, we must first determine whether each random event is being added to one of the bins in the array. Bin numbers within the array are determined by

```
J = INT(6.0*X+1)
```

We can add a (temporary) selective PRINT statement that will tell us whether any bin number is outside the allowable range:

```
IF (J >= 9) THEN
      PRINT *,J
END IF
```

These statements are added just after the bin assignment statement and will tell us whether the program attempts to access any bin whose index number is greater than 8.

When the program is executed with the above modification, we observe that bin numbers greater than 8 are being accessed. Because such bins do not exist in the array, the simulated events represented by incrementing the bin count are lost; this accounts for our missing events. Having determined this, we must now find the ultimate source of this error. To do so, we can insert appropriate test probes that check for

1. The random variable Y lying outside the interval $(0, 1)$.
2. The random variable X lying outside the interval $(0, 1.167)$. (If X assumes a value in excess of 1.167, the resulting bin number to be accessed (J in the program) will exceed 8.)

Although results with the appropriate probes are not shown (see Problem 8.5), it turns out that Y remains within its interval but X exceeds 1.167, which subsequently causes J to exceed 8. The difficulty is easily remedied by adding statements to exclude values of X beyond 1.167; actually, a limit of 1.3 is used to be sure that a bin value of 8 can be achieved after the truncation that occurs in the FORTRAN 90 intrinsic INT function. The final program is shown below. In addition to the limit on X, the DO loop is designed to ensure that 1000 values are simulated by making the variable I into a *counter* that terminates the loop when it reaches 1000.

```
        PROGRAM STREET_TRAFFIC
! THIS PROGRAM IS INTENDED TO REPRODUCE TRAFFIC FLOW ON A STREET.
! ULTIMATELY, IT MIGHT BE CONVERTED INTO A SUBROUTINE AND USED IN
! PROGRAMS TO STUDY DESIGN OF A TRAFFIC CONTROL SYSTEM.
!
! DECLARATIONS
        IMPLICIT NONE
        REAL :: X,Y
        INTEGER,DIMENSION(8) :: CARS_PER_HOUR
        INTEGER :: I,J
!
! START OF MAIN PROGRAM
!
        CARS_PER_HOUR = (/0,0,0,0,0,0,0,0/)
        CALL RANDOM_SEED
        I=0
        DO;IF (I == 1000)EXIT
                CALL RANDOM_NUMBER(Y)
                X = -(1.0/2.0)*LOG(1.0 - Y)
                IF (X < 1.3) THEN
                        J = INT(6.0*X+1)
                        CARS_PER_HOUR(J) = CARS_PER_HOUR(J)+1
                        I=I+1
                END IF
        END DO
        PRINT *,"THE NUMBER OF CARS PER HOUR IS"
        PRINT *, CARS_PER_HOUR
        END PROGRAM STREET_TRAFFIC
```

When the program is once again executed, the results become

```
        THE NUMBER OF CARS PER HOUR IS
        297 209 189 112 80 52 47 14
```

and the total number of simulated events is 1000.

EXAMPLE 8.7 Complete Testing/Debugging of a Program

In order for robots to carry out useful work, they must be designed so that they can avoid obstacles. They must be able to follow the contour of a solid object in order to get to a station on the factory floor or to be able to deliver mail. The outline of a scheme for accomplishing obstacle avoidance is shown in Fig. 8.6. There are three elements to the algorithm:

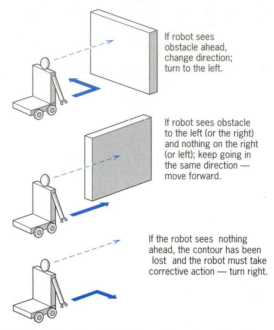

If robot sees obstacle ahead, change direction; turn to the left.

If robot sees obstacle to the left (or the right) and nothing on the right (or left); keep going in the same direction — move forward.

If the robot sees nothing ahead, the contour has been lost and the robot must take corrective action — turn right.

FIGURE 8.6   The scheme for implementing an obstacle avoidance algorithm.

- If the robot detects ("sees") an object directly ahead, corrective action is necessary. In this case, the robot will turn to the left.
- If the robot sees an obstacle to the left and nothing to the right in the space immediately ahead, it can proceed to move forward. Alternatively, the obstacle may appear on the right and nothing on the left; the robot will also proceed forward in this case.
- If the robot sees nothing directly ahead, then it has lost sight of the perimeter (outline) of the obstacle and must turn right in an attempt to regain its orientation to the object.

A pseudocode summary for the program that will realize the alogrithm and provide for program testing follows.

```
program robot
{User enters extent of the site}
{User supplies plan view of obstacle}
{User enters initial position of the robot}
do
      If (robot facing north and obstacle ahead) then
            turn west.
      Else if (robot facing north and nothing ahead) then
            turn east.
      else move robot forward.
      end if
      If (robot facing east and obstacle ahead) then
            turn north
      Else if (robot facing east and nothing ahead) then
            turn south
```

```
      else move robot forward.
      end if
      If (robot facing south and obstacle ahead) then
            turn east
      Else if (robot facing south and nothing ahead) then
            turn west
      else move robot forward.
      end if
      If (robot facing west and obstacle ahead) then
            turn south
      Else if (robot facing west and nothing ahead) then
            turn north
      else move robot forward.
      end if
end do (when robot returns to initial position)
print robot position and orientation
end program robot
```

The FORTRAN 90 source code is shown below.

```
       PROGRAM ROBOT
! THIS PROGRAM ACCEPTS INPUTS FROM THE USER; THESE DESCRIBE AN       &
!    OBJECT
! WHOSE OUTLINE A ROBOT IS TO FOLLOW. THE ROBOT ACCOMPLISHES THIS      &
!    BY
! SENSING THE BOUNDARIES OF THE OBJECT AND TURNING SO AS TO REMAIN
! OUTSIDE THE OBJECT AS IT TRAVERSES THE PERIMETER.
!
! DECLARATIONS
!
     INTEGER, DIMENSION (:,:), ALLOCATABLE :: OBJECT
     INTEGER :: X,Y
     INTEGER, DIMENSION (2) :: ROBOT_POSITION,START
     CHARACTER (LEN=1) :: ROBOT_DIRECTION
     LOGICAL :: MOVE
!
! MAIN PROGRAM STARTS HERE
!
ACCEPT 1'S AND 0'S FROM USER WHICH DEFINE THE OBJECT
!
     WRITE (*,"(T10,A)",ADVANCE='NO'                            &
              "PLEASE SET THE OVERALL DIMENSIONS OF THE SITE "
     READ (*,"(I2)") X,Y
     ALLOCATE (OBJECT(X,Y))
     WRITE (*,"(T10,A)") "ENTER OBJECT OUTLINE"
     READ *,((OBJECT(I,J),I=1,X),J=1,Y)
! SET THE STARTING POSITION OF THE ROBOT
     WRITE (*,"(T10,A)") "ENTER THE ROBOT'S POSITION "
     READ (*,"(I2)")ROBOT_POSITION
     WRITE (*,"(T10,A)") "ENTER THE ROBOT'S DIRECTION (N,E,S,W)"
     READ (*,"(A)")ROBOT_DIRECTION
     START = ROBOT_POSITION
! ROBOT TRAVERSES THE OBJECT UNTIL IT RETURNS TO ITS STARTING     &
!    POINT
```

```fortran
        DO
          CALL TURN_OR_MOVE ROBOT                               &
              (ROBOT_POSITION,ROBOT_DIRECTION,OBJECT,MOVE)
          PRINT "(T10,2I5,TR2,A)", ROBOT_POSITION,ROBOT_DIRECTION
          IF (MOVE .EQV. .TRUE.) THEN
              IF (ROBOT_POSITION(1) == START(1) .and.          &
                  ROBOT_POSITION(2) == START(2)) THEN
                  EXIT
              END IF
          END IF
        END DO
!
        CONTAINS
!
        SUBROUTINE TURN_OR_MOVE_ROBOT                           &
              (ROBOT_POSITION,ROBOT_DIRECTION,OBJECT,MOVE)
! THIS SUBROUTINE DETERMINES WHETHER TO MOVE THE ROBOT OR SIMPLY
! HAVE THE ROBOT LOOK IN ANOTHER DIRECTION ("TURN")
        INTEGER, DIMENSION(2), INTENT(INOUT) :: ROBOT_POSITION
        CHARACTER, INTENT(INOUT) :: ROBOT_DIRECTION
        LOGICAL, INTENT(OUT) :: MOVE
        INTEGER, DIMENSION (:,:), INTENT(IN) :: OBJECT
        SELECT CASE (ROBOT_DIRECTION)
        CASE('N')
            IF (OBJECT(ROBOT_POSITION(1),ROBOT_POSITION(2)) == 1    &
               .AND.
              OBJECT(ROBOT_POSITION(1)+1,ROBOT_POSITION(2)) ==  1)   &
                 THEN
              ROBOT_DIRECTION = 'W'
              MOVE = .FALSE.
            ELSE IF (OBJECT(ROBOT_POSITION(1),ROBOT_POSITION(2))     &
               == 0 .AND. &
              OBJECT(ROBOT_POSITION(1)+1,ROBOT_POSITION(2)) ==  0)   &
                 THEN
              ROBOT_DIRECTION = 'E'
              MOVE = .FALSE.
            ELSE
              ROBOT_POSITION(2)=ROBOT_POSITION(2)-1
              MOVE = .TRUE.
            END IF
        CASE('W')
            IF (OBJECT(ROBOT_POSITION(1),ROBOT_POSITION(2)) == 1     &
               .AND. &
              OBJECT(ROBOT_POSITION(1),ROBOT_POSITION(2)+1) ==  1)    &
                 THEN
              ROBOT_DIRECTION = 'S'
              MOVE = .FALSE.
            ELSE IF(OBJECT(ROBOT_POSITION(1),ROBOT_POSITION(2)) ==   &
                0 .AND. &
                 OBJECT(ROBOT_POSITION(1),ROBOT_POSITION(2)+1) ==    &
                     0) THEN
              ROBOT_DIRECTION = 'N'
              MOVE = .FALSE.
            ELSE
```

```
            ROBOT_POSITION(1)=ROBOT_POSITION(1)-1
            MOVE = .TRUE.
         END IF
  CASE('S')
     IF(OBJECT(ROBOT_POSITION(1),ROBOT_POSITION(2)+1) == 1      &
          .AND. &
        OBJECT(ROBOT_POSITION(1)+1,ROBOT_POSITION(2)+1) ==   1)      &
            THEN
        ROBOT_DIRECTION = 'E'
        MOVE = .FALSE.
     ELSE IF(OBJECT(ROBOT_POSITION(1),ROBOT_POSITION(2)+1) == 0      &
          .AND. &
        OBJECT(ROBOT_POSITION(1)+1,ROBOT_POSITION(2)+1) ==   0)      &
            THEN
        ROBOT_DIRECTION = 'W'
        MOVE = .FALSE.
     ELSE
        ROBOT_POSITION(2)=ROBOT_POSITION(2)+1
        MOVE = .TRUE.
        END IF
  CASE('E')
     IF(OBJECT(ROBOT_POSITION(1)+1,ROBOT_POSITION(2)) == 1      &
          .AND.  &
           OBJECT(ROBOT_POSITION(1)+1,ROBOT_POSITION(2)+1) ==       &
              1) THEN
        ROBOT_DIRECTION = 'N'
        MOVE = .FALSE.
     ELSE IF(OBJECT(ROBOT_POSITION(1)+1,ROBOT_POSITION(2)) == 0      &
          .AND. &
           OBJECT(ROBOT_POSITION(1)+1,ROBOT_POSITION)+1) ==   0)      &
              THEN
        ROBOT_DIRECTION = 'S'
        MOVE = .FALSE.
     ELSE
        ROBOT_POSITION(1)=ROBOT_POSITION(1)+1
        MOVE = .TRUE.
     END IF
     END SELECT
     END SUBROUTINE TURN_OR_MOVE_ROBOT
     END PROGRAM ROBOT
```

Important elements of the program include the following:

- The principal data structure in this program is an array named OBJECT which contains a plan view of the object using a series of 1's and 0's. A 1 signifies part of the obstacle, and a 0 indicates empty space.

- Two identifiers (variables) are associated with the robot, namely, ROBOT_POSI-TION and ROBOT_DIRECTION. The position variable is an array whose entries are the X and Y coordinates of the robot. The direction is a character variable that can take values of N, E, S, or W corresponding to north (facing), east, south, or west.

- Because the extent of the entire site is not restricted prior to entry by the user, the ALLOCATE attribute is used. Within the declaration section, the array is defined as:

  ```
  INTEGER, DIMENSION (:,:), ALLOCATABLE :: OBJECT
  ```

  Two colons (":") appear within the dimension parameter to alert the compiler to the fact that this is going to be a two-dimensional array. However, no limits are assigned; instead, the key word ALLOCATABLE advises the compiler that suitable dimensions will be specified during execution. In the program, this is accomplished by the following three statements, with the last one actually initiating allocation of appropriate memory space within the computer:

  ```
  WRITE (*,"(T10,A)",ADVANCE='NO'                               &
         "PLEASE SET THE OVERALL DIMENSIONS OF THE SITE "
  READ (*,"(I2)") X,Y
  ALLOCATE (OBJECT(X,Y))
  ```

  The array OBJECT will have dimensions of X and Y which have been entered by the user.

- The subroutine TURN_OR_MOVE_ROBOT commits the algorithm depicted in Fig. 8.6 to its software equivalent. The case structure is used in this example. The block of code that is executed depends on the value of robot_direction (e.g., N for north, E for east, S for south, W for west). For each case, the orientation (direction) of the robot is changed if there is an object ahead or an empty space ahead; otherwise, the robot's position is moved forward in the direction it was originally proceeding. The site is sampled (sensed) according to the sketch shown in Fig. 8.7, which depicts the case for a robot initially facing north; other directions test appropriate cells within the array OBJECT according to the following list:

Initial direction of robot	Test cell indices
West	(I, J) and $(I, J + 1)$
South	$(I, J + 1)$ and $(I + 1, J + 1)$
East	$(I + 1, J)$ and $(I + 1, J + 1)$

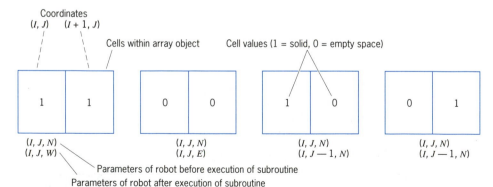

FIGURE 8.7 Sketch of how SUBROUTINE TURN_OR_MOVE_ROBOT carries out its boundary detection scheme.

The source code as shown above has already been cleared of syntactical errors.

Several syntactical errors were uncovered by the compiler and are worth noting in order to illustrate part of a complete debugging process.

Originally, the statement used to enter the outline of the object appeared as

```
READ *,(OBJECT((I,J),I=1,X) J=1,8)
```

which is intended to accept array integers from a user according to a sequence in which the column index varies more rapidly than the low index—for example, $(1, 1), (1, 2), \ldots (1, m), (2, 1). \ldots$ The statement uses an implied DO loop to accomplish this input. The compiler detected an error in this statement. What is missing is a comma, and the statement should be

```
READ *,(OBJECT((I,J),I=1,X), J=1,Y)
```

A second syntactical error was generated by the following statement in the original source:

```
IF (ROBOT_POSITION == START) THEN
              EXIT
```

The expression to be satisfied by the IF statement must be a scalar quantity. However, as written, it attempts to equate two arrays. It was modified as follows:

```
IF (ROBOT_POSITION(1) == START (1)  .AND.        &
      ROBOT_POSITION(2) == START (2)) then
          EXIT
```

which resolved the error.

Finally, the original source code contained the following statement:

```
IF (OBJECT(ROBOT_POSITION(1),ROBOT_POSITION(2)) .AND.  &
      OBJECT(ROBOT_POSITION(1)+1,ROBOT_POSITION(2)) == 1) THEN
      —
```

which generated a compiler error message indicating "inconsistent use of OBJECT." The reason for this error can be seen by noting that the expression to be satisfied (within the if clause) is intended to compare two different cells within the array OBJECT. However, ".AND." is a logical operation that requires logical operands. As written (above) this is not the case. This statement was rewritten as

```
IF (OBJECT(ROBOT_POSITION(1),ROBOT_POSITION(2)) == 1 .AND.  &
    OBJECT(ROBOT_POSITION(1)+1,ROBOT_POSITION(2)) == 1) THEN
      —
```

which has the proper form.

Execution of the compiled program generated the following results.

```
PLEASE SET THE OVERALL DIMENSIONS OF THE SITE  13  12
```

```
          Enter object outline
0,0,0,0,0,0,0,0,0,0,0,0,0,0
0,0,0,0,0,0,0,0,0,0,0,0,0,0
0,0,0,1,1,0,0,0,0,0,0,0,0,0
0,0,0,1,1,1,1,1,1,0,0,0,0,0
0,0,0,0,1,1,1,1,1,0,0,0,0,0
0,0,0,0,1,1,1,1,1,1,1,0,0,0
0,0,0,0,0,1,1,1,1,1,1,0,0,0
0,0,0,1,1,1,1,1,1,1,1,0,0,0
0,0,0,1,1,1,1,1,0,1,1,0,0,0
0,0,0,1,1,1,1,1,0,0,0,0,0,0
0,0,0,0,0,0,0,0,0,0,0,0,0,0
0,0,0,0,0,0,0,0,0,0,0,0,0,0
          ENTER THE ROBOT'S POSITION
3
9

          ENTER THE ROBOT'S DIRECTION (N,E,S,W)
E
          3      9   N
          3      8   N
          3      7   N
          3      7   E
          4      7   E
          5      7   E
          5      7   N
          5      6   N
          5      6   W
          4      6   W
          4      6   N
          4      5   N
          4      4   N
          4      4   W
          3      4   W
          3      4   N
          3      3   N
          3      2   N
          3      2   E
          4      2   E
          5      2   E
          5      2   S
          5      3   S
          5      3   E
          6      3   E
          7      3   E
          8      3   E
          9      3   E
          9      3   S
          9      4   S
          9      5   S
          9      5   E
         10      5   E
         11      5   E
         11      5   S
         11      6   S
```

11	7	S
11	8	S
11	9	S
11	9	W
10	9	W
9	9	W
9	9	N
9	8	N
9	8	W
8	8	W
8	8	S
8	9	S
8	10	S

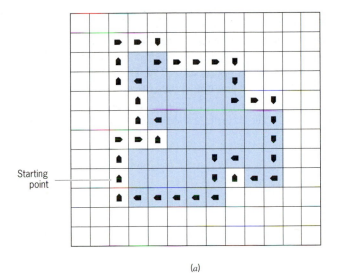

(a)

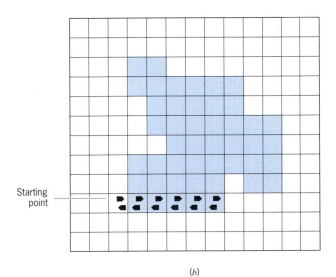

(b)

FIGURE 8.8 Results of the object tracing program. (a) Successful tracking; (b) An algorithmic limitation.

```
8    10   W
7    10   W
6    10   W
5    10   W
4    10   W
3    10   W
3    10   N
3     9   N
```

The site is specified to be a 13 by 12 array and the object "outlined" using 1's and 0's as indicated above. The robot's initial position is set at the array (coordinate) position $(3, 9)$ and is facing east (E). The program generates the sequence of robotic positions indicating sequential coordinate (array) positions and directions. A sketch of the object and the path followed by the robot is shown in Fig. 8.8a. Notice that the robot appears to (partially) traverse the solid part of the object; this is an artifact of the way in which coordinates are determined in the program and not a failure of the algorithm. The results of a second execution of the program in which the algorithm does, however, fail are sketched in Fig. 8.8b; in this case, the only change in input data was the original position of the robot, which is set at $(3, 10, E)$ as opposed to $(3, 9, E)$ in the original case. The robot "sees" an edge, continues along the edge until it detects empty space, turns to the right twice, and retraces its original steps to the starting point where the program is terminated. This is clearly a limitation in the algorithm; modification is left to the reader (see Problem 8.10).

PROBLEMS

8.1 Cite two general ways in which programs with no absolutely correct answer might be tested.

8.2 Write a program that calculates the weight of the steel door shown in Fig. 8.1. The program must have the following characteristics:

- The user enters the dimension as well as the units of width, length, depth, and density of the material.
- The program converts all dimensions and parameters to common units.
- The program displays user-entered values together with their proper units.
- The program displays the final weight of the object (door).

8.3 **(a)** Modifying PROGRAM ASCENDING_SORT (Example. 8.4) so that the numbers are sorted in descending order. Name the program DESCENDING_SORT and test it using the numbers shown in Example 8.4.

(b) Modify the program so that it will sort in either ascending or descending order. Prompt the user for the order and execute the program accordingly.

8.4 A program fragment is intended to assign a value to y according to the following formula:

$$y = \frac{1}{2\pi} \sqrt{\frac{A}{B}}$$

The following code is inserted into the program. (Data declarations are omitted for simplicity.)

```
PI = 3.14159
Y = (1.0/2.0 * PI) * SQRT (A / B)
```

Is this correct?

8.5 Refer to PROGRAM STREET_TRAFFIC (Example 8.6)

(a) Show that when the variable X lies outside the range $(0, 1.167)$, the corresponding bin number lies outside the range $(1, 8)$.

(b) Write appropriate test probe statements to check for the random variable Y lying outside the interval $(0, 1)$.

(c) Repeat part (b) for the random variable X lying outside the interval $(0, 1.25)$.

8.6 The following source code is submitted to the compiler.

```
PROGRAM ERROR
IMPLICIT NONE
REAL :: X,Y
REAL,PARAMETER :: A = 1.0,
                  B = 2.0
X = A + B
Y = A - B
PRINT *, A
PRINT *, B
END PROGRAM ERROR
```

The compiler returns the following messages.

```
Error: Syntax error at line 4
       ***Invalid item in type declaration
Error: Implicit type for B at line 5
       [FTN90 terminated - errors found by pass 1]
```

Explain what is wrong.

8.7 It is required to test all items in a one-dimensional array for a particular value starting at the highest index. The following program is proposed to do this:

```
PROGRAM SCAN_ARRAY
! DECLARATIONS
      INTEGER, DIMENSION(10) :: TEST_ARRAY
      INTEGER :: TEST_VALUE, I
!
! START OF MAIN PROGRAM
!
      TEST_VALUE = 5
      TEST_ARRAY = (/1,2,3,4,5,6,7,8,9,10/)
      DO I = 10,1
        IF (TEST_ARRAY(I)==TEST_VALUE) THEN
            PRINT *, I
        END IF
      END DO
END PROGRAM SCAN_ARRAY
```

(a)   Will the compiler display any error messages?

(b)   What is displayed when all syntax errors are eliminated and the program executes?

8.8   In each case, compare the algebraic and FORTRAN 90 statements. If they are not equivalent, indicate the correct FORTRAN 90 statement.

$$Y = \cfrac{1}{1+\cfrac{1}{1+\cfrac{1}{x}}} \qquad Y = 1.0/(1.0+1.0/1.0+1/X)$$

(b)   If the sides of a triangle are a, b, and c, and s is given by

$$s = \frac{a+b+c}{2}$$

Then the area of the triangle is given by

$$\text{Area} = \sqrt{s(s-a)(s-b)(s-c)}$$

The FORTRAN 90 statement for this is

```
S = (A + B + C)/2.0
AREA = SQRT(S(S-A)(S-B)(S-C))
```

(c)   (x and y are both greater than 5.0.)
FORTRAN 90 equivalent

```
(X .AND. Y > 5.0)
```

(d)   Consider name to be character type.

To assign the expression Bill's Hat to Name, use the following FORTRAN 90 statement.

```
NAME = 'BILL"S HAT
```

8.9   A falling body is subject to two forces: Gravity tends to accelerate the falling object, and a frictional force (tending to hold back the body) is generated by air resistance. An equation that describes the model and that determines the velocity, V, at any point in time is given by the following equation:

$$V = \frac{gm}{c}\left(\frac{t}{3.75+t}\right)$$

where

V = velocity of the falling body in m/sec

g = gravitational acceleration (9.8 m/sec^2)

m = mass of the falling body, which is assumed to be 69.2 kg for this example

c = coefficient of drag (12.5 kg/sec)

FORTRAN 90 source code to determine the velocity of a falling body with the given parameters for a period of 15 seconds follows.

```
        PROGRAM FALLING_BODY
! THIS PROGRAM CALCULATES THE VELOCITY OF A FALLING BODY AS A
! FUNCTION OF TIME. FORCES OF THE BODY INCLUDE GRAVITY AND DRAG
! WHICH IS CALCULATED AS -C*V WHERE C IS THE DRAG COEFFICIENT
! AND V IS THE VELOCITY.
!
! DECLARATIONS
!
        REAL, PARAMETER :: G = 9.8,                 &
                           M = 69.2,                &
                           C = 12.5
        REAL :: T,V
        INTEGER :: I
!
        PRINT "(T10,A,TR10,A)",  "TIME","VELOCITY"
        PRINT "(T10,A,TR10,A)",  "====","========"
        T = 1.0
        DO I=1, 15
            V = G*M/C*(T/3.75+T)
            PRINT "(T10,F4.1,TR12,F6.1)", T,V
            T = T + 1.0
        END DO
        END PROGRAM FALLING_BODY
```

The program compiles successfully and executes with the following results.

TIME	VELOCITY
====	========
1.0	68.7
2.0	137.4
3.0	206.2
4.0	274.9
5.0	343.6
6.0	412.3
7.0	481.0
8.0	549.8
9.0	618.5
10.0	687.2
11.0	755.9
12.0	824.6
13.0	893.4
14.0	962.1
15.0	1030.8

The results appear to be suspicious because a velocity of 1030.8 m/sec seems extraordinarily high. Real data are acquired from a falling body with the same mass, and the results are:

Time	Velocity
1	11.4
2	18.9
3	24.1
4	28.0

5	31.0
6	33.4
7	35.3
8	36.9
9	38.3
10	39.5
11	40.5
12	41.3
13	42.1
14	42.8
15	43.4

Why are the "real-world" results so different?

8.10 Suggest an algorithm that improves the operation of the robot in program robot (Example 8.7). Develop the procedure in the form of pseudocode so that the robot may start from any point in the site, find the object, and navigate the periphery successfully.

8.11 Will the following two FORTRAN 90 statements produce identical results?

```
PRINT *, SIN(1.0)/COS(1.0)
PRINT *, TAN(1.0)
```

9

Numerical Applications

PART I: SIMULATION

9.1 THE ROLE OF SIMULATION IN DESIGN

The phrase "simulation in design" may signify several different activities. In Chapter 7 we presented a program for designing Chebychev filters. After completing a design, we could

1. submit it to the manufacturing department for production of a quantity of filters;
2. send the design to the laboratory to have a prototype constructed to validate the design; or
3. write a program that would calculate the frequency response—that is, the variation in output of the filter in decibels versus an input voltage that is constant in amplitude but variable in frequency.

The third choice involves a simulation; nothing is constructed, but the behavior of a device is simulated to predict the performance of the actual device. Simulation is valuable because it is a quicker and less costly method of testing performance than construction. The third method is *one* way of simulating performance. Figure 9.1, which illustrates use of this method, shows the frequency response of a low-pass Butterworth filter designed by a program similar to that presented in Sec. 7.11.2. The design specification was a cut-off frequency of 10 Hz and at least 21 dB of attenuation at 20 Hz. The graph indicates that the design is satisfactory, and either a prototype will be built and tested or we will go directly into production. There is another method of simulation that is very relevant when

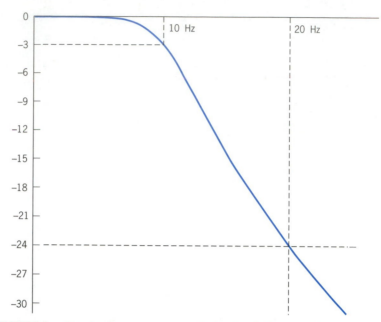

FIGURE 9.1   Plot of the frequency response of a fourth order low pass (LP) Butterworth filter.

we wish to observe how the performance of a component or device is influenced by events that have probabilistic behavior. This method involves the use of random numbers and is often called *Monte Carlo simulation*. One tool that is useful in probabilistic calculations is a histogram.

9.2 HISTOGRAMS

Let us assume that we manufacture 1 million resistors and that our specification is 1000 ohms ±15%. Thus, the expected range of the values of resistance is 850 ohms to 1150 ohms. Let us also assume that the values of the resistors are uniformly distributed over this range. Suppose we draw a random sample of 10,000 resistors from the production run, measure them, and sort them into five groups of resistance values: 850–910; 910.001–970; 970.001–1030; 1030.001–1090; and 1090.001–1150. Each of these groups has a range of 60 ohms (within 0.001 ohm). Because the "parent" population is uniformly distributed, we would also expect the random sample to be *approximately* uniformly distributed. That means that we expect to find about 2000 resistors in each group. When we count the actual number of samples in various ranges, the result is called a *frequency distribution*. A general procedure for generating a frequency distribution from a random population is to determine the smallest and largest value in the population, and then divide the difference between these values by an integer. This integer establishes the number of *class intervals*. Then, the number of items in each interval must be determined.

Let us discuss a program that calculates a frequency distribution. The program, HISTO2, and a run are as follows.

```
MODULE HISTO
IMPLICIT NONE
REAL:: U(4000),S,XMIN, DIST(20)
```

```
                 INTEGER:: N,K,KK,I,J
                 END MODULE HISTO
                 PROGRAM HISTO2
                 USE HISTO
                 CALL RANDOM_SEED
                 N = 4000
                 DO KK = 1,N
                    CALL RANDOM_NUMBER(U(KK))
                 U(KK) = 200.0*U(KK) + 100.0
                 END DO
                 CALL RANK
                 S = 5.0/(U(N) - U(1))
                 WRITE(*,"(A,F10.5)") 'U MAX =', U(N)
                 WRITE(*,"(A,F10.5)") 'U MIN =', U(1)
                 WRITE(*,"(A,F7.3)") 'S = ',S
                 WRITE(*,"(/A/)")'     *    *    *'
                 XMIN = S*U(1) - 1.0
        DO I = 1,20
                    DIST(I) = 0.0
                 END DO
                 DO J = 1,N
                   K = S*U(J) - XMIN
                    IF(K == 0) THEN
                    K = K + 1
                    ELSE IF(K == 6) THEN
                    K = K -1
                    ENDIF
                    DIST(K) = DIST(K) + 1.0
                 END DO
                 WRITE(*,*)     INTERVAL FREQUENCY'
                  DO I = 1,5
                       WRITE(*,"(9X,I4,7X,F5.0)") I,DIST(I)
        END DO
                 END PROGRAM HISTO2
                 SUBROUTINE RANK
                 USE HISTO
                  DO I = 1,N - 1
                   MAX = N - I
                    DO J = 1,MAX
                     IF(U(J) > U(J+1)) THEN
                               TEMP = U(J)
                               U(J) = U(J+1)
                               U(J+1) = TEMP
                       ENDIF
                      END DO
                  END DO
                 RETURN
                 END
```

In this program, the frequency distribution of 4000 scaled, uniformly distributed random numbers is calculated. The random numbers are scaled to produce numbers that are defined by $200 \pm 50\%$. Five class intervals were used. Recall that a random number generator produces random numbers that are approximately uniformly distributed over the range 0 to 1. We can scale them so that they range from a minimum value of A to a maximum value of B. To do this, the random numbers generated by the RNG are multiplied as follows.

$$U_s = (B - A)U + A$$

where U_s denotes scaled random numbers and U denotes the random numbers generated by the random number generator. In program HISTO2, the following values are chosen: $B = 300$ and $A = 100$. Thus, $B - A = 200$. The random numbers are stored in the array $U(KK)$ and then scaled by means of the statement

$$U(KK) = 200.0*U(KK) + 100.0$$

As a result of this scaling, when $U(KK)$ on the right side of the equation is equal to 0, then the scaled random number is 100.0; when it is 1.0, the scaled random number is $200.0 + 100.0 = 300.0$.

Subroutine RANK determines the maximum and minimum values of the scaled random numbers and stores the maximum value in $U(N)$ and the minimum value in $U(1)$. N is the total number of random numbers that generated.

As a result of the scaling, we expect the random numbers to range from a minimum of 100.0 to a maximum of 300 and expect the *range*, $U(N) - U(1)$, to be *approximately* $300.0 - 100.0 = 200$. The number of class intervals was arbitrarily chosen to be 5; the program has to examine each random number and assign it to a class interval that is designated by a number from 1 to 5. The count is stored in DIST(K) where K is $1, 2, 3, 4, 5$. The assignment is carried in loop DO $J = 1, N$ by means of the variable K. In loop DO $J = 1, N$ there is the statement

1. $$K = S*U(J) - XMIN$$

XMIN has been previously defined:

2. $$XMIN = S*(U(1) - 1$$

By using (2) to replace XMIN in (1), we get the equation

3. $$K = S*[U(J) - U(1)] + 1$$

Examining program HISTO2, we note that

$$S = 5.0/[U(N) - U(1)]$$

Substituting the value of S in K, we obtain

$$K = 5 \frac{U(J) - U(1)}{U(N) - U(1)} \tag{9.1}$$

In Eq. (9.1) the number of intervals, namely, 5, is multiplied by a quantity that varies from 0 to 1; this quantity, when increased by one, produces a class interval.

To show this procedure, let us calculate some values of K. As shown above:

$$K = S*[U(J) - U(1)] + 1$$

From the trial run, $S = 0.025$ and $U(1) = U$ minimum $= 100.00034$.

Suppose that a random number, $U(J)$, is 110.80. Then,

$$K = 0.025(110.80 - 100.00034) + 1 = 0.269915 + 1 = 1$$

Therefore, DIST$(K) =$ DIST(1) is incremented by 1. Next, suppose that $U(J) = 170.21$. In this case,

$$K = 0.025(170.21 - 100.00034) + 1 = 1.75524 + 1 = 2$$

DIST(2) is incremented by 1.

In the trial run, shown below, we see that $U(N)$, the maximum scaled random number, is 299.98511 and $U(1)$, the minimum scaled number, is 100.00034. The range, $U(N) - U(1) = 199.985$.

```
RUN
U MAX = 299.98511
U MIN = 100.00034
S =  0.025
```

                    ⋆   ⋆   ⋆

                 INTERVAL FREQUENCY

                    1   828.

                    2   765.

                    3   862.

                    4   802.

                    5   743.

Because the numbers are uniformly distributed, ideally the number in each interval should be 800. In the trial run, this expectation is met only approximately. Use of more random numbers would produce a result that is closer to the ideal. If the frequency distribution is plotted as a function of the interval in the form of a bar graph, the graph is called a histogram. Figure 9.2 shows a histogram for this example.

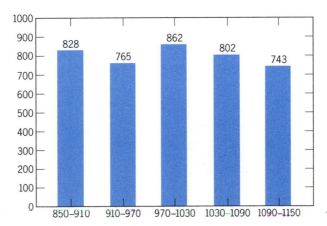

FIGURE 9.2   Bar graph of the distribution of values from a sample of resistors.

9.3 SIMULATING THE PERFORMANCE OF AN ELECTRONIC AMPLIFIER (*Electrical Engineering*)

The design of an electronic device may involve circuits containing hundreds or perhaps even thousands of components. The design process implicitly assumes that each component meets its specification. However, it is well known that all components have a tolerance. We discussed this subject in the previous example with regard to resistors that have a tolerance of 10 percent. Similar variations apply to every component specified in the design. To further complicate the situation, the variations in the components have a probabilistic distribution. In general, the aggregation of all these possible variations may make it difficult for the designer to predict within acceptable limits the actual performance of the device, even though the design itself is correct. We might ask why not purchase resistors and other components with a variation of only $\pm 1\%$ from the nominal value. When there are dozens or even hundreds of components in a device specifying narrow specifications such as $\pm 1\%$, the cost of the product will increase greatly. In some cases, it may not be feasible to manufacture the components to so narrow a tolerance.

Constructing one prototype of the product and testing it will verify the design but will not demonstrate the variation in performance that may occur when thousands of the product are manufactured. One method of determining the variation of the product is by simulation.

In order to be able to present a program of modest length, we will illustrate the process of simulation by using as an example a small device: a simple amplifier. By limiting the number of components and allowing only a few of them to vary, we will avoid being swamped by detail and so we can then focus on the nature of the simulation.

One important measure of the performance of an amplifier is the *voltage gain*. A signal is applied to the input of the amplifier, and, typically, an enlarged replica of that signal appears at the output. The ratio of the voltage at the output to the voltage at the input is called the voltage gain. For the amplifier, whose performance we will study, the voltage gain is given by Eq. (9.2).

$$A_v \frac{V_{\text{out}}}{V_{\text{input}}} = \frac{-h_{fe}R_L}{h_{ie} + (h_{ie}h_{oe} - h_{fe}h_{re})R_L} \tag{9.2}$$

Program AMPLIFY2, shown below, calculates the voltage gain according to this formula using the nominal values of the parameters and also taking into account variations in two of the parameters. In the calculation, the minus sign in Eq. (9.2) is ignored because it only concerns phase, not magnitude. The minus sign means that, as the input signal becomes more positive, the output signal becomes more negative; as the input signal becomes more negative, the output becomes more positive.

```
        MODULE AMPLIFY
        IMPLICIT NONE
        REAL::HIE,HRE,HOE,HFENOM,RL,AVNOM, AVMAX,AVMIN,HFE,Y
        REAL, DIMENSION(4000)::AV,X
        INTEGER:: N,I,J, MAX
        END MODULE AMPLIFY
        PROGRAM AMPLIFY2
    !   THIS PROGRAM CALCULATES THE AMPLIFICATION OF AN
    !   AMPLIFIER WITH RL AND HFE EACH UNIFORMLY DISTRIBUTED.
        USE AMPLIFY
```

```
      N = 1000
      HIE = 1500.0
      HRE = 3.0E-04
      HOE = 20.0E-06
      HFENOM = 80.0
      RL = 5000
      AVNOM = (HFENOM*RL)/(HIE + (HIE*HOE - HFENOM*HRE)*RL)
      WRITE(*,*)'AVONOM = ',AVNOM
       WRITE(*,*)'   *    *    *'
      CALL RANDOM_SEED
      DO I = 1,N
       CALL RANDOM_NUMBER(Y)
       RL = (1000.0)*Y + 4500.0
       HFE = 32.0*Y + 64.0
       AV(I) = (HFE*RL)/(HIE + (HIE*HOE - HFE*HRE)*RL)
      END DO
      CALL RANK
       WRITE(*,*)'AVMAX = ', AV(N),' AVMIN = ',AV(1)
       WRITE(*,"(A/A/)")'   *    *    *',' *    *    *'
      END PROGRAM AMPLIFY2
!
      SUBROUTINE RANK
      USE AMPLIFY
       DO I = 1, N-1
        MAX = N-1
         DO J = 1,MAX
          IF(X(J) > X(J+1)) THEN
              TEMP = X(J)
              X(J) = X(J+1)
               X(J+1) = TEMP
         END IF
        END DO
       END DO
      END
```

OUTPUT OF RUN

```
AVNOM =     2.6143790E+02
***
AVMAX =     3.5043457E+02        AVMIN =    1.8611957E+02
***
***
```

The two parameters that are varied are R_L and h_{fe}. The values of R_L are assumed to be uniformly distributed between 4500 and 5500 ohms. The values of h_{fe} are assumed to be uniformly distributed between 64 and 96. For the simulation, 1000 random numbers are used. The trial run shows that the nominal voltage gain A_{vnom} is about 261. However, when the variations of R_L and h_{fe} are taken into account, the voltage gain varies between a minimum value of 186 and a maximum of 350. Thus, the minimum gain is about 40 percent less than the nominal gain and the maximum is about 33 percent greater than the nominal gain. Without the benefit of the simulation, it would have been difficult to predict these variations.

9.4 ONE-DIMENSIONAL RANDOM WALK; A MODEL OF DIFFUSION (*Chemistry*)

In this section, we illustrate the use of random numbers in simulating a process called a one-dimensional random walk. We use the one-dimensional random walk to produce a simplified model of *diffusion*. Diffusion is a process in which particles migrate from a region of high concentration to a region of lower concentration. For example, if a bottle of perfume is opened in a corner of a room, the scent is soon detected throughout the room. If there is no air motion in the room, the scent spreads by diffusion. Diffusion is the result of the *random* motion of molecules. All the molecules undergo random thermal motion and have collisions with other molecules. However, the net result is that the molecules are dispersed throughout the room until they are uniformly distributed. As mentioned above, the process of diffusion involves random motion and thus probability is involved. In our discussion, we will need two terms used in probability—independence and mutually exclusive events; we will now define these terms.

When we state that two events, A and B, are *independent*, we mean that the occurrence of one of them does not affect the probable occurrence of the other. If the probability of the occurrence of A is P(A) and the probability of the occurrence of B is P(B), then the probability of both occurring is P(A)P(B).

EXAMPLE 9.1 Independence

A subassembly of a certain electronic device consists of a diode and a resistor. The diode is randomly drawn from a bin containing 100 diodes, 15 of which are defective. Let P(D) denote the probability that the diode is defective. Then, P(D) is given by Eq. (9.3),

$$P(D) = \frac{15}{100} \tag{9.3}$$

The resistor is drawn from a bin containing 500 resistors, 25 of which are defective. Let P(R) equal the probability of drawing a defective resistor. The probability that the resistor is defective is given in Eq. (9.4).

$$P(R) = \frac{25}{500} \tag{9.4}$$

Drawing a resistor from a bin and drawing a diode from another bin are independent events. Therefore, this probability is given by Eq. (9.5).

$$P(D)P(R) = \frac{15 \cdot 25}{100 \cdot 500} \tag{9.5}$$

Two events are said to be *mutually exclusive* if they cannot occur at the same time. If A and B are mutually exclusive, then the probability that both events occur is P(A) + P(B).

EXAMPLE 9.2 Mutually Exclusive Events

Consider a standard card deck of 52 cards. We define a face card as King, Queen, or Jack. There are a total of 12 face cards, and the probability of drawing a face card is

$P(\text{FACE}) = 12/52$. There are four aces in the deck, and the probability of drawing an ace is $P(\text{ACE}) = 4/52$. The events "drawing an ace" and "drawing a face card" are mutually exclusive. Therefore:

$$P(\text{card drawn is an ace or a face card}) = 4/52 + 12/52 = 16/52$$

We now return to our dicussion of diffusion. Obviously, diffusion is a three-dimensional process. Here, however, we will consider a model for diffusion that is simplified by dealing with only one dimension, namely, x. This is called a *one-dimensional* random walk because we are limiting motion to the x direction. After using the model to predict the position of a particle after three units of time, we will discuss a program that uses random numbers to simulate and validate the model.

Consider a particle that is located, at time $t = 0$, at the origin of the coordinate axes, and that is constrained to move along the x axis in either the positive or the negative direction. The following assumptions will be made:

1. At the end of each unit time interval, the particle must move a unit length in either the positive or negative x direction. For convenience, we will call a unit length a "step."

2. The probability, p, of taking one step in the negative x direction is equal to the probability of taking a step in the positive x direction, and $p = 1/2$.

Let us calculate the probabilities of various events in this sample space. As previously mentioned, at the beginning of the process, $(t = 0)$, the particle is at $x = 0$, and there is an equal probability, $p = \frac{1}{2}$, that the particle will move to either $x = 1$ or $x = -1$. Therefore, at $t = 1$, there are two possible events with equal probabilities:

1. The probability that the particle is at $x = 1$ is equal to 1/2.

2. The probability that the particle is at $x = -1$ is equal to 1/2.

Note that the sum of probabilities for all possible events that can occur is equal to 1. The sum of probabilities for all possible events at any given time will always be 1. This is a very useful check on calculations. In summary, at $t = 1$, the particle will be either at $x = 1$ or at $x = -1$, with a probability of fi for either event.

Now let us consider the set of events at $t = 2$ or, in equivalent terms, after two steps have been taken. If a particle is at $x = 1$, it may move with probability p to either $x = 2$ or $x = 0$; if a particle is at $x = -1$, it may move with probability p to either $x = -2$ or $x = 0$. Therefore, at $t = 2$, there are the following probabilities:

The probability that the particle moved from $x = 0$ to $x = 1$ and then to $x = 2$: $(\frac{1}{2})(\frac{1}{2}) = \frac{1}{4}$

The probability that the particle moved from $x = 0$ to $x = -1$ and then to $x = -2$: $(\frac{1}{2})(\frac{1}{2}) = \frac{1}{4}$

The probability that the particle moved from $x = 0$ to $x = 1$ and then to $x = 0$: $(\frac{1}{2})(\frac{1}{2}) = \frac{1}{4}$

The probability that the particle moved from $x = 0$ to $x = -1$ and then to $x = 0$: $(\frac{1}{2})(\frac{1}{2}) = \frac{1}{4}$

If we consider the last two probabilities, we see that there are two mutually exclusive ways in which the event "started at $x = 0$ and returned to $x = 0$" can occur. Therefore, the probability of this event is $\frac{1}{4} + \frac{1}{4} = \frac{1}{2}$. That is, the probability of this event is obtained by adding the probabilities of the two mutually exclusive ways in which it can occur. Note that the sum of all the probabilities of the events at $t = 2$ is $\frac{1}{2} + \frac{1}{4} + \frac{1}{4} = 1$.

We see that at the second step the possible positions of the particle are $x = 0$, with probability of $\frac{1}{2}$; $x = 2$, with probability of $\frac{1}{4}$; and $x = -2$ with probability of $\frac{1}{4}$. At the third step the possible positions are $x = 3, x = -3, x = 1, x = -1$.

Let us calculate the probabilities at the third step.

1. The probability that a particle moved to $x = 0$ at the second step and moved to $x = -1$ at the third step is $(\frac{1}{2})(\frac{1}{2}) = \frac{1}{4}$.

2. The probability that a particle moved to $x = -2$ at the second step and moved to $x = -1$ at the third step is $(\frac{1}{4})(\frac{1}{2}) = \frac{1}{8}$.

(1) and (2) are mutually exclusive; therefore, the probability that at step 3 the particle is at $x = -1$ is $\frac{3}{8}$.

3. The probability that a particle moved to $x = 0$ at the second step and moved to $x = +1$ at the third step is $(\frac{1}{2})(\frac{1}{2}) = \frac{1}{4}$.

4. The probability that a particle moved to $x = +2$ at the second step and moved to $x = +1$ at the third step is $(\frac{1}{4})(\frac{1}{2}) = \frac{1}{8}$.

(3) and (4) are mutually exclusive; therefore, the probability that at step 3 the particle is at $x = +1$ is $\frac{1}{4} + \frac{1}{8} = \frac{3}{8}$.

5. The probability that a particle moved to $x = -2$ at the second step and moved to $x = -3$ at the third step is $(\frac{1}{4})(\frac{1}{2}) = \frac{1}{8}$.

6. The probability that a particle moved to $x = +2$ at the second step and moved to $x = +3$ at the third step is $(\frac{1}{4})(\frac{1}{2}) = \frac{1}{8}$.

As the number of steps increases, the calculations become tedious. So now let us turn to a program that simulates the one-dimensional random walk. The program, RANWALK, is as follows.

```
      PROGRAM RANWALK
!     THIS PROGRAM SIMULATES A ONE DIMENSIONAL RANDOM WALK
!     WHICH IS USED TO MODEL DIFFUSION
      IMPLICIT NONE
      REAL, DIMENSION(10000):: POS
      REAL, DIMENSION(0:10000):: DISTRIB
      REAL::Y,XN,PROB,SUMPROB
      INTEGER::N,I,J,II,L,K,M
      CALL RANDOM_SEED
      WRITE(*,*)'ENTER NUMBER OF RANDOM NUMBERS WANTED'
      READ(*,*) N
      XN = N
      WRITE(*,*)'NUMBER OF RANDOM NUMBERS', N
      DO I = 1,N
      POS(I) = 0.
      END DO
!     NOTE NESTED LOOPS
      DO J = 1,6
       DO I = 1, N
       CALL RANDOM_NUMBER(Y)
        IF(Y <= 0.500) THEN
        POS(I) = POS(I) - 2.0
        END IF
        POS(I) = POS(I) + 1.0
```

```
      END DO
       DO II = 0,N-1
       DISTRIB(II) = 0.0
      END DO
       DO L = 1,N
        K = ABS(POS(L))
        DISTRIB(K) = DISTRIB(K) + 1.0
      END DO
      WRITE(*,"(A/)")'      STEP    DISTANCE   PROBABILITY'
       SUMPROB = 0
       DO M = 0,J
         PROB = DISTRIB(M)/XN
         WRITE(*,"(,4X,I6,5X,I6,6X,F9.4)") J,M , PROB
         SUMPROB = SUMPROB + PROB
       END DO

 !       WRITE(*,"(/5X,A,F9.4)")'TOTAL PROBABILITY =  ', SUMPR
       END DO
 END PROGRAM RANWALK
```

Random numbers uniformly distributed from 0 to 1 are used to assign positions to the particles in the following way. If a random number is less than or equal to 0.500, then a particle is moved one step in the negative x direction; if the random number is greater than 0.500, then the particle is moved one step in the positive x direction. The motion of the particle is symmetrical in that, at each step, the probability $p(d)$ that the particle has moved to $+d$ is equal to the probability $p(-d)$ that it has moved to $-d$. We will take advantage of this fact by specifying only the probability $P(D) = p(d) + p(-d)$ that the particle is at a particular *distance* from the origin at any given step. In the program, the position of the particles is stored in the variable POS(I). The program gives the user the option of specifying the number of random numbers to be used. In the trial run, which will be discussed later, 10,000 random numbers were used.

Now, let us examine the loop DO J. The index, J, ranges from 1 to 6 and counts the number of steps. Six steps are sufficient to validate the model. There are four nested DO loops within DO J. The first nested loop, DO I = 1, N generates 10,000 random numbers, each of which is successively stored in Y. As a result of the IF statement, if Y is equal to less than 0.5000, POS(I) is decreased by 2. Then, the last statement increases POS(I) by 1. If Y is greater than 0.5, then POS(I) is not decreased; it is only increased. For example, suppose J = 1. This is the first step of the random walk. First, I, the index of the loop, equals 1. Suppose Y is less than 0.5000. Then, after the first iteration of the loop POS(1) $= -1.00$. Now $I = 2$. Suppose that Y is greater than 0.5000, then POS(2) = 1. After 10,000 random numbers have been generated, an exit from the loop occurs, and we expect that *approximately* 5000 members of the array POS(I) are equal to $+1$ and *approximately* 5000 are equal to -1.

With J remaining at a value of 1, loop DO L calculates the frequency distribution. In this loop, the variable K is assigned a value based on the *magnitude* of POS(L). This achieves our goal of dealing only with distance. At step 1, the particle is always at a distance of 1; therefore, K remains at 1 through 10,000 iterations. After K is assigned a value, the statement

$$DISTRIB(K) = DISTRIB(K) + 1$$

is executed. Therefore, at exit from the loop, DISTRIB(1) = 10000.

In loop DO M, the probabilities at each step are calculated and summed. Note that the index of the loop, M, varies from 0 to J. M is used to specify distance. At step 1 (J = 1), M varies from 0 to 1, thus specifying $x = 0$ or $x = |1|$, respectively. For J = 1, as we just saw, DISTRIB(1) = 10000; DISTRIB(0) = 0. Therefore, the statement PROB = DISTRIB(M)/XN results in values as follows:

$$\text{Step 1: M} = 0, \quad \text{distance} = 0; \quad \text{PROB} = 0;$$
$$\text{M} = 1, \quad \text{distance} = 1; \quad \text{PROB} = 1.0$$

The results at steps 2, 3, 4, and 5 follow the same general pattern. The trial run is shown below. Note that the sum of the probabilities at each step is 1.0000. Also note that the probability of a particle being at $x = 0$ decreases from 0.4979 at step 2 to 0.3104 at step 6. If the simulation were extended to a larger number of steps, this probability would decrease further.

RUN

NUMBER OF RANDOM NUMBERS 10000

STEP	DISTANCE	PROBABILITY
1	0	0.0000
1	1	1.0000

TOTAL PROBABILITY =   1.0000

STEP	DISTANCE	PROBABILITY
2	0	0.4979
2	1	0.0000
2	2	0.5021

TOTAL PROBABILITY =   1.0000

STEP	DISTANCE	PROBABILITY
3	0	0.0000
3	1	0.7459
3	2	0.0000
3	3	0.2541

TOTAL PROBABILITY =   1.0000

STEP	DISTANCE	PROBABILITY
4	0	0.3823
4	1	0.0000
4	2	0.4894
4	3	0.0000
4	4	0.1283

TOTAL PROBABILITY =   1.0000

STEP	DISTANCE	PROBABILITY
5	0	0.0000
5	1	0.6226
5	2	0.0000
5	3	0.3116
5	4	0.0000
5	5	0.0658

TOTAL PROBABILITY =   1.0000

```
STEP    DISTANCE   PROBABILITY
  6        0         0.3104
  6        1         0.0000
  6        2         0.4713
  6        3         0.0000
  6        4         0.1857
  6        5         0.0000
  6        6         0.0326
    TOTAL PROBABILITY =     1.0000
```

9.5 SIMULATING THE DISTRIBUTION OF THE TOTAL RESISTANCE OF THREE RESISTORS IN SERIES
(Electrical Engineering)

Let us consider a situation that might occur in the production of some electronic device. The supervisor is preparing to ask the assembly line to install a 6000-ohm resistor in the device when she is informed that the purchasing agent forgot to order the resistors. However, there are 2000-ohm resistors in stock, and there is room in the chassis to use three 2000-ohm resistors in series. The resistors have a specification of 2000 ohms ±10%. The permissible deviation of a component from its specification is called the *tolerance*. Using three resistors in series will be satisfactory, provided that the result is 6000 ohms ±10%. The question is, Will the three resistors in series yield a 6000-ohm resistor that meets the tolerance?

To find the answer, a simulation will be used. It will be assumed that the values of the resistors are governed by the uniform probability distribution. The program for performing the simulation, RESISTOR, and the trial run are shown below. The RNG is used to generate random numbers that are stored in variable U and scaled; this is done by the inner of a pair of nested loops, DO J = 1, 3.

```
      MODULE RESIST
      IMPLICIT NONE
      REAL,DIMENSION(1000)::DISTRIB,RS
      REAL:: B,S,RSMAX,RSMIN,XMIN,WINT,TEMP
      INTEGER::I,K,N,J,MAX,MIN
      END MODULE RESIST
      PROGRAM RESISTOR
!     SIMULATION OF THE VARIATION OF THE TOTAL RESISTANCE OF
!     THREE RESISTORS CONNECTED IN SERIES. RESISTORS ARE
!     SPECIFIED TO BE 2000 OHMS PLUS OR MINUS 10%.
      USE RESIST
      N = 1000
      CALL RANDOM_SEED
      DO I = 1, N
        DO J = 1,3
          CALL RANDOM_NUMBER(U)
          RS(I) = RS(I) + 1800.0 + 400.0*U
        END DO
      END DO
      CALL RANK
      WRITE(*,"(A,F9.3,A,F9.3/)")'RSMAX =',RSMAX,'  RSMIN =', RSMIN
```

```
S = 10.0/(RSMAX − RSMIN)
XMIN = S*RSMIN −1.0
WINT = 1.0/S
DO J = 1,N
 K = S*RS(J) − XMIN
  IF(K == 0) K = K + 1
 IF(K == 11) K = K −1
 DISTRIB(K) = DISTRIB(K) + 1
 END DO
 WRITE(*,*)'   INTERVAL          RANGE             FREQ'
 B = RSMIN + WINT
 DO K = 1, 10
 WRITE(*,"(10X,I3,9X,F9.3,F9.3,11X,F6.0)")K,RSMIN,B,DISTRIB(K)
  RSMIN = RSMIN + WINT
  B = B + WINT
 END DO
 END
 SUBROUTINE RANK
 USE RESIST
  DO I = 1,N−1
   MAX = N − I
     DO J = 1,MAX
     IF(RS(J) > RS(J+1)) THEN
         TEMP = RS(J)
         RS(J) = RS(J+1)
         RS(J+1) = TEMP
      ELSE
       CYCLE
      END IF
     END DO
   END DO
  RSMIN = RS(1)
  RSMAX = RS(N)
 END
```

RUN

```
RSMAX = 6539.625   RSMIN = 5453.055
    INTERVAL          RANGE           FREQ
       1        5453.055   5561.712        9.
       2        5561.712   5670.369       44.
       3        5670.369   5779.025       99.
       4        5779.025   5887.682      146.
       5        5887.682   5996.339      202.
       6        5996.339   6104.996      205.
       7        6104.996   6213.652      159.
       8        6213.652   6322.309       99.
       9        6322.309   6430.966       28.
      10        6430.966   6539.623        9.
```

Within this loop, the scaling is done by

$$RS(I) = RS(I) + 1800.0 + 400.0* U(I)$$

Thus, RS(I) varies from 1800 to 2200 ohms.

Executing loop DO J three times is equivalent to adding three resistors (combining them in series). This procedure is performed 1000 times. The results shown above are interesting. The *maximum* value attained by the three resistors in series is 6550.56 ohms, and the *minimum* value is 5460.12. The first is within $6000 + 10\% = 6600$ ohms; the second is within $6000 - 10\% = 5400$ ohms. The histogram is perhaps equally interesting. About 80 percent of the resistors are found in intervals 3, 4, 5, 6, and 7, which represents an even smaller range. The conclusion is that using three resistors in series will not result in a violation of the desired tolerance of $\pm10\%$; in fact, the result is a somewhat narrower tolerance.

9.6 ADDITIONAL EXAMPLES OF THE USE OF THE MONTE CARLO METHOD

We will now discuss the use of random numbers in geometric applications such as the calculation of area. We will assume that the generation of a random number simulates the throw of a dart at a target. The target will consist of a rectangle that encloses a figure, the area of which is to be calculated.

EXAMPLE 9.3 Program MONTE1

In this example, the area to be found is that of a quadrant of a circle with radius $r = 1$. The center of the circle is at the origin of the x-y axes. Therefore, the equation of the circle is

$$x^2 + y^2 = 1$$

It will be assumed that if a dart is thrown (a random number is generated), it must strike either the quadrant of the circle or that part of the rectangle that encloses the quadrant but is outside of the quadrant. Denote the area of the quadrant by A_q and the area of the rectangle A_r. It is assumed that the probability of a dart hitting an area is proportional to the size of the area. Thus, it also is reasonable to assume that the probability of hitting the quadrant is the ratio of the area of the quadrant to the area of the rectangle. Therefore,

$$P(\text{hit } A_q) = \text{probability of hitting the quadrant} = A_q/A_r \tag{9.6}$$

and

$$A_q/A_r = N_{\text{hits}}/N_t \tag{9.7}$$

where N_{hits} refers to the number of darts that hit the quadrant and N_t refers to the total number of darts thrown (total number of random numbers genrated). Therefore,

$$A_q = A_r \frac{N_{\text{hits}}}{N_t} \tag{9.8}$$

The quadrant of the circle is enclosed by a rectangle with dimensions 1×1. Since the random numbers lie between 0 and 1.0, we do not have to scale them. We can claim a hit if $x^2 + y^2 \leq 1.0$. Let us examine program MONTE1, shown below, which calculates the area of the quadrant.

Within loop DO K, the random number generator is called; on each pass through the loop, a random number is assigned to X and another random number is assigned to Y. If (X**2 + Y**2) exceeds 1, the quadrant has been missed and CYCLE is executed; otherwise, the variable HIT is increased by 1. After 4000 iterations, the loop is terminated and AREA = HIT/4000.0. As shown by the result of the run, the area is found to be 0.79250. The exact value of the quadrant is $\pi r^2/4 = 0.785398$. Thus, the simulation is within 1 percent of the exact value.

```
PROGRAM MONTE1
!    CALCULATION OF THE AREA OF A QUADRANT OF A CIRCLE
IMPLICIT NONE
REAL:: X, Y, HIT, AREA
INTEGER:: K
CALL RANDOM_SEED
DO K = 1,4000
  CALL RANDOM_NUMBER(X)
  CALL RANDOM_NUMBER(Y)
  IF(X**2 + Y**2 > 1.0) THEN
    CYCLE
  ELSE
   HIT = HIT + 1.0
  END IF
END DO
  AREA = HIT/4000.0
  WRITE(*,"(A,F12.5)")'AREA OF QUADRANT = ',AREA
END PROGRAM MONTE1
```

OUTPUT OF RUN

```
AREA OF QUADRANT =     0.79250
```

EXAMPLE 9.4 Program MONTE2

In this example, we compute the area bounded by $y = 8/(x^2 + 4)$, $x^2 - 4y = 0$, and the y axis, shown in Fig. 9.3. The two curves intersect at (2, 1). The area is enclosed by a square 2×2.

Program MONTE2 shown below computes the area. The random numbers are scaled by multiplying them by 2, so that they are in range 0 to 2.0 rather than 0 to 1.0. This is necessary because in the area of interest the curves pass through $x = 2$ or $y = 2$. Note that $A_r = 4$, so HIT/4000 is multiplied by 4.0 (see Eq. 9.8).

The program calculates the area to be 2.484. The exact answer with six significant figures is 2.47493.

```
PROGRAM MONTE2
!    CALCULATION OF THE AREA BETWEEN 4Y = X**2 AND
!    Y*(X**2 + 4) = 8 IN FIRST QUADRANT.
IMPLICIT NONE
REAL:: X, Y, HIT, AREA
INTEGER::
CALL RANDOM_SEED
DO K = 1,4000
```

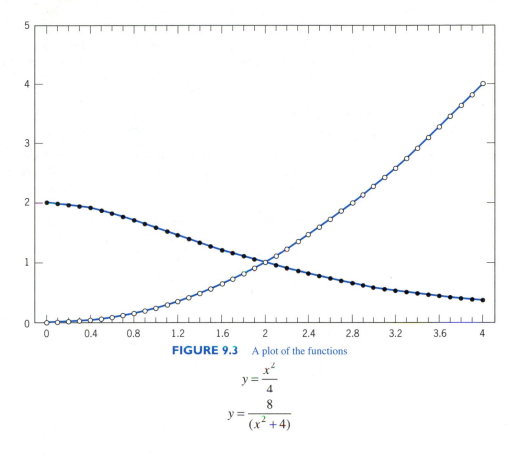

FIGURE 9.3   A plot of the functions

$$y = \frac{x^2}{4}$$

$$y = \frac{8}{(x^2 + 4)}$$

```
CALL RANDOM_NUMBER(X)
X = 2.0*X
CALL RANDOM_NUMBER(Y)
Y = 2.0*Y
IF((Y*(X**2 + 4.0))<= 8.0.AND.(X**2 - 4.0*Y)<= 0) THEN
   HIT = HIT + 1.0
     END IF
END DO
 AREA = 4.0*HIT/4000.0
 WRITE(*,"(A//)")'AREA BETWEEN 4Y = X**2 & Y*(X**2 + 4)'
 WRITE(*,"(10X,A,F12.5)")'AREA = ',AREA
END PROGRAM MONTE2
```

OUTPUT OF RUN

```
AREA =  2.484
```

PART II: SOME TOOLS FOR ESTIMATION

Let us consider a situation in which an engineer or scientist has performed an experiment and collected data, and then plots the data. It is known that the physical law that the experiment was demonstrating should show a linear relation between the variables x and y of the form $y = a + bx$. However, because of experimental error and possibly instrument inaccuracy, it is found that it is not possible to draw a straight line that will pass through all the data. The problem is to find a straight line that most closely approximates the data.

EXAMPLE 9.5 Program LEASTA, LEAST SQUARES: LINEAR FIT

The method of least squares enables one to draw a straight line that is the "best fit"; that is, the straight line comes as close as possible to each point. Possibly this line will not pass through any of the points. One method of drawing such a line, which is called a *regression line,* is by the *method of least squares.*

The principle on which the method of least squares is based is as follows. When a straight line is drawn through the region of the data points, there will, in general, be a difference, δ_i, between the ordinate of the line y_1 and the ordinate of a data point y_i. This can be expressed as

$$\delta_i = y_i - (a + bx_i)$$

The difference δ_i for each point is computed, and the sum of the squares of these quantities is computed as shown in Eq. (9.9).

$$E = \sum_{i=1}^{n} \delta_1^2 = (y_1 - a - bx_1)^2 + (y_2 - a - bx_2)^2 + \ldots$$

$$+(y_n - a - bx_n)^n \tag{9.9}$$

For a straight-line fit, the least-squares method requires that the parameters a and b be chosen so that the sum of the squares of the deviations between the y value of the data and the corresponding ordinates of the fitted line are as small as possible. This is accomplished by calculating the first partial derivatives with respect to a and b and then equating these derivatives to zero. The equations are solved with the results shown in Eqs. (9.10) and (9.11).

$$a = \frac{\sum_{i=1}^{n} y_i \sum_{i=1}^{n} x_i^2 - \sum_{i=1}^{n} x_i \sum_{i=1}^{n} x_i y_i}{\Delta} \tag{9.10}$$

$$b = \frac{n \sum_{i=1}^{n} x_i y_i - \sum_{i=1}^{n} x_i \sum_{i=1}^{n} y_i}{\Delta} \tag{9.11}$$

where

$$\Delta = n \sum_{i=1}^{n} x_i^2 - \left(\sum_{i=1}^{n} x_i \right)^2$$

Suppose that we have n data points (x_i, y_i) and we wish to find a best-fit straight line by the method of least squares. The coefficients a and b are obtained from Eqs. 9.10 and 9.11. A program for calculating a and b, LEASTA, is as follows.

```
MODULE REGRESS
IMPLICIT NONE
```

```
        REAL,DIMENSION(20)::X,Y
        REAL:: A,B,AA,AB, SUMX,SUMY,DELTA,SUMXY
        INTEGER :: I,N
        END MODULE REGRESS
        PROGRAM LEASTA
!       THIS PROGRAM CALCULATES COEFFICIENTS OF A REGRESSION
!       LINE BY LEAST SQUARES
        USE REGRESS
        WRITE(*,*)'ENTER THE NUMBER OF DATA PAIRS(N)'
        READ(*,*)N
        WRITE(*,*)'ENTER THE X DATA'
        READ(*,*)(X(I), I = 1,N)
        WRITE(*,*)'ENTER THE Y DATA'
        READ(*,*)(Y(I), I = 1,N)
        CALL LST
        WRITE(*,"(A,I5/)")'COEFFICIENTS, LINEAR FIT OF ',N,' DATA
           PAIRS'
        WRITE(*,"(/A,F9.4,A,F9.4)")'A = ',A,' B = ',B
        END PROGRAM LEASTA
        SUBROUTINE LST
        USE REGRESS
        SUMX = 0
        SUMY = 0
        SUMXX = 0
        SUMXY = 0
        DO I = 1, N
         SUMX = SUMX + X(I)
         SUMY = SUMY + Y(I)
         SUMXX = SUMXX + X(I)**2
         SUMXY = SUMXY + X(I)*Y(I)
        END DO
        DELTA = N*SUMXX - SUMX**2
        A = (SUMY*SUMXX - SUMX*SUMXY)/DELTA
        B = (N*SUMXY - SUMX*SUMY)/DELTA
        END SUBROUTINE LST
```

The calculations shown in Eqs. (9.10) and (9.11) are carried out in subroutine LST(XX, YY, NN, AA, BB). The dummy arguments XX, YY, NN, AA, BB correspond to the variables X, Y, N, A, B in the main program. As shown by the declarations in the subroutine, data for XX, YY, and NN are supplied by the main program and have INTENT(IN). The data for AA and BB are calculated by the subroutine and are returned to the main program. Therefore, they have INTENT(OUT). The summations shown in the equations for a and b are performed in the loop DO I = 1, NN and are stored in four variables with the descriptive names SUMX, SUMY, SUMXX, and SUMXY. Then, DELTA, AA, and BB are calculated.

The result of a sample run is as follows.

```
The INPUT Data are

N = 6
x: {3.05, 4.29, 5.41, 6.7, 8.71, 10.55}
y: {4.09, 5.8, 6.8, 8.11, 10.45, 12.69}
```

The **OUTPUT** is

```
COEFFICIENTS, LINEAR FIT    6
 DATA PAIRS


A = 0.7500   B = 1.1222
```

Therefore, the equation that represents a least-squares linear fit to the data is

$$y = 0.750 + 1.11222x$$

Note that the first coefficient, A, denotes the constant term in the equation.

EXAMPLE 9.6 Program LEASTB (*Civil Engineering*)

Let us briefly consider an application of the least-squares method to data collected in the study of vehicular traffic flow. Two variables that are used to describe traffic flow are u, the speed of vehicles expressed in miles per hour, and d, the density of vehicles expressed in vehicles per mile. The relation between these variables is empirical; among the relations proposed and that we will use is

$$d = d_m e^{-u/u_m} \tag{9.12}$$

where d_m and u_m are parameters to be determined. If we make a logarithmic transformation of Eq. (9.12), we obtain

$$\ln d = \ln d_m - (u/u_m)$$

The values of the constants d_m and u_m can be determined by making a least-squares fit to the collected data. By comparing the logarithmic equation with the standard form $y = a + bx$, it is seen that

$$y = \ln d$$
$$a = \ln d_m$$
$$b = -1/u_m$$
$$x = u$$

The values of a and b can be determined by a small modification of program LEASTA which we discussed above. The first modification is the calculation of the natural logarithm of each value of density in order to satisfy the relation $y = \ln d$. Then subroutine LST is called, and the values of a and b are returned to the main program. The parameters d_m and u_m can be calculated as follows.

$$d_m = e^a$$
$$u_m = -1/b$$

The revised program, LEASTB, is shown below. LEASTB is a revision of LEASTA for use in the study of traffic flow. In LEASTB, we will enter values of speed for X and values of traffic density for Y. After the data have been entered, a logarithmic transformation of the density data is carried out in loop DO K. A call to subroutine LST returns values of a and b to the main program, and d_m and u_m are calculated. A sample run follows.

```
MODULE LINEAR
IMPLICIT NONE
REAL,DIMENSION(20)::X,Y
REAL::A,B,UM,DM,SUMX,  SUMY,SUMXX,SUMXY,DELTA
```

```
          INTEGER ::I,N,K
          END MODULE LINEAR
          PROGRAM LEASTB
    !     THIS PROGRAM CALCULATES COEFFICIENTS OF A REGRESSION
    !     LINE BY LEAST SQUARES
          USE LINEAR
          WRITE(*,*)'ENTER THE NUMBER OF DATA PAIRS(N)'
          READ(*,*)N
          WRITE(*,*)'ENTER THE X DATA'
          READ(*,*)(X(I), I = 1,N)
          WRITE(*,*)'ENTER THE Y DATA'
          READ(*,*)(Y(I), I = 1,N)
          DO K = 1, N
           Y(K) = ALOG(Y(K))
          END DO
          CALL LST                        !      (X,Y,N,A,B)
          UM = -1./B
          DM = EXP(A)
          WRITE(*,"(A,I5/)")'COEFFICIENTS, LINEAR FIT OF ',N,' DATA   &
              PAIRS'
          WRITE(*,"(/A,F9.4,A,F9.4)")'A = ',A,' B = ',B
          WRITE(*,"(/A,F10.4,A,F10.4)"'DM = ',DM,'  UM = ',UM
          END PROGRAM LEASTB
          SUBROUTINE LST                  !(XX, YY, NN, AA, BB)
          USE LINEAR
          SUMX = 0
          SUMY = 0
          SUMXX = 0
          SUMXY = 0
          DO I = 1, N
            SUMX = SUMX + X(I)
            SUMY = SUMY + Y(I)
            SUMXX = SUMXX + X(I)**2
            SUMXY = SUMXY + X(I)*Y(I)
          END DO
          DELTA = N*SUMXX - SUMX**2
          A = (SUMY*SUMXX - SUMX*SUMXY)/DELTA
          B = (N*SUMXY - SUMX*SUMY)/DELTA
          END SUBROUTINE LST
```

RUN

THE **INPUT** DATA ARE

X: {52,43,51,35,55,41}
Y: {34,60,80,94,96,102}

THE **OUTPUT** IS
COEFFICIENTS, LINEAR FIT OF   6
 DATA PAIRS

 A =   5.14187 B = −0.0186
 DM =   172.2049 UM =   53.7159

From these results, the following relation between u and d is obtained:

$$d = 172e^{-u/53.7}$$

It is possible to use the method of least squares to obtain fits to data using functions that are not linear. Before we study this case, we will discuss the solution of systems of linear equations.

PART III: TOOLS FOR INTERPOLATION AND ESTIMATION

9.7 LAGRANGE'S INTERPOLATION FORMULA

Lagrange's formula is given by Eq. (9.13).

$$P_x(x) = \frac{(x-x_0)(x-x_1)\cdots(x-x_m)}{(x-x_k)} \qquad (k = 0, 1, 2, \ldots, m)$$

Lagrange's formula is

$$y = \sum_{k=0}^{m} \frac{y_k P_k(x)}{P_k(x_k)} \tag{9.13}$$

We will illustrate the use of this formula by two examples. We use two pairs of data in the first example and three pairs in the second. Later, we will relate these calculations to a FORTRAN program.

CALCULATION 1 Using the Lagrange Formula

Interpolation using two pairs of data is

x	0.1	0.3
y	1.8074	1.465

The calculation using the Lagrange formula is

$$y = 1.8074 \frac{(0.2-0.3)}{(0.1-0.3)} + 1.465 \frac{(0.2-0.1)}{(0.3-0.1)}$$

$$= 0.9037 + 0.725$$

$$= 1.632$$

The answer is $y = 1.6362$. The "exact" answer is 1.6298 (rounded to five significant figures).

CALCULATION 2 Using The Lagrange Formula

Interpolation using three pairs of data is

x	0.1	0.3	0.6
y	1.8074	1.465	1.0486

We wish to find y for $x = 0.2$ using the data above.

$$y = 1.8074 \frac{(0.2-0.3)(0.2-0.6)}{(0.1-0.3)(0.1-0.6)} + 1.465 \frac{(0.2-0.1)(0.2-0.6)}{(0.3-0.1)(0.1-0.6)}$$

$$+ 1.0486 \frac{(0.2-0.1)(0.2-0.3)}{(0.6-0.1)(0.6-0.3)}$$

$$= .72296 + 0.97666 - 0.06991 = 1.62971$$

This answer, 1.62971, is closer to the exact value than was obtained by the previous calculation in which two pairs of data were used.

EXAMPLE 9.7 Program LAGRAN2, Interpolation by the Lagrange Formula

Program LAGRAN2 performs interpolation.

```
      PROGRAM LANGRAN2
!     PROGRAM USES THE LAGRANGE FORMULA FOR INTERPOLATION
      IMPLICIT NONE
      REAL,DIMENSION(10)::X,Y, XX
      REAL:: XK, ZXJ,A, B, P, ZX, C,FUN, Q
      INTEGER::NXI, K, M, MM, NLDP, NUDP,I, J
      DATA X/0.1, 0.3, 0.6, 1.0, 1.2, 1.5, 1.8, 2.0, 2.3, 2.5/
      DATA Y/1.8074,1.465,1.0486,0.6457,0.4972,.3265,.2055,.1462, &
           .0819, .0518/
      WRITE(*,*) 'ENTER THE NO. OF VALUES TO BE INTERPOLATED'
      READ(*,*) NXI
      WRITE(*,*)' ENTER THE X VALUES TO BE INTERPOLATED'
       READ(*,*) (XX(K),K = 1,NXI)          ! VALUES INTERPOLATED
       WRITE(*,*)'VALUES INTERPOLATED', (XX(K),K = 1,NXI)
      WRITE(*,*)'ENTER LOWER LIMIT OF THE DATA PAIRS'
      READ(*,*) NLDP
      WRITE(*,*)'ENTER UPPER LIMIT OF THE DATA PAIRS'
      READ(*,*)NUDP
      WRITE(*,"(/A/)")'TABULATED X DATA '
      DO M = NLDP,NUDP
      WRITE(*,"(F10.5)") X(M)
      END DO
      WRITE(*,"(/A/)")'TABULATED Y DATA '
      DO MM = NLDP,NUDP
      WRITE(*,"(F10.5)") Y(MM)
      END DO
      WRITE(*,"(//4X,A,6X,A,12X,A/)")'X,INTERP.','Y LAGRANGE', &
          'EXACT'
!
      DO K = 1,NXI
       C = 0
       XK = XX(K)
       DO I = NLDP,NUDP
         ZX = X(I)
          P = 1.0
            DO J = NLDP,NUDP
                IF(I == J) THEN
                CYCLE
```

```
                ELSE
                ZXJ = X(J)
                A = (XK- ZXJ)/(ZX -ZXJ)
                P = P*A
                END IF
            END DO
                B = P*Y(I)
                C = C + B
            END DO                    !END DO K = 1,NXI
        Q = FUN(XX(K))
        WRITE(*,"(/2X,F10.5,8X,F10.5/)") XK,C,Q
        END DO
        END PROGRAM LAGRAN2
        REAL FUNCTION FUN(ZZ)
        FUN = 2.0*EXP(-ZZ)*COS(0.5*ZZ)
        END FUNCTION FUN
```

For convenience, the available data (x_i, y_i) are stored in two DATA statements, one for X(I) and the other for Y(I). In this program, we are using a known function to obtain data to illustrate the procedure. The data are obtained by evaluating

$$y = 2.0*\exp(-x)*\cos(0.5*x)$$

at various values of x which are *not* equally spaced. This is because the Lagrange method does not require equispaced intervals. In the program, this polynomial is evaluated by use of the function subprogram FUN. By use of this subprogram, we can compare the results of the interpolation with the exact value.

The user supplies only the following data:

1. The number of y values to be found by interpolation.
2. The x value(s) for which y values are sought.
3. The number of data pairs to be used in the interpolation. This number is given by entering the upper and lower limits of the positions in the array of the x values to be used in the interpolation. This enables the user to select precisely the data that are to be used.

In the program, the lower limit is called NLDP, and the upper limit is called NUDP. As stated above, the tabulated data—that is, the data stored in the DATA statements—are X(I) and Y(I). The values to be interpolated are stored in XX.

The calculations are performed by the three nested loops DO K, DO I, and DO J. It is useful to see how the program performs the calculations shown in Calculations 1 and 2.

Program Calculation of Example 1

One value is to be interpolated; therefore, NXI = 1. The value to be interpolated is $x = 0.2$, so XX(1) = 0.2.

The lower and upper limits are entered. Two of the tabulated data are to be used, so NLDP = 1 and NUDP = 2. Therefore, the data pairs to be used are

$$X(1) = 0.1, \quad Y(1) = 1.8074$$
$$X(2) = 0.3, \quad Y(2) = 1.465$$

We will step through the three nested loops referred to above.

Loop DO K = 1, NXI

  As NXI = 1, the result is: DO K = 1, 1

  C = 0

  XK = XX(1) $\equiv x_1 \equiv x_I$. We use the notation x_I to remind us that this value is to be interpolated.

Loop DO I = NLDP, NUDP, which is equivalent to DO I = 1, 2.

  Initially, I = 1. Therefore, ZX = X(I) $\equiv x_1$ and $P = 1.0$ are executed.

Loop DO J = NLDP, NUDP, which is equivalent to DO J = 1, 2

  At this point J = 1 and I = 1. Because J = I, CYCLE is executed, and J is incremented. Therefore, ZXJ = X(J) = X(2) $\equiv x_2$

$$A = (XK - ZXJ)/(ZX - ZXJ) = (x_I - x_2)/(x_1 - x_2)$$
$$= (0.2 - 0.3)/(0.1 - 0.3) = (-0.1)/(-0.2) = 0.5$$
$$P = P*A = 0.5$$
$$B = P*Y(I) = (0.5)Y(1) = (0.5)(1.8074) = 0.9037$$
$$C = C + B = 0.9037$$

Return to loop DO K = 1, 1. This loop has been satisfied, K remains at a value of 1, and in loop DO I, I is incremented to its maximum value of 2; ZX = X(2) = x_2; P = 1.0. Loop DO J again begins at its initial value of J = 1, and ZXJ = X(J) = X(1) ; x_1. XK remains at its previous value of x_I.

$$A = (XK - ZXJ)/(ZX - ZXJ) = (x_I - x_1)/(x_2 - x_1) = (0.2 - 0.1)/(0.3 - 0.1) = 0.5$$
$$P = P*A = (1.0)(0.5) = 0.5$$
$$B = P*Y(I) = (0.5)*Y(2) = (0.5)(1.465) = 0.7325$$
$$C = C + B = 0.9037 + 0.7325 = 1.6362$$

This result is the same as the one we obtained in Calculation 1.

Program Calculation of Example 2

One value is to be interpolated; therefore, NXI = 1. Again, $x_i = 0.2$, and the value of XX(1) = 0.2.

  The lower and upper limits are entered. Three of the tabulated data are to be used, so NLDP = 1 and NUDP = 2. Therefore, the data pairs to be used are

$$X(1) = 0.1, \qquad Y(1) = 1.8074$$
$$X(2) = 0.3, \qquad Y(2) = 1.465$$
$$X(3) = 0.6, \qquad Y(3) = 1.0486$$

Again, we will step through the three nested loops.

Loop DO K = 1, *NXI*

  As NXI = 1, the result is: DO K = 1, 1

  C = 0

  XK = XX(1) $\equiv x_1 \equiv x_I$.

Loop DO I = NLDP, NUDP, which is equivalent to DO I = 1, 3.

  Initially, I = 1. Therefore, ZX = X(I) $\equiv x_1$ and $P = 1.0$ are executed.

Loop DO J = NLDP, NUDP, which is equivalent to DO J = 1,3

At this point $J = 1$ and $I = 1$. Because $J = I$, CYCLE is executed, and J is incremented to a value of 2. Therefore, $ZXJ = X(J) = X(2) \equiv x_2$

$$A = (XK - ZXJ)/(ZX - ZXJ) = (x_I - x_2)/(x_1 - x_2)$$
$$= (0.2 - 0.3)/(0.1 - 0.3) = (-0.1)/(-0.2) = 0.5$$
$$P = P*A = 0.5$$

J is incremented to its maximum value, namely, 3, and $ZXJ = X(J) = X(3) \equiv x_3$. ZX remains at its value of x_1.

$$A = (XK - ZXJ)/(ZX - ZXJ) = (x_I - x_3)/(x_1 - x_3)$$
$$= (0.2 - 0.6)/(0.1 - 0.6) = (-0.4)/(-0.5) = 0.8$$
$$P = P*A = (0.5)(0.8) = 0.4$$

Loop DO J has been satisified and an exit occurs. Then,

$$B = P*Y(I) = (0.4)Y(1) = (0.4)(1.8074) = 0.72296$$
$$C = C + B$$
$$= 0 + 0.72296 = 0.72296$$

Return to loop DO K = 1, 1. This loop has been satisfied, K remains at a value of 1, and XK remains at a value of $XX(I) = XX(1) \equiv x_I$

In loop DO I, I is incremented to 2;

$$ZX = X(I) = X(2) = x_2; \qquad P = 1.0.$$

Loop DO J again begins at its initial value of $J = 1$, and $ZXJ = X(J) = X(1) = x_1$. XK remains at its previous value of x_I.

$$A = (XK - ZXJ)/(ZX - ZXJ) = (x_I - x_1)/(x_2 - x_1)$$
$$= (0.2 - 0.1)/(0.3 - 0.1) = 0.5$$
$$P = P*A = (1.0)(0.5) = 0.5$$
$$B = P*Y(I) = (0.5)*Y(2) = (0.5)(1.465) = 0.7325$$

J is incremented to a value of 2. However, now $J = I$, and CYCLE is executed. Therefore, J is incremented to its maximum value of 3, and $ZXJ = X(J) = X(3)$; x_3.

$$A = (XK - ZXJ)/(ZX - ZXJ) = (x_I - x_3)/(x_2 - x_3)$$
$$= (0.2 - 0.6)/(0.3 - 0.6) = (-0.4)(-0.3) = 4./3.$$
$$P = P*A = (0.5)(4./3.) = 0.666666$$

After exit from loop DO J:

$$B = P*Y(I) = P*Y(2) = (0.666666)(1.465) = 0.97666$$
$$C = C + B = 0.72296 + 0.97666 = 1.69962$$

Since loop DO K has been satisified, XK remains at its previous value, x_I. The program branches to DO I, and I is incremented to its maximum value, I = 3. We are now beginning the final cycle.

$$ZX = X(I) = X(3) \equiv x_3$$
$$P = 1.0$$

In loop DO J, J is at its initial value, 1.

$$ZKJ = X(J) = X(1) \equiv x_1$$

$$A = (XK - ZXJ)/(ZX - ZXJ) = (x_I - x_1)/(x_3 - x_1)$$
$$= (0.2 - 0.1)/(0.6 - 0.1) = (0.1)/(0.5) = 1./5.$$
$$P = P*A = (1.0)(0.2) = 0.2$$

J is incremented to 2.
$$ZXJ = X(J) = X(2) \equiv x_2$$

$$A = (XK) - ZXJ)/(ZX - ZXJ) = (x_I - x^2)/(x_3 - x_2)$$
$$= (0.2 - 0.3)/(0.6 - 0.3) = (-0.1)/(0.3) = -1./3.$$
$$P*A = (0.2)(-1./3.) = -0.2/3.$$
$$P = P*Y(I) = P*Y(3) = ((-0.2)/3.)(1.0486) = -0.06991$$
$$C = C + B = 1.69962 - 0.06991 = 1.6297$$

This result is the same as the one we obtained in Calculation 2.

Some trial runs of program LAGRAN2 follow.

RUN 1. Interpolate for $x = 0.2$ using three data pairs. (This example was done previously by a calculator.)

INPUT

The value to be interpolated: $x = 0.2$

The desired pairs of data are obtained by specifying NLDP = 1 and NUDP = 3.

OUTPUT

TABULATED X DATA
  0.10000
  0.30000
  0.60000

TABULATED Y DATA
  1.80740
  1.46500
  1.04860

X, INTERP.	Y LAGRANGE	EXACT
0.20000	1.62972	1.62928

RUN 2. Interpolate for $X = 0.5$ and for $X = 0.8$

INPUT

The values to be interpolated are $x = 0.5$ and $x = 0.8$.
The desired pairs of data are obtained by specifying NLDP = 2 and NUDP = 5.

OUTPUT

TABULATED X DATA
  0.30000

0.60000
1.00000
1.20000

TABULATED Y DATA
1.46500
1.04860
0.64570
0.49720

X, INTERP.	Y LAGRANGE	EXACT
0.50000	1.17538	1.17535
0.80000	0.82767	0.82771

9.8 ESTIMATION BY TAYLOR SERIES

The Taylor series provides a means of estimating a function in terms of the value of the function at one point and its derivatives at another. The Taylor series for $f(x_{i+1})$ is given by Eqs. (9.14a) and (9.14b):

$$f(x_{i+1}) = f(x_i) + f'(x_i)(x_{i+1} - x_i) + f''\frac{(x_i)}{2!}(x_{i+1} - x_i)^2 + f'''\frac{(x_i)}{3!}(x_{i+1} - x_i) + \cdots$$

$$+ \frac{f^{(n)}(x_i - x_{i+1})^n}{n!} + R_n \qquad (9.14a)$$

where R_n denotes the remaining terms of the series.

$$f(x_{i+1}) = f(x_i) + f'(x_i)h + \frac{f''(x_i)}{2!}h^2 + \frac{f'''(x_i)}{3!}h_3 + \cdots$$

$$+ \frac{f^{(n)}(x_i)}{n!}h^n + R_n \qquad (9.14b)$$

If we let $h = x_{i+1} - x_i$ in Eq. (9.14b), we obtain the somewhat more compact form of Taylor series shown in Eq. (9.15).

$$f(x_{i+1}) = f(x_i) + f'(x_i)h + \frac{f''(x_i)h^2}{2!} + \frac{f'''(x_i)h^3}{3!} + \cdots \qquad (9.15)$$

We will now illustrate the use of these equations.

Calculation

Calculate the value of $\exp(-x_{i+1})$ where $x_{i+1} = 1$ and $h = 0.4$; also calculate $\exp(-x_i)$.
As $h = x_{i+1} - x_i$, $\quad x_i = 1 - 0.4 = 0.6$; $\quad \exp(-x_{i+1}) = 0.367879$; $\quad \exp(-x_i) = 0.548811$

EXAMPLE 9.8 Program TAYLOR1

Program TAYLOR1 performs the calculation. In the program, the first term of the Taylor series is calculated and stored in E(0). Then, within loop DO N, other terms of the series are successively added to E(0), producing a sequence of increasingly improved approximations. When the loop has been satisfied, the various approximations as well as the direct calculation of exp(−1) are printed. The output of the run, which follows the program, shows that for N = 5 the series has produced a very close approximation to the exact values.

```
PROGRAM TAYLOR1
IMPLICIT NONE
REAL:: TRUE, H, XI
REAL:: E(0:10)
INTEGER:: N,L,FACT
H = 0.4           !THE STEP SIZE
XI = 0.6
TRUE = EXP(-1.0)
DO N = 1, 5
E(N) = E(N -1 ) + (-1)**N*EXP(-XI)*H**N/FACT(N)
END DO
WRITE(*,"(6X,A,4X,A/)")'TAYLOR TERMS','RESULT'
DO L = 0,5
 WRITE(*,"(7X,I4,9X,F12.8)") L, E(L)
END DO
WRITE(*,"(/A,F12.8)")'EXACT VALUE =', TRUE
END PROGRAM TAYLOR1
INTEGER FUNCTION FACT(M)
FACT = 1.0
DO J = 1,M
 IF(M == 0.OR.M ==1) THEN
 EXIT
END IF
 FACT = FACT*J
END DO
END FUNCTION FACT
```

TRIAL RUN

OUTPUT

```
TAYLOR TERMS    RESULT
0               0.54881161
1               0.32928696
2               0.37319189
3               0.36733791
4               0.36792331
5               0.36787649

EXACT VALUE = 0.36787945
```

PART IV: INTEGRATION

9.9 INTEGRATION BY SIMPSON'S RULE

There are many integrals for which it is not possible to find a solution in closed form. When an integral cannot be evaluated in closed form, an approximation can be obtained by *numerical* integration. Among the many methods of numerical integration are: (1) divide the area of interest into rectangular strips and add these subareas; (2) divide the area into trapezoidal strips and add these subareas; and (3) approximate the curve under which the area is to be calculated by parabolic arcs and add the subareas under these arcs; the last is Simpson's rule. This method can probably be best understood by a derivation, so we will present that first. Later, we will show the rectangular approximation, which is a simpler method and is adequate in many cases.

A definite integral $\int_a^b f(x)dx$ can be interpreted as the area under the curve $y = f(x)$ over the interval a to b, where a and b are points on the x axis. Simpson's rule is based on the concept that the curve $y = f(x)$ can be divided into segments that can be approximated by an arc of a parabola. The area bounded by the curve is divided into an *even* number, N, of subareas, each of width h. A pair of subareas is shown in Fig. 9.4. The equation of the parabola is $y = Ax^2 + Bx + C$. We integrate this function between the limits $M - h$ and $M + h>$, as shown in Fig. 9.4, and we obtain Eq. (9.16):

$$\text{area} = \int_{M-h}^{M+h} (Ax^2 + Bx + C)dx = \left(\frac{A}{3}\right)x^3 + \left(\frac{B}{2}\right)x^2 + Cx\Big|_{M-h}^{M+h} \tag{9.16}$$

After substituting limits and simplifying, we obtain Eq. (9.17):

$$\text{area} = \left(\frac{h}{3}\right)[A(6M^2 + 2h^2) + B(6M) + 6C] \tag{9.17}$$

Figure 9.4 shows that the parabola passes through the points $(M - h, y_1)$, (M, y_2), and $(M + h, y_3)$. The values of the equation $y = Ax^2 + Bx + C$ at the left end, midpoint, and right end are, respectively,

$$y_1 = A(M-h)^2 + B(M - h) + C \tag{9.18}$$
$$y_2 = AM^2 + BM + C \tag{9.19}$$
$$y_3 = A(M + h)^2 + B(M + h) + C \tag{9.20}$$

Adding y_1 to y_3 yields

$$y_1 + y_3 = 2AM^2 + 2h^2 + 2BM + 2Ah^2 + 2C \tag{9.21}$$

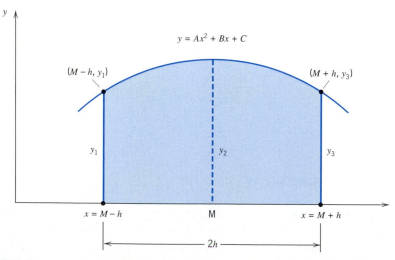

FIGURE 9.4   Definition of an interval with respect to a parabola ($y = Ax^2 + Bx + C$) in order to be able to perform numerical integration.

Finally, adding $4y_2$ to Eq. (9.21) yields

$$y_1 + 4y_2 + y_3 = 6AM^2 + 2h^2 + 6BM + 2Ah^2 + 6C$$
$$= A(6M^2 + 2h^2) + B(6M) + 6C \qquad (9.22)$$

By use of Eq. (9.22), we see that we can rewrite Eq. (9.17) as

$$\text{area} = (h/3)[y_1 + 4y_2 + y_3] \qquad (9.23)$$

Equation (9.23) can be used to calculate the area under the curve $y = f(x)$ and bounded by the x axis between limits a and b and two ordinates. As mentioned above, in applying Simpson's rule, this area is divided into an even number of subareas, each of width h. Then Eq. (9.23) is used to calculate the area of successive pairs of subareas:

$$\text{area} = (h/3)(y_1 + 4y_2 + y_3) + (h/3)(y_3 + 4y_4 + y5) + \cdots + (h/3)(y_{n-1} + 4y_n + 4y_{n+1})$$

After factoring $(h/3)$ and regrouping, the result is Eq. (9.24)

$$\text{area} = (h/3)[y_1 + 4(y_2 + y_4 + y_6 + \cdots + y_n) + 2(y_3 + y_5 + y_7 + \cdots + y_{n-1}) + y_{n+1}] \qquad (9.24)$$

We will show two examples of integration by Simpson's rule. One is presented in this section and a second in Sec. 9.10.

EXAMPLE 9.9 Program INTEGR2, Integrating $f(x) = x^2\exp(2x)$

In this program, the function $f(x) = x^2 \exp(2x)$ is integrated. This function is defined within function subprogram $FNX(X)$. If desired, the program can be used to integrate another function simply by changing one statement within FNX. In the examples presented here, we have arbitrarily used eight subareas. Of course, if it is important to check the effect of this decision, one can increase the value of n, say in steps of 2, and thereby find out how much of a change results. (See Problem 9.9 at the end of the chapter.)

```
        PROGRAM INTEGR2
!       THIS PROGRAM INTEGRATES BY USE OF SIMPSON'S RULE
        IMPLICIT NONE
        REAL::A,B,SIMPS
        INTEGER::N
        WRITE(*,*)'ENTER LOWER,THEN UPPER LIMIT'
        READ(*,*)A,B
        WRITE(*,"(A,F10.2,5X,A,F10.2)")'A = ',A,'B = ',B
        WRITE(*,*)'ENTER NUBER OF STRIPS
        READ(*,*)N
        CALL SIMPSON(A,B,N,SIMPS)
        WRITE(*,"(A,F14.6)")'VALUE OF THE INTEGRAL = ',SIMPS
        END PROGRAM INTEGR2
        REAL FUNCTION FNX(X)
        FNX = X**2*EXP(-X**2)
        END
        SUBROUTINE SIMPSON(E,F,N,SIM)
        REAL,INTENT(IN)::E,F
        INTEGER, INTENT(IN)::N
        REAL, INTENT(OUT):: SIM
        M = N-1
        MM = M - 1
        H = (F - E)/N
```

```
      PARSUM = 0
      ODD = 0
      CONST = FNX(E) + FNX(F)
         DO I = 1,M,2
          DX = H*I
         PARSUM = PARSUM + 4.0*FNX(E + DX)
         END DO
          DO J = 2,MM,2
           DX = H*J
           ODD = ODD + 2.0*FNX(E + DX)
          END DO
          SIM = H/3.0*(CONST + ODD + PARSUM)
       END SUBROUTINE SIMPSON

RESULT OF RUN

A =    0.00  B =   5.00
VALUE OF THE INTEGRAL =    0.449320
*    *    *    *
```

9.10 DOUBLE INTEGRATION

Under some circumstances it is necessary to perform numerical integration of double integrals. One example is the calculation of probabilities when some event depends on two random variables. (This is called a joint probability distribution.) It is possible to use Simpson's rule to evaluate double integrals by applying it successively in the x and y directions. The formula for carrying out this integration is

$$I \approx (HX)(HY)/9[F_1 + F_3 + F_7 + F_9 + 4(F_2 + F_4 + F_6 + F_8) + 16F_5] \qquad (9.25)$$

The region of integration is divided into four rectangles, each of which has dimensions HX by HY. The integrand must be evaluated at nine points of the subdivided region as shown in Fig. 9.5.

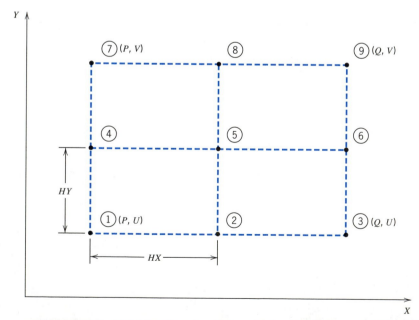

FIGURE 9.5 Definition of a region of integration for performing numerical integration of double integrals.

In Eq. (9.25), F_1 represents the integrand evaluated at point 1, F_2 represents the integrand evaluated at point 2, and so forth. Equation (9.25) is first used to obtain a preliminary estimate of the double integral that is called TEST in the program. The intervals *HX* and *HY* are then halved. As a result, the region is subdivided in 16 rectangles, equivalent to four grids, each of which is similar to the original grid. These smaller grids are then evaluated by means of Eq. (9.22), and the results are summed. This constitutes a second evaluation of the double integral. If the magnitude of the difference between the first and second evaluations is less than a preassigned number, the procedure is halted. If not, the intervals *HX* and *HY* are again halved and the calculation proceeds. An example of double integration follows.

EXAMPLE 9.10 Program **INTEGTWO, DOUBLE INTEGRATION**

```
PROGRAM INTEGTWO
!   DOUBLE INTEGRATION BY USE OF SIMPSON'S RULE
REAL::A,B,C,D
WRITE(*,*)'ENTER LIMITS OF X INTEGRAL'
READ(*,*)A,B
WRITE(*,*)'ENTER LIMITS OF Y INTEGRAL'
READ(*,*)C,D
WRITE(*,"(A,3X,2F10.2)")'X LIMITS = ',A,B
WRITE(*,"(A,3X,F10.2)")'Y LIMITS = ',C,D
CALL SIMPS(A,B,C,D,SIM,N)
WRITE(*,"(A,F14.6)")'THE VALUE OF THE DOUBLE INTEGRAL = ',SIM
WRITE(*,*)'NO. OF ITERATIONS IN SIMPS = ',N
END PROGRAM INTEGTWO
REAL FUNCTION FXY(X,Y)
FXY = EXP(-(X + Y))
END
SUBROUTINE SIMPS(P,Q,U,V,SIM,N)
REAL,INTENT(IN)::P,Q,U,V
REAL,INTENT(OUT)::SIM
INTEGER,INTENT(OUT)::N
N = 1
HX = (Q - P)/2.0
HY = (V - U)/2.0
XS = P
XMID = XS + HX
XEND = XMID + HX
YS = U
YMID = YS + HY
YEND = YMID + HY
F1 = FXY(XS,YS)
F2 = FXY(XMID,YS)
F3 = FXY(XEND,YS)
F4 = FXY(XS,YMID)
F5 = FXY(XMID,YMID)
F6 = FXY(XEND,YMID)
F7 = FXY(XS,YEND)
F8 = FXY(FXMID,YEND)
F9 = FXY(XEND,YEND)
TEST = (F1 + F3 + F7 + F9 + 4.*(F2 + F4 + F6 + F8) + 16.*F5)
TEST = HX*HY/9.*TEST
DO K = 1,N
```

```
      SIM = 0
      N = 2*N
      HX = HX/2.0
      HY = HY/2.0
      XS = P
      XMID = XS + HX
      XEND = XMID + HX
      DO I = 1, N
       YS = U
       YMID = YS + HY
       YEND = YMID + HY
      F1 = FXY(XS,YS)
      F2 = FXY(XMID,YS)
      F3 = FXY(XEND,YS)
       DO J = 1, N
                   F4 = FXY(XS,YMID)
                   F5 = FXY(XMID,YMID)
                   F6 = FXY(XEND,YMID)
                   F7 = FXY(XS,YEND)
                   F8 = FXY(XMHx,YEND)
                   F9 = FXY(XEND,YEND)
      SIM = SIM + HX*HY/9.*(F1 + F3 + F7 + F9 + 4.*(F2+F4+F6+F8)+16.*F5)
      F1 = F7
      F2 = F8
      F3 = F9
      YMID = YEND + HY
      YEND = YMID + HY
      END DO
      XS = XEND
      XMID = XS + HX
      XEND = XMID + HX
      END DO
      IF(ABS(TEST-SIM)<0.0001.OR.N>128) THEN
         EXIT
      END IF
      END DO
      END SUBROUTINE SIMPS

RESULT OF RUN
X LIMITS =     0.00  1.00
Y LIMITS =     1.00  2.00
THE VALUE OF THE DOUBLE INTEGRAL =     0.147002
NO. OF ITERATIONS IN SIMPS = 2
```

The results show that after N was increased from 8 to 16 and SIM was compared to TEST, the difference between them was less than 0.0001. Therefore, the program was halted.

PART V: INTRODUCTION TO THE DISCRETE FOURIER TRANSFORM (*Civil, Electrical, and Mechanical Engineering*)

With the advent of reasonably priced high-speed computers and the design of algorithms that speed their computation, the analysis of signals has become a major research tool. The analysis of signals, called spectral analysis, is being used in diverse areas such as the study of the effects of waves on the vibration of ships; of noise on the performance of electrical guidance systems; and of the shock waves resulting from an earthquake. Next, we will study one topic associated with this important subject, the discrete Fourier transform.

9.11 ANALOG AND DIGITAL SIGNALS

We may define a signal as a function of time which conveys information. A signal may originate from a variety of sources, including the human body. Several electrical signals can be obtained from the body. One signal can be obtained by connecting wires to the surface of the scalp; with the aid of suitable instrumentation, the signal can be viewed. A graphic record of this signal is called an electroencephalogram, commonly called the EEG. This particular signal provides information about the activity of the brain. A second signal can be obtained by connecting wires to the chest. A graphic record of this signal is called an electrocardiogram, commonly called the EKG. This signal provides information about the electrical activity of the heart. A drawing of the EKG is shown in Fig. 9.6. For comparison, a sinusoid is also shown. The shape of the EKG is quite irregular compared to the smooth shape of the sinusoid. The shape of signals is called the *waveform*.

9.12 FOURIER SERIES

The French mathematician Jean Baptiste Fourier (1768–1830) derived a theorem stating that periodic waveforms can be expressed as a summation of sinusoids of differing frequencies plus, possibly, a constant. This summation is called a *trigonometric* Fourier series. A Fourier series contains an infinite number of terms. The general expression for a Fourier series is given by Eq. (9.26):

$$f(t) = a_0 + \sum_{n=1}^{\infty} (a_n \cos n\omega t + b_n \sin n\omega t) \tag{9.26}$$

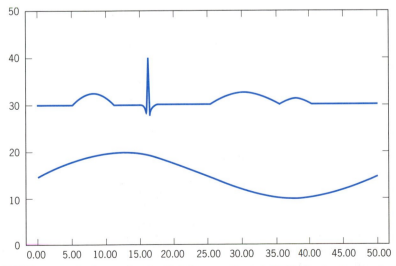

FIGURE 9.6   A sketch of one cycle of an ideal electrocardiograph (EKG) signal and one cycle of a sine wave for comparison purposes.

It should be noted that a periodic function continues to time $t = \infty$.

An example of a Fourier series (the signal is the output of a half-wave rectifier) is:

$$f(t) = a_0 + b_1 \sin \pi t - a_1 \cos 2\pi t - a_2 \cos 4\pi t - a_3 \sin 6\pi t + \ldots$$

where

$a_0 = 1/\pi = 0.3183098$

$b_1 = 1/2 = 0.5$

$a_1 = 2/(3\pi) = 0.2122065$

$a_2 = 2/(15\pi) = 0.0424413$

$a_3 = 2/(35\pi) = 0.0181891$

This is called the trigonometric Fourier series because, except for the dc component, the terms are either sine or cosine. The term a_0 is the dc component. (The frequency is zero.) For some signals, this component will have a zero amplitude. The sinusoid of lowest frequency, b_1, $\sin \pi t$, is called the fundamental, and the terms of higher frequencies are called harmonics. In general, the amplitude of the fundamental, b_1, is higher than the amplitude of any of the harmonics, and the amplitudes of successive terms decrease; that is, a_1 is larger than a_2 and a_2 is larger than a_3, and so forth.

Using Fourier's theorem, it is possible to analyze periodic waveforms and determine the constituents. A listing or a graph of the various components of $f(t)$ showing the frequency and magnitude of each component is called a *discrete* spectrum. For example, the spectral listing for $f(t)$ shown above is:

$$0.3183098, 0; \quad 0.5, \pi t; \quad 0.2122065, 2\pi t; \quad 0.0424413, 4\pi t; \quad 0.0181891, 6\pi t; \ldots$$

The frequency in the spectral listing above is in radians per second.

Usually, the spectrum is displayed in the form of a bar graph. Because the Fourier series is infinite, not all of its terms can be listed. However, as the amplitudes of the higher frequency terms decrease, a frequency is reached at which the amplitude of the remaining terms is negligible. One topic of interest in a Fourier analysis is the determination of what each spectral component contributes to the power delivered to a 1-ohm resistor.

9.13 THE EXPONENTIAL FOURIER SERIES

Leonhard Euler, a Swiss mathematician, made several contributions to number theory, geometry and calculus. One contribution is the theorem stated in Eqs. (9.27), (9.28a) and (9.28b).

Euler's theorem states that $\sin n\omega t$ and $\cos n\omega t$ can be expressed in the forms:

$$\cos n\omega t = (e^{jn\omega t} + e^{-jn\omega t})/2 \tag{9.27}$$

$$\sin n\omega t = (e^{jn\omega t} - e^{-jn\omega t})2j \tag{9.28a}$$

$$= (-0.5j)e^{jn\omega t} + (0.5j)e^{-jn\omega t} \tag{9.28b}$$

Equation (9.28b) shows that the factors in parentheses that multiply the exponentials are complex conjugates. We will encounter the same property in our discussion of the discrete Fourier transform. We will call terms that multiply the exponentials, such as $(-0.5j)$ and $(0.5j)$, c_n and c_{-n}, respectively.

Euler's theorem can be used to convert a trigonometric Fourier series to the exponential form. For example, suppose that the first two terms of the Fourier series of a signal are

$$f(t) = \cos \omega t + \sin 3\omega t + \ldots$$

Using Euler's theorem, we replace sin and cos and obtain

$$f(t) = 0.5e^{j\omega t} + 0.5e^{-j\omega t} - 0.5je^{j3\omega t} + 0.5e^{-j3\omega t}$$

We now group the terms positive frequency with positive frequency and negative with negative.

$$f(t) = \text{(additional negative frequency terms)} + c_0 \text{ (dc term)} + 0.5je^{-j3\omega t}$$
$$+ 0.5e^{-j\omega t} + 0.5e^{j\omega t} - 0.5je^{j3\omega t} \ldots + \text{(additional positive frequency terms)}$$

This is how the exponential form of the Fourier series normally appears: positive frequency terms in one group and negative frequency terms in the other. If we draw a graph showing the amplitude of the components, the terms with negative frequency will appear to the left of the y axis and the amplitudes of the terms with positive frequency will appear to the right of the y axis. Of course, we can convert the exponential form to the trigonometric form.

The general expression for the exponential Fourier series is given by Eq. (9.29):

$$f(t) - c_0 + \sum_{n=1}^{\infty} c_n e^{jn\omega t} + \sum_{n=1}^{\infty} c_{-n} e^{-jn\omega t} \tag{9.29}$$

When we use the discrete Fourier transform, we often wish to convert exponential Fourier series to trigonometric form. This can be done using the following relations:

$$a_n = c_n + c_{-n} \tag{9.30}$$
$$b_n = j(c_n - c_{-n}) \tag{9.31}$$

Equations (9.30) and (9.31), respectively, show that the terms a_n are the amplitudes of the cos terms of the Fourier series and the terms b_n are the amplitudes of the sin terms of the Fourier series.

9.14 THE FOURIER TRANSFORM

The Fourier transform is used to calculate the spectrum of a *nonperiodic analog signal*. The Fourier transform is given by Eq. (9.32):

$$F(j\omega) = \int_{-\infty}^{\infty} f(t) e^{-j\omega t} dt \tag{9.32}$$

Unlike the Fourier series which produces a spectrum of *discrete* frequencies, the Fourier transform produces a continuous spectrum. For example, if $f(t) = e^{-at}$, then by integration we obtain

$$F(j\omega) = 1/(a + j\omega)$$

The inverse Fourier transform is given by Eq. (9.33)

$$x(t) = \int_{x=-\infty}^{\infty} X(f) \exp(+j\omega t) df \tag{9.33}$$

9.15 THE DISCRETE FOURIER TRANSFORM (DFT)

Up to this point we have been discussing *analog* signals. An analog signal is a continuous function of time and amplitude. We now want to use the discrete Fourier transform (DFT) to analyze a signal that has been stored in a computer. Initially, we will assume that the signal being studied is periodic. Later, we discuss the possibility of modifying this assumption. To use the DFT, we will have to change from a continuous time signal to a discrete time signal. Let us see what is involved in obtaining a discrete time signal.

The term *quantization* refers to the representation of a variable by a finite set of values. A *discrete-time* signal is defined only at discrete times 0, T, $2T$, $3T$, ... Therefore, the variable time has been quantized. If a discrete-time signal can assume a continuous range of amplitudes, it is called a *sampled-data* signal. A *digital* signal is a signal in which *both* time and amplitude are quantized. A digital signal can be obtained by connecting the signal source to a device called an *analog to digital (A/D) converter*. The A/D converter accepts information from a source at a predetermined rate called the sampling frequency. This frequency determines the time, T, between samples. The reciprocal of T is called the sampling frequency f_s; that is, $f_s = 1/T$. T has to be sufficiently small to collect enough samples, so that the spectrum can be correctly computed. The A/D converter converts each sample to a binary number that is stored in a *register* whose capacity is a certain number of bits. A particular number of bits determines the number that can be stored. Adding (or subtracting a bit) changes the number that can be stored by an increment determined by the number of available bits. Because the increment is a specific quantity, a change of one bit produces a "jump" (a quantum change) in the magnitude of the number that can be stored. The larger the number of bits, the greater the accuracy of the converter. The binary number is transferred from the register of the converter to a computer and stored in the computer's memory. The procedure for setting up the A/D converter involves selecting the value of f_s as well as the number of samples, N, to be collected. The product NT is the duration of the signal that is to be sampled.

As stated above, T has to be chosen sufficiently small in order to compute the spectrum correctly. The sampling frequency, f_s, is related to the spectral content of the signal that is being analyzed in the following way. Assume that the highest frequency component of the signal is f_H. Then the sampling frequency must satisfy

$$f_s \geq 2f_H \tag{9.34}$$

or, in terms of T,

$$T \leq 1/(2f_H) \tag{9.35}$$

If Eq. (9.34) or (9.35) is not satisified, the DFT will produce spectral components that are *not* in the signal. This error is called *aliasing*.

In addition to the sampling frequency, another factor that must be taken into account is *frequency resolution*. Resolution is the frequency separation between the components of the spectrum. We will denote the frequency resolution Δf. It is given by

$$\Delta f = 1/(NT) \tag{9.36}$$

For example, if $T = 0.0001$ sec and $N = 500$, then the resolution will be 1/0.05 or 20 Hz. Suppose that a certain signal has a spectrum such that the significant frequencies are 5, 15, 30, 40, 60, and 75 Hz. If $\Delta f = 20$ Hz, only the 30- and 60-Hz components will be detected. In this case, the resolution must be 5 Hz if all the frequencies are to be detected.

By studying Eqs. (9.34) and (9.35), we note that a higher sampling frequency is obtained by making T smaller; but Eq. (9.35) shows that a smaller value of T makes the resolution worse. To improve frequency resolution, the product NT in the denominator of Eq. (9.36) must be larger. If T has already been selected and cannot be increased, then N must be increased in order to obtain the desired resolution. In the example above, if we increased N to a value of 2000, then $NT = (0.0001)(2000) = 0.2$ and $\Delta f = 5$ Hz.

Note that the value of T selected above, namely, 0.0001 sec, corresponds to a sampling frequency of 1000. This means that the highest frequency component of the signal should be no more than 500 Hz. For the signal being discussed, the highest significant frequency is 75 Hz; thus, the value of T is satisfactory.

It has been stated that the value of T must be chosen on the basis of the highest frequency component of the signal that is being analyzed. This implies that this information is known *before* the DFT has been computed. When this not the case, the signal can be filtered by use of an analog low-pass filter that will remove all signal components above some selected frequency. This will ensure that aliasing does not occur. After filtering, the signal is said to be *band-limited* because the frequency band has been truncated.

Suppose that a signal has been digitized with a particular value of N and T and it is believed that the chosen resolution is not adequate to obtain a complete spectrum from the DFT. We can attempt to repeat the sampling process using different values for N and T. If this is not feasible, we can improve the resolution of the signal by a method known as *zero padding*. Space limitation prevents discussion of this method.

A final point about the sampling process is that the number of samples stored should span an *integral* number of cycles. Failure to do so results in spectral errors. This is called leakage. Leakage occurs because the *truncated* signal becomes the basis for the DFT. For example, suppose that about $2\frac{1}{}$ cycles of signal are sampled and the DFT is calculated. Then that length of signal becomes a *new* periodic signal, and its DFT is computed. Recall our comment that the DFT periodically extends any signal for which it computes the spectrum. For a periodic waveform, which generally is available for a time sufficiently long for its observation, it is usually feasible to observe and capture the signal for an integral number of cycles.

The discrete Fourier transform is a method for calculating the Fourier transform of a discrete or a digital signal. The resulting spectrum is discrete; it consists of a finite number of discrete frequencies. The DFT is defined by Eq. (9.37)

$$X(m) = \frac{1}{N} \sum_{k=0}^{N-1} x(k) e^{[-j2\pi mk/N]} \tag{9.37}$$

where

$x(k), k; = 0, 1T, 2T, \ldots, (N-1)T$ are signal samples spaced T sec apart

$X(m), m = 0, 1, 2, \ldots, N-1$ are the spectral components calculated by the DFT

Hereafter, we will omit T and use the notation $k = 0, 1, 2, \ldots$; the parameter T will be understood. In general, $X(m)$ is a complex value; however, usually either the real part is zero or the imaginary part is zero. $X(0)$ is never a complex number. If $X(0)$ is nonzero, then it is real and it represents a dc component of the signal. The components of $X(m)$ form an *exponential* Fourier series with a finite number of terms. The series consists of the coefficients c_n and c_{-n} only; the exponentials $e^{jn\omega t}$ and $e^{-jn\omega t}$ are not displayed. The frequency is obtained by calculating $m\Delta f$. Except for $X(0)$, the terms of $X(m)$ must be paired with $X(N-m)$ in order to obtain *each spectral component in trigonometric form*. The frequency domain is translated to the right along the x axis so that the components $X(m)$ range from $m = 0$ to $m = N-1$. The positive frequency components are found in the range $1 \le m \le (N/2) - 1$; the negative frequency components are found in the range $(N/2) + 1 \le m \le N-1$. The value $m = 0$ denotes dc. The value $m = N/2$ represents a frequency called the *folding frequency* and is denoted by f_0. It separates the positive frequency terms from the negative frequency terms.

One property of $X(m)$ is that, when the real parts are zero but the terms have a nonzero imaginary part, then

$$X(N-m) = *X(m)$$

One positive frequency component combined with a component of the same frequency, but with negative sign, form one spectral component which will be either a sine or a cosine, depending on whether the components are real or imaginary.

When $X(m)$ consists of only a real part—that is, the imaginary part is zero—then $X(m) = X(N-m)$. In this case, as indicated by Eq. (9.26) $X(N-m)$ is simply added to $X(m)$ and the result is the amplitude of a cosine term. When $X(m)$ has only an imaginary part, then $X(m)$ and $X(N-m)$ are combined in accordance with Eq. (9.27).

Because of the relations between $X(m)$ and $X(N-m)$, it is sufficient to print only the components in the range

$$0 \le X(m) \le N/2 - 1$$

The values of $X(m)$ higher than the folding frequency can be deduced.

This procedure for combining the components above the folding frequency with the components below the folding frequency is illustrated below. As noted above, the frequency of any component is given by $m(\Delta f)$.

Another property of the DFT is that the frequency function $X(m)$ which it produces is periodic. In addition, the DFT treats all signals as if they were periodic; that is, a signal that has a finite duration is treated as if it were periodic and had an infinite duration.

EXAMPLE 9.11 The Result of a DFT Calculation

Assume that a DFT has been computed for a certain signal using $N = 32$ and $T = 1/1600$ sec. For $T = 1/1600$, the sampling frequency is 1600 Hz. Thus, the highest frequency contained in the signal has been assumed to be 800 Hz. Since $NT = 32/1600$, the frequency resolution is $1/NT = 50$ Hz. The results of the DFT are shown below. Only those values of m are listed which have nonzero components.

Note that the highest frequency component is found to be 700 Hz.

m	frequency	$X(m)$
2	100	$0.5 + j0.0$
6	300	$0.0 - j0.40$
10	500	$0.3 + j0.0$
14	700	$0.0 - j0.20$
	800*	
18		$0.0 + j0.20$
22		$0.3 + j0.0$
26		$0.0 + j0.40$
30		$0.5 + j0.0$

*Folding frequency.

Now we will combine terms $X(m)$ below the folding frequency with terms $X(N-m)$ above the folding frequency. Note that both $X(2)$ and $X(30)$ are real numbers and are equal. As the terms are real, the result will be the amplitude of a cosine. We also observe that $X(10)$ and $X(22)$ are real and equal; they, too, will be combined to give the amplitude of a cosine. On the other hand, $X(26) = *X(6)$; when these terms are combined, the result will be the amplitude of a sine. This is also true for $X(14)$ and $X(18)$. These results are indicated by Eqs. (9.30) and (9.31).

Thus,

$$X(2) + X(32 - 2) \text{ yields} \quad 1.0 \cos[2\pi(100)t]$$
$$X(10) + X(22) \text{ yields} \quad 0.6 \cos[2\pi(500)t]$$

The other terms are complex; these produce a sine function:

$$j[X(6) - X(26)] = j[-j0.40 - j0.40] = j[-j0.80] = 0.80$$

The result is

$$0.8 \sin[2\pi(300)t]$$

Finally

$$j[X(14) - X(18)] = j[-j0.20 - j0.20] = j[-j0.40] = 0.40$$

The result is

$$0.40 \sin[2\pi(700)t]$$

Let us now discuss the inverse DFT briefly. The *inverse* DFT operates on the spectral components $X(m)$ and *recovers* the original signal. The *inverse* discrete Fourier transform (IDFT) is given by Eq. (9.38):

$$x(k) = \sum_{m=0}^{N-1} X(m)e^{[j\pi mk/N]} \tag{9.38}$$

Let us compare the formula for the DFT with the formula for the IDFT. We note the following.

1. In the formula for the DFT, factor $(1/N)$ multiplies the summation.
2. The DFT has a negative sign in the exponential function; the IDFT has a positive sign.
3. In the DFT, the summation involves the *real* samples $x(k)$.

In the IDFT, the summation involves the *complex* components $X(m)$. We will return to this subject later and also provide examples of the computation of the IDFT.

9.16 GENERATING A SAMPLED DATA SIGNAL

Our present goal is to present a FORTRAN program for computing the DFT. We will test the program using various sampled data signals. Our immediate aim is to show how to obtain sampled data signals for use in the DFT program.

Suppose that the signal to be studied is

$$f(t) = \cos(200\pi t) + 0.8 \sin(600\pi t) + 0.6 \cos(1000\pi t) + 0.40 \sin(1400\pi t)$$

This signal is band-limited, and we already know the spectral components. Nevertheless, we can use this signal to test the DFT program once we convert the signal to sampled data form. We will use $N = 32$ and $T = 1/1600$. Then, the continuous time variable t must be replaced by KT where T is the time between samples and $k = 0, 1, 2, 3, \ldots, N - 1$. After replacing t by $KT = K/1600$, the result is

$$f(t) = \cos(\pi k/8) + 0.8 \sin(3\pi k/8) + 0.6 \cos(5\pi k/8) + 0.4 \sin(7\pi k/8)$$

EXAMPLE 9.12 Program DISCRETE_FT1, Calculating the DFT of a Band-limited Signal

Program DISCRETE_FT1, which computes the DFT, is shown in this subsection. First, let us examine the main features of the program. The sampling frequency is 1600 Hz, and the number of samples is 32. Thus, the resolution is 50 Hz.

The loop DO K = 0, N − 1 generates the samples of the signal and stores them in the variable SIG(K). The signal itself is stored in the function subprogram SIGNAL(K). It is useful to store the signal in a function subprogram because this makes it possible to change the signal without disturbing the rest of the program.

The calculation of the DFT is performed by the nested loops DO M and DO K. The outer loop sets a value of M. After the value of M is set, the inner loop sums

$$x(k)e^{-j2\pi mk/N} \quad \text{for} \quad 0 \le k \le N - 1$$

Note that the exponential is computed by means of the intrinsic function CEXP.

```
      PROGRAM DISCRETE_FT1
!     THIS PROGRAM CALCULATES THE DFT OF A PERIODIC SIGNAL
      IMPLICIT NONE
      REAL, DIMENSION (0:31):: SIG, XREAL,XIMAG
      REAL:: SIGNAL
      INTEGER N, K, M, J
      COMPLEX :: A, X
      REAL:: Q
      REAL,PARAMETER :: PI = 3.1415926
      N = 32
!     GENERATE THE SAMPLED DATA SIGNAL
      DO K = 0, N-1
        SIG(K) = SIGNAL(K)
      END DO
      WRITE(*,*)' M    XREAL(M)   XIMAG(M)'
!     CALCULATE THE DFT
      DO M = 0, N-1
        X = CMPLX(0,0)
        Q = -2.0*PI*M/N
        DO J = 0, N-1
          A = CMPLX(0, Q*J)
            X = X + SIG(J)*CEXP(A)
          END DO
          XREAL(M) = REAL(X)/N
          XIMAG(M) = AIMAG(X)/N
            WRITE(*,"(I4,2F12.2)") M,XREAL(M),XIMAG(M)
        END DO
      END PROGRAM DISCRETE_FT1
      REAL FUNCTION SIGNAL(K)
      IMPLICIT NONE
      REAL :: P8
```

```
INTEGER :: K
P8 = 3.1415926/8.0
SIGNAL=COS(P8*K)+.8*SIN(3.*P8*K)+.6*COS(5.*P8*K)+.4*SIN &
    (7.*P8*K)
END
```

A trial run is shown in below. It is seen that the results are identical to those calculated in Example 9.11 because the data used in the example were the same as those that the DFT calculated in the program.

RUN of program DISCRETE_FT1

M	XREAL(M)	XIMAG(M)
0	0.00	0.00
1	0.00	0.00
2	0.50	0.00
3	0.00	0.00
4	0.00	0.00
5	0.00	0.00
6	0.00	-0.40
7	0.00	0.00
8	0.00	0.00
9	0.00	0.00
10	0.30	0.00
11	0.00	0.00
12	0.00	0.00
13	0.00	0.00
14	0.00	-0.20
15	0.00	0.00
16	0.00	0.00
17	0.00	0.00
18	0.00	0.20
19	0.00	0.00
20	0.00	0.00
21	0.00	0.00
22	0.30	0.00
23	0.00	0.00
24	0.00	0.00
25	0.00	0.00
26	0.00	0.40
27	0.00	0.00
28	0.00	0.00
29	0.00	0.00
30	0.50	0.00
31	0.00	0.00

*   *   *   *   *

EXAMPLE 9.13 Program DISCRETE_FT2: Calculating the DFT of a Signal That Is Not Bandlimited

A *rectifier* is a device that converts alternating current to direct currents. Two popular forms of this device are the half-wave rectifier and the full-wave rectifier. In this exam-

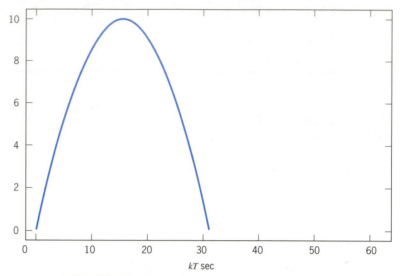

FIGURE 9.7   Graph of the output of a half-wave rectifier.

ple, we assume that the voltage 10 sin(200πt) is applied to a half-wave rectifier. This signal has a peak amplitude of 10 V and a frequency of 100 Hz. Usually, the output is connected to a filter that removes most of the harmonics. We are examining the *unfiltered*
output, shown in Fig. 9.7. This output is the positive half of the sine waveform that was
applied to the input of the rectifier.

The trigonometric Fourier series for the output of the rectifier can be calculated and
is found to be

$$f(t) = 10/\pi + 5 \sin(200\pi t) + [20/(-3\pi)]\cos(400\pi t) + [20/(-15\pi t)]\cos(800\pi t)$$
$$+ [20/(-35\pi t)]\cos(1200\pi t) + [20/(-63\pi t)]\cos(1600\pi t) + \dots$$
$$= 3.1831 + 5.0 \sin(200\pi t) - 2.1221 \cos(400\pi t) - 0.4244 \cos(800\pi t)$$
$$- 0.1819 \cos(1200\pi t) - .1010 \cos(1600\pi t) - \dots$$

It is seen that the amplitudes of the harmonics fall quite rapidly beyond the 600 Hz component.

Now we will compute the DFT for this signal. To do so, we must first generate the
sampled data form of the signal. We will use $N = 64$ and $T = 1/6400$ for this calculation.

With $T = 1/6400$, we have allowed for a maximum frequency component of 3200 Hz
in the signal. With $N = 64$ and $T = 1/6400$, the frequency resolution is 100 Hz. As stated
above, the signal is the positive half of one cycle of a sine waveform. For this computation, we have modified the program shown above. The modified program, DIS-
CRETE_FT2, is shown below. In function subprogram SIGNAL we have defined SIG-
NAL as a sampled data version of 10.0*sin(200πt) by replacing *t* by *KT*. As we can see
from the Fourier series, the amplitudes of components beyond 800 Hz are small, so our
choice of sampling frequency is adequate. The function subprogram SIGNAL is called
twice. First, it is called in loop DO K = 0, 31. As N = 64, this loop will generate the positive half cycle (32 samples) of the sine wave. The next loop, DO K = 32, 63, assigns a
value of zero to the next half cycle (the next 32 samples) of the sine wave. This assignment is necessary in order to generate the waveform correctly.

```
        PROGRAM DISCRETE_FT2
!       THIS PROGRAM CALCULATES THE DFT OF THE UNFILTERED
```

```
!    OUTPUT OF A HALF WAVE RECTIFIER
     IMPLICIT NONE
     REAL, DIMENSION(0:64) :: SIG, XREAL,XIMAG
     REAL :: SIGNAL, Q
     INTEGER :: N, K, M
     COMPLEX :: A, X
     REAL, PARAMETER ::PI = 3.141592
     N = 64
!    GENERATE THE SAMPLED DATA SIGNAL
     DO K = 0, 31
       SIG(K) = SIGNAL(K)
     END DO
     DO K = 32,63
       SIG(K) = 0
     END DO
!    CALCULATE THE DFT
     WRITE(*,*)' M    XREAL(M)   XIMAG(M)'
     DO M = 0, N-1
      X = CMPLX(0,0)
      Q = -2.0*PI*M/N
      DO K = 0, N-1
         A = CMPLX(0, Q*K)
         X = X + SIG(K)*CEXP(A)
       END DO
         XREAL(M) = REAL(X)/N
         XIMAG(M) = AIMAG(X)/N
     END DO
       DO M = 0, 31
         WRITE(*,"(I4,2F12.2)") M,XREAL(M),XIMAG(M)
       END DO
     END PROGRAM DISCRETE_FT2
     REAL FUNCTION SIGNAL(K)
     IMPLICIT NONE
     REAL :: P32
     INTEGER :: K
     P32 = 3.1415926/32
     SIGNAL = 10.0*SIN(P32*K)
     END
```

Next, the results of a run are shown. The following table compares the results obtained from use of the DFT with the results of the Fourier series computation. The results are seen to be in close agreement.

	Results of DFT*			Fourier Series
M	Frequency	XREAL(M)	XIMAG(M)	
0	0	3.18	0	3.183
1	100	0	−2.50	5.00
2	200	−1.06	0	−2.122
4	400	−0.21	0	−0.4244
6	600	−0.09	0	−0.1819
8	800	−0.05	0	−0.1010

*Only positive frequency, nonzero components are shown.

Note that the results shown for M = 1, 2, 4, 6, 8 are *half* of the value shown for the comparable Fourier series values because the positive frequency components *have not been combined* with the negative frequency components.

9.17 A SUBPROGRAM THAT COMPUTES THE DFT AND THE IDFT

Earlier, we noted some differences between the formulas for the DFT and the IDFT. Because there are only a few differences, it is reasonable to investigate the possibility of writing a subroutine subprogram that can compute *either* the DFT or the IDFT. We have to find a way to get around the differences that we noted. One way that suggests itself is by means of the dummy arguments used to define the subroutine. For example, if one of the arguments is SIGN, then we call the subroutine using the values +1 or −1 for sign, depending on whether we want the IDFT or the DFT. The multiplier (1/N) that was used for the DFT but that had a value of 1 for the IDFT can be provided for by using the dummy argument FACTOR. We can call the subroutine using either the value (1/N) or the value 1 for FACTOR. The next difference is somewhat more subtle. In the DFT, there is a summation of the terms $x(k)$ where $x(k)$ represents a sequence of *real* numbers that define the signal. In the IDFT, there is a summation of the terms $X(m)$, where $X(m)$ is a sequence of *complex* numbers that define the spectrum of the signal. What argument can we use which will accept *both* real and complex numbers? The answer is that we should use a *complex* argument. Then, in order to make real signals compatible with that argument, we will make the signal complex but with *zero imaginary parts*.

EXAMPLE 9.14 Program DISCRETE_FT5, Computing the DFT and the IDFT

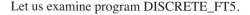

Let us examine program DISCRETE_FT5.

```
        PROGRAM DISCRETE_FT5
!       THIS PROGRAM CALCULATES THE DFT & IDFT OF THE UNFILTERED
!       OUTPUT OF A FULL WAVE RECTIFIER WITH T = 1/6400 SEC.
!
        IMPLICIT NONE
        REAL:: W,P64, AN
        INTEGER :: N, K, M
        COMPLEX, DIMENSION(0:512):: DFT, IDFT, X
        REAL,PARAMETER ::PI = 3.14159265
        P64 = PI/64
        N = 128
        AN = N
!       GENERATE THE SAMPLED DATA SIGNAL
        DO K = 0, 63
          X(K) = CMPLX(10.0*SIN(P64*K),0.0)
        END DO
        DO K = 64, 127
          W = 10.0*ABS(SIN(P64*K))
          X(K) = CMPLX(W, 0)
        END DO
```

```
CALL FOURIER(-1.0, N, PI, AN, X, DFT)    !SIGNAL IN, DFT OUT
CALL FOURIER(+1.0, N,PI,1.0, DFT, IDFT)  !DFT IN, IDFT OUT
WRITE(*,*)'  M     DFT,REAL  DFT,IMAG    IDFT,MAGNIT.'
DO M = 0, 64, 2
  WRITE(*,"(I5,7X,2F11.5,6X,2F11.5)")M, DFT(M),CABS(IDFT(M))
END DO
END PROGRAM DISCRETE_FT5
SUBROUTINE FOURIER(SIGN, N, PI, FACTOR, FOURIN, FOUROUT)
IMPLICIT NONE
INTEGER:: I,J,N
REAL:: Q, PI
REAL, INTENT(IN) :: SIGN,FACTOR
COMPLEX, DIMENSION(0:512),INTENT(IN) :: FOURIN
COMPLEX, DIMENSION(0:512),INTENT(OUT):: FOUROUT
COMPLEX:: A
DO I = 0, N-1
 Q = 2.0*SIGN*PI*I/N
 DO J = 0, N-1
  A = CMPLX(0,0, Q*J)
  FOUROUT(I) = FOUROUT(I) + FOURIN(J)*CEXP(A)/FACTOR
 END DO
END DO
END SUBROUTINE FOURIER
```

In this program, two DO loops are used to define the signal. However, the signal is complex, with its imaginary part equal to zero. The subroutine

$$FOURIER(SIGN, N, PI, FACTOR,FOURIN, FOUROUT)$$

implements the DFT or the IDFT, depending on the value of SIGN and the value of FACTOR used in the CALL. To illustrate the procedure, subroutine FOURIER is called twice. The first time, CALL FOURIER(−1.0, N, PI, AN, X, DFT) is used. A result of this call, a value of −1.0, is transmitted to SIGN, and the variable X transmits the signal to the variable FOURIN. The output of the subroutine is transmitted to variable DFT by the dummy variable FOUROUT.

The second call is CALL FOURIER(+1.0, N, PI, 1.0, DFT, IDFT). Because we want to compute the IDFT, a value of +1.0 is used for SIGN and 1.0 is used for FACTOR. The DFT, previously computed by subroutine FOURIER, is now the input to the subroutine and the subroutine returns the IDFT to the main program.

The results of the run are shown below. To save space, the loop DO M = 0, 64, 2 is used; thus, only alternate values of the DFT and IDFT are printed. Because there are only even harmonics, no information is lost by this procedure. In addition, a portion of the IDFT is shown. Enough data are seen to identify a half cycle of a sine wave of amplitude 10.0.

RUN

M	DFT,REAL	DFT,IMAG	IDFT,MAGNIT.
0	6.36492	0.00000	0.00008
2	−2.12334	0.00000	0.98020
4	−0.42569	0.00000	1.95094
6	−0.18317	0.00000	2.90291

8	−0.10233	0.00000	3.82690
10	−0.06559	0.00000	4.71406
12	−0.04582	0.00000	5.55572
14	−0.03395	0.00000	6.34396
16	−0.02628	0.00000	7.07110
18	−0.02103	0.00000	7.73017
20	−0.01729	0.00000	8.31470
22	−0.01453	0.00000	8.81925
24	−0.01244	0.00000	9.23884
26	−0.01081	0.00000	9.56943
28	−0.00953	0.00000	9.80788
30	−0.00851	0.00000	9.95189
32	−0.00767	0.00000	10.00002
34	−0.00698	0.00000	9.95182
36	−0.00642	0.00000	9.80780
38	−0.00594	0.00000	9.56934
40	−0.00554	0.00000	9.23878
42	−0.00521	0.00000	8.81921
44	−0.00493	0.00000	8.31472
46	−0.00469	0.00000	7.73009
48	−0.00449	0.00000	7.07102
50	−0.00432	0.00000	6.34386
52	−0.00419	0.00000	5.55565
54	−0.00407	0.00000	4.71392
56	−0.00398	0.00000	3.82685
58	−0.00391	0.00000	2.90284
60	−0.00386	0.00000	1.95091
62	−0.00384	0.00000	0.98014
64	−0.00383	0.00000	0.00003

9.18 NONPERIODIC SIGNALS

We have shown that the DFT treats all sampled-data signals as periodic. Now, we wish to consider the possibility of obtaining an *approximation* to the Fourier transform of a nonperiodic signal by use of the DFT.

Let us recall the Fourier transform, Eq. 9.32. We will discretize it by replacing t by kT. In addition, we will approximate the integral by a rectangular approximation consisting of strips of area $T[x(kT)]$. The integral will be replaced by a summation. The result is shown in Eq. (9.39):

$$X(\omega) \approx \sum_{0}^{N-1} T[x(kT)]e^{(-j\omega kT)}$$

(9.39)

Using this result as a guide, we will use T as a value for the dummy variable FACTOR when we call the subroutine FOURIER, which was used in program DISCRETE_FT5 in computing the DFT of a *nonperiodic* signal. There is one more consideration. The Fourier transform yields a continuous spectrum. With the DFT, only a discrete frequency spectrum can be achieved. However, we have seen that the frequency resolution can be controlled by a choice of T and N.

Next, we will discretize the inverse Fourier transform, Eq. (9.29), by replacing f by $m\Delta f$ and replacing the integral by a summation. The result is Eq. (9.40).

$$x(t) \approx \Delta f \sum_{0}^{N-1} X(m\Delta f) \exp(+jm\Delta ft) \tag{9.40}$$

We note that we have a factor $\Delta f = 1/NT$ multiplying the summation. When calculating the IDFT of a nonperiodic function, we will use $1/NT$ for the dummy variable FACTOR. We will illustrate these concepts in the following example.

EXAMPLE 9.15 Program DISCRETE_FT6, the DFT of the Nonperiodic Signal $10te^{-t}$

We will calculate the DFT of the signal $10te^{-t}$, assuming that it begins at time $t = 0$. Although this signal is not periodic, it has the property that it extends to $t = \infty$. This is not a problem because the amplitude of the signal decays quite rapidly. In the program to be discussed, N = 200 and T = 0.04. Thus, the signal is sampled for 8 seconds. At $t = 8$ sec, the amplitude of the signal is only 0.033546. This amplitude may be considered to be negligible. Program DISCRETE_FT6 and a trial run, shown here, calculate the DFT and the IDFT of the signal. Note that the IDFT closely approximates the signal.

```
      PROGRAM DISCRETE_FT6
!     THIS PROGRAM CALCULATES THE DFT OF 10*t*EXP(-t)
!     T = 0.04 SEC; N = 200; NT = 8 SEC; DELTA-F = 0.125 HZ
      IMPLICIT NONE
      INTEGER ::K, M, N
      REAL:: AN, DW,DFTMAG(0:512),MIDFT(0:512),FMAG(0:512)
      COMPLEX :: DFT(0:512),IDFT(0:512),X(0:512)
      REAL, PARAMETER :: PI = 3.14159265,T =0.04
      N = 200
      AN = N
!     CALCULATE THE DISCRETE SIGNAL FOR THE DFT/IDFT
      DO K = 0, N-1
       X(K) = CMPLX(10.0*T*K*EXP(-T*K), 0.0)
      END DO
!     CALCULATE MAGNITUDE OF THE ANALOG FOURIER TRANSFORM
       DW = 2.0*PI*(1.0/(T*N))
      DO K = 0, N-1
        FMAG(K) = 10.0/(1.0 + (DW*K)**2)
      END DO
      CALL FOURIER(-1.0, N, PI, 1.0/T, X, DFT)
      WRITE(*,*)'  M     DFT,REAL    FMAG    MAG-IDFT'
      CALL FOURIER(+1.0, N, PI, AN*T, DFT, IDFT)
      DO M = 0, 40
      DFTMAG(M) = CABS(DFT(M))
      MIDFT(M) = CABS(IDFT(M))
      WRITE(*,"(I5,5X,F9.5,3X,F9.5,3X,F9.5)")M,DFTMAG(M),FMAG(M), &
          MIDFT(M)
      END DO
      END PROGRAM DISCRETE_FT6
      SUBROUTINE FOURIER(SIGN, N, PI, FACTOR, FOURIN, FOUROUT)
      IMPLICIT NONE
      INTEGER ::I, J, N
      REAL:: Q,PI
      REAL,INTENT(IN) :: SIGN, FACTOR
      COMPLEX, DIMENSION(0:512),INTENT(IN):: FOURIN
```

```
COMPLEX, DIMENSION(0:512),INTENT(OUT):: FOUROUT
COMPLEX:: A
DO I = 0, N-1
 FOUROUT(I) = CMPLX(0.0,0.0)
END DO
DO I = 0, N-1
 Q = 2.0*SIGN*PI*I/N
 DO J = 0, N-1
 A = CMPLX(0.0,Q*J)
 FOUROUT(I) = FOUROUT(I)+ FOURIN(J)*CEXP(A)/FACTOR
 END DO
END DO
END SUBROUTINE FOURIER
```

RUN

M	DFT,REAL	FMAG	MAG-IDFT
0	9.96793	10.00000	0.00000
1	6.16577	6.18486	0.38431
2	2.87613	2.88400	0.73848
3	1.52307	1.52633	1.06430
4	0.91879	0.91999	1.36343
5	0.60882	0.60896	1.63747
6	0.43137	0.43091	1.88791
7	0.32109	0.32024	2.11621
8	0.24813	0.24704	2.32368
9	0.19747	0.19621	2.51164
10	0.16091	0.15952	2.68128
11	0.13369	0.13220	2.83376
12	0.11288	0.11132	2.97017
13	0.09662	0.09501	3.09150
14	0.03869	0.08203	3.19878
15	0.07323	0.07153	3.29287
16	0.06465	0.06292	3.37467
17	0.05753	0.05578	3.44499
18	0.05156	0.04978	3.50462
19	0.04650	0.04470	3.55427
20	0.04217	0.04036	3.59462
21	0.03845	0.03662	3.62636
22	0.03522	0.03338	3.65008
23	0.03240	0.03055	3.66638
24	0.02992	0.02806	3.67578
25	0.02774	0.02587	3.67880
26	0.02580	0.02392	3.67593
27	0.02408	0.02218	3.66764
28	0.02253	0.02063	3.65434
29	0.02114	0.01923	3.63644
30	0.01989	0.01798	3.61434
31	0.01876	0.01684	3.58837
32	0.01773	0.01580	3.55889
33	0.01680	0.01486	3.52619
34	0.01595	0.01400	3.49059
35	0.01516	0.01321	3.45236
36	0.0144	0.01249	3.41176

37	0.01379	0.01182	3.36904
38	0.01318	0.01121	3.32442
39	0.01263	0.01064	3.27812
40	0.01211	0.01012	3.23034

For purposes of comparison with the DFT, the magnitude of the Fourier transform has been calculated. Using Eq. (9.32), we find the Fourier transform to be

$$F(\omega) = \frac{1}{(1 + j\omega)^2}$$

Its magnitude is

$$|F(\omega)| = \frac{1}{1 + \omega^2}$$

In the program, this is evaluated using the expression

$$\text{FMAG(K)} = 10.0/(1.0 + (\text{DW*K)**2})$$

Note that ω has been replaced by its discrete form, DW = 2.0*PI*(1.0/T*N) where (1.0/T*N) represents Δf. With T = 0.04 and N = 200, the resolution is 1/8 = 0.125 Hz. Although the DFT produces a discrete, not a continuous, spectrum, the results of the trial run show that this resolution is sufficient, so that the DFT provides a good approximation to the value produced by the Fourier transform.

In the printout, the results of the IDFT are shown from $t = 0$ (K = 0) to $t = 1.6$ sec (K = 40). It can be seen that the signal has a peak value at about 1.0 sec. The IDFT data have been plotted and are shown in Fig. 9.8. The IDFT is shown to be a good representation of the signal.

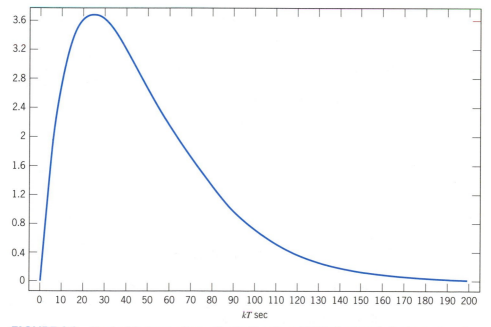

FIGURE 9.8   Graph of the inverse discrete Fourier Transform (IDFT) of a nonperiodic signal whose time domain response is $10te^{-4}$.

PROBLEMS

9.1 Two dice are rolled. We are interested in the probabilities that the sum of the dots on the uppermost faces is a particular number. The solution to this problem can be obtained by creating an array such as the one shown here. In the array we call one die A and the other B.

A/B	1	2	3	4	5	6
1	1, 1	1, 2	1, 3	1, 4	1, 5	1, 6
2	2, 1	2, 2	2, 3	2, 4	2, 5	2, 6
3	3, 1	3, 2	3, 3	3, 4	3, 5	3, 6
4	4, 1	4, 2	4, 3	4, 4	4, 5	4, 6
5	5, 1	5, 2	5, 3	5, 4	5, 5	5, 6
6	6, 1	6, 2	6, 3	6, 4	6, 5	6, 6

Note that there are 36 pairs of numbers. Each pair represents a possible result from rolling the two dice. To find the sum of the dots on a particular roll, the two numbers must be added. Suppose we want the probability that the sum will be 6. We observe the following pairs in the array: $(1, 5)$; $(2, 4)$; $(3, 3)$; $(4, 2)$; $(5, 1)$.

Of the 36 pairs, these five pairs are the only ones that produce a sum of 6. The probability of obtaining a sum of 6 is the ratio of all the events (cases) in which the sum is 6 divided by the total number of events, namely, 36. Therefore, $P(\text{sum} = 6)$ = 5/36 = 0.138889 (to six significant figures). We could calculate the other possible sums in a similar way. However, we are interested in a computer solution of this problem.

Write a program that calculates the probability of all the possible sums resulting from the roll of two dice. Use 5000 random numbers.

9.2 When studying data, it is often helpful to use some quantity that is computed from the data. Such computed quantities are called *statistics*. Baseball batting averages are an example. We will discuss only the statistics called the *average,* the *variance,* and the *standard deviation.*

The concept of an average is familiar to most of us. We will define the average of a set of n data denoted by X_i:

$$\text{AVG} = \{\textstyle\sum X_i\}/n$$

where $i = 1, n$

The variance is a measure of the "spread" of the data about the average. It is defined as

$$\text{VAR} = \{\textstyle\sum (X_i - \text{AVG})^2\}/n$$

where $i = 1, n$

The standard deviation, SDEV, is defined as the positive square root of the variance.

Occasionally, we scale data. For example, we often wish to scale random numbers. If we have a set of random numbers R, the scaled set R_s where $R_s = aR + b$ will have a standard deviation such that

$$(\text{SDEV})_s = a(\text{SDEV})$$

The constant b does not affect the standard deviation.

Write a program that scales 3000 random numbers so that the minimum value is 100 and the maximum value is 300. (These data might represent resistors whose values are uniformly distributed between 100 and 300 ohms.) The program should compute the average and standard deviation of the numbers.

9.3   As previously discussed, random number generators produce numbers that are uniformly distributed from 0 to 1. For some simulations, random numbers are needed which follow other probabilistic variations—for example, the normal distribution, also called the Gaussian distribution. The mathematicians Box and Muller proved that the following formula transformed uniformly distributed random numbers into normally distributed random numbers, with an average of approximately zero and a standard deviation of 1.0 (often called standard normal numbers):

$$\text{NORM} - \left[\sqrt{-2.0\text{LOG}(X)}\right]\left[\cos(2.0\pi(Y))\right]$$

where X and Y are uniformly distributed random numbers.

Write a program that generates 3000 normal numbers by the use of the Box and Muller formula and scales them so that the standard deviation is approximately 50 and the average is 200. Note that if 200 is added to each normal random number, the average of the set of numbers will increase from 0 to about 200, but the standard deviation is not affected. (See the discussion in Problem 9.2.)

Calculate the average and standard deviation of these numbers.

9.4   In the previous problem, we used the Box and Muller formula to transform uniformly distributed random numbers into standard normal numbers. Another way of achieving this result is to use the *central limit theorem* which can be stated as follows. Let $X_1, X_2, X_3, \ldots$ be a sequence of uniformly distributed random variables with mean (average) A and standard deviation S. Then

$$\lim_{n \to \infty} \frac{X_1 + X_2 \cdots + X_n - nA}{S\sqrt{n}}$$

Theoretically, n should go to infinity; however, good results are obtained using a relatively small value of n. By good results, we mean that the average of the normal numbers obtained is close to zero and the standard deviation is approximately 1.0. These are the theoretical values for the standard normal distribution.

In the formula given above, values for n, A and S must be supplied. The parameter n is the number of random numbers which will be summed to produce each normal number. We will generate *each* normal number by adding 20 random numbers. Therefore $n = 20$. The random numbers that we are adding are uniformly distributed, and uniformly distributed numbers have an average, A, which is 0.5, and their standard deviation S is equal to 1 over the square root of 12.

The result of adding each group of 20 random numbers will be stored in SUM. Then, using the formula, obtain a normal random number by the operation shown above, namely,

$$\text{RNORM}(K) = (\text{SUM} - 10.0)/\text{SQRT}(20.0/12.0)$$

The quantity 10 in the numerator is equal to $nA = (20)(0.5)$. The denominator is the product of the standard deviation and the square root of n.

Generate 2000 normal random numbers using this procedure. Then calculate the average and standard deviation of the numbers.

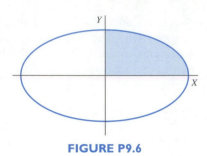

FIGURE P9.6

9.5 Write a program that calculates

$$f = \frac{1}{2\pi\sqrt{LC}}$$

where L and C are each uniformly distributed as follows.

The minimum value of L is 0.3 henry; the maximum value of L is 0.4 henry. The minimum value of C is 0.2 microfarads; the maximum value of C is 1.1 microfarads.

Use 4000 random numbers and use the subroutine RANK, which is used in program HISTO2 to find the largest and the smallest frequency.

9.6 **(a)** Use random numbers to calculate the area under the ellipse $x^2 + 4y^2 = 36$ in the first quadrant. (See Fig. P9.6.)

Note: Scale x and y so that their ranges will cover the appropriate part of the first quadrant.

(b) What is the theoretical value of the answer?

9.7 Use random numbers to calculate the area under the unit normal density function

$$y = \frac{1}{\sqrt{2\pi}} e^{-x^2/2}$$

from $x = -3$ to $x = +3$. Although this function extends to minus infinity and plus infinity, the limits specified above include more than 99 percent of the area. (See Fig. P9.7.)

Suggestions: Scale x so that the random numbers will vary from $x = -3$ to $x = +3$. Scale y so that the random numbers will vary from

$$y = 0 \qquad \text{to} \qquad y = \frac{1}{\sqrt{2\pi}}$$

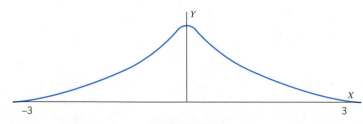

FIGURE P9.7

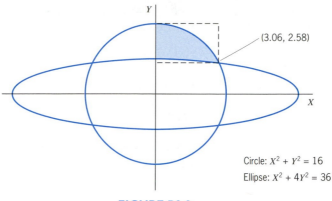

FIGURE P9.8

9.8 Use random numbers to calculate the area in the first quadrant between the circle $x^2 + y^2 = 16$ and the ellipse $x^2 + 4y^2 = 36$. (See Fig. P9.8.)

9.9 Use random numbers to calculate the area in the first quadrant between the parabola $y = 4.0x - x^2$ and the line $y = x$. (See Fig. P9.9.)

Suggestion: Using the figure as a guide, generate random x, random y, and scale them appropriately. Let Y1 denote the scaled y values; let $Y1A = 4.0*X - X**2$ and $Y2A = X$ where X is the scaled value of X. There is NO hit IF(Y1>Y1A.OR. Y1<Y2A). Otherwise, there is a hit.

9.10 Modify program INTEGR2 to integrate

$$x^2 \sqrt{x^3 + 1}$$

from 0 to 2. Use N = 8 (eight subareas).

9.11 Revise the program you wrote for Problem 9.10 as follows. As previously, integrate using eight subareas (N = 8). Store this result in variable TEST. Then, double the value of N, and integrate and store the result in SIM. Again double the value of N and repeat the calculation. The procedure should be halted when the

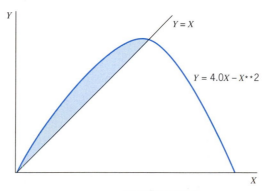

FIGURE P9.9

magnitude of (TEST − SIM) is less than 0.0001 or if N exceeds 64. When this occurs, print the value of SIM and the value of N.

9.11 Modify program INTEGTWO to integrate $x(1.0 + 3.0y^2)$ using the limits given.

For x: 0 to 1.5

For y: 0 to 1.0

9.12 It is instructive to compute the DFT by "hand" at least once to get an appreciation for the calculation.

Assume that the following sampled data are available to you.

$$x(k) = (10., 7.07, 0, -7.07, -10., -7.07, 0, 7.07)$$

Note that k goes from 0 to 7.

These data were acquired using a sampling frequency of 400 Hz. Using $N = 8$, you can calculate the frequency resolution. From Eq. (9.37), calculate $X(m)$, $m = 1$, and $m = 2$. After calculating $X(1)$, deduce the value of $X(7)$.

Hint: There is no dc component, so $X(0) = 0$. Recall that $X(N − m) = X^*(m)$. In this example, all values of $X(m)$ are real, so $X(N − m) = X(m)$.

9.13 Using the results of Problem 9.12, calculate the sampled datum $x(1)$ using Eq. (9.38).

When substituting values of $X(m)$ into Eq. (9.38), they should be the final values you obtained—that is, the values obtained after multiplying by $(1/N) = (1/8)$. Your answer should correspond to $x(1)$ of the set $x(k)$ given in Problem 9.12.

9.14 In Sec. 9.15, it was stated that if the sampling frequency did not satisfy Eq. (9.34) or if its equivalent T did not satisfy Eq. (9.35), *aliasing* would occur. The purpose of this problem is to illustrate aliasing.

Assume that there is a signal

$$x(t) = 4.0 \cos(10\pi t) + 2.0 \cos(30\pi t) + \cos(90\pi t)$$

Convert it to sampled data form using $T = 1/42$ sec. Let $N = 42$ and compute the DFT and the magnitude of the IDFT. In observing the output of the program, note that the data indicate spectral components of 3, 5, and 15 Hz. The 45-Hz component in the original signal has been lost.

In the IDFT data, can you explain the fact that the magnitude of the IDFT is 7.0 at $t = 0$?

9.15 Section 9.17 showed how to use subroutine FOURIER to compute either the DFT or the IDFT. It was stated that a real signal should be treated as a complex signal, with the complex part set to zero.

In Sec. 9.18 nonperiodic signals were discussed. It was pointed out that for such a signal, when computing the DFT, T is used for the dummy variable FACTOR. When computing the IDFT, NT is used for FACTOR. See, for example, program DISCRETE_FT6.

Finally, it should be recalled that, to avoid periodic extension, the signal should be padded with zeros.

Write a program that computes the DFT of a positive pulse. Then, it computes the IDFT. Use T = 0.04. Define the pulse using two DO loops. In the first loop, use index K = 0, 29 and set the amplitude of the pulse at a value of 1.0. Then follow this by a DO loop with index K = 30, 249 and set the amplitude at 0. The second loop is the zero padding. Thus, the pulse is defined by 250 points (N = 250), the majority of which are zero.

Print only the magnitude of the DFT and the magnitude of the IDFT. It will be sufficient to print 40 points. The magnitude of the IDFT should be 1.0 from M = 0 to M = 1.0. Thereafter, the magnitude should be zero. Because of roundoff error, some points may have a value of 0.99999 rather than 1.0.

10

Graphing Data and Design Applications

Five topics with scientific or engineering importance are briefly introduced in this chapter. These topics are: graphic representation of data, use of queuing theory for project planning, databases for maintaining data, expert systems, and computer solutions of differential equations. The examples presented in this chapter are intended to introduce these topics and to demonstrate how FORTRAN 90 programs may be used to support the underlying principles.

10.1 GRAPHIC REPRESENTATION OF DATA

The graphical presentation of results for engineering and scientific problems may be significantly more informative than the simple tabulation of conclusions produced by FORTRAN 90 programs. An image tends to summarize events in a way that lists of numbers may not be able to do without further interpretation. For example, the possibility of a functional relationship between two variables is readily discernible by graphing the values of one variable against the other. Because there are minor variations in computed results—even when a strict functional relationship exists between variables—clear correlations may not be immediately obvious, while graphical presentation greatly enhances the relationship. In yet other circumstances, individual datum points are "not relevant"; what is important is the general trend of the results. Examples can be found in those problems that include probabilistic phenomena. Two alternatives for graphical presentation of FORTRAN 90 results are discussed in this chapter:

- A relatively simple one that can be readily incorporated directly into a FORTRAN 90 program.

- One that can be used to communicate with a separate software product (with its own graphics capability).

EXAMPLE 10.1 Design Aids to Environmental Control (*Engineering Management*).

Environmental control of temperature, whether in the home, the factory, or the office, is most important to our comfort, our ability to relax, and our productivity. A computer can help to design a temperature control system. Often, it is too costly to build a prototype of a product or system before verifying that it will work successfully. Figure 10.1 depicts the environmental temperature control problem to be addressed. The temperature in the building depends on what happens to heat buildup (or reduction) within the building. Heat enters the building from the outside (sun) and from heat sources within the building such as machines, people, and the heating system. Heat is removed from the building through the walls, the normal exits (windows, smokestacks, doors), people departing, and the cooling system if one exists. The design problem consists of deciding on the best way to keep the temperature in the building constant.

Graphical presentation of the building's temperature, the desired temperature, and the state of the heating/cooling system, as a function of time, greatly enhances the designer's ability to judge the system response.

There are at least three different ways to maintain the temperature within the building:

- *On-off system* If the temperature falls below the desired temperature, turn on the heat and leave it on until the temperature goes above the desired setting.
- *Proportional control* Use a variable heat source. Adjust the amount of heat to be added to the building, that amount being proportional to the difference between

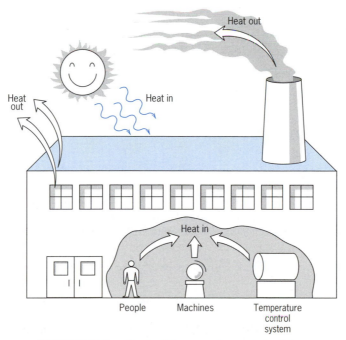

FIGURE 10.1   Sketch of the temperature control problem.

the actual temperature and the desired temperature (*set point*). A modified form of this system is one in which the building is cooled whenever the temperature rises above the desired level.

- *Bang-bang* Supply heat to the building at the maximum rate until the actual temperature is very close to the set point. Should the actual temperature rise above the set point, the building is cooled at the maximum rate. When the actual temperature falls to an acceptable level, turn off the cooling system. (The maximum addition or subtraction of heat in the manner described above leads to the designation of this method as "bang-bang.")

Figure 10.2 demonstrates how these three environmental control alternatives work. In the program that follows (program *HVAC*), only the on-off system will be studied. (Recall that HVAC stands for *H*eating, *V*entilation, *A*ir *C*onditioning, which is an important subdiscipline within engineering.) The constraints of the design problem are as follows.

1. The temperature is determined once each (simulated) minute. The value of the variable used to represent temperature depends on what has occurred since the last sample (iteration). It is calculated using the following formula:

   ```
   NEW_TEMP = OLD_TEMP+HEAT_ADDED−HEAT_LOSSES+OTHER_HEAT
   ```

   where

   ```
   OLD_TEMP = Temperature at the last sampling.
   HEAT_ADDED = Heat added to the environment if the heating
        system was turned on.
   HEAT_LOSSES = Heat lost through walls, etc.
   OTHER_HEAT = Heat added by machines that have been turned on
        or by people entering the building.
   ```

2. The variable HEAT_ADDED is 0 if the heating system is off and 0.75 if it is on; 0.75 is an arbitrary (empirical) factor in this example.

3. The heating system is considered to be off if

   ```
   OLD_TEMP > DESIRED_TEMP + 1
   ```

   and to be on if

   ```
   OLD_TEMP < DESIRED_TEMP − 1
   ```

   where DESIRED_TEMP is the desired temperature or set point at which to heat the building. (We accept a temperature error of ±1 degree in this example; hence, the heating system is turned on (or off) if it is within 1 degree of the set point.)

4. HEAT_LOSSES are expressed by the following.

   ```
   0.02 * (OLD_TEMP − OUTSIDE_TEMP)
   ```

   where OUTSIDE_TEMP is the temperature outside the building. This equation is a model of heat losses.

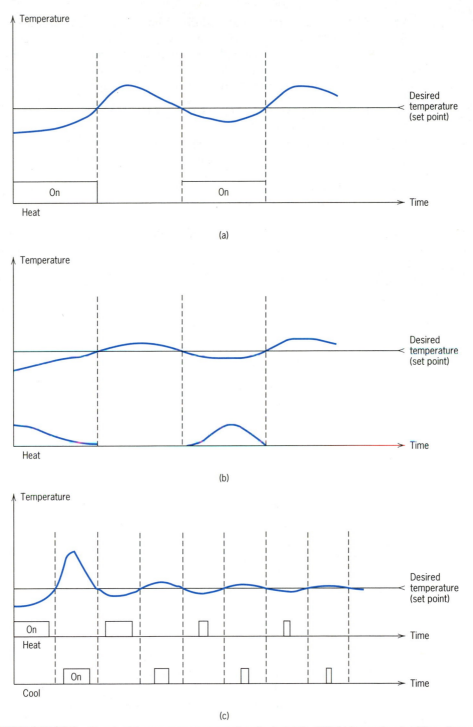

FUGURE 10.2 Sketch of three temperature control methods. (a) On-Off; (b) Proportional; (c)Bang-bang.

5. OTHER_HEAT represents additional heat gains: New machines may be installed or turned on, or people may enter the building; this represents a net introduction of heat into the building. Alternatively, there may not be any change from one measurement to the next. Uniformly distributed random numbers are used to set the value of OTHER_HEAT according to the following rules:

- There are no net changes 10 percent of the time. For these cases, OTHER_HEAT is assigned a value of 0.

- For the remaining 90 percent of the time, OTHER_HEAT has a constant value of 0.11. Assume that the starting value for the variable OTHER_HEAT is 0.11.

6. The DESIRED_TEMP is 24 (°C). The OUTSIDE_TEMP is 0; the initial building temperature is 15 (°C).

The program can be summarized by the following pseudocode description. (In the FORTRAN 90 source code, pseudocode statements can be used to advantage as comments within the program.)

```
program HVAC
{initialize variables}
{query the user for the duration of the simulation}
{display ("print") an axis on the monitor (or to a file)}
do (for the duration of the simulation)
        determine if heat is to be on or off;
        send a value for set point to the graph;
        send a value for the simulated temperature result;
        print one line of the graph;
{call random number to determine value for heat added by
        machines turned on and people entering building}
end do
end program HVAC
```

The goal of this program is to display the variation of building temperature as a function of (simulated) time on the computer's monitor together with the temperature set point. This allows the user to see the dynamic response of the building's temperature, under heating system control, as it approaches the desired temperature. The steps carried out within the DO loop described in the pseudocode above permit the user to visualize the dynamic response of the system.

- The computer determines whether the heat is on or off according to problem constraint 3 cited previously.

- The ordinate values of the (temperature) variables to be displayed are stored in an array, with each array location corresponding to a single value of temperature. The operation "send a value for set point to the graph" is carried out by storing a symbol—a mark—in the array location that corresponds to the desired temperature.

- The array location corresponding to the building temperature is assigned a character value. The temperature itself is calculated as shown in constraint 1 above.

- One line of the graph is displayed by printing the contents of the array on the monitor. The marks stored in the array will be displayed at both the building temperature and the set point.

- A random number is generated to determine the value for OTHER_HEAT as noted in constraint 5.
- The loop is repeated for each (simulated) time iteration. The loop terminates when the index reaches a number that corresponds to the duration of the simulation. (This last parameter is set interactively by the user at the start of the program.)

The program uses the initial values for the building temperature, the outside temperature, and the heating system parameters, and generates simulated results as a function of time without additional data. It makes use of the MODULE PORTRAIT_GRAPH and the SUBROUTINE STRIP_CHART, which generates the graphical record. This record corresponds to an image that can be regarded as a matrix of cells or positions on the monitor, which can be filled with CHARACTER data in such a way as to produce an image. (See Fig. 10.3). A graph of the sample-by-sample results of the building temperature is stored in a file (called "CHART.DOC"), which can be used to generate a printed copy once the program has been executed. The FORTRAN 90 source code for the simulation program is shown below:

```
        PROGRAM HVAC
! THIS SIMULATES ENVIRONMENTAL (TEMPERATURE) CONTROL OF A BUILDING
! SUBJECT TO VARIOUS "RANDOM" ADDITIONS AND SUBTRACTIONS OF HEAT       &
        AT
! SUCCESSIVE SAMPLES OF THE BUILDING'S TEMPERATURE. IF THE       &
        TEMPERATURE
! IS BELOW THE SET POINT, THEN THE HEAT IS CONSIDERED TO BE TURNED       &
        ON.
! ALL TEMPERATURES ARE IN DEGREES C
!
```

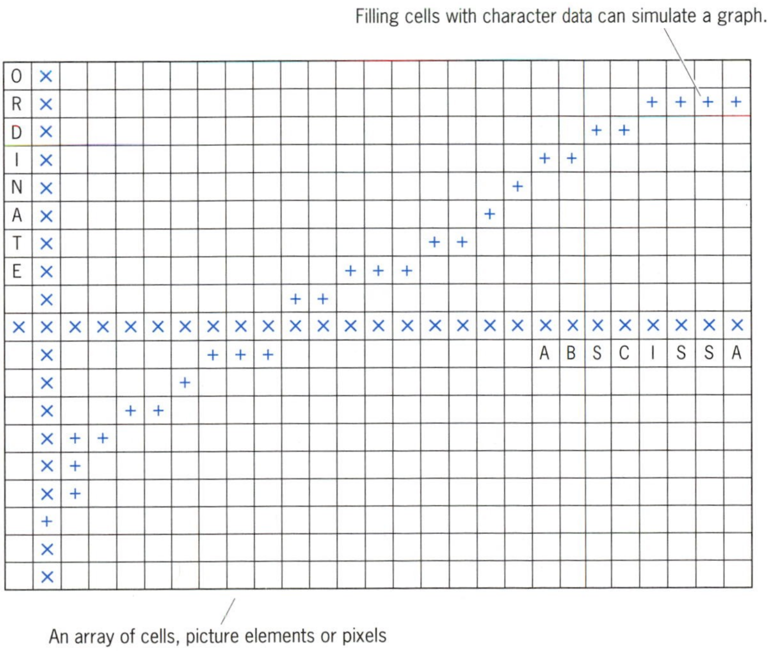

Filling cells with character data can simulate a graph.

An array of cells, picture elements or pixels

FIGURE 10.3   An array structure is used to create an image of a graph.

```
! DECLARATIONS
!
        USE PORTRAIT_GRAPH
        IMPLICIT NONE
        REAL :: OLD_TEMP, HEAT_ADDED, HEAT_LOSSES, OTHER_HEAT,    &
            NEW_TEMP
        REAL, PARAMETER :: DESIRED_TEMP = 24.0
        REAL, PARAMETER :: OUTSIDE_TEMP = 0.0
        INTEGER :: RUN_LENGTH,I
!
!       INITIALIZE VARIABLES
!
        OTHER_HEAT = 0.11
        OLD_TEMP = 15.0
        HEAT_ADDED = 0.75
        CALL RANDOM_SEED

OPEN(2,FILE="B:CHART.DAT",STATUS='UNKNOWN',POSITION='REWIND')
!
! QUERY USER FOR DURATION OF THE SIMULATION
!
        PRINT"(T5,A)", 'HOW LONG SHOULD THE SIMULATION RUN?'
        WRITE (*,"(T5,A)", ADVANCE = 'NO')                        &
                'EACH ITERATION SIMULATES ONE MINUTE:'
        READ "(I3)", RUN_LENGTH
!
! PRINT AN AXIS ON THE GRAPH
!
        AXIS = .TRUE.
        PRINT_COMMAND = .FALSE.
        CALL STRIP_CHART
        AXIS = .FALSE.
!
! RUN THE SIMULATION FOR THE DURATION DEFINED BY RUN_LENGTH
!
        DO I = 1,RUN_LENGTH
            HEAT_LOSSES = 0.02*(OLD_TEMP - OUTSIDE_TEMP)
            NEW_TEMP = OLD_TEMP + HEAT_ADDED - HEAT_LOSSES +      &
                OTHER_HEAT
            OLD_TEMP = NEW_TEMP
!---DETERMINE IF HEAT IS TO BE ON OR OFF----!
        IF (NEW_TEMP > (DESIRED_TEMP + 1.0)) THEN
            HEAT_ADDED = 0.0
        ELSE IF (NEW_TEMP <= (DESIRED_TEMP - 1.0)) THEN
            HEAT_ADDED = 0.75
        END IF
!---SEND A DATUM POINT AND DESIRED_TEMP TO THE STRIP CHART----!
        RANGE = 69.0
        CURVE_VALUE = DESIRED_TEMP
        CURVE_SYMBOL = '.'
        CALL STRIP_CHART
        CURVE_VALUE = NEW_TEMP
        CURVE_SYMBOL = '='
        CALL STRIP_CHART
```

```
!---PRINT ONE LINE OF THE CHART----!
        PRINT_COMMAND = .TRUE.
        CALL STRIP_CHART
        PRINT_COMMAND = .FALSE.
!---COMPUTE A NEW RANDOM VALUE FOR OTHER_HEAT----!
        CALL RANDOM_NUMBER (OTHER_HEAT)
        IF (OTHER_HEAT > 0.1) THEN
            OTHER_HEAT = 0.11
        ELSE
            OTHER_HEAT = 0.0
        END IF
        END DO
        CLOSE(2)
        END PROGRAM HVAC
```

FORTRAN 90 statements that have already been described can be readily used to create graphical images on the monitor. The program statements needed to accomplish these images are included in MODULE PORTRAIT_GRAPH. An important aspect of constructing an image is the data structure that is needed. (The basic FORTRAN 90 data structure that supports this arrangement is the *array*.) To create graphs directly using FORTRAN 90, we need only fill the array with appropriate characters and then write (or print) the array directly to the monitor or to a file if this is appropriate.

The module is composed substantially of SUBROUTINE STRIP_CHART, which generates an image using the technique depicted in Fig. 10.3. The graph will be created with a vertical orientation (in contrast to the horizontal arrangement in Fig. 10.3). Such a graph is called a *strip chart* and is useful because the abscissa may have virtually unlimited extent. The program includes the following parameters (together with a brief explanation of their purpose):

- **IMAGE_ARRAY** This variable retains (an array) of 70 characters that will generate one line of the graph. The elements of the array are filled in accordance with the category of data (e.g., creating the Y axis [ordinate]).

- **AXIS** This logical variable instructs the subroutine to fill the array with the characters that generate an ordinate axis if its value is .TRUE. when the subroutine is called. A plus sign (+) is used to create an image of an axis. After storing and displaying an image of the axis, the array elements are erased (blanked) to prepare them for the next command.

- **CURVE_VALUE** and **RANGE** These variables work together to compute the array location in which to mark the datum. The array location, given by the integer variable COLUMN, is computed as

$$COLUMN = NINT(CURVE\_VALUE/RANGE*69.0) + 35$$

The intrinsic function NINT rounds the argument to the nearest integer. The integer nearest to the value of the datum (CURVE_VALUE), scaled according to the RANGE of the curve being plotted, is computed. The image has a maximum range of 69 locations. An offset of 35 is added to this computed value in order to locate the point relative to the origin that is considered to be at the center (of the monitor).

- **CURVE_SYMBOL** The user specifies the symbol to be used for the graph by assigning a character to this variable.

- **PRINT_COMMAND** If this logical variable is .TRUE. at the time the subroutine is invoked, then one line of the graph is printed and displayed. The array is then cleared (erased).

The source code for MODULE PORTRAIT_GRAPH follows:

```
MODULE PORTRAIT_GRAPH
LOGICAL :: AXIS,PRINT_COMMAND
REAL :: CURVE_VALUE,RANGE
CHARACTER :: CURVE_SYMBOL
CHARACTER, DIMENSION (1:70) :: IMAGE_ARRAY

!     CONTAINS
!
      SUBROUTINE STRIP_CHART
! THIS SUBROUTINE ACCEPTS DATA SIMILAR TO A STRIP CHART
! RECORDER AND DISPLAYS THE INFORMATION IN PORTRAIT
! (VERTICAL) ORIENTATION ON THE MONITOR. THE ORDINATE ORIGIN IS
! CONSIDERED TO BE AT POSITION 35 OF THE SCREEN.
!
! DECLARATIONS
      INTEGER :: I,COLUMN
!
! IF THE LOGICAL VARIABLE AXIS IS PRESENT, PRINT AN ORDINATE AXIS;
!    ELSE IF THE PRINT COMMAND EXISTS THEN PRINT THE PRESENT
!     VALUES OF ALL CURVES,
!    ELSE CREATE AN IMAGE OF A POINT ON THE CURVE
!
      IF (AXIS.EQV..TRUE.) THEN
          DO I=1,70
              IMAGE_ARRAY(I) = '+'
          END DO
          PRINT"(T2,70A)", IMAGE_ARRAY
          WRITE (2,"(T2,70A)") IMAGE_ARRAY
          DO I = 1,70
              IMAGE_ARRAY(I) = ' '
          END DO
      ELSE IF (PRINT_COMMAND .EQV..TRUE.) THEN
          PRINT"(T2,70A)", IMAGE_ARRAY
          WRITE (2,"(T2,70A)") IMAGE_ARRAY
          DO I = 1,70
              IMAGE_ARRAY(I) = ' '
          END DO
      ELSE
          IMAGE_ARRAYS(35) = '+'
          COLUMN = NINT(CURVE_VALUE/RANGE*69.0) + 35
          IMAGE_ARRAY(COLUMN) = CURVE_SYMBOL
      END IF
END SUBROUTINE STRIP_CHART
END MODULE PORTRAIT_GRAPH
```

The results of the simulation are shown in Fig. 10.4. The response of the system is clearly depicted. A period (.) is used for the temperature set point, and the equal sign (=) is the symbol for the simulated temperature. A 50-minute time interval was simulated,

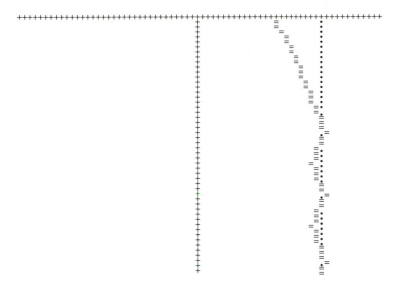

FIGURE 10.4   Results of the environmental control design problem.

and the building temperature reaches a relatively stable state in approximately 20 minutes. The other heating/cooling alogrithms described above could be simulated by modifying the program HVAC. In addition to a system's ability to maintain the set point temperature, the designer will be interested in the efficiency of the system (e.g., "How much does the heating/cooling system cost to operate?"). Questions of this nature could be addressed by further program modifications.

EXAMPLE 10.2 Plotting FORTRAN 90 Results Using a Spreadsheet

Graphs with greater resolution than those graphs described in Example 10.1 are possible if a spreadsheet software applications package is used. Shown here is an example in which results are stored in a file; the contents of this file are then used with a spreadsheet to create a graph of the data.

In this example, we show how to obtain a high-resolution graph of the low-pass magnitude frequency response of a type of filter called the *Elliptic* filter. This type of filter has a ripple in the passband as well as a large ripple in the stopband as shown in Fig. 10.5, which is a high-resolution graph as described below. The feature that makes the Elliptic filter more useful in some applications is that its transition from passband to stopband is much steeper, for a given order, n, then is provided by other filters. (See, for example, the type I Chebychev filter described in Chapter 7.)

The FORTRAN 90 source code for calculating the amplitude response of an Elliptic filter is as follows.

```
        PROGRAM ELLIPTIC_FILTER
!       LP ELLIPTIC N = 5
        IMPLICIT NONE
        COMPLEX HD1,HD2,HD3,H
        REAL:: W,NUM,A1,A2,Y
        OPEN(2, FILE = 'B:ELLIP.DAT')
        DO W = 0, 200.0, 0.5
```

```
A1 = -W**2 + 23829.
A2 = -W**2 + 13784.
   NUM = 0.11118*(110.0)*A1*A2
   HD1 = CMPLX(7665. - W**2, 42.2*W)
   HD2 = CMPLX(11064. - W**2, 7.107*W)
   HD3 = CMPLX(47.48, W)
   H = NUM/(HD1*HD2*HD3)
   Y = 20.0*LOG10(CABS(H))
   WRITE(*,*)W,Y
   WRITE(2,*)W,Y
END DO
CLOSE(2)
END PROGRAM ELLIPTIC_FILTER
```

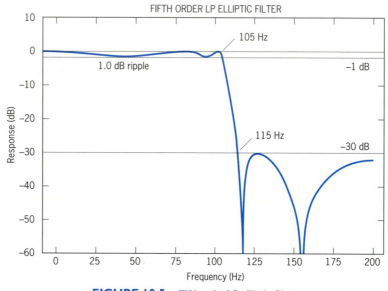

FIGURE 10.5   Fifth order LP elliptic filter.

Note the presence of the communication statements that direct the results to a file (in addition to the display on the monitor):

```
OPEN(2, FILE = 'B:ELLIP.DAT')
WRITE(2,*)W,Y
CLOSE(2)
```

A series of 401 points (the DO loop index runs from 0 to 200 in increments of 0.5) are calculated, and for each iteration the variables W and Y are written into the file B:EL-LIP.DAT. A graph of this information requires considerable resolution and serves as the input data for the applications software discussed below.

A number of spreadsheet applications products are available; the one used in this case is Lotus 1-2-3 (Release 3.1). This program, like many of its competitors, employs a series of commands (like subroutine procedures in FORTRAN 90) that permit a user to perform calculations or generate graphs. These commands are executed by invoking a menu, with an associated list of choices, and selecting the appropriate action. Selecting a particular menu item might in turn produce a second menu (or *submenu*) from which choices are made.

A spreadsheet consists of a very large matrix of cells. Within these cells, numbers or textual information can be entered. In addition, calculations can be performed on the numbers in the cells and the results assigned to other cells. The spreadsheet uses the keyboard to control these events; two keys are particularly important:

- The key marked "/": this key invokes the menu system which, in turn, provides control for all spreadsheet operations.
- The key marked "Esc"—the *Escape* key: depressing this key returns the user to the previous operation. Thus, if some operation is inadvertently initiated, it may be halted by depressing the Escape key. In addition, if a given procedure requires several steps, the Escape key allows the user to backtrack to earlier stages.

A simplified schematic drawing of menu choices in Lotus 1-2-3 is shown in Fig. 10.6. The menu system is quite extensive, and only those menus and submenus relevant to the discussion below are included.

In order to graph the data generated in PROGRAM ELLIPTIC_FILTER, the following steps are carried out:

- Initiate the spreadsheet program.
- Import data from the file B:ELLIP.DAT into the spreadsheet.
- Select the graphing operation.
- Determine the parameters of the graph.
- Print the graph.

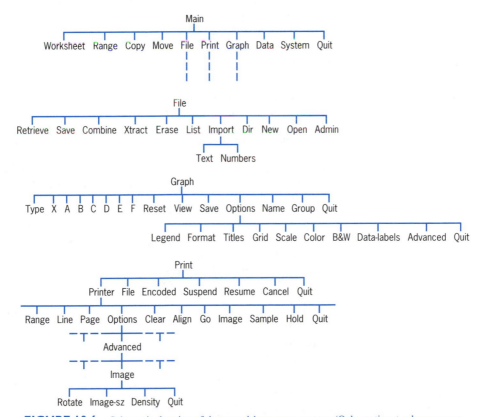

FIGURE 10.6   Schematic drawing of the spreadsheet menu system. (Only pertinent submenus are expanded.)

The first step, initiating the spreadsheet, varies according to the type of computer and operating system (OS) being used. Some OSs (e.g., DOS) may require a text command such as "Lotus"; others (e.g., Windows) require the user to select (point) to an icon (picture) of the spreadsheet using the computer's mouse in order to initiate operation.

The remainder of the steps are summarized in Table 10.1. In the table, making a

Table 10.1   Spreadsheet Steps for Creating a High Resolution Graph

Function	Procedure
Import data.	• Use the Arrow keys to select cell a1. ("a" is the designation of a column and "1" corresponds to a row number in the array of cells.)
	• Invoke the spreadsheet menu ("/").
	• Select the FILE submenu.
	• Select the IMPORT submenu.
	• Choose the NUMBERS option.
	• Type "B:ELLIP.DAT" when prompted for the name of the data file. (B:ELLIP.DAT was created when PROGRAM ELLIPTIC_FILTER was executed). Once the Enter key validates this choice, the data from the file are imported into the spreadsheet and the data (numbers) will be displayed starting in cell a1.
Select the graphing operation.	• Invoke the main menu ("/").
	• Select the GRAPH submenu.
	• Choose the TYPE option from the submenu.
	• Select a LINE graph.
	• Select X (the abscissa values). Enter the range of X coordinates by typing "a1..a401". (The abscissa values extend from cells a1 to a401.)
	• Select A, the curve to be plotted.
	• Specify the range of ordinate values to be plotted by typing "b1..b401".)
Determine the parameters. (Submenu sequence selections are separated by dashes ("-").)	• GRAPH-OPTIONS-FORMAT: select LINES only, as opposed to other possible choices such as showing the datum points without a connecting curve. For the LINES choice, the datum points themselves are not marked; this produces a "clean" image that would otherwise be cluttered with a marker at each of the 401 data points.
	• GRAPH-OPTIONS-TITLES: The user can specify titles for the graph, the X axis, and the Y axis. In this case the title "FIFTH ORDER LP ELLIPTIC FILTER" is entered for the first line of the graph title, the X axis is labeled "FREQUENCY(Hz)", and the Y axis is labeled "RESPONSE(DB)."
	• GRAPH-OPTIONS-SCALE: Choose the SKIP option. By "skipping" points on the X axis, the graph will become less cluttered. In this case, choose a skip factor of 20. Another option in the SCALE submenu allows the user to override the default settings for the Y axis scale. Set the lower limit of the scale to −60 and the upper limit to be 10, and instruct the spreadsheet to use the MANUAL settings for the Y axis.
	• GRAPH-OPTIONS-GRID: This allows the user to include grid lines on the graph. Choose only VERTICAL grid lines.
Print the graph.	• Invoke the main menu ("/").
	• Select PRINT submenu.
	• Choose PRINTER submenu.
	• Choose IMAGE submenu.
	• Select CURRENT option.
	• Select GO option which appears (automatically) when previous step is validated.

choice is carried out by using the Arrow keys ($\rightarrow$ or $\leftarrow$) to highlight a menu choice or option selection and then depressing the Enter key of the computer to validate the choice and initiate action.

Other graphic enhancements, such as the presence of horizontal lines at -1 and -30, and various notes (e.g., "1.0 dB RIPPLE"), are included in Fig. 10.5. These additions can be understood by referring to the spreadsheet User's Manual. Other spreadsheets have similar capabilities and characteristics, any of which can be used to create good-quality, high-resolution graphs.

10.2 A TOOL FOR ENGINEERING PLANNING (MANAGEMENT/INDUSTRIAL ENGINEERING)

There are numerous scientific and engineering applications wherein the computer plays a significant role in system analysis. These include problems in social science, behavioral science, transportation, manufacturing, geophysics, medicine, power generation and distribution, electronics, mechanics, environmental engineering, computer-integrated manufacturing (CIM), and communications, including those involving local area (computer) networks or LANs. One tool used to analyze such systems is referred to as *Queuing theory*.

The description of a *queuing* problem is straightforward and is representative of many real-world applications. (One meaning of the "queue" is "a line or file of people or things waiting to be served or brought into service.")

- "Customers" (see Table 10.2 below) arrive to receive service.
- These customers are serviced by a "server"—a single server in this case—and when service is complete, they depart.

This description applies to one server and is therefore referred to as the *single server* (SS) problem. Each instance of service consists of a number of events (e.g., a customer arrives to be serviced and is placed at the end of the queue). Examples of such applications are summarized in the table.

The queuing problem may be described as follows.

- The customer may arrive and find the server idle, in which case service is immediate.

Table 10.2   Single Server Queuing Systems

Example	Customers	Servers
Assembly line (manufacturing)	Items being manufactured	Workers, machines
Airport	Airplanes, passengers	Runways, check-in stations, personnel
Hospital	Patients	Doctors, nurses, machines, beds
Computer system	Tasks, procedures	CPU, Memory, I/O
Communications	Calls, callers, messages	Lines (including trunks), circuits, operators
Bank	Customers	Tellers
Transportation	Ships, cargo	Tugs, docks, loading/unloading facilities

- A customer arrives and finds the server busy and must therefore wait in a line or queue.
- Service must be completed in a finite amount of time. After being served, the customer leaves. If there is a line, the next customer in the line receives service.
- The queue is a *First-In-First-Out* (FIFO), or alternatively stated, First-Come-First-Served organization. (This is not necessarily realistic; for example, if the application is a computer installation, then the president's job may be fifth in the queue but will often go to the head of the line because of priority. We will not include this possiblity.)
- Customers do not arrive in a regular pattern (at equispaced time intervals). Instead, they arrive at randomly varying intervals.
- Customers are serviced in randomly varying intervals of time because servers do not always complete tasks in the same amount of time. (E.g., a message on a computer local area network (LAN) varies in length and therefore requires the communication line for differing periods of time.)

When using the computer to study such applications a number of questions may be addressed. Computer results change dramatically with minor changes in the problem statement. The user must judge the answers by determining whether they make sense.

- What is the average waiting time for customers in the queue?
- What is the average number of customers in the queue? This helps to determine the necessary resources (such as the number of docks in an oil transportation system).
- How busy is the server? Can we complete the design with fewer workers or do we need more servers?

In an SS application, the computer schedules events of the type described above (e.g., a customer arrives, a customer is serviced) in accordance with an appropriate random function. These events are put on and taken off lists (e.g., a list of customers waiting to be serviced.). The computer subsequently updates the state of the system according to the event on the list. One additional "event" must be scheduled, namely, the point at which the application should terminate.

The arrival times of the customers are specified as the elapsed time between customers and are referred to as *interarrival* times. Specific interarrival times will be designated as A with an appropriate subscript given to identify the first, second, third, and so on, such as

$$A_1, A_2, A_3, \ldots$$

These are random events and are considered to be *random variables* (RVs). Each can be regarded as if it were drawn from a series of bowls with numbers (time delays) in them. Each bowl might have a different grouping (*distribution*) of numbers. However, in this example, it is assumed that the distributions are identical. Furthermore, each interarrival time has no influence or bearing on the one that comes before or after; we refer to these as *independent* events.

In a similar way, the time required to service a customer is also an independent, identically distributed, random variable with specific service times noted by

$$S_1, S_2, S_3, \ldots$$

The program ends when the nth customer enters service. This means that the $(n-1)^{\text{st}}$ customer completes service, leaves the system, and the next—customer n—moves up to enter service. The time at which the program ends is also a random variable because it is a function of two other random variables—the interarrival times and the service times.

When the computer is used to analyze such systems, a number of performance measures can be examined, including

- The time delay that customers experience in the queue after the nth customer enters service. (For example, how long, on average, must an oil tanker wait before being filled? This datum must be factored into the operating costs of a tanker fleet.)
- The (expected) number of customers in the queue over the course of the analysis. (Such a calculation would, for example, give insight into what types of anchorage and harbor facilities are needed for a petroleum station.)
- Server utilization—the proportion of time that the server is busy (not idle).

The results noted above are RVs; their outcomes depend on a series of random events. Therefore, each has a range of outcomes with, in general, an unknown distribution. One of the more important measures of RVs with unknown distributions is to determine its central tendency, and one important calculation is the *mean* value of the RV. An estimate of the mean value or central tendency of a RV can be obtained by calculating its *average* value. For example, we can obtain a measure of the expected value of the delay time in the queue as follows.

Let D_i be the delay of customer i in the queue; each customer will have a different experience (delay in the queue). The average delay, $\overline{D}$, is calculated as follows.

$$\overline{D}(n) = \frac{\sum\limits_{i=1}^{n} D_i}{n}$$

In order to calculate the expected number of customers in the queue (and not served), we need to define additional quantities:

$Q(t) =$ the number of customers in the queue at time t.

$T(n) =$ the elapsed time for n delays in the queue—the (simulated) time to complete the execution of the SS application.

Note that $0 < t \leq T(n)$. Figure 10.7 shows the outcomes of a typical SS application. From this, a number of parameters can be determined. Let p_k be the proportion of time that $Q(t) = k$. From the figure we conclude that

$$p_k = \frac{t_a + t_b}{T(n)} = \sum \frac{T_k}{T(n)}$$

where T_k is the time during which there are k customers in the queue. We can now determine the average number of unserved customers in the queue ($\overline{q}$)

$$\overline{q}(n) = \sum\limits_{i=0}^{\infty} i P_i$$

or

$$\overline{q}(n) = \frac{\sum\limits_{i=0}^{\infty} i T_i}{T(n)}$$

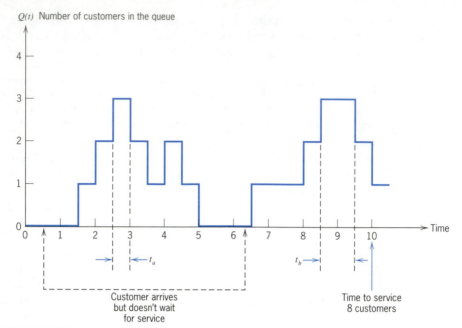

$Q(t)$ Number of customers in the queue

FIGURE 10.7 Number of customers on a single server queue as a function of time (sample). The program terminates when 8 customers are considered to be serviced. It includes customers who do not wait for service upon arrival.

From Fig. 10.7 we can calculate the following:

$$T_0 = (1.5 - 0) + (6.5 - 5.0) = 3.0$$
$$T_1 = (2.0 - 1.5) + (4.0 - 3.5) + (5.0 - 4.5) + (8.0 - 6.5) = 3.0$$
$$T_2 = (2.5 - 2.0) + (3.5 - 3.0) + (4.5 - 4.0) + (8.5 - 8.0) + (10.0 - 9.5) = 2.5$$
$$T_3 = (3.0 - 2.5) + (9.5 - 8.5) = 1.5$$
$$T_i = 0 \text{ for } i \geq 4$$

Therefore,

$$\sum_{i=0}^{\infty} iT_i = 12.5$$

and

$$\bar{q} = (8) = \frac{12.5}{10.0} = 1.25$$

Alternatively, the average may be calculated by finding the area under a curve and dividing by the interval over which it is computed. For example, in the case of the average number of customers on the queue,

$$\sum iT_i$$

is the area under $Q(t)$. The average is then calculated by dividing this term by $T(n)$. In general,

$$\bar{q}(n) = \frac{\displaystyle\int_0^{T(n)} Q(t)\, dt}{T(n)}$$

Utilization is the proportion of time that the server is busy. It too is a random variable, and its average can be found from the proportion of time that the server is busy. Let

$$B(t) = \begin{cases} 1 & \text{if server is busy} \\ 0 & \text{if server is idle} \end{cases}$$

$B(t)$ is called the *server busy* function. Having determined $B(t)$ we can compute the average utilization as

$$\bar{u} = \frac{\displaystyle\int_{0}^{T(n)} B(t)\, dt}{T(n)}$$

Utilization is an important parameter in queuing applications because values near 100 percent indicate that a potential bottleneck exists.

Having described the important considerations in queuing theory, two additional factors must be considered if a FORTRAN 90 program is to be developed, namely, the data structure and the algorithm. The data structure must make provision for

- The server status: busy = 1, idle = 0.
- The number of customers in the queue.
- Arrival times of customers (in order to calculate how long a customer remains in the queue).
- The time of the last event (in order to calculate areas as required by the formulas shown above).
- A clock so that Δt can be found to calculate areas under curves.
- The number of customers that have been admitted to service so that we know when to terminate the system simulation.
- Total delay in order to compute the estimate of average customer delay.
- The area under $Q(t)$
- The area under $B(t)$
- A list of events from which to determine what is the next event to be processed.

These data parameters might be represented as a scoreboard as shown in Fig. 10.8; the scoreboard is updated after each event is processed. Two important pseudocode segments portray *customer arrival* and *customer departure* events.

```
customer arrival event
{schedule the next arrival event}
If (server is not busy)
      then
              set delay=0 for this customer and gather statistics
              add 1 to the number of customers delayed
              set server busy = 1
              schedule a departure event for this customer.
      else
              add 1 to the number in the queue
              if (queue not full)
                    then
                            store time of arrival of this customer
                    else
                            write error message and stop
              end if
      end if
end customer arrival event
```

```
customer departure event
if (queue is empty)
        then
                make the server idle (B = 0)
                eliminate departure event from consideration
        else
                subtract 1 from number of customers in the queue
                compute delay of customer entering service and gather
                    statistics
                add 1 to the number of customers delayed
                schedule a departure event for this customer
                move each customer in queue up one place (if any remain).
end if
end customer departure event.
```

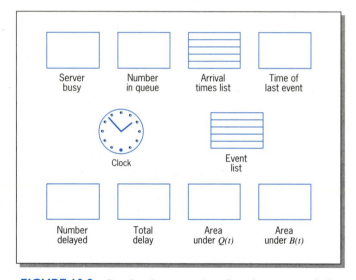

FIGURE 10.8   Scoreboard representation of queuing system analysis.

EXAMPLE 10.3 A FORTRAN 90 Program for a Queue

 The source code for a queuing application is shown below. The main program consists of a series of subroutines that are invoked as needed. The sequence is summarized in the fol-

Table 10.3   Subroutines for Queuing Program

Subroutine Name	Summary
RANDOM_SEED	Initializes random function generator.
INITIALIZE	Initializes parameters of queuing model.
DETERMINE_NEXT_EVENT	Updates time; determines if next event (in time) on event list is arrival or departure.
STATISTICAL_UPDATE	Finds Δt since last event; updates areas under $Q(t)$ and $B(t)$.
ARRIVAL_EVENT	As described in pseudocode in text.
DEPARTURE_EVENT	As described in pseudocode in text.
PRINTOUT	Displays results of analysis.

lowing table. The subroutines DETERMINE_NEXT_EVENT, STATISTICAL_UP-DATE, ARRIVAL_EVENT, and DEPARTURE_EVENT are contained in a DO loop that is repeated until 1000 customer services have been completed. The intrinsic function RANDOM_NUMBER is used extensively to generate events such as the arrival or departure of a customer. Subroutines are used for customer arrival and customer departure.

```fortran
      PROGRAM QUEUE
! THIS PROGRAM CAN BE USED TO ANALYZE SYSTEMS WHICH ARE
! MODIFIED WITH CUSTOMERS, SERVERS, AND THEIR INTERACTIONS.
!
! MEANINGS OF PROGRAM VARIABLES
! Q_AREA = RUNNING TOTAL OF AREA UNDER Q(T) CURVE.
! B_AREA = RUNNING TOTAL OF AREA UNDER B(T) CURVE.
! SERVER BUSY = STATUS OF SERVER; BUSY = 1, IDLE = 0.
! DELAY = CUSTOMER DELAY IN THE QUEUE.
! NEXT_EVENT = STORES WHETHER EVENT IS ARRIVAL OR DEPARTURE
! NUMBER_IN_QUEUE = NUMBER OF CUSTOMERS IN THE QUEUE.
! COMPLETED_DELAYS = NUMBER OF CUSTOMERS WHO HAVE COMPLETED THEIR
!      DELAYS.
! ARRIVAL_TIME = TIME OF ARRIVAL OF ITH CUSTOMER IN THE QUEUE
!      (LIMIT=100)
! CLOCK = CURRENT TIME.
! TIME_OF_LAST EVENT = TIME OF THE LAST EVENT.
! TOTAL_DELAY = RUNNING SUM OF DELAYS.
! NO_OF_OBSERVATIONS = NUMBER OF CUSTOMER DELAYS TO BE OBSERVED
! TIME_OF_NEXT_ARRIVAL = RANDOM EVENT SIGNALING NEXT ARRIVAL TIME
! TIME_OF_NEXT DEPARTURE = RANDOM EVENT SIGNALING NEXT DEPARTURE
! TIME
!
! FORMAL DECLARATIONS
!
      IMPLICIT NONE
      CHARACTER (LEN=1) :: NEXT_EVENT
      REAL :: CLOCK,                       &
           TIME_OF_LAST_EVENT              &
           TOTAL_DELAY,                    &
           Q_AREA,                         &
           B_AREA,                         &
           DELAY,                          &
           TIME_OF-NEXT_ARRIVAL,           &
           TIME_OF-NEXT_DEPARTURE
      REAL, DIMENSION (1:100) :: ARRIVAL_TIME
      INTEGER :: SERVER_BUSY,NUMBER_IN_QUEUE,COMPLETED_DELAYS
      INTEGER,PARAMETER :: NO_OF_OBSERVATIONS = 1000
!
! START OF THE MAIN PROGRAM
!
      OPEN(2,FILE='B:QUEUE.DAT',STATUS='UNKNOWN',       &
           POSITION='REWIND')
      CALL RANDOM_SEED
      CALL INITIALIZE
      DO
           CALL DETERMINE_NEXT_EVENT
           CALL STATISTICAL_UPDATE
           IF (NEXT_EVENT == 'A') THEN
```

```
                       CALL ARRIVAL_EVENT
              ELSE
                       CALL DEPATURE_EVENT
              END IF
      IF(COMPLETED_DELAYS >= NO_OF_OBSERVATIONS) EXIT
      END DO
      CALL PRINTOUT
      CLOSE(2)
!

      CONTAINS
!

      SUBROUTINE INITIALIZE
! INITIALIZE VARIABLES AND FORCE ARRIVAL EVENT TO PRECEDE
! DEPARTURE EVENT (AS THERE SHOULD BE NO CUSTOMERS ON THE
! EVENT LIST WHEN THE ANALYSIS BEGINS).
      CLOCK = 0.0
      SERVER_BUSY = 0
      NUMBER_IN_QUEUE = 0
      TIME_OF_LAST_EVENT = 0.0
      COMPLETED_DELAYS = 0
      TOTAL_DELAY = 0.0
      Q_AREA = 0.0
      B_AREA = 0.0
      CALL GET_A_TIME (1.0,TIME_OF_NEXT_ARRIVAL)
      TIME_OF_NEXT_DEPARTURE = 1.0E+10
      END SUBROUTINE INITIALIZE
!

      SUBROUTINE DETERMINE_NEXT_EVENT
! THIS DETERMINES IF THE NEXT EVENT IS AN ARRIVAL OR A
! DEPARTURE EVENT. IT ALSO UPDATES THE CURRENT TIME (CLOCK)
      IMPLICIT NONE
      IF (TIME_OF_NEXT_ARRIVAL <= TIME_OF_NEXT_DEPARTURE) THEN
          NEXT_EVENT = 'A'
          CLOCK = TIME_OF_NEXT_ARRIVAL
      ELSE
          NEXT_EVENT = 'D'
          CLOCK = TIME_OF_NEXT_DEPARTURE
      END IF
      END SUBROUTINE DETERMINE_NEXT_EVENT
!

      SUBROUTINE STATISTICAL_UPDATE
! THIS SUBROUTINE PERFORMS THE FOLLOWING TASKS: FIND TIME CHANGE SINCE
! LAST EVENT; UDPATE TIME OF LAST EVENT; UPDATE AREA UNDER Q(T); UPDATE
! AREA UNDER B(T)
      IMPLICIT NONE
      REAL :: DELTA_T
      DELTA_T = CLOCK - TIME_OF_LAST_EVENT
      TIME_OF_LAST_EVENT = CLOCK
      Q_AREA = Q_AREA + NUMBER_IN_QUEUE*DELTA_T
      B_AREA = B_AREA + DELTA_T*REAL(SERVER_BUSY)
      END SUBROUTINE STATISTICAL_UPDATE
!

      SUBROUTINE ARRIVAL_EVENT
      IMPLICIT NONE
      CALL GET_A_TIME(1.0,TIME_OF_NEXT_ARRIVAL)
```

```fortran
      TIME_OF_NEXT_ARRIVAL = CLOCK + TIME_OF_NEXT_ARRIVAL
      IF(SERVER_BUSY == 1) THEN
           NUMBER_IN_QUEUE = NUMBER_IN_QUEUE + 1
           IF(NUMBER_IN_QUEUE > 100) THEN
               PRINT*,'   QUEUE OVERFLOW ERROR.'
               PRINT*,'   CLOCK = ',CLOCK
           END IF
           ARRIVAL_TIME(NUMBER_IN_QUEUE) = CLOCK
      ELSE
           SERVER_BUSY = 1
           COMPLETED_DELAYS = COMPLETED_DELAYS + 1
           CALL GET_A_TIME(0.5,TIME_OF_NEXT_DEPARTURE)
           TIME_OF_NEXT_DEPARTURE = TIME_OF_NEXT_DEPARTURE + CLOCK
      END IF
      END SUBROUTINE ARRIVAL_EVENT
!

      SUBROUTINE DEPARTURE_EVENT
      IMPLICIT NONE
      INTEGER :: J
      IF (NUMBER_IN_QUEUE == 0) THEN
           SERVER_BUSY = 0
           TIME_OF_NEXT_DEPARTURE = 1.0E+10
      ELSE
           NUMBER_IN_QUEUE = NUMBER_IN_QUEUE - 1
           DELAY = CLOCK - ARRIVAL_TIME(1)
           TOTAL_DELAY = TOTAL_DELAY + DELAY
           COMPLETED_DELAYS = COMPLETED_DELAYS + 1
           CALL GET_A_TIME(0.5,TIME_OF_NEXT_DEPARTURE)
           TIME_OF_NEXT_DEPARTURE = CLOCK + TIME_OF_NEXT_DEPARTURE
           DO J = 1,NUMBER_IN_QUEUE
               ARRIVAL_TIME(J) = ARRIVAL_TIME(J+1)
           END DO
      END IF
      END SUBROUTINE DEPARTURE_EVENT
!

      SUBROUTINE PRINTOUT
      IMPLICIT NONE
      WRITE (2,'(T20,A)')'ANALYSIS OF QUEUING SYSTEM'
      WRITE (2,'(T10,A,T40,F5.2,T47,A)')                            &
           'MEAN INTERARRIVAL TIME',1.00,'MINUTES'
      WRITE (2,'(T10,A,T40,F5.2,T47,A)')                            &
           'MEAN SERVICE TIME',0.50,'MINUTES'
      WRITE (2,'(T10,A,T40,I4)')                                    &
           'NUMBER OF CUSTOMERS',1000
      WRITE (2,'(T10,A,T40,F5.2,T47,A)')                            &
           'AVERAGE DELAY',TOTAL_DELAY/REAL(COMPLETED_DELAYS),      &
           'MINUTES'
      WRITE (2,'(T10,A,T40,F5.2)')                                  &
           'AVERAGE NUMBER IN QUEUE',                               &
           Q_AREA/CLOCK
      WRITE (2,'(T10,A,T40,F5.2)')                                  &
           'UTILIZATION FACTOR',                                    &
           B_AREA/CLOCK
      WRITE (2,'(T10,A,T40,F7.2,TR3,A)')                            &
           'ANALYSIS ENDED AT',                                     &
```

```
        CLOCK,                                              &
        'MINUTES'
    END SUBROUTINE PRINTOUT
!

    SUBROUTINE GET_A_TIME(MEAN_TIME,TIME)
! RETURNS A RANDOM TIME WHICH IS EXPONENTIALLY DISTRIBUTED
!

    SUBROUTINE GET_A_TIME(MEAN_TIME,TIME)
! RETURNS A RANDOM TIME WHICH IS EXPONENTIALLY DISTRIBUTED
! WITH A MEAN GIVEN BY MEAN_TIME.
    IMPLICIT NONE
    REAL,INTENT(IN) :: MEAN_TIME
    REAL,INTENT(OUT) :: TIME
    REAL :: X
    CALL RANDOM_NUMBER (X)
    TIME = -MEAN_TIME*LOG(X)
    END SUBROUTINE GET_A_TIME
!
END PROGRAM QUEUE
```

Typical results are shown below; these have been stored in a file ("B:QUEUE.DAT"), they may be displayed on the monitor by adding statements of the form WRITE(*,*), and so on.

```
    Analysis of queuing system
    Mean interarrival time              1.00 minutes
    Mean service time                   0.50 minutes
    Number of customers         1000
    Average delay                       0.44 minutes
    Average number in queue             0.43
    Utilization factor                  0.47
    Analysis ended at           1021.89 minutes
```

10.3 DATABASES FOR MAINTAINING DATA

Data are a vital resource for scientists and engineers as well as for the business community. Data are as important as the instruments, machines, and materials needed for the achievement of scientific or industrial goals. Unless organized and used efficiently, data alone do not have any genuine value. When this resource is utilized efficiently, data become transformed into *knowledge*. The resultant data structures are known variously as *databases* (DBs) or information bases. A sampling of applications includes:

- *Maintenance Management Systems* These systems assist in the automation and planning of tasks in manufacturing, utility, institutional, and hospital environments. The DB stores maintenance labor, work order backlog, planning aids, equipment history records, preventative maintenance, and report data.
- *Geophysical Research* Information is required to describe the propagation of energy travel through geophysical models. Such information exists in the form of geological profiles, including horizon depths, seismic travel times, and geological densities. This information can be subsequently used to predict the presence of "hydrocarbon traps" (gas and/or oil deposits) and geophysical responses to earthquakes.

- *Industrial Training* Using a DB that includes organization of manufacturing facilities (e.g., assembly-line profiles, production, and material handling), engineers and other employees may receive industrial training, even though they may have limited computer experience.
- *Integrated Circuit Analysis* A DB facilitates the analysis of parametric test data on integrated circuits. Such analysis is useful for electronic circuit design. The DB stores the test data from a wide range of integrated circuits.

Other, more familiar DB applications include credit transactions, Universal Product Codes (e.g., for inventory control and marketing), airline reservation systems, and medical systems (e.g., recording/billing, diagnosis, drug interaction).

An important emerging technological application is the role of the DB in *expert systems*. The DB or knowledge base contains facts and practical, or heuristic, information relating to a given area of expertise. (A simple example (Example 10.4) related to automated troubleshooting of equipment is provided later in this chapter.)

A DB is a nonredundant collection of interrelated data items that can be shared by several different subsystems or users. Although a DB normally includes a collection of files that embody the information, we will restrict the term *DB* to mean a single file. In its simplest form a DB can be viewed as a table wherein

- Each row of the table is called a *record* (and is also called a *tuple*).
- Each item in a record is an *attribute* or *field*.
- An attribute has certain characteristics; it has a name (field name) and it has a type (e.g., numeric, logical, character).

Other properties of a DB that should be noted include the following.

- Each entry (cell) in a record contains only one value.
- Each attribute (column) has a distinct name.
- The order of attributes is not important.
- The record order is not important.
- No duplicate records are permitted; each row must be distinct in at least one attribute.

A user can query the DB; the attribute on which the query is based is called the *key*. Because a relational DB has no duplicate records (tuples), it is always possible for a program to distinguish rows. There must be at least one key on which to uniquely distinguish records, and that is known as the *primary key*.

The DB described here involves the classification of chemicals. It is useful for chemical engineers, environmental engineers, physicians, and scientists.

A chemical substance can be characterized according to its reaction to certain tests, one of which is the way in which it responds to incident light—that is, how the chemical passes or reflects light. A sample absorbs the light energy according to the characteristics of the particular chemical compound. The accompanying table (Table 10.4) indicates how a series of eight chemical compounds might respond to three tests as well as their response to incident light ("absorbance"). The parameters (Parm_1, Parm_2, Parm_3) represent three different tests that are performed on the substances. The example is restricted to a small number of factors to minimize complexity; in many cases there are many more parameters. In addition, the response to the various tests is limited to either a high ("hi") or low ("lo") reaction. In the table, the units of absorbance are considered to be arbitrary (e.g., a reading on a meter).

Table 10.4   A Simple Database of Test Responses

Compound	Parm_1	Parm_2	Parm_3	Absorbance
chem_1	lo	lo	lo	0.115
chem_2	hi	lo	lo	0.130
chem_3	lo	hi	lo	0.123
chem_4	hi	hi	lo	0.135
chem_5	lo	lo	hi	0.130
chem_6	hi	lo	hi	0.165
chem_7	lo	hi	hi	0.125
chem_8	hi	hi	hi	0.160

The design goals of this database system are

- To maintain a file system of test records similar to the one shown above. Maintenance of records should include facilities to edit records (make modifications to a particular test result), add records to the file system, and delete records entirely from the file system.
- Permit a user to "query" the file system looking for records with particular characteristics.

One of the first design decisions that must be made is to determine what data structure will support these goals. A reasonable structure for each test would be a derived data type (discussed in Chapter 3) in the form of a *record* with the following organization:

```
TYPE TEST
      CHARACTER(LEN=10) :: SAMPLE_ID
      CHARACTER(LEN=8) :: TEST_DATE
      REAL, DIMENSION(1:4) :: SCORES
END TYPE TEST
```

Having defined such a record, we create a variable of that type in order to communicate with the records within the file—read from, or write to, the file.

```
TYPE(TEST) :: TEST_SAMPLE
```

In summary, each test sample will include an identification (SAMPLE_ID), the date on which the sample was tested (TEST_DATE) with the format *mm/dd/yy*, and the array of four items that stores the test values (SCORES).

Here is a pseudocode representation of the program.

```
{Prompt the user for desired operation
          add_record
          delete_record
          edit_record};}
If (choice==add_record) then
      {prompt user for sample information}
      {add record to end of the file};
endif;
IF (choice==delete_record) then
      {prompt user for record identification}
```

```
            {read sequential file into temporary buffer (memory
               location)
                  one record at a time;
                        IF (record==record to be expunged) then
                              do not copy to file
                        else
                              copy record back to file;
                        end if;}
endif;
If (choice==edit) then
        {prompt user for record identification}
        {search file for designated record}
        {display record contents}
        {prompt user for changes}
        {return record to file}
endif;
end program;
```

The complete Fortran 90 source code is shown below.

```
        MODULE COMMON_DATA
          TYPE TEST
              CHARACTER(LEN=10) :: SAMPLE_ID
              CHARACTER(LEN=8) :: TEST_DATE
              REAL, DIMENSION(1:4) :: SCORES
          END TYPE TEST
          TYPE(TEST) :: TEST_SAMPLE
          INTEGER :: IOS
          INTEGER,PARAMETER :: END_OF_FILE = -1
          CHARACTER (LEN = 3) :: ANSWER
          CHARACTER (LEN = 10) :: CHEM_TO_DELETE,CHEM_TO_EDIT
          END MODULE COMMON_DATA
!
      PROGRAM CHEM_DB
!     THIS PROGRAM MAINTAINS A FILE SYSTEM FOR A DATABASE OF    &
!         CHEMICALS
! DECLARATIONS
      IMPLICIT NONE
      INTEGER :: CHOICE
!
! START OF THE MAIN PROGRAM
! SOME INITIALIZATIONS NEEDED
      CHOICE = 0
! PROMPT THE USER FOR A CHOICE; GET CHOICE; IF AN ERROR, REPEAT.
      DO; IF(CHOICE == 1 .OR. CHOICE == 2 .OR. CHOICE == 3) EXIT
      PRINT"(A,//,A,//,A,//,A,//A)","  CHEMICAL FILE FACILITY
          CHOICES", &
                   "(1) ADD A NEW TEST RECORD",   &
                   "(2) DELETE A TEST RECORD",    &
                   "(3) EDIT A TEST RECORD",      &
                   "(4) RETURN TO OS"
      WRITE (*,"(/,A)",ADVANCE="NO") " PLEASE CHOOSE A NUMBER "
      READ (*,"(I1)") CHOICE
      END DO
```

```
      !
      ! DETERMINE USER'S CHOICE AND CALL EITHER ADD, DELETE, OR EDIT
      ! SUBROUTINES
            SELECT CASE (CHOICE)
            CASE (1)
      ! ADD A NEW TEST RECORD
                CALL ADD_A_TEST
            CASE (2)
      ! DELETE A TEST
                CALL DELETE_A_TEST
            CASE (3)
      ! EDIT A TEST
                CALL EDIT_A_TEST
            END SELECT
      !
            CONTAINS
      !
            SUBROUTINE ADD_A_TEST
      !     THIS SUBROUTINE ADDS A TEST TO THE DATABASE
            USE COMMON_DATA
      !         PROMPT USER FOR THE NEW RECORD
                WRITE (*,"(A)",ADVANCE="NO") &
                 " SAMPLE ID (10 CHARACTERS) = "
                READ (*,"(A)") TEST_SAMPLE % SAMPLE_ID
                WRITE (*,"(A)",ADVANCE="NO") &
                 " TEST DATE (MM/DD/YY) = "
                READ (*,"(A)") TEST_SAMPLE % TEST_DATE
                WRITE (*,"(A)",ADVANCE="NO") &
                 " ENTER (4) TEST VALUES"
                READ(*,"(F6.3)") TEST_SAMPLE % SCORES (1:4)
      !         OPEN COMMUNICATION TO THE FILE FOR ADDING A TEST
                OPEN (UNIT=2,FILE="B:CHEMS",POSITION="APPEND",&
                 FORM="FORMATTED",ACCESS="SEQUENTIAL", &
                 ACTION="READWRITE",STATUS="UNKNOWN")
      !         APPEND RECORD TO THE FILE
                WRITE (2,"(A,A,4F6.3)") TEST_SAMPLE
                ENDFILE (2)
      !         CLOSE COMMUNICATION
                CLOSE(2)
            END SUBROUTINE ADD_A_TEST
      !
            SUBROUTINE DELETE_A_TEST
            USE COMMON_DATA
      !         PROMPT USER FOR SAMPLE_ID; PROVIDE FOR ABORT
                ANSWER = "NO"
                DO; IF (ANSWER == "YES") EXIT
                 WRITE (*,"(A)",ADVANCE="NO") "PLEASE ENTER SAMPLE_ID "
                 READ (*,"(A)") CHEM_TO_DELETE
                 WRITE (*,"(A)",ADVANCE="NO") "ARE YOU SURE? "
                 READ (*,"(A)") ANSWER
                END DO
      !         OPEN COMMUNICATION; READ THROUGH FILE; DELETE RECORD
      !         USE TEMPORARY FILE
                OPEN (2,FILE="B:CHEMS", ACCESS="SEQUENTIAL")
```

```
        OPEN (9,STATUS="SCRATCH",ACCESS="SEQUENTIAL")
         DO
         READ(2,"(A,A,4F6.3)",IOSTAT=IOS)   &
           TEST_SAMPLE % SAMPLE_ID,    &
           TEST_SAMPLE % TEST_DATE,    &
           TEST_SAMPLE % SCORES
         IF(IOS == END_OF_FILE)EXIT
         IF(TEST_SAMPLE % SAMPLE_ID /= CHEM_TO_DELETE) THEN
         WRITE(9,"(A,A,4F6.3)")       &
           TEST_SAMPLE % SAMPLE_ID,    &
           TEST_SAMPLE % TEST_DATE,    &
           TEST_SAMPLE % SCORES
         END IF
        END DO
!       UPDATE DATABASE; REWIND TEMP; CLOSE AND REOPEN
!       PERMANENT FILE AS REPLACEMENT; COPY TEMP TO CHEMS
        CLOSE (2)
        OPEN (2,FILE="B:CHEMS",ACCESS="SEQUENTIAL", &
                  STATUS="REPLACE")
        REWIND (9)
        IOS = 0
        DO
         READ(9,"(A,A,4F6.3)",IOSTAT=IOS)     &
                 TEST_SAMPLE % SAMPLE_ID,  &
                 TEST_SAMPLE % TEST_DATE,  &
                 TEST_SAMPLE & SCORES
         IF(IOS == END_OF_FILE)EXIT
         WRITE (2,"(A,A,4F6.3)")        &
                 TEST_SAMPLE % SAMPLE_ID,  &
                 TEST_SAMPLE % TEST_DATE,  &
                 TEST_SAMPLE % SCORES
        END DO
!       CLOSE COMMUNICATION
        CLOSE (2)
        CLOSE (9)
     END SUBROUTINE DELETE_A_TEST
!
     SUBROUTINE EDIT_A_TEST
! THIS SUBROUTINE ALLOWS A UESR TO EDIT A TEST
     USE COMMON_DATA
! PROMPT USER FOR SAMPLE_ID
        WRITE (*,"(A)",ADVANCE="NO") "PLEASE ENTER SAMPLE_ID"
        READ (*,"(A)") CHEM_TO_EDIT
! OPEN COMMUNICATION; READ THROUGH FILE; STOP IF SAMPLE_ID FOUND.
        OPEN (2,FILE="B:CHEMS",ACCESS="SEQUENTIAL")
        OPEN (9,STATUS="SCRATCH",ACCESS="SEQUENTIAL")
         DO
          READ(2,"(A,A,4F6.3)",IOSTAT=IOS)    &
            TEST_SAMPLE % SAMPLE_ID,      &
            TEST_SAMPLE % TEST_DATE,      &
            TEST_SAMPLE % SCORES
         IF(IOS == END_OF_FILE) EXIT
         IF(TEST_SAMPLE % SAMPLE_ID == CHEM_TO_EDIT) THEN
          WRITE (*,"(A,A)", ADVANCE="NO")      &
```

```
                    TEST_SAMPLE % SAMPLE_ID,          &
                    " ENTER NEW VALUE "
                  READ (*,"(A)") TEST_SAMPLE % SAMPLE_ID
                  WRITE (*, "(A,A)", ADVANCE="NO")      &
                    TEST_SAMPLE % TEST_DATE,       &
                    " ENTER NEW VALUE "
                  READ (*,"(A)") TEST_SAMPLE % TEST_DATE
                  PRINT"(A,/,4(F6.3,TR2))",            &
                    " THE TEST RESULTS FOLLOW, ENTER NEW VALUES", &
                    TEST_SAMPLE % SCORES
                  READ (*, "(F6.3)") TEST_SAMPLE % SCORES(1:4)
                END IF
                WRITE (9,"(A,A,4F6.3)")          &
                    TEST_SAMPLE % SAMPLE_ID,     &
                    TEST_SAMPLE & TEST_DATE,      &
                    TEST_SAMPLE % SCORES
              END DO
! UPDATE DATABASE; REWIND TEMP; CLOSE AND REOPEN
! PERMANENT FILE AS REPLACEMENT; COPY TEMP TO CHEMS
            CLOSE (2)
            OPEN (2,FILE="B:CHEMS",ACCESS="SEQUENTIAL",&
                STATUS="REPLACE")
            REWIND (9)
            IOS = 0
            DO
              READ (9,"(A,A,4F6.3)",IOSTAT=IOS)    &
                    TEST_SAMPLE % SAMPLE ID,     &
                    TEST_SAMPLE % TEST_DATE,     &
                    TEST_SAMPLE % SCORES
              IF(IOS == END_OF_FILE)EXIT
              WRITE (2,"(A,A,4F6.3)")            &
                    TEST_SAMPLE % SAMPLE_ID,     &
                    TEST_SAMPLE % TEST_DATE,     &
                    TEST_SAMPLE % SCORES
            END DO
! CLOSE COMMUNICATION
            CLOSE (2)
            CLOSE (9)
       END SUBROUTINE EDIT_A_TEST
!
END PROGRAM CHEM_DB
```

Aspects of the program to note in particular include the following:

- The program is organized as a series of subroutines. Each subroutine supports one of the desired recordkeeping tasks—add a test, delete a test, and edit a test result.

- The appropriate subroutine is invoked by means of an interactive menu procedure that prompts the user for the choice to be made. The menu procedure is controlled by a DO loop that displays the choices on the monitor. The DO loop provides a simple way to limit the user to the allowed choices. The loop terminates if the variable CHOICE—the user response—is either 1 or 2 or 3, in which case control is transferred to the next part of the program (the CASE construct). However, if the user enters some other (unrecognized) integer, the entire menu is redisplayed.

- User response, which is assigned to the integer variable CHOICE, determines which subroutine is called. This is accomplished using a SELECT CASE statement. (See Chapter 6, Sec. 6.4.) The specific SELECT CASE statement used in the program is

```
SELECT CASE (CHOICE)
CASE (1)
      CALL ADD_A_TEST
CASE (2)
      CALL DELETE_A_TEST
CASE (3)
      CALL EDIT_A_TEST
      END SELECT
```

If the variable CHOICE—the value assigned by user response—assumes a value of 1, then the statement block following "CASE (1)" is executed. The block of code that follows that phrase is "CALL ADD_A_TEST," and the subroutine "ADD_A_TEST" is thereby invoked. Once the subroutine is completed, control is transferred back to the SELECT statement, which immediately transfers control to the statement following the "END SELECT" phrase.

- All subroutines need access to certain common data. In particular, each subroutine requires a declaration (definition) of the variable TEST_SAMPLE as well as the variables IOS (where a file operation status is returned), ANSWER (which is assigned "yes" or "no" responses by the user), and the names of the test results involved in the task (e.g., CHEM_TO_DELETE, CHEM_TO_EDIT). All of this information is conveniently passed from the calling program—the main program—to the subroutines by means of a MODULE construct (discussed in Chapter 7). All the variables that are common to the subroutines are declared within the MODULE statement. Within each subroutine is the statement USE COMMON_DATA which alerts the compiler to the existence of the data to be used in the subroutine. This saves code (declarations), which otherwise would have to be repeated in each subroutine.

The subroutines themselves are straightforward implementations of the pseudocode; these can be reviewed without extensive explanation. In general, these subroutines involve four steps:

```
{Prompt the user for data appropriate to the operation
    (add,delete,edit)}
{open communications to the file}
{operate on the file}
{close communication to the file}
```

All test results are retained in a file named "CHEMS" which is stored on drive B: of the computer system. (The particular drive to be used is system dependent, but most PCs include a floppy drive with the designation "B:". It is useful to use this drive for "work disks" so that the main [hard] drive does not become cluttered with too many applications programs. The main secondary storage system should be reserved for such applications programs as the FORTRAN 90 compiler, the editor program, etc.).

When adding a new chemical to the DB, the subroutine ADD_A_TEST opens communication to file with "POSITION="APPEND" " as an option because it is required to append a new record onto the DB. To accomplish deletion of a record from the DB, the subroutine DELETE_A_TEST implements the following pseudocode:

```
{open communication to the file named "CHEMS"}
{open communication to a temporary or "scratch" file}
{read a record from "CHEMS"}
repeat
If (record does not match record to be deleted) then
      copy record to scratch file
end if;
until (end of file record in "CHEMS" file is encountered);
{copy contents of scratch file to file named "CHEMS"}
{close communication to "CHEMS" and "scratch files}
```

Program CHEM_DB was compiled and executed; it was run eight times, with option 1 ("Add a new test record") being selected each time in order to create the following file:

```
chem_1    01/15/95 0.000 0.000 0.000 0.037
chem_2    04/06/91 0.000 0.000 1.000 0.144
chem_3    12/19/93 0.000 1.000 0.000 0.071
chem_4    02/04/92 0.000 1.000 1.000 0.638
chem_5    08/25/91 1.000 0.000 0.000 0.073
chem_6    07/14/94 1.000 0.000 1.000 0.034
chem_7    03/04/93 1.000 1.000 0.000 0.198
chem_8    10/19/90 1.000 1.000 1.000 0.108
```

The program was executed once again, and this time option 2 was selected; the test record for chem_1 was deleted. Finally, the program was executed one last time, and the test record for the chem_8 was edited to simulate entry of an updated test record. (We omit the resulting file for the sake of brevity.) Having to execute the program repeatedly for each choice is not a convenient arrangement. Problem 10.7 asks the reader to modify the program so that options may be repeated until the user no longer needs to access the file records.

10.4 EXPERT SYSTEMS

A DB generally includes two forms of knowledge: facts (e.g., the chemical test results), and rules of the form, *if p then q* or $p \rightarrow q$. In the latter case, both p and q are considered to be *predicates* (phrases) whose truth or falsity can be established. The rule $p \rightarrow q$ can be restated as follows:

"If the predicate p is found to be true then it follows that q is true." Simple examples of rules include

If (valve_1 is not open) then (waste water will not empty).

If (object is a bird) the (object has wings).

If (object is human) then (object is mortal).

If (leg is broken) then (leg is severely swollen).

If (system output is 0) then (short circuit or open circuit exists).

If (stress exceeds elastic limit) then (design is not conservative).

The rules may refer to practical or heuristic information—so-called rules of thumb. (As an example of heuristic information, consider the case in which a size 18 wire might be routinely used when the current it carries exceeds 100 milliamperes regardless of other considerations.)

Rules permit us to "search" the DB to see if we can find a circumstance that fits a given predicate p. If the computer finds a predicate p in the DB that fits the circumstances, then the rule can be applied (or "fired"), and we can conclude that q must be true. In most circumstances, more than one rule is fired; that is, more than one rule of the form $(p \rightarrow q)$ has a p value that matches the input.

EXAMPLE 10.4 Troubleshooting a Simple Electric Network

In the example to be provided, we have initially limited our DB to three rules that, we will demonstrate, get fired as single entities. This provides an example of the use of DBs in expert systems while not unduly complicating the model.

The example to be presented involves finding a defect in a simple electric network. (Programs of the type to be described can be extended to more complex devices.) To develop a computer-based "expert" system, the designer normally observes how a human expert accomplishes the same task and then seeks to use this process within the program. The human expert usually has a series of rules or tests that are applied to the problem to find the appropriate answer. Consider the following problem: An attenuator circuit (see Fig. 10.9) is to be automatically maintained and/or tested by computer. In normal operation, a voltage is applied to the input terminals, and an attenuated, or reduced, voltage appears at the output terminals. The relationship between output and input is given by

$$\text{output} = A * \text{input}$$

$$A = \frac{R_2}{(R_1 + R_2)} = \text{attenuation factor}$$

The attenuation factor, A, is always less than 1 in normal operation. A computer program (e.g., an "expert" system) is to be developed to help the technician diagnose potential problems with such circuits. After consultations with numerous engineers and techni-

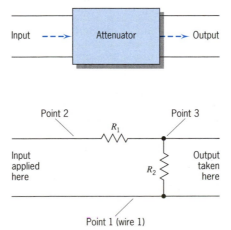

FIGURE 10.9   The attenuator circuit to be maintained with the aid of an expert system.

cians, the expert system designer can make the following observations regarding the rules that real experts apply to this simple circuit to determine if it is functioning properly:

1. It is best to isolate the attenuator from any other circuitry in order to determine proper operation.

2. A known voltage should be applied to the input terminals.

3. If the output voltage is "reasonably" close to

$$\text{ATTENUATION\_FACTOR} * \text{INPUT\_VOLTAGE}$$

we can conclude that the attenuator is operating properly.

4. If the output is 0, it is very likely that either R_1 is open (infinite) or R_2 is shorted (0 ohms); both conditions can exist simultaneously. It is also possible that both R_1 and R_2 are open.

5. If the value of the output voltage is equal to or "close to" the value of the input voltage, then there is a strong possibility that R_1 is shorted or R_2 is open, or both.

6. If the value of the output voltage has an undefined value (for example, the meter has a changing reading), it is likely that both R_1 and R_2 are open. It is also possible that the meter is malfunctioning.

7. If the value of the input signal cannot be set from the energy supply, it is very likely that both R_1 and R_2 are shorted.

8. If the diagnosis is not correct, then the problem is not obvious, and the cause is unknown at the time of the test.

Items 3 through 8 can be converted to rules of the form described above ($p \rightarrow q$). Additional rules can be appended or removed, or existing rules can be modified, as experience is gained with a particular expert system. The rules will be stored in a DB file named "rulebase." The data structure for a rule will consist of a record type named "rule." Three fields are included in each rule record: an integer field with the number of the rule; a character field representing the first part (the presumption p) of the rule; and a second character field that contains the rule's conclusion (q). One example of this (corresponding to 4 above) is

rule_number: 01

presumption (p): The attenuation factor is very low signifying a malfunction; this is specified as "Atten < Amin."

conclusion (q): $R1$ is open, $R2$ is shorted, or both conditions exist.

A pseudocode representation of the program follows.

```
program expert_system
{Prompt user for initial instructions}
{Ask user to enter measured values}
{Determine attenuation_factor}
{Make judgement about attenuation_factor}
{open communication to DB file "rulebase"}
while (record <> EOF)
        {read a rule_record}
        If (rule_record presumption (p of rule) is satisfied by
           attenuation_factor)
              then
```

```
                    {print conclusion}
        end if
        {Ask user to verify conclusion}
        {Retain answer}
end while;
if (no solution found)
        then
                {print acknowledgement of failure}
else if (too many conclusions found)
        then
                {print confusion}
else if (results confirmed)
        then
                {print acknowledgement}
end if
end program expert_system
```

In general, more than one rule may be applicable when the DB is searched. Sometimes rules lead to conflicting conclusions, but on other occasions the results may be consistent. The complete rule base for the example is shown in Fig. 10.10. This file can be generated in a variety of ways—for example, develop a program similar to the one described to maintain the file for chemicals (including facilities for adding, deleting, and editing records); or use an editor program similar to the one described in Chapter 2 to carry out maintenance procedures. (The second approach was used in this instance.) Because of the format used for each field, the presumption and conclusion of each rule appear to "run together," but the computer can readily distinguish these as described in the program.

```
01      Atten < AminR1 may be open or R2 may be shorted or both.
02      Atten < AminBoth R1 and R2 may be open.
03      Atten < AmaxR1 may be shorted or R2 may be open or both.
04  Output undefined.Both R1, R2 open; possible meter malfunction.
05 Can't adjust input.Both R1, R2 shorted; possible meter malfunction.
```

FIGURE 10.10   The DB used for an expert system to diagnose problems in an electrical attenuator network.

The FORTRAN 90 source code follows.

```
    PROGRAM EXPERT_SYSTEM
! THIS IS AN EXAMPLE OF AN EXPERT SYSTEM WHICH TROUBLESHOOTS
! A SIMPLE ELECTRICAL NETWORK—AN ATTENUATOR CIRCUIT
!
! DECLARATIONS
!
    TYPE RULE
        INTEGER :: RULE_NUMBER
        CHARACTER (LEN = 20) :: P
        CHARACTER (LEN = 50) :: Q
    END TYPE RULE
!
    TYPE(RULE) :: TEST_RULE
    CHARACTER (LEN = 1) :: ANSWER
```

```
        REAL :: INPUT_VOLTAGE, OUTPUT_VOLTAGE
        REAL :: ATTENUATION_FACTOR,ATTEN_THEORETICAL
        REAL :: R1,R2
        REAL,PARAMETER :: UPPER_LIMIT = 1.0
        REAL,PARAMETER :: LOWER_LIMIT = 0.0
        CHARACTER (LEN = 20) :: JUDGEMENT
        INTEGER,PARAMETER :: END_OF_FILE = -1
        INTEGER :: IOS
        INTEGER :: NUMBER_OF_RULES_FIRED,NUMBER_OF_CONFIRMATIONS
  !
  ! START OF THE MAIN PROGRAM
  !
  ! INITIAL INSTRUCTIONS TO THE USER
        PRINT"(A)",                                        &
        "    TO BEGIN DEBUGGING THE ATTENUATOR YOU SHOULD FIRST", &
        "    REMOVE IT FROM THE SYSTEM AND MEASURE THE SIGNAL",  &
        "    AT THE INPUT. TO MEASURE A SIGNAL, PLACE THE",  &
        "    REFERENCE LEAD OF THE METER OR OSCILLOSCOPE ON POINT",  &
        "    1 (GROUND TERMINAL). NEXT, PLACE THE MEASUREMENT",  &
        "    LEAD ON POINT 2."
        WRITE (*,"(A)",ADVANCE="NO")                        &
        "    PLEASE REPORT YOUR MEASUREMENT:"
        READ (*,"(F5.2)") INPUT_VOLTAGE
        PRINT "(A)",                          &
        "    NOW, PLACE MEASUREMENT LEAD ON OUTPUT (POINT 3)"
        WRITE (*,"(A)",ADVANCE="NO")                  &
        "    AND REPORT YOUR MEASUREMENT:"
        READ (*,"(F5.2)") OUTPUT_VOLTAGE
  ! ASK FOR VALUES FOR R1 AND R2
        WRITE (*,"(A)",ADVANCE="NO")                  &
           "PLEASE ENTER A VALUE FOR R1;"
        READ (*,"(F11.3)") R1
        WRITE (*,"(A)",ADVANCE="NO")                  &
           "PLEASE ENTER A VALUE FOR R2:"
        READ (*,"(F11.3)") R2
  ! CALCULATE THEORETICAL ATTENUATION FACTOR
        ATTEN_THEORETICAL = R2/(R1+R2)
  ! COMPUTE ACTUAL ATTENUATION FACTOR
        ATTENUATION_FACTOR = OUTPUT_VOLTAGE/INPUT_VOLTAGE
  ! MAKE JUDGEMENT ABOUT ATTENUATION_FACTOR
        IF (INPUT_VOLTAGE == -1.0) THEN
           JUDGEMENT = " CAN'T ADJUST INPUT."
        ELSE IF (OUTPUT_VOLTAGE >= 100.0) THEN
           JUDGEMENT = " OUTPUT UNDEFINED."
        ELSE IF ((ATTENUATION_FACTOR <= LOWER_LIMIT) .AND.    &
           (ATTENUATION_FACTOR > -1.0)) THEN
           JUDGEMENT = "     ATTEN < AMIN"
        ELSE IF (ATTENUATION_FACTOR >= UPPER_LIMIT) THEN
           JUDGEMENT = "     ATTEN > AMAX"
        ELSE IF ((ATTENUATION_FACTOR > 1.2*ATTEN_THEORETICAL).OR.    &
           (ATTENUATION_FACTOR < 0.8*ATTEN_THEORETICAL)) THEN
           JUDGEMENT =" OUT OF TOLERANCE."
        ELSE
           JUDGEMENT = " ATTENUATION IS O.K."
        END IF
```

```
          PRINT "(A)",JUDGEMENT
! OPEN FILE "RULEBASE"
          OPEN (2,FILE = "B:RULEBASE",ACCESS="SEQUENTIAL",        &
              STATUS="OLD",POSITION="REWIND")
! START OF DO LOOP WHICH: READS RULEBASE FILE; FINDS MATCHING
!     RULE,
! IF POSSIBLE; ASKS USER FOR CONFIRMATION; PRINTS APPROPRIATE
! MESSAGES.
          NUMBER_OF_RULES_FIRED = 0
          NUMBER_OF_CONFIRMATIONS = 0
          DO
          READ(2,"(I2,A,A)",IOSTAT=IOS)                &
              TEST_RULE % RULE_NUMBER,                  &
              TEST_RULE % P,                   &
              TEST_RULE % Q
          IF(IOS == END_OF FILE) EXIT
          IF(TEST_RULE % P == JUDGEMENT) THEN
              PRINT "(T10,A,I2,A)","RULE NUMBER",        &
                  TEST_RULE % RULE_NUMBER, " STATES THAT IF"
              PRINT"(T10,A,A,/,T10,A)", TEST_RULE % P, " THEN ",    &
                  TEST_RULE % Q
              PRINT "(T10,A,)","PLEASE CHECK THE INDICATIONS."
              NUMBER_OF_RULES_FIRED = NUMBER_OF_RULES_FIRED + 1
              WRITE (*,"(T10,A)",ADVANCE="NO")
                  "DO YOU CONFIRM THE FINDINGS (Y OR N)?"
              READ "(A)", ANSWER
              IF (ANSWER == 'Y') THEN
               NUMBER_OF_CONFIRMATIONS = NUMBER_OF_CONFIRMATIONS + 1
              END IF
          END IF
          END DO
! MAINTENANCE_GENIE SUMMARIZES RESULTS:
          IF (NUMBER_OF_RULES_FIRED == 0 .OR.        &
              (NUMBER_OF_RULES_FIRED == 1 .AND.        &
              NUMBER_OF_CONFIRMATIONS == 0)) THEN
            PRINT "(T10,A0)",                &
            "THIS ONE HAS ME STUMPED; GET YOURSELF A REAL EXPERT."
          ELSE IF (NUMBER_OF_RULES_FIRED >= 1 .AND.      &
              NUMBER_OF_CONFIRMATIONS == 1) THEN
            PRINT "(T10,A)",                &
            "THE MAINTENANCE GENIE IS RIGHT AGAIN; GLAD TO HAVE
                HELPED."
          ELSE IF (NUMBER_OF_RULES_FIRED > 1 .AND.        &
              NUMBER_OF_CONFIRMATIONS > 1) THEN
            PRINT "(T10,A)",                    &
             "WE SEEM TO BE CONFUSED; FURTHER CHECKING NEEDED."
          END IF
          CLOSE (2)
          END PROGRAM EXPERT_SYSTEM
```

Important characteristics of the program to note include the following:

- A derived data type, namely, RULE, is created to support the data structure of each record in the (rule) DB. (Derived data types are discussed in Chapter 3.)

- Two parameters are used to represent the upper and lower limits of the attenuation factor. When the measured attenuation is outside these limits, then the network is defined as exhibiting a malfunction. Parameter statements are useful because such limits can be readily changed without having to perform extensive editing in the body of the program.

- Two variables are defined to keep track of how well the expert system functions; these variables are NUMBER_OF_RULES_FIRED and NUMBER_OF_CON-FIRMATIONS. The meanings, respectively, are: the number of rules in the DB for which the presumption agrees with the computer's initial judgement about the attenuation factor, and the number of times the user confirms the conclusions. These variables will be set equal to 0 before the records are examined. They will be used to draw conclusions about the expert system's results.

- The program's logic can be readily followed by referring to the pseudocode as well as the comments within the source code.

The following table (Table 10.5) provides the logic for the number of rules that are fired and the number of confirmations observed.

Two complete interactive user dialogues are shown in Fig. 10.11. In Fig. 10.11a the user enters measurements of 1 for input and 0 for output. This triggers rules 1 and 2, both of which correspond to the judgement that Atten < Amin but do so for different reasons. Both signify malfunctions of the attenuator network. The user confirms the first result (R_1 open or R_2 shorted, or both) by responding with "Y" to the prompt. The user rejects the second conclusion that both R_1 and R_2 are open.

The other rules in the DB do not fire; consequently, once the entire file has been searched, the number_of_rules fired is 2, while the number_of_confirmations is 1. The table above indicates that this is equivalent to a successful diagnosis, and the computer responds with a "user-friendly" comment about the skill of the "Maintenance Genie." Figure 10.11b is a second example in which both the input and output read the same value, indicating a possible malfunction. In this case only one rule of the DB is invoked, and again the (simulated) malfunction is correctly identified.

Several logical omissions in the program can be observed:

- There is no judgement within the program which would correspond to rules 04 or 05.

- In addition, there is no provision for an attenuator in which the resistors are neither open nor shorted but have a value that is not appropriate. In other words, the attenuation factor is not 0 or 1 but some value not intended by the designer because an improper resistor has been used for either $R1$, $R2$, or both.

- It is possible that a resistor has not failed; rather, wire 1, shown in Fig. 10.9 is open. Symptoms for this condition might be observed, but the rule of the DB includes no provision for this case.

Table 10.5 Summary of Conclusions for Expert System

Number_of_Rules_Fired	Number_of_Confirmations	Conclusion
1	0	Computer is unable to draw conclusions.
0	NA	Computer is unable to draw conclusions.
>= 1	1	Successful diagnosis.
>1	>1	Computer has drawn conflicting conclusions.

```
To begin debugging the attenuator you should first
remove it from the system and measure the signal
at the input. To measure a signal, place the ref-
erence lead of the meter or oscilloscope on point
1 (ground terminal). Next, place the measurement
lead on point 2.
Please report your measurement: 1.0
Now, place measurement lead on output (point 3)
and report your measurement: 0.0
   rule number 1 states that if
         Atten < Amin then
   R1 may be open or R2 may be shorted or both.
   Please check the indications.
   Do you confirm the findings (Y or N)? Y
   rule number 2 states that if
         Atten < Amin then
  R1 and R2 may be open.
  Please check the indications.
  Do you confirm the findings (Y or N)? N
  The Maintenance Genie is right again; glad to have helped.
```

(*a*)

```
To begin debugging the attenuator you should first
remove it from the system and measure the signal
at the input. To measure a signal, place the ref-
erence lead of the meter or oscilloscope on point
1 (ground terminal). Next, place the measurement
lead on point 2.
Please report your measurement: 1.0
Now, place measurement lead on output (point 3)
and report your measurement: 1.0
   rule number 3 states that if
         Atten > Amax
   R1 may be shorted or R2 may be open or both.
   Please check the indications.
   Do you confirm the findings (Y or N)? Y
   The Maintenance Genie is right again; glad to have helped.
```

(*b*)

FIGURE 10.11   Monitor display for expert system example. (a) Case for 0 output; (b)Case for same output as input.

Such additions and/or modifications to the rule base may result from experience with the expert system.

10.5 DIFFERENTIAL EQUATIONS

Digital computer solutions of mathematical equations are needed in order to predict or understand how a *system* behaves. The term *system* designates a collection of objects with well-defined relations or interactions between the objects. For example, the solar system is a system in these circumstances; the sun and planets are the objects, and the gravitational forces define the interactions. Many additional examples of systems have been provided throughout this text. A *model* includes a mathematical or logical description of the system which can be realized by writing a FORTRAN 90 program incorporating the relations between the structural objects in the form of ASSIGNMENT and CONTROL statements. The examples presented here focus on problems that benefit from computer solution of differential equations and that are very important for describing dynamic system performance.

EXAMPLE 10.5 Computer Solution of a First-Order Differential Equation (DE): Euler Method

Because the computer requires a small but finite time to perform calculations, and because it has finite resolution, it is considered to be a *discrete* machine. Although differential equations (DEs) can be continuous in time (or any other independent variable), the computer can only *approximate* solutions because it is a discrete device. The approximate solution closely approaches the continuous solution if small increments are used. Many computer algorithms for solving DEs are based on linear approximations. One of these methods is called *Euler's method*. (See Fig. 10.12.)

Suppose that we have a first-order differential equation as follows:

$$\frac{dx}{dt} + Ax = B$$

or

$$\frac{dx}{dt} = B - Ax = f(x,t)$$

where A, B may either be constant or functions of x and/or t, in which case the solution to the DE would be nonlinear. Next, consider that we know some initial

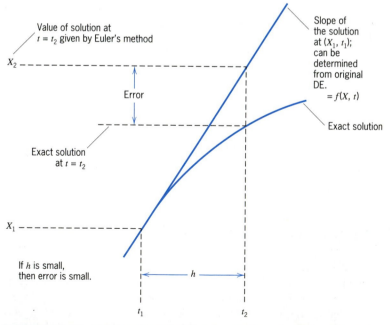

FIGURE 10.12   Euler's method for the solution of a first-order differential equation.

point (t_1, x_1) on the curve of the solution. We can now find a new point on the solution curve (t_2, x_2) by proceeding as follows.

$$x_2 = x_1 + hf(x,t)$$

and

$$t_2 = t_1 + h$$

The parameter h is called the step size. The slope of the line (dx/dt) is assumed to be constant over the entire interval h. These equations provide a solution for the DE at t_2.

Each subsequent value of y depends on the previous value of t and x, and the slope at the previous point. The solution to a DE by the Euler method is a series of straight-line segments. Although the Euler solution diverges from the exact solution, the error may be minimized by choosing a step size, h, that is small. (In order to determine whether a particular value of h is sufficiently small, it must be decreased and the new solution compared with the previous solution; such a test increases computing time.)

The sequence of steps in the Euler method (sometimes called the *simple marching method*) is summarized as follows.

$$x_{n+1} = x_n + h(B_n - A_n x_n) \tag{1}$$
$$x_{n+1} = (1 - hA_n)x_n + hB_n \tag{2}$$
$$x_{new} = (1 - hA_{old})x_{old} + hB_{old} \tag{3}$$

Equation (3) provides the basis for a computer program in which *old* represents the values at $t = t_n$ and *new* represents the values at $t = t_{n+1}$. Equation (3) is derived from Eq. (2) by replacing the subscript n by *old* and the subscript $n+1$ by *new*. A pseudocode description of the iterative process is

```
do
{Evaluate A, B}
{Calculate a new value of dx/dt from (dx/dt)new = B - Axold}
{Calculate a new value of x from xnew = xold + h(dx/dt)new}
end do
```

The first-order DE to be solved by computer using the Euler method is

$$\frac{dx}{dt} + x = 1$$

with $x = 0$ at $t = 0$

Make the following substitutions into Eq. (3) above:

$$A = 1 \quad \text{and} \quad B = 1$$
$$(dx/dt) = 1 - x$$
$$x_{n+1} = (1 - h)x_n + h$$

If h is chosen to be 0.1, this last equation becomes

$$x_{n+1} = 0.9\, x_n + 0.1$$

and is the Euler solution to the original differential equation. The FORTRAN 90 source code for solving this equation is shown below. Note that the exact solution to the original DE is

$$x = 1 - e^{-t}$$

Within the program, exact values are also computed as well as the error resulting from the specified step size. These are summarized in the results.

```
      PROGRAM EULER_METHOD
! THIS PROGRAM SOLVES THE DIFFERENTIAL EQUATION (DX/DT) + X = 1
! WITH INITIAL CONDITIONS (X=0 AT T=0). IT USES THE EULER OR
! "MARCHING METHOD."
! THE VARIABLES ARE DEFINED:
! T = THE INDEPENDENT VARIABLE (TIME).
! X = THE DEPENDENT VARIABLE
! H = STEP SIZE
! ERROR = THE DIFFERENCE BETWEEN THE APPROXIMATE AND EXACT ANSWERS
! THE DISCRETE EULER EQUATION FOR THIS DE IS X(N+1) = 0.9*X(N) + H
! THE STEP H MAY BE VARIED AND THE ERROR STUDIED. IN THIS CASE THE
! STEP SIZE IS CHOSEN TO BE 0.1 AND T VARIES FROM 0 to 1.5. THE
! EXACT ANSWER IS X = 1 - EXP(-T)
!
! FORMAL DECLARATIONS
!
      IMPLICIT NONE
      REAL,DIMENSION(0:15) :: X,EXACT,ERROR,T
      INTEGER :: I,N
      INTEGER,PARAMETER :: LAST = 15
      REAL,PARAMETER :: H = 0.1
! INITIALIZE VALUES
      X(0) = 0.0
      EXACT(0) = 0.0
      ERROR(0) = 0.0
! FILL VALUES FOR T
      DO N = 0,LAST
          T(N) = 0.1*REAL(N)
      END DO
! COMPUTE EULER APPROXIMATIONS
      DO N = 1,LAST
          X(N) = (1.0-H)*X(N-1) + H
      END DO
! COMPUTE EXACT VALUES
      DO N = 0,LAST
          EXACT (N) = 1.0 - EXP(-T(N))
      END DO
! COMPUTE THE ERROR
      DO I = 1,LAST
          ERROR(I) = (EXACT(I) - X(I))/EXACT(I)
      END DO
! DISPLAY THE RESULTS
      WRITE (*,'(T10,A,T20,A,T35,A,T56,A)')              &
          'T'                                       &
          'X=1-EXP(-T)',                              &
          'X(N+1)=0.X*(N)+1',                         &
          'ERROR'
      WRITE (*,'(A)')                                   &
       '======================================================'
      DO I = 0,LAST
          WRITE(*,'(T10,F5.2,T20,F10.6,T35,F10.6,T56,F6.3)') &
```

```
        T(I),EXACT(I),X(I),ERROR(I)
    END DO
    END PROGRAM EULER_METHOD
```

The results are

T	$X = 1 - \text{EXP}(-T)$	$X(N + 1) = 0.9X(N) + 1$	ERROR
0.00	0.000000	0.000000	0.000
0.10	0.095162	0.100000	−0.050
0.20	0.181269	0.190000	−0.048
0.30	0.259181	0.271000	−0.045
0.40	0.329679	0.343900	−0.043
0.50	0.393469	0.409509	−0.040
0.60	0.451188	0.468558	−0.038
0.70	0.503414	0.521703	−0.036
0.80	0.550671	0.569532	−0.034
0.90	0.593430	0.612579	−0.032
1.00	0.632120	0.651321	−0.030
1.10	0.667128	0.686189	−0.028
1.20	0.698805	0.717570	−0.026
1.30	0.727468	0.745813	−0.025
1.40	0.753403	0.771232	−0.023
1.50	0.776869	0.794108	−0.022

EXAMPLE 10.6 Runge-Kutta Solutions

Analysis of dynamic systems is greatly improved (with respect to error) by the use of the *Runge-Kutta* (R-K) solution of DEs. The proof of this method will not be discussed; rather, the method will be described with an example to demonstrate its use.

We want to solve

$$\frac{dx}{dt} + Ax = B$$

with an appropriate boundary (initial) condition. The coefficients A and B may be functions of x and t. First, rewrite the equation as

$$f(t, x) = \frac{dx}{dt} = B - Ax$$

A set of four Runge-Kutta (R-K) equations are formed from $f(t, x)$ as follows.

$$Q_1 = hf(t_n, x_n)$$
$$Q_2 = hf\left(t_n + \frac{h}{2}, x_n + \frac{Q_1}{2}\right)$$
$$Q_3 = hf\left(t_n + \frac{h}{2}, x_n + \frac{Q_2}{2}\right)$$
$$Q_4 = hf(t_n + h, x_n + Q_3)$$

Once these four functions (Q_1, Q_2, Q_3, and Q_4) have been evaluated, the solution at interval $(n + 1)$ can be computed from the solution at n from the following weighted average:

$$x_{n+1} = x_n + \frac{1}{6}(Q_1 + 2Q_2 + 2Q_3 + Q_4)$$

A system described by a DE will produce a nonlinear result when one or more of the coefficients in the equation depends on the independent or dependent variables. In one case this can be represented as follows:

$$\frac{dx}{dt} + A(x,\,t)x(t) = B(x,\,t)$$

(with an associated initial condition). A specific example of this can be seen in Fig. 10.13, which shows a simple electric network consisting of a resistor and an inductor. In the absence of nonlinear effects, the DE governing the current that flows in the circuit is given by

$$L\frac{di}{dt} + iR = E$$

after the switch is closed and $i = 0$ at $t = 0$.

However, resistance depends not only on the resistive material but also on the temperature of that material. As current flows through the resistive material, it heats the material and thus changes its resistance. As a result, the resistance R is a function of the dependent variable i. For this example, assume that R varies with i according to the following relationship:

$$R = (A + Bi^2)$$

and, after substitution into the original DE, the equation that governs this situation is

$$\frac{di}{dt} + \frac{B}{L}i^3 + \frac{A}{L}i = \frac{E}{L}$$

and

$$i = 0 \quad \text{at} \quad t = 0$$

Nonlinear DEs are often difficult to solve analytically, but, using the R-K method, it is possible to obtain a solution. The FORTRAN 90 program shown below was used to find the response of the current in this network as a function of time after the switch is closed.

The parametric values for the network are chosen as follows:

$$E = 200 \text{ volts}$$
$$L = 3 \text{ henries}$$
$$A = 100 \text{ ohms}$$
$$B = 50 \text{ ohms/amp}^2$$

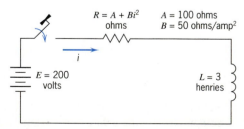

FIGURE 10.13   A nonlinear circuit to be analyzed by the Runge-Kutta method.

This is a straightforward application of the R-K method as previously described with

$$f(i, t) = \frac{di}{dt} = \frac{E}{L} = \frac{B}{L}i^3 - \frac{A}{L}i$$

```
      PROGRAM NON_LINEAR
! USING THE R-K METHOD, THE DYNAMIC CIRCUIT RESPONSE OF A
! NONLINEAR
! NETWORK MAY BE COMPUTED.
!
! DECLARATIONS
!
      IMPLICIT NONE
      REAL, PARAMETER :: STEP_SIZE = .002
      REAL, DIMENSION (0:25) :: CURRENT, TIME
      REAL :: Q1,Q2,Q3,Q4
      INTEGER, PARAMETER :: LAST = 25
      INTEGER :: I !INDEX FOR VARIOUS DO LOOPS
      REAL,PARAMETER :: E=200.0          !VOLTS
      REAL,PARAMETER :: L = 3.0          !HENRIES
      REAL,PARAMETER :: A = 100.0        !OHMS

      REAL,PARAMETER :: B = 50.0            !OHMS/AMP**2
      OPEN(2,FILE='B:NONLINR.DAT',STATUS='UNKNOWN',POSITION='REWIND')
! INITIALIZE VALUES
      CURRENT(0) = 0.0
! FILL VALUES FOR THE INDEPENDENT VARIABLE T
      DO I = 0, LAST
          TIME(I) = STEP_SIZE*REAL(I)
      END DO
! COMPUTE R-K SOLUTION TO THE NONLINEAR DE
      DO I = 1,LAST
        Q1 = STEP_SIZE*                          &
          (E/L-(B/L)*(CURRENT(I-1)**3)-(A/L)*(CURRENT(I-1)))
        Q2 = STEP_SIZE*                          &
          (E/L-(B/L)*(CURRENT(I-1)**3)-(A/L)*(CURRENT(I-))+Q1/2.0)
        Q3 = STEP_SIZE*                          &
          (E/L-(B/L)*(CURRENT(I-1)**3)-(A/L)*(CURRENT(I-))+Q2.0)
        Q4 = STEP_SIZE*                          &
          (E/L-(B/L)*(CURRENT(I-1)**3)-(A/L)*(CURRENT(I-1))+Q3)
! COMPUTE (ESTIMATE) THE SOLUTION AT THE NEXT ITERATION POINT BY
! CALCULATING A WEIGHTED AVERAGE OF Q1, Q2, Q3, AND Q4
        CURRENT(I) =                             &
          CURRENT(I-1)+(1.0/6.0)*(Q1+2.0*Q2+2.0*Q3+Q4)
      END DO
! DISPLAY THE RESULTS
      DO I = 0,LAST
          WRITE(2,'(T10,F5.2,T20,F10.6)')        &
          TIME(I),CURRENT(I)
      END DO
      CLOSE(2)
      END PROGRAM NON_LINEAR
```

The results are graphed (see Fig. 10.14) using the high-resolution techniques previously described. Also shown on the graph is the dynamic response when the resistor is consid-

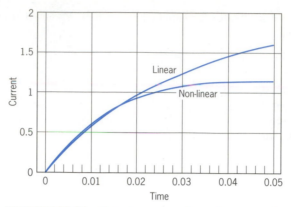

FIGURE 10.14 Dynamic response of a nonlinear network.

ered to be constant; this condition is the linear case. Solution of nonlinear problems such as the one just described is greatly eased by the power of the R-K method, the digital computer, and the FORTRAN 90 programming language.

PROBLEMS

10.1 Modify program HVAC to include a marker that indicates when the heating system is turned on. For convenience, this marker can be located at −15 on the strip chart.

10.2 Simulate the *proportional control* heating system described in Example 10.1.

10.3 Simulate the *bang-bang* environmental control system described in Example 10.1.

10.4 Discuss the results of the three environmental control systems. Your discussion should concentrate on those factors that will help to decide which system to install.

10.5 Modify the program HVAC so that it is used to simulate an environment to be cooled rather than heated. Test the simulation for an *on-off* control algorithm.

10.6 In program QUEUE, the time of arrival of customers is a random event that is exponentially distributed with a mean of 1 minute. Departure events are similarly distributed but have a mean time of 0.5 minute. Rerun the program but alter subroutine GET_A_TIME, so that arrival times are uniformly distributed (equally likely) between 0 minute and 2 minutes and departure events are uniformly distributed between 0 and 1 minute. (The mean customer interarrival time remains 1 minute, and the mean service time remains at 0.5 minute as in program QUEUE.) Compare the uniformly distributed analysis to the exponentially distributed analysis.

10.7 Modify program CHEM_DB in the following way: Add an option—call it (4)—with the prompt message "Return to OS." If the user chooses this option, terminate the program. Otherwise, after successful execution of any of the other options, redisplay the menu in order to permit a user to perform repeated additions, deletions, or edit operations on the DB file.

10.8 **(a)** Write a program that sorts the records in the file CHEMS according to the following pseudocode algorithm:

```
program sort_chems
{open file "chems"; sequential,read}
{read table of 8 chemicals (Section 10.3) into an array of
    records of type test}
do I = 1,8
{scan the list for the toxin with the (next) smallest
    "value"}
{interchange that toxin and all its parameters with the one
    presently at the top of the
array using a pointer or index to identify the position}
{increment the pointer or index to the top of the array}
end do
end program sort_chems
```

Notes: In FORTRAN 90, character strings can be compared and such comparison is based on the collating (ordering) sequence of the characters. For example, a logical term such as 'AA' < 'AAA' will produce the logical result .true.. The chemicals in the list are readily compared using the relational operators previously described. Make use of temporary locations to interchange entities within a common list. Generically, interchange is represented as follows (with ← representing assignment or a data transfer operation):

temp register ← source object
source object ← destination object
destination ← temp register

(b) As described in (a), the algorithm is limited to the eight toxins in the file. Describe how you would modify the data structure so that a sorting program could be arranged to handle any number of records.

10.9 Draw a flow diagram for program EXPERT_SYSTEM discussed in Sec. 10.4.

10.10 Consider the expert system DB. Does the rule base provide alternatives (rules) for all possible conditions of the resistors R_1 and R_2? Explain your answer fully.

10.11 Add a provision in the expert system for a case in which the attenuation factor is outside a 20 percent tolerance limit and which would suggest that one or both of the resistors have the wrong value.

10.12 Add a provision in the expert system for a case in which the ground wire—wire 1 in Fig. 10.9—is open.

10.13 Add judgements in the expert system program to account for rules 04 and 05 in the rule DB.

10.14 Study the effect of the step size h on the solution to the DE.

$$\frac{dx}{dt} + x = 1$$
$$\text{with} \quad x = 0 \quad \text{at} \quad t = 0$$

using the Euler method as described in Sec. 10.5. Let t vary between 0 and 1.5. Compute the average error for each value of h and plot the error versus the step size. Use the step sizes of $0.01, 0.03, 0.05, 0.075$, and 0.1. (Use high-resolution graphing if possible.)

10.15   The Euler method for solving DEs may be summarized as follows.

• Given a DE

$$\frac{dy}{dx} = f(x, y)$$

and an initial condition (e.g., $y = 0$ when $x = 0$),

• Knowing the initial condition, we can solve for y at other values of x according to the following (iterative) equations.

$$y_2 = y_1 + hf(x_1, y_1)$$
$$x_2 = x_1 + h$$

Solve the following DE:

$$\frac{dy}{dx} = \frac{2y}{x+1} + \frac{x}{x+1}$$

$$\text{with} \quad x_1 = 0, \qquad y_1 = 0$$

(a)   Solve this equation by the Euler method using a calculator. (Solve for $y_1, y_2,$ y_3, and y_4 using a value of $h = 0.02$.)

(b)   Write a FORTRAN 90 program to solve this problem. Calculate the results from $x = 0$ to $x = 0.06$ with step size $= 0.02$. Compare the Euler solution to the exact solution of this DE:

$$y = 0.5(x + 1)^2 - x - 0.5$$

and to the results shown in part (a).

Glossary

Algorithm	A sequence of actions that accomplishes a task.
Append	Addition of information to the end of an existing file.
Application program	A program intended for some purpose other than management of the computer.
Argument	A variable to which either a logical or a numerical value may be assigned.
Array	An entity with the dimension attribute. (See also Dimension.)
ASCII	An acronym for the American Standard Code for Information Interchange; used by computers to represent characters.
Attribute	A characteristic of a data type or data structure; a word that describes the way a variable is treated.
Bit	A binary digit (0 or 1).
Branching	Unless a control construct is encountered, program statements are executed in the order in which they appear in a program unit. An example:

```
IF( X>Y ) GO TO 200
     A = 37.5 + C
```

Here, if $X<Y$, then the statement $A = 37.5 + C$ will be executed. However, if $X > Y$, then the program will branch to the statement associated with the label 200.

Byte	A set of 8 bits.
Character	A letter, number, or symbol such as ! or *.
Code	The program statements.
Comment statement	A nonexecutable statement in a program that explains the logic or otherwise helps a reader to understand the program's statements.
Compiler	A program that translates a program written in a high-level language into a form that can be executed by the computer.

Computer	A machine that can interact with the external world, perform various calculations, and store the results, partial results, as well as the sequence of operations to be performed.
Concatenation	An operation consisting of the sequential combination of two or more strings.
Constant	A value that does not change during program execution.
Construct	A sequence of statements starting with DO, IF, or CASE and ending with an appropriate terminating statement. For example, for DO, the terminating statement is END DO.
Counter	A numeric variable that is periodically incremented during execution of the program. Often it is used to keep track of the number of iterations of a loop.
Cursor	A character that appears on the monitor and that indicates where the next character entered from the keyboard will appear.
Data	The information acted upon by a program.
Declaration	A nonexecutable statement that specifies the attributes of a program element. For example, INTEGER::LIST. Another example is EXTERNAL MULMATRIX.
Dimension	An attribute of an array. An array must be declared by putting the dimension attribute in a TYPE statement followed by a range of subscripts. For example: `REAL, DIMENSION(-1,11):: A,B` Thus, A(−1),B(−1),A(0),B(0),A(1),B(1), . . . , A(10),B(10),A(11),B(11) are members of the array.
Direct access file	A file organized so that any record may be accessed for reading or writing without processing all the preceding records.
Disk operating system	A collection of programs that manage computer files.
Double precision number	A numeric variable with an increased resolution. The number of active digits is installation dependent.
DO-WHILE loop	A programming control structure that supports repeated execution of a group of statements.
Dummy argument	The name by which arguments are specified in the name of the subroutine or function subprogram and are known within the subroutine or function subprogram. For example: FUNCTION FACT (M). The main program might call FACT as follows: ANS = FACT (K). The value of K will be transmitted to the dummy argument M.
Edit	The process of appending, deleting, or otherwise modifying the contents of a file. Normally, this is accomplished with the aid of an Editor applications program.
Endless loop	A LOOP control structure with no terminating condition or for which the terminating condition never occurs.
Entity	In general, a thing that has individual existence. In FORTRAN 90 a thing such as a variable, a constant, a subprogram, a type, a construct, and so on.
Executable	An adjective used with FORTRAN statements or constructs. It means that the statement or construct is a request to perform a specific task. Examples of executable statements: `READ(*,*) X` `C = A + B` `IF(AMOUNT < 0) EXIT` A DECLARATION statement is an example of a nonexecutable statement. For example, REAL::KOUNT. Here, the declaration REAL specifies an attribute of the variable KOUNT. Another example: DIMENSION A(10,10) specifies the "shape" of an array.
File	A collection of data with a common name. The file consists of records that are, in turn, composed of fields.

Flag	A variable whose value signals the occurrence of some event. For example, a flag is used to terminate a sequence of operations or the existence of an unusual event (e.g., an attempt is made to divide by zero).
Flowchart	A graphic representation of program logic.
Function	A prewritten subroutine that performs an operation and returns a single value.
Hard copy	Output from a printer.
Hardware	The physical parts of a computer system.
Input	Data entered into a computer program.
Integer	A positive or negative whole number.
K	Stands for kilo, which corresponds to 10^3. When applied to the computer, it normally stands for 1024.
Label	A number with one to five digits which is used to identify a statement. Two statements in the same program unit may not have the same label. Some examples of labels:

      Example 1. 90 CONTINUE
      Example 2.   GO TO 100
                100 ALPHA = 2.0*PI

Lexical token	Basic units of the language; may consist of one or more characters. Labels, names, and operator symbols are tokens. Thus, $A + B = C$ contains the tokens $A, +, B, =$, and C. The variable names STUDENTS and COMPONENT are tokens.
Logic error	An error in the algorithm or logic of a program.
Loop	A section of code that is repeated.
Menu	A display of operations that a program can perform. The user may select an operation by striking a key or by making a mouse action.
Merge	A process that combines two or more files.
Module	A group of related code statements.
Monitor	A device that displays information to a user.
Nested loop	A Loop structure contained within another Loop structure.
Null string	An empty string (that contains no characters).
Numeric variable	A storage area in memory arranged to retain numbers.
Operator	A symbol that denotes a computation usually involving two operands. Examples of operators are *,/,**, + for numeric operands and .NOT., .AND., .OR. for logical operands.
Output	Results generated by a computer program.
Precision	The number of digits used to represent a numeric variable.
Procedure	Defined by a sequence of statements that expresses a computation which may be invoked as a subroutine or function during program execution.
Program	A logical sequence of operations to be performed by a computer in solving a problem or processing data. Also, the coded instructions and data for such a sequence.
Program unit	Includes one of the following:

    (a) main program
    (b) subprogram (subroutine or function)
    (c) module
    (d) block data

Prompt	A message displayed by a program which requests (data) input or some other operator action.
Pseudocode	A list of statements written in a form similar to a computer program but with less stringent rules of syntax.

Random access memory	The portion of computer memory in which all data can be accessed (for reading or writing purposes) in the same amount of time.
Real number	A number that includes a decimal component.
Recursive functions	A function that calls or invokes itself.
Reserved words	Words with special meaning to the FORTRAN 90 compiler.
Scoping unit	A portion of a program in which a name has a fixed meaning; for example, a type declaration or a subprogram.
Sequential file	A file in which records are stored in consecutive order and from which they must also be retrieved in the same order.
Soft copy	Program results that are displayed on the computer's monitor.
Source code	A form of the computer program prior to compilation.
String	A group of data composed of letters, numbers, and other symbols.

Appendix A

APPENDIX A
SUMMARY OF MS-DOS COMMANDS (PARTIAL)

COMMAND (mnemonic)	Purpose	Example
APPEND	Instructs DOS to search additional paths when looking for a file. (See PATH command for another command of this type.)	append=a:\experim.ent DOS will look in drive a: if it does not find the file experim.ent in the current directory.
ASSIGN	Redirects references from one drive to another.	assign a=c A reference to drive a: will be redirected to drive c:
ATTRIB	Allows a file to be marked for reading only (protected) or for archiving purposes.	attrib +r experim.ent Marks the file experim.ent for reading only; cannot be overwritten.
BACKUP	Allows user to make backup copies of disk files—creates an archive of the file(s) in question.	backup c:experim.ent a: Creates a backup version of the file experim.ent on drive a:
BUFFERS	DOS allocates memory space for disk/file transfers.	buffers=20 Some software applications packages require user to set aside disk buffers in memory.
CALL	A batch command that executes one batch file from within another.	call nextone The batchfile nextone will be executed; when completed, control returns to the batchfile that invoked nextone.

COMMAND (mnemonic)	Purpose	Example
CD (CHDIR)	Changes current directory or displays current directory's path.	cd a:\datadir Changes current directory to the directory designated datadir on drive a:
CHKDSK	Reports on status of directories and subdirectories on a disk.	chkdsk/f With the /f option, DOS will correct certain types of disk errors if they are encountered.
CLS	Clears screen and moves cursor to upper left corner of monitor.	cls
COMP	Compares contents of one file with those of another; reports mismatches.	comp file1.txt file2.txt
COPY	Copies an existing file; combines two or more into a single file; transfers data between peripheral devices and files.	copy c:file1.txt prn: Copies the file named file1.txt on drive c: to the printer (prn):—in other words, prints the contents of the file.
DATE	Displays current date; can be used to change the date.	date
DEL	Deletes (erases) one or more files from a disk—alternate form for erase.	del junk
DEVICE	Used to install a device driver; can only be used within a file called config.sys	device=mouse Adds the mouse driver.
DIR	Lists directory entries (some or all files and subdirectories).	dir/w Lists all files in multicolumn arrangement so that they fit on a single screen (with no scrolling).
DISCOMP	Compares the contents of two floppy diskettes.	diskcomp a: b: Compares diskettes in drives a: and b:; if a mismatch exists, the track and side where mismatches occur will be displayed.
DISKCOPY	Used to copy contents of one floppy diskette onto another.	diskcopy a: b: Copies one track at a time from a: to b:; all preexisting data on b: ("target diskette") will be overwritten.
ERASE	Erases one or more files from a disk.	erase c:\expdata\test Erases the file "test" in the root of the subdirectory named expdata.
FILES	Sets aside memory for handling files; can only be used in the file called config.sys.	files=20 Some applications programs/packages require the user to set aside space for 20 file handlers.
FIND	Searches for a given string of alphanumeric characters—a string—in a file or files.	find/n "sample" c:\expdata\test Locates any lines containing the text "sample" in the file named test in the subdirectory named "expdata."
FORMAT	Makes disks ready to work with DOS.	format a:/s/v Formats the disk (floppy) in drive a:, adds system files (/s option) which allows the floppy to "boot the system"; allows user to name the volume (/v option).

COMMAND (mnemonic)	Purpose	Example
GRAPHICS	Permits the user to print whatever is on the screen when the Shift key and the Prt Scrn key are depressed simultaneously.	graphics
KEYB	Loads a keyboard device driver that supports non-U.S. keyboards.	keybd fr Loads a driver for a French keyboard.
MEM	DOS will display memory is being used.	mem DOS will report how much memory is used and how much is available in the system
MKDIR	Creates a subdirectory.	mkdir c:\expdata\trials Creates a new subdirectory in the subdirectory named expdata; this subdirectory is named trials.
MODE	May perform any of the following: set mode of operation of parallel printer, color display adaptor, protocol for asynchronous communications port, and various (program) coding designations.	mode com1: 9600,e,8,1,, The asynchronous communications port com1: is set to communicate at 9600 (baud), with even parity (e), having 8 code bits per work, with 1 stop bit. The repeated comma instructs DOS not to retry communication when the line is busy (use "p" if retry is desired).
MORE	Outputs 23 lines of data at a time.	More < bigfile Allows one screenful of bigfile to be displayed at a time.
PATH	Instructs DOS as to the directories and subdirectories to search to find executable files.	path=c:\first;c:\second;c:\third DOS will first search subdirectory "first" in the c: drive, then subdirectory "second," and finally subdirectory "third."
PRINT	Prints a list of file(s).	print fileone filetwo file3 DOS will print the indicated files while concurrently peforming other tasks.
PROMPT	Sets the prompt that the user sees when DOS is ready to accept commands.	prompt pg This form of the DOS command will produce the current directory followed by the symbol >.
RECOVER	Recovers data from files or an entire disk that has bad sectors or a damaged file directory.	recover abadfile Only data in the undamaged sectors are recovered; this is a limited DOS facility with more powerful commercial products being available (PC-Tools, Norton Utilities, Mace Utilities).
RENAME	Renames a file.	rename new old The file "new" is renamed to "old."
REPLACE	Replaces or adds files.	replace a:source b: Replaces a file named "source" on drive b: with the file "source" on drive a:

COMMAND (mnemonic)	Purpose	Example
RESTORE	Restores one or more files from one disk to another.	restore a:backup1 Restores the file "backup1" on drive a: to current drive (normally c:) if it was stored with the backup command at some time in the past.
RMDIR	Deletes a subdirectory.	rmdir temp The subdirectory temp will be removed, but only after all files in the subdirectory have been erased.
TIME	Displays current time and allows user to change it if desired.	time
TREE	Displays directory paths.	tree a: /f All directories and subdirectories in drive a: will be listed; the /f option will also list the files.
TYPE	Displays the contents of a file on the screen.	type a:testresu.lts
VER	Displays the version of DOS that is installed on the system.	ver
VOL	Displays the name of the volume (disks) if one was assigned.	vol a:

Appendix B

APPENDIX B
SUMMARY OF MS-DOS EDIT KEY FUNCTIONS

Key	Purpose
← (on keypad)	Move cursor one position to the left.
→	Move cursor one position to the right.
↑	Move cursor one line up.
↓	Move cursor one line down.
^enter	Move cursor to beginning of next line of text.
End key	Move cursor to end of the current line of text.
Del[1]	Delete character to the left of the cursor.
^←[2]	Mover cursor one word to the left.
^→	Move cursor one word to the right.
PgUp	Move the cursor to the previous page of text.
PgDn	Move the cursor to the next page of text.
Alt	Activate the menu at the top of the screen.
Shft ←[3]	Select or highlight character to the left.
Shft →	Select or highlight character to the right.
Shft ^ ←	Select or highlight word to the left.
Shft ^ →	Select or highlight word to the right.
Shft ↓	Select or highlight current line of text.
Shft ↑	Select or highlight previous line of text.
Shft ^ Home	Select all text from present position to start of file.

Key	Purpose
Shft ^ End	Select all text from current position to end of file.
Ins	Change from insert mode to overwrite mode, or vice versa.
Shft Del	Delete selected text and move to clipboard (cut out text).
Shft Ins	Copy contents of clipboard to position indicated by the cursor (paste).
Del	Delete selected text.
^ Ins	Copy selected text to the clipboard (without erasing it).
^L or F3	Find next occurrence of indicated text.
^Q	Search for text.

[1]Del is the Delete key or Erase key sometimes indciated by ← on the key in the main keyboard area.
[2]^ is a symbol for the key marked Ctrl (Control key). Hold it down while striking the next key shown in the table; then release both.
[3]Shft is a symbol for the Shift key. Hold it down while striking the next key shown in the table; then release both.

Solutions to Selected Problems

Chapter 1

Problem 1.4

dir > prn:

Problem 1.5

A group of data with a common name.

Problem 1.8

(a) 8.41

(b) 856.29

(c) 6.81

(d) 1.768

(e) 124.0 (The difference of the first two numbers is precise to one decimal place, and the product of the last two numbers is good to three significant digits. The final answer is good to one decimal place.)

Problem 1.10

(a) $11011011 = 2^0+2^1+2^3+2^4+2^6 + 2^7 = 1+2+8+16+64+128 = 219$

(b) $10.11 = 2^1+2^{-1}+2^{-2} = 2+0.5+ 0.25 = 2.75$

Problem 1.12

$10011001 = 1001\ 1001 = 99(\text{hex}) = 9(16^1)+9(16^0) = 144+9 = 153$

Direct conversion is accomplished as follows:

$10011001 = 1+8+16+128 = 153$

This confirms the first method.

Chapter 2

Problem 2.3

(a) A simple program for calculating the square root is shown below. It includes three well-defined processes: prompt the user for the data; perform the calculations; and print the results.

```
      PROGRAM ROOT
! This program is shown without extensive comments
      REAL:: X,RESULT
! Start of the main program
! Prompt the user for the number and read his/her response
      PRINT *, ' This program finds the square root of the number    &
         that you &
      enter from the keyboard.'
      PRINT *, 'Please enter the number '
      READ *, X
! Calculate the square root
      RESULT = sqrt(x)
! Print the result
      PRINT *, 'The square root of ',X,' is ',RESULT
      END PROGRAM ROOT
```

Chapter 3

Problem 3.1

```
                  PROGRAM HEATVAL
            !     HEATING VALUE OF A SOLID FUEL, BTU/LB
                  IMPLICIT NONE
                  REAL:: HV,C,H,O,S
                  WRITE(*,*)'ENTER PER CENT SULPHUR'
                  READ(*,*)S
                  WRITE(*,*)'PER CENT SULPHUR  ',S
                  WRITE(*,*)'ENTER PER CENT HYDROGEN'
                  READ(*,*)H
                  WRITE(*,*)'PER CENT HYDROGEN  ', H
                  WRITE(*,*)'ENTER PER CENT OXYGEN'
                  READ(*,*)O
                  WRITE(*,*)'PER CENT OXYGEN  ',O
                  WRITE(*,*)'ENTER PER CENT CARBON'
                  READ(*,*)C
                  WRITE(*,*)'PER CENT CARBON  ',C
                  HV = 145.0*C + 620.0*(H - O/8.) + 40.*S
                  WRITE(*,*)'HEATING VALUE OF FUEL, BTU/LB',HV
                  END PROGRAM HEATVAL

            RUN

            PER CENT SULPHUR      0.8700000
            PER CENT HYDROGEN       5.1599998
            PER CENT OXYGEN      9.1899996
            PER CENT CARBON     74.5100021
            HEATING VALUE OF FUEL, BTU/LB   1.3325726E+04
```

Problem 3.3

```
      PROGRAM RADIATE
!     STEFAN-BOLTZMANN RADIATION LAW
      IMPLICIT NONE
      REAL:: EB,T
      WRITE(*,*)'ENTER TEMPERATURE IN DEGREES FAHRENHEIT'
      READ(*,*)T
      WRITE(*,*)'TEMPERATURE IN DEGREES FAHRENHEIT',T
      EB = 0.1714E-08*(T + 460.0)**4
      WRITE(*,*)'ENERGY RADIATED =  ',EB
      END PROGRAM RADIATE
```

RUN

```
TEMPERATURE IN DEGREES FAHRENHEIT  2.0000000E+02
ENERGY RADIATED =   3.2522699E+02
```

Problem 3.6

```
      PROGRAM STIRLING
!     APPROXIMATION TO THE FACTORIAL CALCULATION
      IMPLICIT NONE
      REAL::N, NFACT
      REAL, PARAMETER::PI = 3.145927
      WRITE(*,*)'ENTER THE VALUE N'
      READ(*,*)N
      WRITE(*,*)'THE VALUE OF N WHOSE FACTORIAL IS WANTED: ',N
      NFACT = N**N*SQRT(2.*PI*N)/EXP(N)
      WRITE(*,*)'STIRLING APPROX TO N FACTORIAL = ',NFACT
      END PROGRAM STIRLING
```

RUN

```
THE VALUE OF N WHOSE FACTORIAL IS WANTED:  20.0000000
STIRLING APPROX TO N FACTORIAL =    2.4244578E+18
```

Problem 3.9

```
      PROGRAM TORQUE
!
      IMPLICIT NONE
      REAL, PARAMETER:PI = 3.1415927
      REAL::HP,RPM,S,T,D
      WRITE(*,*)'ENTER THE HORSEPOWER'
      READ(*,*)HP
      WRITE(*,*)'HORSEPOWER = ',HP
      WRITE(*,*)'ENTER THE ROTATIONAL SPEED,REV/MIN'
      READ(*,*)RPM
      WRITE(*,*)'RPM = ', RPM
      WRITE(*,*)'ENTER THE ALLOWABLE SHEAR STRSS,LB/SQ-IN'
      READ(*,*)S
      WRITE(*,*)'ALLOWABLE SHEAR STRESS = ',S
```

```
T = (HP*63000)/RPM
D = (16.*T/(PI*S))**(1.3.)
WRITE(*,*)'REQUIRED SHAFT DIAMETER = ',D,' IN'
END PROGRAM TORQUE
```

RUN

```
HORSEPOWER =   6.0000000E+02
RPM =  85.0000000
ALLOWABLE SHEAR STRESS =   6.0000000E+03
REQUIRED SHAFT DIAMETER =   7.2270980 IN
```

Chapter 4

Problem 4.1

The following table proves that only 25 binary digits are needed to send the message in the example described in Sec. 4.1.1.

Symbol	No. of Times It Occurs	No. of Binary Digits in the Code	Total No. of Digits
7	8	1	8
5	4	2	8
3	2	3	6
1	1	3	3
			25

Problem 4.3

The following program tests the ES edit descriptor.

```
PROGRAM TEST_ES_DESCRIPTOR
REAL :: X
DO
READ "(F6.3)", X
PRINT "(ES12.5)", X
END DO
END PROGRAM TEST_ES_DESCRIPTOR
```

The results are

```
6.891
  6.89100E+00
−0.4
−4.00000E−01
.0456
  4.56000E−02
9854.2
  9.85420E+03
```

To terminate the program, simply enter any nonnumeric character such as an "a." The program ends with a run time error—"Invalid character in real input field Program terminated by fatal I/O error." Depressing the Control key and Break key simultaneously will also work.

Problem 4.8

```
0.10500E + 02
105.000E − 01
```

Problem 4.10

A typical short program is

```
PROGRAM TEST
REAL :: W,X,Y,Z
INTEGER :: I
I = 55
W = −1.24
X = 10.50
Y = 124.6
Z = 90.65
PRINT *, I,W,X,Y,Z,"OK"
END PROGRAM TEST
```

with the following typical results:

```
bb55bb−1.2400000bb10.5000000bbb1.2460000E+02bb90.6500015bOK
```

Notice that 90.65 reproduces as 90.6500015, the result of the inaccuracy of its internal representation well as the default format.

Chapter 5

Problem 5.2

```
PROGRAM CALCSIN
!   CALCULATION OF SINE OF AN ANGLE BY USE OF SERIES
IMPLICIT NONE
REAL::X,SINEFN,FACT,Y
INTEGER::N,I,K,J
WRITE(*,*)'ENTER THE ANGLE IN DEGREES'
READ(*,*)X
Y = X
X = X*3.14159265/180
WRITE(*,*)'ENTER THE NUMBER OF TERMS TO BE USED'
READ(*,*)N
SINEFN = 0
DO I = 1,N
FACT = 1.0
    K = 2*I − 1
DO J = 1,K
    FACT = FACT*J
END DO
SINEFN = SINEFN + (−1)**(I+1)*X**K/FACT
END DO
WRITE(*,*)'THE NUMBER OF TERMS USED IN THE SERIES =',N
WRITE(*,"(A,F10.5)")'THE ANGLE IN DEGREES',Y
WRITE(*,"(A,F10.5)")'THE SINE OF THE ANGLE = ',SINEFN
END PROGRAM CALCSIN
```

```
RUN

THE NUMBER OF TERMS USED IN THE SERIES = 10
THE ANGLE IN DEGREES 30.00000
THE SINE OF THE ANGLE =   0.50000
```

Problem 5.6

```
        PROGRAM ADSORPT
!    USE OF FREUNDLICH EQUATION
        IMPLICIT NONE
        INTEGER::I
        REAL::A1,A2,R1,R2,C,Y1,R,A,X1
        A1 = 5; A2 = 10.0
        R1 = 70; R2 = 93
        X1 = R1/A1
        Y1 = 1.0 -(R1/100)
        C = ALOG((R1*A2)/(R2*A1))/ALOG((100-R1)/(100-R2))
        WRITE(*,*)'C = ',C
        WRITE(*,"(4X,A,4X,A)")'A(ppm)','R %'
        WRITE(*,"(F8.1,F10.2)")A1,R1
        WRITE(*,"(F8.1,F10.2)")A2,R2
        DO I = 950,995,5
         R = I
         R = R/10
         A = R/EXP(ALOG(X1) + C*(ALOG(1.-R/100) - ALOG(Y1)))
         WRITE(*,"(F8.1,F10.2)")A,R
        END DO
        END PROGRAM ADSORPT
```

```
RUN
C =   0.2810736


A(ppm)      R %
  5.0      70.00
 10.0      93.00
 11.2      95.00
 11.6      95.50
 12.1      96.00
 12.6      96.50
 13.2      97.00
 14.0      97.50
 15.0      98.00
 16.3      98.50
 18.4      99.00
 22.5      99.50
```

Problem 5.11

```
        PROGRAM MAGFIELD
!

        IMPLICIT NONE
        INTEGER::J
        REAL::COSTH1,L,X,COSTH2,RAD,N,I,B
```

```
WRITE(*,*)'ENTER THE LENGTH OF THE COIL(METERS)'
READ(*,*)L
WRITE(*,"(A,2X,F7.1/)")'LENGTH OF COIL = ',L
WRITE(*,*)'ENTER THE RADIUS OF THE COIL(METERS)'
READ(*,*)RAD
WRITE(*,"(A, 2X, F7.1/)")'RADIUS OF COIL = ',RAD
WRITE(*,*)'ENTER THE CURRENT'
READ(*,*)I
WRITE(*,"(A,2X,F7.1/)")'CURRENT = ',I
WRITE(*,*)'ENTER THE NUMBER OF TURNS PER METER'
READ(*,*) N
WRITE(*,"(A,2X,F10.1/)")'NUMBER OF TURNS PER METER = ',N
WRITE(*,"(3X,A,6X,A)")' X','TESLA'
DO J = 0, 20
     X = J
     X = J/100.
COSTH1 = (0.5*L + X)/SQRT(RAD**2 + (0.5*L + X)**2)
COSTH2 = (0.5*L - X)/SQRT(RAD**2 + (0.5*L - X)**2)
B = 0.5*N*I*(COSTH1 + COSTH2)
WRITE(*,"(F8.2,3X,F10.3)")X,B
END DO
END PROGRAM MAGFIELD
```

RUN

LENGTH OF COIL =   0.1

RADIUS OF COIL =   0.0

CURRENT =   4.0

NUMBER OF TURNS PER METER =   1500.00

X	TESLA
0.00	5970.223
0.01	5966.471
0.02	5951.558
0.03	5904.585
0.04	5678.663
0.05	2996.257
0.06	313.624
0.07	86.972
0.08	38.602
0.09	21.255
0.10	13.223
0.11	8.899
0.12	6.327
0.13	4.686
0.14	3.581
0.15	2.806
0.16	2.245
0.17	1.826
0.18	1.508
0.19	1.261
0.20	1.066

Problem 5.13

```
       PROGRAM MAPPING
!      MAPPING A RECTANGLE FROM THE Z TO THE W PLANE
       IMPLICIT NONE
       INTEGER::I,J
       REAL::X,Y
       REAL, PARAMETER::PI = 3.14159265
       COMPLEX:: Z,W
       X = 0
       WRITE(*,"(8X,A,10X,A,11X,A,11X,A)")' X',' Y','U','V'
       DO I = 1,2
       Y = 0
         DO J = 1,11
         Z = COMPLX(X,Y)
         W = SQRT(2.)*Z*CEXP((0,1.0)*PI/4.)
         Y = Y + 0.2
         WRITE(*,"(1X,4F12.3)")Z,W
         END DO
       X = 2.0
       END DO
       END PROGRAM MAPPING
```

RUN

X	Y	U	V
0.000	0.000	0.000	0.000
0.000	0.200	−0.200	0.200
0.000	0.400	−0.400	0.400
0.000	0.600	−0.600	0.600
0.000	0.800	−0.800	0.800
0.000	1.000	−1.000	1.000
0.000	1.200	−1.200	1.200
0.000	1.400	−1.400	1.400
0.000	1.600	−1.600	1.600
0.000	1.800	−1.800	1.800
0.000	2.000	−2.000	2.000
2.000	0.000	2.000	2.000
2.000	0.200	1.800	.200
2.000	0.400	1.600	.400
2.000	0.600	1.400	.600
2.000	0.800	1.200	2.800
2.000	1.000	1.000	3.000
2.000	1.200	0.800	3.200
2.000	1.400	0.600	3.400
2.000	1.600	0.400	3.600
2.000	1.800	0.200	3.800
2.000	2.000	0.000	4.000

Chapter 6

Problem 6.1

```
       PROGRAM PROB6_1
!      FINDING THREE DB FREQUENCY OF NETWORK
```

```
IMPLICIT NONE
INTEGER::K
REAL::X,THREEDB,POLY
DO K = 18000,20000
 X = K
 X = X/10000
 THREEDB = ABS(POLY(X))
   IF(THREEDB<=1.0E-2)EXIT
END DO
WRITE(*,"(A,F9.5,3X,A,F9.5)")'THREE DB FREQ = ',X,'FN. =     &
     ',POLY(X)
END PROGRAM PROB6_1
REAL FUNCTION POLY(Z)
POLY = Z**6 - Z**4 - 3.73*Z**2 - 25.9
END
```

RUN

```
        THREE DB FREQ =  1.94640  FN. = -0.00936
```

Problem 6.4

```
        PROGRAM RELIABLE
    !
        IMPLICIT NONE
        INTEGER::I
        REAL:: Q
        Q = 0
        DO I = 1,1000000
            IF(0.95 -(1.0 - Q)**100>=0)EXIT
        Q = Q + 0.000001
        END DO
        WRITE(*,"(A,I8/)")'I = ',I
        WRITE(*,"(A,F12.6)")'Q = ',Q
        END PROGRAM RELIABLE
```

RUN

```
    I =    514
    Q =    0.000513
```

Problem 6.6

```
PROGRAM ETHYLENE
!   PRODUCTION OF ETHYL ALCOHOL
IMPLICIT NONE
INTEGER::I
REAL::NA, TEST
DO I = 1,1000
NA = I
NA = NA/1000
TEST = NA*(1.6 - NA)/((1-NA)*(0.6- NA))
IF(0.156- TEST<= 0) THEN
        EXIT
```

```
           END IF
           END DO
           WRITE(*,"(A,I8//)")'NO. OF ITERATIONS',I
           WRITE(*,"(A,F10.4)")'NO. OF MOLS OF ALCOHOL FORMED =',NA
           END PROGRAM ETHYLENE
```

RUN

```
NO. OF ITERATIONS   53
NO. OF MOLS OF ALCOHOL FORMED =  0.0530
```

Problem 6.9

```
           PROGRAM ACCELER
       !
           INTEGER::I
           REAL::T,X
           T = 2.0
           DO I = 1,1000
                X = 12.*T**2 -(1./6.)*T**3 - 0.5*T**4 - 4*T
                IF(X>=37.3)EXIT
                T = T + 0.1
           END DO
           WRITE(*,*)'T = ',T
           WRITE(*,*)'X = ',X
           END PROGRAM ACCELER
```

RUN

```
           X =    70.8885  T =   2.800
```

Chapter 7

Problem 7.1

```
           PROGRAM UNITVEC
       !   CALCULATION OF UNIT VECTORS
           IMPLICIT NONE
           REAL,DIMENSION(10)::C,CUNIT
           INTEGER::I,J,N
           CHARACTER*3::CHOICE
           DO
           WRITE(*,*)'TO END THE PROGRAM TYPE BYE'
           WRITE(*,*)'OR TO CONTINUE TYPE YES'
           READ(*,*) CHOICE
           IF(CHOICE=='BYE') EXIT
           WRITE(*,*)'ENTER THE NUMBER OF COMPONENTS OF VECTOR C'
           READ(*,*)N
           WRITE(*,*)'ENTER COMPONENTS OF VECTOR C ON ONE LINE'
           READ(*,*)(C(I),I = 1,N)
           WRITE(*,*)'VECTOR C:'
           WRITE(*,"(7F7.0/)")(C(I),I = 1,N)
           CALL VECTOR(N,C,CUNIT)
```

```
WRITE(*,"(A/)")'UNIT VECTORS'
WRITE(*,"(7F10.4/)")(CUNIT(J),J = 1,N)
CYCLE
END DO
END PROGRAM UNITVEC
SUBROUTINE VECTOR(NN,CC, CCUNIT)
REAL,DIMENSION(10),INTENT(IN)::CC
REAL,DIMENSION(10),INTENT(OUT)::CCUNIT
INTEGER,INTENT(IN)::NN
SUM = 0.0
DO I = 1,NN
    SUM = SUM + CC(I)*CC(I)
END DO
SUM = SQRT(SUM)
DO K = 1,NN
    CCUNIT(K) = CC(K)/SUM
END DO
END
```

RUN

```
VECTOR C:
1. -1. 3. 2.
UNIT VECTORS
.2581 -0.2581 0.7745 0.5163
- - - - -
VECTOR C:
2. 3. 6. -5. 4. - 7.
UNIT VECTORS
0.1696 0.2544 0.5089 -0.4240 0.3392 - 0.5937
```

Problem 7.2

```
PROGRAM BINTODEC
!
INTEGER,DIMENSION(1:10)::BIN
INTEGER::I,J,N
REAL::ANSWER
CHARACTER*3::CHOICE
DO
WRITE(*,*)'ENTER BYE IF YOU WISH TO STOP, OR'
WRITE(*,*)'ENTER YES TO CONTINUE'
READ(*,*)CHOICE
IF(CHOICE == 'BYE') EXIT
WRITE(*,*)'ENTER, N,THE NUMBER OF DIGITS IN THE BINARY NO.'
READ(*,*)N
WRITE(*,*)'ENTER BINARY NO. DIGITS SEPARATED BY COMMA'
READ(*,*)(BIN(I),I = 1,N)
WRITE(*,"(A)")'BINARY NUMBER TO BE CONVERTED'
WRITE(*,"(10I2//)") (BIN(J),J = 1,N)
CALL BTODEC(N,BIN,DEC,ANSWER)
WRITE(*,"(A,F14.0)")'DECIMAL EQUIVALENT',ANSWER
CYCLE
END DO
```

```
END PROGRAM BINTODEC
SUBROUTINE BTODEC(NN,BINAR,DECIM,DECIMAL)
INTEGER, DIMENSION(1:10),INTENT(IN) ::BINAR
INTEGER,DIMENSION(1:10),INTENT(OUT)::DECIM
REAL,INTENT(OUT)::DECIMAL
DECIM(NN) = BINAR(NN)
DO K = NN-1, 1 ,-1
DECIM(K) = BINAR(K) + 2*DECIM(K+1)
WRITE(*,*)DECIM(K),K
END DO
DECIMAL = DECIM(1)
END SUBROUTINE BTODEC
```

RUNS

```
BINARY NUMBER TO BE CONVERTED
1 1 0 0 1 1
DECIMAL EQUIVALENT       51.

_ _ _ _ _
BINARY NUMBER TO BE CONVERTED
1 1 0 1 1 1 1
DECIMAL EQUIVALENT      123.
```

Problem 7.8

```
      PROGRAM ELLIPTIC
!     CALCULATION::ELLIPTIC INTEGRAL OF FIRST KIND
      IMPLICIT NONE
      REAL::K, ANSWER,E1
      INTEGER::I
      K = 0.1
      WRITE(*,"( 6X,A,12X,A)")'K','K(k)'
      DO I = 1,5
      ANSWER = E1(K)
      WRITE(*,"(3X,F5.1,5X,F12.7)")K,ANSWER
      K = K + 0.2
      END DO
      END PROGRAM ELLIPTIC
      REAL FUNCTION E1(G)
      U = 1.0 - G**2
      E1 = 1.38629 + U*(.111972 + .0725296*U)-ALOG(U)*(.5 +   &
          U*(.1213478 + 0.0288729))
      END
```

RUN

```
  K          K(k)
 0.1     1.5747483
 0.3     1.6082939
 0.5     1.6873198
 0.7     1.8505195
 0.9     2.2879488
```

Problem 7.10

```
PROGRAM PERSYM
!    VALUES OF THE PERMUTATION SYMBOL
     IMPLICIT NONE
     INTEGER::I,J,K
     REAL::EPS
     WRITE(*,"(8X,A,13X,A,14X,A,16X,A/)")'I','J','K','EPS'
     DO I = 1,3
          DO J = 1,3
               DO K = 1,3
               CALL PERM(I,J,K,EPS)
          WRITE(*,"(7X,I2,12X,I2,13X,I2,13X,F6.0)") I,J,K,EPS
               END DO
          END DO
     END DO
     END PROGRAM PERSYM
     SUBROUTINE PERM(II,JJ,KK,EPS)
     INTEGER,INTENT(IN)::II,JJ,KK
     REAL,INTENT(OUT)::EPS
     DO L = 1,27
          IF(II==JJ.OR.II==KK.OR.JJ==KK) THEN
               EPS = 0
          EXIT
          ELSE IF(II==1.AND.JJ==2.AND.KK==3) THEN
               EPS = 1
          EXIT
               ELSE IF(II==2.AND.JJ==3.AND.KK==1) THEN
               EPS = 1
          EXIT
          ELSE IF(II==3.AND.JJ==1.AND.KK==2) THEN
               EPS = 1
          EXIT
          ELSE
               EPS = -1
          EXIT
          END IF
          END DO
          END
```

RUN

I	J	K	EPS
1	1	1	0.
1	1	2	0.
1	1	3	0.
1	2	1	0.
1	2	2	0.
1	2	3	1.
1	3	1	0.
1	3	2	-1.
1	3	3	0.
2	1	1	0.
2	1	2	0.

2	1	3	-1.
2	2	1	0.
2	2	2	0.
2	2	3	0.
2	3	1	1.
2	3	2	0.
2	3	3	0.
3	1	1	0.
3	1	2	1.
3	1	3	0.
3	2	1	-1.
3	2	2	0.
3	2	3	0.
3	3	1	0.
3	3	2	0.
3	3	3	0.

Chapter 8

Problem 8.1

1. The user can compare program results with existing ("real-world") models. If a totally equivalent system does not exist, then the closest known available model may be used.

2. Include certain tests and/or constraints that must be satisfied. For example, if the program includes probabilistic data, then the probabilities of all possible outcomes should add up to 1.

Problem 8.4

It is not correct. As written, the algebraic equivalent is

$$y = \frac{1}{2} \pi \sqrt{\frac{A}{B}}$$

The correct statement is

$$y = (1.0/(2.0 * \text{pi}))*\text{sqrt}(A/B)$$

or

$$y = 1.0/(2.0 * \text{pi})*\text{sqrt}(A/B)$$

will also work. The latter works because of the order in which computations are carried out.

Problem 8.6

The error message "Invalid item in type declaration" is puzzling. There appears to be nothing wrong with the statement. On closer examination, however, one finds that a continuation symbol has been omitted from the statement. Without this symbol, the compiler interprets the comma as a statement terminator; this is the "Invalid item" in the type declaration. The next line is viewed as an *assignment statement* for b. Since b has not been properly declared, the compiler produces the "implicit type" error message.

Problem 8.11

Mathematically, $\sin(x)/\cos(x)$ and $\tan(x)$ are equivalent. The computer, however, computes the sin, cos, and tan as the sum of a series; this introduces a deviation from the exact answer. Calculating $\sin(x)/\cos(x)$ introduces an additional error. Slightly different answers were observed; for the first the answer was 1.5574079, and for the second 1.5574077. Although these answers are very close, this problem illustrates one way in which unexpected results can be introduced into a program when perfectly correct mathematical substitutions are used.

Chapter 9

Problem 9.1

```
      PROGRAM TWODICE
!     SIMULATION OF THE ROLL OF TWO DICE
      IMPLICIT NONE
      REAL,DIMENSION(12)::DIST
      INTEGER,DIMENSION(2)::ROLL
      REAL::P,X
      INTEGER:: DIE1,DIE2,K,I,L,M
      DO K = 1,12
       DIST(K) = 0
      END DO
       CALL RANDOM_SEED
      DO I = 1,5000
          DO M = 1,2
              CALL RANDOM_NUMBER(X)
              IF(X >= 0) ROLL(M) = 1
              IF(X >= 0.166666) ROLL(M) = 2
              IF(X>= 0.333333) ROLL(M) = 3
              IF(X>= 0.500000) ROLL(M) = 4
              IF(X>= 0.666666) ROLL(M) = 5
              IF(X>= 0.833333) ROLL(M) = 6
          END DO
          DIE1 = ROLL(1)
          DIE2 = ROLL(2)
          L = DIE1 + DIE2
          DIST(L) = DIST(L) + 1
      END DO
      WRITE(*,"(A,6x,A,8x,A)")' SUM OF POINTS','FREQUENCY',    &
          'PROBABILITY'
      DO I = 1,12
          P = DIST(I)/5000
          WRITE(*,"(2X,I5,10X,F10.0,6X, F12.6)")I,DIST(I),P
      END DO
      END PROGRAM TWODICE
```

RUN

SUM OF POINTS	FREQUENCY	PROBABILITY
1	0.	0.000000
2	147.	0.029400
3	276.	0.055199
4	425.	0.085000
5	585.	0.117000
6	710.	0.142000
7	844.	0.168800
8	675.	0.135000

9	542.	0.108400
10	413.	0.082599
11	265.	0.052999
12	118.	0.023600

Problem 9.5

```
        PROGRAM MONTE8
!       CALCULATION OF FREQUENCIES OF RESONANT CIRCUIT
!       L & C UNIFORMLY DISTRIBUTED
        IMPLICIT NONE
        REAL:: L,C,FREQU
        REAL, PARAMETER::PI = 3.1415926
        INTEGER:: K,N
        COMMON FREQU(5000),N
        N = 4000
        CALL RANDOM_SEED
        DO K = 1,N
            CALL RANDOM_NUMBER(L)
            L = 0.1*L + 0.3
            CALL RANDOM_NUMBER(C)
            C = 0.2E-06*C + 0.9E-06
            FREQU(K) = 1.0/(2.0*PI*SQRT(C*L))
        END DO
         CALL RANK
         WRITE(*,"(A,F10.5)")'MAX FREQU =',FREQU(N)
         WRITE(*,"(A,F10.5)")'MIN FREQU =',FREQU(1)
        END PROGRAM MONTE8
        SUBROUTINE RANK
         COMMON FREQU(5000),N
         DO I = 1, N-1
            MAX = N - I
            DO J = 1, MAX
                IF(FREQU(J)>FREQU(J + 1)) THEN
                TEMP = FREQU(J)
                FREQU(J) = FREQU(J+1)
                FREQU(J + 1) = TEMP
                END IF
            END DO
         END DO
         END SUBROUTINE RANK
```

RUN

```
MAX FREQU = 306.11780
MIN FREQU = 240.08765
```

Problem 9.6

```
        PROGRAM MONTE5
!       CALCULATION OF THE AREA UNDER QUADRANT
!       OF ELLIPSE
        IMPLICT NONE
        REAL:: X, Y, HIT, AREA,A
```

```
REAL, PARAMETER::PI = 3.1415926
INTEGER:: K
HIT = 0;   A = 18.0
CALL RANDOM_SEED
DO K = 1,5000
 CALL RANDOM_NUMBER(X)
 X = 6.0*X
 CALL RANDOM_NUMBER(Y)
 Y = 3.0*Y
 IF(X**2 + 4.0*Y**2 < 36.0) THEN
    HIT = HIT + 1.0
      END IF
END DO
 AREA = A*(HIT/5000.0)
 WRITE(*,"(A//)")'AREA UNDER QUADRANT OF ELLIPSE'
 WRITE(*,"(10X,A,F12.5)")'AREA = ',AREA
END PROGRAM MONTE5
```
RUN

```
AREA UNDER QUADRANT OF ELLIPSE
AREA =  14.29560
```

Theoretical value of area:
AREA OF QUADRANT OF ELLIPSE = $\pi AB/4 = \pi(6)(3)/4 = 14.137$
Note: $A = 6$ = semimajor axis $B = 3$ = semiminor axis

Problem 9.10

```
PROGRAM INTEGR3
! INTEGRATION OF X**2*(SQRT(X**3+1)) BY SIMPSON'S RULE.
IMPLICIT NONE
REAL::A,B,SIM
INTEGER::N
WRITE(*,*)'ENTER LOWER,THEN UPPER LIMIT'
READ(*,*)A,B
WRITE(*,*)'ENTER NUMBER OF STRIPS'
READ(*,*)N
CALL SIMPSON(A,B,N,SIM)
WRITE(*,"(A,F14.6)")'VALUE OF THE INTEGRAL = ',SIM
END PROGRAM INTEGR3
REAL FUNCTION FNX(X)
FNX = X**2*SQRT(X**3 + 1)
RETURN
END
SUBROUTINE SIMPSON(E,F,N,SIM)
M = N-1
MM = M - 1
H = (F - E)/N
PARSUM = 0
ODD = 0
CONST = FNX(E) + FNX(F)
    DO I = 1,M,2
    DX = H*I
```

```
            PARSUM = PARSUM + 4.0*FNX(E + DX)
            ENDO DO
              DO J = 2,MM,2
                DX = H*J
                ODD = ODD + 2.0*FNX(E + DX)
              END DO
       SIM = H/3.0*(CONST + ODD + PARSUM)
           END SUBROUTINE SIMPSON
      RUN
```

$$\text{VALUE OF THE INTEGRAL} = \quad 5.778192$$

Problem 9.12

Hand calculation of DFT.

$$X(m) = x(0)e^{(-j\pi m/4)} + x(1)e^{(-j\pi m/4)} + x(3)e^{(-j3\pi m/4)} + x(4)e^{(-j\pi m)} + x(5)e^{(-j5\pi m/4)} + x(7)e^{(-j7\pi m/4)}$$

Note that $x(2) = x(6) = 0$

With $m = 1$, we obtain

$$X(1) = 10 + (5 - j5) - (-5 - j5) + 10 - (-5 + j5) + (5 + j5) = 40$$
$$\text{As } N = 8, X(1) = 5$$
$$\text{Also, } X(7) = X(1) = 5.$$

The frequency resolution is $1/NT = 1/(8/200) = 25$ Hz.

By similar calculation, you can show that

$$X(2) = X(3) = X(4) = X(5) = X(6) = 0$$

Chapter 10

Problem 10.10

Consider the table shown below which includes all possible combinations of an open resistor (1 = open in the table) and a shorted resistor (0 = short in the table):

R1	R2	Appropriate Rule(s)
0	0	1, 3, 5
0	1	3
1	0	1
1	1	1, 2, 3, 4

From the table note that all possible combinations of part failures will show up in at least one rule.

Problem 10.11

That provision is already in program EXPERT_SYSTEM. Notice—in the section identified by the comment "!MAKE JUDGEMENT ABOUT ATTENUATION_FACTOR"—the following code fragment:

```
ELSE IF ((ATTENUATION_FACTOR > 1.2*ATTEN_THEORETICAL) .OR.  &
         (ATTENUATION_FACTOR < 0.8*ATTEN_THEORETICAL)) THEN
         JUDGEMENT =" OUT OF TOLERANCE."
```

Index